NEIKIRK-NEWKIRK-NIKIRK

VOLUME 1

HERITAGE BOOKS

AN IMPRINT OF HERITAGE BOOKS, INC.

Books, CDs, and more—Worldwide

For our listing of thousands of titles see our website
at
www.HeritageBooks.com

Published 2008 by
HERITAGE BOOKS, INC.
Publishing Division
100 Railroad Ave. #104
Westminster, Maryland 21157

International Standard Book Number: 978-0-7884-0773-4

Neikirk, Newkirk, Nikirk and Related Families

Volume One

The Descendants of
MATHEUSE CORNELISSEN VAN NIEUWKERCKE
Born c.1600 in Holland
and
JOHANN HEINRICK NEUKIRK
Born c.1674 in Germany

William Neal Hurley, Jr.

HERITAGE BOOKS
2008

ALSO BY W. N. HURLEY, JR.

Available from the publisher: Heritage Books, Inc.

Neikirk-Newkirk-Nikirk, Volume 2

Hurley Families in America, Volume 1

Hurley Families in America, Volume 2

John William Hines 1600, And His Descendants

Maddox, A Southern Maryland Family

Pratt Families of Virginia

Lowder Families in America

Our Maryland Heritage Series:

   Book One: The Fry Families

   Book Two: The Walker Families

   Book Three: The Fulks Families

"By coming to know the invisible past through the visible present, we may finally be able to locate ourselves in the total scheme."

- Dr. Curtis M. Hinsley, Jr.

A WORD OF CAUTION

The information reported is as accurate as we could make it from the records studied. However, we recognize that it is virtually impossible to report such an extensive amount of data without an error creeping in some place. Occasionally, we may have reported a date of birth, which is in reality the date of christening, or vice versa. Obviously, they should be close. In many cases, we will report dates as approximate, but they should lead you to the general time frame, so that you may distinguish between individuals with the same name. Much of what appears here was reported by other researchers or family members, and we have not personally verified it from contemporary records. They are, of course, just as prone to a mistake as we are. The information should, however, be accurate enough to guide you in your own personal research. Good luck, forgive our occasional error, and please share with us any corrections or further data you may uncover.

Throughout the text, I have used terms which should caution the reader: such as, apparently; may have been; reportedly; about; possibly; could be; and similar terminology, to indicate that the information given has either not been verified by extant contemporary records, or appears to fit a given set of circumstances which, of themselves, are believed to be correct.

CREDITS

Photographic technical preparation by Bob White.
Comprint, Gaithersburg, Maryland.

AND A WORD OF THANKS

There are many individuals who should be recognized for their contribution to this work; and a few very special ones. For several years, Gilbert K. Alford, Jr., and his wife, Mary, published *Newkirk Notes,* a periodic journal of news and information about the family, but had to stop a few years ago. In 1990, I contacted them, and they generously provided me with back issues, and gave permission to use the information. This study draws heavily on their earlier work, and from contacts made with others listed in the various issues of the journal. When I last contacted them, Gil and Mary lived in Florissant, Missouri.

One of my most faithful and prolific correspondents over the years has been Marjorie Judd, of Emporia, Kansas. Marjorie has provided me with extensive research on the Neikirk families of southwest Virginia and Kentucky, and their descendants, the Wampler families.

Marjorie put me in touch with Leroy Nikirk of Alvord, Texas, who generously provided information on a whole branch of the family bearing that name spelling.

Also, in 1990, I made contact with Cathrine Auble, from Republic, Ohio. She is descended from the Neikirks of Hagerstown, Maryland, on two sides of her family, through the Sheeley and Barnheisel families. The amount of information that she furnished is staggering.

In Hagerstown, Maryland, the ancestral home of many members of the family, I found extensive records in the local library, and at the Washington County Historical Society. For a number of years, Joseph C. Neikirk had researched the family, but a few years ago had a stroke, and was unable to continue. He gave me his research notes, from which many family connections were derived.

There were many others, and many gracious people in libraries, courthouses and historical societies who shared their time and knowledge; and their patience. Without them, this work would not have been possible.

CONTENTS

**The Dutch Newkirks: Descendants of Matheuse
Cornelissen Van Nieuwkercke of Holland.**

**The Palatines: Descendants of Johann Heinrick
Neukirk, born c.1674 in Germany**

viii

INTRODUCTION

The Neikirk families, and their descendants, with whom we are related, appear to have originated in Pennsylvania in the early 1700s. We have found, among others, the arrival on September 20, 1738, in Philadelphia, one Hendrick Nikerick, age 32, on board the *Nancy*, William Wallace, Master. *Genealogies of Pennsylvania Families*, from Pennsylvania Genealogical Magazine, Volume II, by Hinman-Sotcher, on page 391, states that Hendrick Nikerick settled in Berks County, and that he had numerous descendants. Some of them remained in the area about Reading, Pennsylvania, and assumed the spelling Newkirk, while those that relocated to Washington County, Maryland, from whom the author is descended, adopted the spelling I am now familiar with, Neikirk or, occasionally, Niekirk or Nikirk.

In 1985, I published a book entitled *The Ancestry of William Neal Hurley, III*, my youngest son, in which the Neikirk families were reported as I then knew them, along with four other major families from whom we are descended. Since that time, additional information has been discovered relative to each of those families, including Neikirk. This study will include all that is now known about the family, including the earlier material, with necessary corrections. It will appear here in much the same order as the original, omitting some of the earlier "color" and concentrating on family lineage.

The Washington County Historical Society Library, located in Hagerstown, Maryland, contains numerous references to the Neikirk family (with its various spellings). Among them are a collection of letters from Thomas J. Neikirk of Chicago in 1912; Mrs Ada Peters Newkirk Ferguson of Lancaster, Ohio, in the early 1900s; Dr. A. B. Newkirk of Los Angeles in c.1902; and George M. Newkirk of Philomath, Oregon in 1903. Unfortunately, some of the notes they refer to do not now appear available, but much of what follows is based on their letters to each other. There are also references to certain publications in the various letters, and I have reviewed those that were available to me.

References are made to various family members in the early 1900s, then living in Jackson County, Indiana; Shiloh, Illinois;

Oxford, Iowa; Alford, Texas; Philadelphia; Missouri; Ohio; Kentucky; and elsewhere. Naturally, the references are all so old that it is nearly impossible to establish a contact.

If it is available to you, the reader is urged to read *The Early History of the Descendants of Henry Newkirk in America*, by Dr. Glen A. Newkirk, 1975, which contains a fascinating history of the early Neikirk families in Germany as early as 1155.

Among the writings of Dr. A. B. Newkirk c.1903, there is a report of a story found in a book entitled *Yarns About Diamonds*.

The story of the "*Star of Africa*" discovered at the Cape of Good Hope, was related thus, by one Mr. Nuncy: Albania was a portion of the Griqua Territory, settled by Dutch Colonists, under terms made with Walterboor; one of the colonists was a Mr. Von Niekirk. Mr. O'Reilly, who was returning from the interior to Colesburg, called upon Mr. Von Niekirk and remained with him over night. In the course of the evening, one of Mr. Von Niekirk's children, a little girl, was playing on the floor with some of the pretty pebbles which are common in the neighborhood of the Vaal River. Mr. O'Reilly's attention was directed to one of the stones, which threw out a very strong light, and which, in Mr. O'Reilly's eyes, seemed unusually bright. He accordingly took it up from the floor and at once offered to buy it from the owner. The simple-minded Boer said that he would "take no money for a stone" but that if Mr. O'Reilly had a mind to it, he could have it. The latter, however, said that he believed it to be a precious stone of value and would not consent to take it for nothing. He gave Mr. Von Niekirk half its estimated value, made by a jeweler at Grahamstown, namely five hundred pounds, and it was subsequently sold to Lilienfield Brothers, of Hopetown, for eleven thousand, two hundred pounds, sterling. Was this the famous Hope Diamond?

There is another interesting article reported in the papers of Dr. A. B. Newkirk, relative to the ancient origins of the family in Europe, similar to reports found in several other publications.

The continuous line of this very old family of Julich begins with the ancestor John Van Neukirchen, Lord of Neuraidt in Oclen, who married, in 1403, Anna Van Nyvenheim, heiress of Gerods, by reason of which it came to pass that their descendants bore the united names and arms of both families. From Julich, the family went to Lower Rhine, acquired in the course of time many hereditary offices, and much wealth, and furnished a number of knights and commanders to the German Order. One branch removed to the Netherlands, while the other remained in the Rhine region. Walter Godfried Van Neukirchen, called Nyvenheim, in the thirteenth generation of the continuous genealogical Lord of Drieberg, Kessel, Mook and Musschienborg, was, by his wife, Elberyina Van Tengnagel Van Gillikum, whom he married in 1703, ancestor of the present branch of the family living in France.

Early Family History

The Neikirk family is a very ancient one, with its origins in Germany and Holland. Like many other families with Germanic names, it has undergone many changes in the way it is spelled and, even today, in the same geographic locations, various groups of the family spell their name differently.

The family is found very early in the history of the Lower Rhine in Germany. In the seventeenth century, this area was under the control of a Count Palatine, granted such authority by the German Emperor; hence the designation of the inhabitants as Palatines. There were towns named Neukirchen in both the county of Grevenbrock and in Moers. Members of the family are also found in the history of Nykerck, Gelderland, as well as in Nieuenkerk, Zeeland, and Niewkerk in the Rhine Province.

The Neikirk family members (by whatever spelling), were members of the Reformed Church, and suffered much from religious persecution. The political leader of the Palatines was Conrad Weiser and the religious leader was the Reverend Joshua Kockerthal. One John Newkirkand reportedly prepared a petition to the King to address the grievances of the Palatines against the Albanians, which was delivered to Conrad Weiser. The outcome of the effort was the violent enmity of the Governor, who attempted to hang all those involved in the petition. As a result, and after suffering the ravages of the Thirty Years War, religious persecution by the French Jesuits, destruction and plunder by King Louis XIV, and an unusually severe winter of 1707/08, many of them immigrated to England, seeking freedom and protection. Apparently that was not very successful, and in 1708 the Reverend Joshua Kockerthal petitioned the London Board of Trade to be sent to America. The result of that petition, and later assistance from Queen Anne, was the great migration of thousands of Palatines, first to New Jersey in 1708, and in 1709 and 1710 to Manhattan Island.

They came in such numbers that the small community of Manhattan could not take care of them, and they removed up the Hudson River to a new settlement at *Livingston Manor* in the valley of the Mohawk and the Schoharie Rivers. It is of some interest to the author to note that the Neikirk families settled at *Hurley*, in Ulster County, New York. Once again, problems arose between these newcomers seeking farms, and the Dutch settlers of the area, and a second Palatine migration occurred. This time, they moved to Pennsylvania, where many of them settled, first in Tolpehocken in Bucks County, and then in areas around that first settlement. The area is now known as the Pennsylvania Dutch country, with its center being Reading. Not far from Reading is the town of Maxatawney in Oley Township, Berks County, where they either formed or joined the Moravian Congregation.

While there is no Neikirk included in the listings of these migrations in 1708 to 1710, *The List of Palatines Remaining in New York in 1710*, contains the names of Johan Henrick Newkirk, 36; Anna Maria, 33; Johannes, 11; John Henrick, dead. Descendants of this family resided mainly in Orange and Ulster Counties, New York. Johannes, or John, son of John Henry (or Johan Heinrick), had eleven children, was fairly wealthy, and died in 1777 near Wallkill. There were other rather early immigrants to America bearing this family name. Among them was Gerret Cornelisse Van Nieuwkercke, born c.1631 in Holland and immigrated to New York aboard the *Moesman*, arriving there April 25, 1659. He brought with him a wife and an infant son, and his descendants are the ancestors of the New Jersey Neikirks, and the New York Neikirks of modern days. Additionally, some of his descendants migrated to Washington County, Pennsylvania, and to Rush County, Indiana.

There was also a Johann Heinrick Neukirch listed on Governor Hunter's ration list of 1710 in New York at the age of 36, born c.1674; with a wife Anna Marie at age 33, born c.1677; and some of their children, including a John at age 8, born c.1702. He also appears in *The Simmendinger List of Names*, and in the Reverend Josiah Kockerthal's *Baptism Records of the Moravian Church in the Mohawk Valley*. We have no further records of this family at this time, nor their relationship to our immediate lineage. It has been suggested that this is the father of our Johann Heinrick Neukirch, but if he is, then he left his infant son in Germany when he immigrated, in that "our" Johann was born c.1708, married in Germany in 1731, and arrived in Philadelphia in 1738.

I have found reports of at least three immigrants, who are possibly related many generations back, but that relationship is not now proven, nor claimed. They included: Mattheuse Cornelissen Van Nieuwkercke (1600), who we classify in our records as head of the Dutch families; Johann Heinrick Neukirch (1674), head of the German Palatines; and Johann Heinrick Neukirch (1708), head of the author's lineage; all treated further in the text.

Origins of Hurley, Ulster County, New York

As has been mentioned, the early Nieuwkirk families that came to America settled in Ulster County, New York, in the valley of the Hudson River. One of the towns in that county is to this day named Hurley, as well as a second town called West Hurley. It is of some interest to the author, since the parents of my father were David Pearson Hurley and Sarah Alberta Clementine Neikirk; they were married in southwest Virginia in 1889.

The first recorded settler in the region which is now Ulster County was Thomas Chambers, who arrived in June of 1652, and arranged to purchase a tract of land from the local Indians, the Warronawanka Tribe, later to become known as the Esopus Indians. Following that first settlement, there were numerous conflicts with the Indians. Between 1660 and 1663, the original Dutch settlement was renamed Wiltwyck and enlarged. A second village was laid out a few miles to the southwest, called Nieuw Dorp. On June 7, 1663, the Esopus Indians attacked the two villages and killed many of the inhabitants, burning the village of Nieuw Dorp to the ground.

In 1664, just after the Second Esopus War, the English took over the Dutch Colonies, and the village of Wiltwyck was given the present name of Kingston. A new village was built and resettled where Nieuw Dorp had stood, and named Hurley. It is quite probable that the town of Hurley derived its name from that of one of the early Governors of New York appointed by the Crown; Sir Francis Lovelace, Baron of Hurley, who served in that capacity from 1668 to 1673.

On March 28, 1708, Queen Anne appointed John, Fourth Lord Lovelace, Governor of New York and New Jersey. He is reported by some as being a grandson of Francis, Lord Lovelace, the first Governor of New York appointed from this family; and by others as being a nephew, although neither is proven. According to Burke's *General Armory*, Sir Richard Lovelace was knighted and made Baron of Hurley in 1627, and the barony was extinguished in 1736. This Richard Lovelace was reportedly a close friend of Sir Francis Drake and amassed a considerable fortune by sharing in Drake's marauding expeditions. The family seat was found at Hurley, in Berkshire. The ancient manor house of Hurley, where many generations of Lovelaces were born, was destroyed by fire in 1835, but the historic name remains, both in England and America.

Ancient Records of the Neikirk Family

In 1990, I made contact with Cathrine Auble, then living at Republic, Ohio. She is a direct lineal descendant of Johann Heinrick Neukirch, born in Hahn, Dusseldorff, Germany, about 1708. She provided me with copies of several sheets of information that had come to her some years earlier, obviously relative to the Neikirk family, but written in what appeared to be German, which she could not translate. I sent the papers to a friend in Hamburg, Germany, and she made the effort to translate it for us, which provides some interesting information. My friend, Elin Ballough, first noted that some of the history relates to the area of Reval, which was originally in Estonia, now occupied by Russia and known as Tallinn. Some of the spelling in this report is going to suffer, due to my problem with reading Elin's writing; and her translation of the very old script.

Elin also commented that her own father studied medicine at a university founded by Gustav Adolph, whose name appears in our report. Elin reports also that it appears the notes were partly translated from Estonian into German, and that some of the words are unknown to her. There were several references to Coats of Arms in the notes, but Elin was unable to translate those, probably due in part to unfamiliarity with the terms used in heraldry. In any case, translation of the papers reads:

"Rhenish Prussia, Lower Rhine. Neukirchen, called Nyvenheim, very old Nobility; in the Netherlands and Dutch East Indies of great wealth. One line received on August 21, 1852 the Royal Prussian title of baron and serves the King. Neukirchen old Rhineland nobility whose main property was Reisberg, Ruchelhoven, and Kessel near Kleve (these latter are near the Dutch border on German side, not far from Dutch town of Nijmegen). They carry their Arms since 1648 and it has been united with that of the Nyvenheim family. The Neikirks of Pomerania (now Poland)...Neukirchen (Neukirch, Niekirch, Nykerk). Johann W. was in 1525 Master of the Order, Walter V. Plattenberg, with 10 and 1/2 haken (something like acres) in the land of Marienburg, now Poland. (Elin notes that there is a verb missing in this translation; probably Johann was given the land by Walter V. Plattenberg, who was the Master of the Order).

Estate of Goldbeck given to hold in fee. The Master of the Order, V. D. Recke, acknowledged this fee to Jurgen, his son in law. One may well assume that Johann W. Neukirchen of the Pomeranian and Altmark family line which was with Rodolfus, the Nijenkerke in 1289 in Pomerania and with Hennig Nyenkerken in 1381 in the area of Uckermark (east of Berlin). On August 6, 1589, King Sigismund III bestowed upon Heinrich Nikirch for his lifetime, Foseenburg or Ketsemoise, with hakens Paggarst and also Rasin. In 1599 he was recognized by the King as belonging to the old nobility. Reference is made that Johann Nykerk, in the year 1555, received a windmill and 5 haken of the Master and landowner, Heinrich von Galen, to use in fee during the time of his life. There were three servants living on the premises of the mill operated by Johann; namely Nicho Telemeggi, Kunter Jacob Reytema, and Mattis Kraw. There was also a fishing ground under the Falle Mill which was called Wachtes, apparently also operated by Johann Neukirch. In 1572, he was called to account for the fish, and the report seems to name the types of fish, but Elin was not able to translate, except that one name "lax" could be "lachs" or salmon. In a 1574 Register of Free Landowners under the Chateau of Reval (today called Tallin in Estonia), Johan Nykerk is called a miller of Falle, and has been (like all other millers) under contract to serve with his own horse on account of his master in war activities and to participate in military expeditions.

In 1574 it is written that Johann Nykerk received this mill from King Erich, together with five haken. In 1575 it is written that he should give money to the town, and two fat pigs. In 1575, there is a Register of those people who have been under fee, and the name of Johan Nykerke appears. He is listed in a group of persons whose property in the name of the Vogdte (magistrate) should be reduced. But, in 1586, it appears that it has been determined that Heinrich and Hans Nykerke received the mill previously from their parents, who already owned the mill, and that they have at all times supported the Swedish Crown, but that they have to pay 30 marks and two fat pigs each year, and that they should seek Royal confirmation concerning the matter. In the Wackenbuch (a book of some sort), in 1620, the Mill by the name of Falle is mentioned to have five haken and 1/2 haken and Eifussling landed property in the name of the Nykerks, and that it is hereditary. It followed then, that Hans Neukirch was the heir which later was acknowledged by a letter from King Carl IX, confirmed by King Gustav Adolph of Sweden on July 31, 1602. Ordered further on November 4, 1610 that the seven and one half haken in the village of Morest, the mill and the two thirds haken and Einfussling land are for him to keep, and that they are hereditary.

Albrecht V. Neukirch sealed in 1324 a Handfeste of the Duke of Bavaria. The sister of the latter was married to Wolf Kellner of Mittersill. Their children sold Neukirchen in 1556."

A few somewhat notable persons holding the name included: Benjamin Neukirch, a renowned German poet, born in Reinke or Renke, a village in Silesia. He studied in Frankfort (either on Oder or Main; there being two Frankforts in Germany), and in Halle and Leipzig. He died in 1556.

Melchior (Neofanius) Neukirch was a protestant preacher and dramatist of the 16th century. His father, Johannes Neukirch, born in Enburg in Gergisdon, arrived in the fall of 1531 at the school of the Hieren of Deventer in the town of Wittenberg. Born in 1540 in Braunschweig; preached in Barem.

On the gable wall of the Catholic Church of Rhondorf on the Rhine, built in 1714, there can be found an inscription reading, *All wish to have God's blessing, 1714, Jacobus Neukirchen and Catherine Weinreich marriage.*

A town of of the name Neukirchen (Stanmetz, Stannitz) can be found in Wassenburg. In the funeral registry of Raitenhaslach in 1260, the Knights Albrecht Neukirchen and Friedrich Neukirchen are mentioned.

The reader is referred to *Genealogies of Pennsylvania Families From The Pennsylvania Genealogical Magazine*, Volume II, by Hinman-Sotcher, Genealogical Publishing Company, Inc., 1982, for detailed information about members of the early families, wherein the writings of Doctor Adamson Bentley Newkirk are found beginning at page 391. The book is available in most Mormon genealogical libraries, and other major libraries.

Notes Relative to Revisions

This revised edition contains a few corrections to the original, together with rather extensive new information on several branches of the family, derived from correspondence since original publication. The author regrets any inconvenience that may have been caused by presentation of erroneous information, or absence of more complete data in the original publication.

A Word About Names; And The Index

As can be seen from the following page, the family name has developed numerous spellings through the years. My research tends to indicate that the descendants of the Dutch families; from Matheuse Cornelissen Van Nieuwkercke, born c.1600; more commonly use the spelling Newkirk. The same is true of the Palatines, descended from Johann Heinrick Neukirk, born c.1674.

These two groups are described for the most part in the text within Chapters 1 through 13 of this Volume 1 of the study.

The descendants of Johann Heinrick Neukirch, born c.1708 appear, however, to have generally used the spelling Neikirk in later generations, although there is some crossing over between the two lines. Additionally, there is a whole group in western Maryland and nearby Pennsylvania who, for reasons known only to history, adopted the spelling Nicarry, or Nicarrick. Yet another group, found primarily in Texas, but also scattered elsewhere, prefer the spelling Nikirk.

All of these families are investigated in Volume 2 of the study, to which reference is made.

Every effort has been made to utilize the name spelling properly in the text, although I will surely have made some mistakes along the way. As can be seen from the following page, if all names are entered just as found in the records, the researcher faces a monumental task of exploring each possible spelling in the index.

In the Index, therefore, I have chosen to use only the spellings Newkirk, Nikirk, or Neikirk (for the groups described), and Nicarry for those using that name. In that way, I believe the reader will find it easier to locate their ancestors if limited to these few possible spellings in the index, recognizing that what appears to be the proper spelling by usage will appear in the text. Each of the spelling variants should be checked in the index.

From Germany and Holland To America

With Variant Name Spellings, Including:

Von Niekirk	Newchurch
Van Niekercke	Nieuwkerke
Van Neikirk	Nieuwkurcke
Van Neukirchen	Van Nieuwkercke
Von Niekerk	Neiukirk
Nyekirk	Neukerch
Nieukerke	Nikirk
Nikerick	Neukerck
Neukirck	Neukirch
Newkirk	Newkirch
Neikirk	Nicerk
Nicarry	Nicarrick

*To be ignorant of what occurred before you were
born is to remain always a child.
For what is the worth of human existence unless
it is woven into the lives of our ancestors?*

- Cicero

CHAPTER 1

Mattheuse Cornelissen Van Nieuwkercke
1600-

This individual lived about twenty-five miles south of the city of Amsterdam, near Nijkerk in the District of Slichtenhorst, Gelderland, Holland, and was born there about 1600. He was one of the descendants of the Newkirks who were in Germany as early as 1153. The Dutch Newkirks probably lived in Holland for several hundred years before they came to the American colonies. He was married November 9, 1630 at Putten, Holland, to Bijtie Gerrits, daughter of Gerrit Aerts. In Holland records, he is reported as Cornelis Killen, son of Kil Hermens. During 1996, we received information from Suzanne Nelson Thomas of Granbury, Texas, a descendant of the Newkirks. She stated that Mattheuse Cornelissen Van Nieuwkercke was born in the early 1600s, and actually came to America, where he served for a time as Magistrate in New Netherlands, the Dutch colony on Manhattan Island. Suffering poor health, and homesick for his family, he returned to his native land and died there. He was the father of at least two sons, who arrived in New Amsterdam, America, on April 25, 1659, aboard the *Moesman*. They were reportedly born in Holland, but with the date of birth of the eldest son being 1631, when the father was not more than thirty years old or so, it seems possible that at least that son may have been in America with his father, returning to Holland with the family, and then once again moving back to America with his own wife and child. The two known sons were:

1. Gerrit Cornelisse Van Nieuwkercke, born c.1631 in Slichtenhorst, Gelderland, Holland; died between February 3, 1686 and March 4, 1695 at Hurley, Ulster County, New York. His descendants are treated immediately following.
2. Mattheus Cornelisse Van Nieuwkercke, born about 1647 in Holland, and died May 12, 1705 in Bergen County, New Jersey. Married first December 14, 1670 to Anna Lubi, and second August 15, 1686 to Catryna Paulus. He was the father of thirteen children, and of whom more in Chapter 10.

Gerrit Cornelisse Van Nieuwkercke
1631-1686/95

This son of Mattheuse Cornelissen Van Nieuwkercke (1600), was born July 24, 1631 in Holland, and immigrated to America on board the *Moesman*, which arrived in New York April 25, 1659. He brought with him a wife, a "sucking child", and his younger brother, Mattheus Cornelisse (then aged 12), and apparently had additional children in America. He died between February 3, 1686 and March, 1695. I have found in the library of the Washington County Historical Society at Hagerstown, Maryland, the papers of Dr. A. B. Newkirk, which contain information about this family. It is reported there that the wife brought to America was Aaltie Gerrits, who was "his wife of record in Nykerk, Holland, if these are the same people." There is a letter dated March 18, 1984, from J. H. M. Putman, of the Genealogische Documentatie Service, Netherlands, which contains interesting information on the family.

It is there reported that Gerrit Cornelisse and Aaltie Gerrits were married in Putten on December 9, 1655; he was the son of Cornelis Killen, she the daughter of Gerrit Jansen. Gerrit Cornelisse was baptized in Putten on July 24, 1631. His father, Matheuse Cornelissen Van Nieuwkercke (known in Holland records as Cornelis Killen, son of Kil Hermens), was married in Putten on November 9, 1630 to Bijtie Gerrits, daughter of Gerrit Aerts. There is one daughter of Gerrit Cornellisen and Aaltie Gerrits registered in the baptismal registers of the Reformed Church at Nijkerk, Disje, baptized July 11, 1658. She must be the "sucking child" as reported in the immigration records.

He may have been married secondly to Chieltje (Charlotte) Cornelissen Slecht about 1661 in New York. Gustave Anjou, in *Ulster County, New York Probate Records*, reports his wife as Hendrikje Paulus. Upon his arrival in America, he located at Flatbush, Long Island, and obtained a small tract of land which he sold March 10, 1665 to Arent Evertse. This tract consisted of eighteen morgens (about thirty-six acres), and is in the heart of the City of Brooklyn; today worth many millions of dollars. Neikirk Street runs through the tract, and that is all that is left to show of who originally settled the area. Some time around March of 1669, he purchased lands in the Hurley Patent, in Ulster County, New York, which was still considered his home when his will was probated March 4, 1695/96. It was dated February 3, 1686, and his wife inherited the entire estate. Reportedly, he signed the will as Gerritt Cornelison, having been known on occasion to use that name as a surname, rather than the more usual Newkirk or a similar derivation of the original family name. His wife was deceased prior to June 30, 1702. He was in Captain Henry Pawling's Company of Foot Militia and, at the April 5, 1670 *Rendevouz*, was reported as being from Hurley. His family consisted of the following children:

1. Disje Van Nieuwkercke, baptized July 11, 1658 in the Reformed Church of Nijkerk, Netherlands, and died in New York after April, 1659
2. Arien Gerritsen Van Nieuwkercke (or Adrian Gerritsen, according to Mormon IGI records), born c.1661 (or more likely 1663) at Midwout, Long Island, New York. Married Lysbeth Lambertse Brink after October 17, 1686, who was baptized February 14, 1666. His wife has been reported as Elizabeth Huybertse, and they are said to be the progenitors of the New York families. They had eight children, and of whom more in Chapter 9.
3. Cornelis Gerretse Van Nieuwkercke, born c.1662, probably at Long Island, New York, and died 1695/96. Married about September 16, 1683 in Ulster County, New York, to Jennetje Jansz Kunst; and of whom more in Chapter 2.
4. Jan or Jan Gerretse Van Nieuwkercke, baptized September 8, 1666 in New York Dutch Church. Married Titjen Deckers July 23, 1687 at Kingston, New York.
5. Neeltje Van Nieuwkercke (Eleanor or Cornelia), born c.1667 in Ulster County, New York, and died at Hurley c.1706. She was married first about 1690 to Peter Crispell, son of Anthony Crispell and Maria Blanshan Crispell. Peter was baptized December 21, 1664 at Kingston, New York, and died c.1695. They had three children.
   a. Anthony Crispell, baptized April 17, 1692; married September 11, 1719 to Lea Roosa, daughter of Heyman Aldertse Roosa and Anna Margaret Roosevelt Roosa. His

will, dated March 9, 1767 at Hurley, and probated August 16, 1771, mentions three children:
(1)   Johannes Crispell.
(2)   Cornelius Crispell.
(3)   Neeltje Crispell; married Dirck Roosa
b. Ariantje Crispell, born June 30, 1694; married March 10, 1712 to Andries Ten Eyck, son of Matthew Ten Eyck and Jenneke Roosa Ten Eyck. They had children:
(1)   Neeltje Ten Eyck, baptized October 15, 1717
(2)   Matthew Ten Eyck, baptized February 21, 1720
(3)   Jannetje Ten Eyck, baptized May 20, 1722
(4)   Petrus Ten Eyck, baptized February 21, 1725
(5)   Andries Ten Eyck, baptized March 19, 1727
(6)   Johannes Ten Eyck, baptized September 9, 1732
(7)   Abraham Ten Eyck, baptized December 21, 1735
(8)   Adrientje Ten Eyck, baptized May 27, 1739
(9)   Marytje Ten Eyck; married Jaques Vanderbeck
c. Johannes Crispell, baptized October 27, 1695; married December 15, 1725 to Anna Margaret Roosa, daughter of Albert Roosa and Aagje Krom Roosa. Children:
(1)   Petrus Crispell, baptized November 26, 1727; died young
(2)   Albert Crispell, baptized November 10, 1728; died young
(3)   Rachel Crispell, baptized October 1, 1732. Married to Petrus Roosa December 11, 1756 and had children
(4)   Arriantje Crispell, baptized August 25, 1734; married April 26, 1758 to Abraham Elmendorf.
(5)   Petrus Crispell, baptized September 19, 1736, and married November 10, 1762 to Gerretje DuBois, daughter of Garret DuBois and Margaret Elmendorf DuBois and had children.
(6)   Elizabeth Crispell, baptized February 24, 1738; married to Cornelius J. Elmendorf.
(7)   Lea Crispell, baptized December 14, 1740
(8)   Albert Crispell, baptized February 13, 1743

(9)   Johannes Crispell, baptized April 21, 1745, and married to Rebecca Roosa. His will was dated May 29, 1809 and probated November 6, 1810. He lived then at Shawangunk, and named two sons and their sisters in his will.

Neeltje Van Nieuwkercke was married second February 18, 1697 to Johannes Schepmoes. He was a son of Dirck Jansen Schepmoes and Maria Willems Schepmoes, and was baptized April 7, 1672 at Kingston. They had one child:

d.   Maria Schepmoes, baptized May 1, 1698, and died 1734. Married May 26, 1720 to Simon Van Wagenen, son of Gerret Aartsen Van Wagenen and Clarissa Evertse Pells. After her death, her husband remarried; they had eight children:

   (1)   Clara Van Wagenen, baptized May 14, 1721; married December, 1743 to Hendrick Krom and had children.

   (2)   Johannes Van Wagenen, baptized November 18, 1722; married first August 2, 1748 to Elizabeth Burhans, widowed daughter of Barent Burhans; and second in 1760 to Helena Kittle. Children to both marriages.

   (3)   Gerret Aartsen Van Wagenen, baptized March 24, 1724; married Annatje Bosch, and had children in Ulster County.

   (4)   Neeltje Van Wagenen, baptized November 6, 1726, married Henrich Bosch and had children.

   (5)   Jacob Van Wagenen, baptized July 7, 1728

   (6)   Maria Van Wagenen, baptized December 21, 1729, married November 23, 1751 Abraham Krom of Ulster County, and had children.

   (7)   Annatje Van Wagenen, baptized February 20, 1732; married to Jonas Schmidt in Ulster County.

   (8)   Sarah Van Wagenen, baptized March 24, 1734; married March 26, 1759 to Henrich Schmidt and had children.

6. Gerretje Van Nieuwkercke (Geraldine), born February 15, 1665 and baptized March 12, 1669 at Kingston, New York; and died after April 3, 1739 at Hurley, New York. Her name has also been reported as being Trintje. Married first to Barent Kunst, son of Jan Barentsen Kunst and Jacomyntje Slecht Kunst. He was baptized at Kingston on January 30, 1667. Barent was the brother of Jannetje Kunst, who married Gerretje's older brother. One child was born to this marriage.

    a. Jacomyntje Kunst, born in Hurley. Married at Kingston June 26, 1713 to Henry Pawling, born c.1689, and died August 30, 1739 in an area that later became Montgomery County, Pennsylvania. He was the youngest son of Henry Pawling and Neeltje Roosa Pawling of Ulster County, New York. He moved from Ulster to a farm near Norristown, and they had seven children:

        (1) Henry Pawling, baptized June 27, 1714 in Ulster County, New York; died c.1792 in Pennsylvania. Married c.1740 to his cousin, Eleanor Pawling, born February 27, 1715, daughter of John Pawling and Aagje DeWitt Pawling.

        (2) Sara Pawling, baptized July 8, 1716

        (3) Elizabeth Pawling, baptized March 22, 1719

        (4) Barent Pawling; married to Elizabeth James, a daughter of Josiah James.

        (5) Levi Pawling, who served as a Colonel in the Revolution, and Judge of Ulster County. Married October 12, 1749 at Kingston to Helena Burhans, baptized May 14, 1732, the daughter of William Burhans and Grietje or Grietjen Ten Eyck (1689) Newkirk Burhans, widow of Gerrit Nieuwkercke (1684).

        (6) John Pawling, baptized December 27, 1732; and married to May 23, 1755 Neeltje Van Keuren. She was the daughter of Thomas Van Keuren and Mary Pawling.

        (7) Elinor Pawling; married before 1746 to James Morgan.

Gerretje Van Nieuwkercke married second Jacob DuBois in 1691/92. He was a son of Louis DuBois and Catherine Blanshan, and was baptized October 9, 1661; and died in 1745. He had first been married March 8, 1689 to Elizabeth Vernooy, by whom he had a daughter in 1690. Eleven children were born to this second marriage of both, in Ulster County, New York:

b. Barent DuBois, baptized May 3, 1693, died at Pittsgrove, Salem County, New Jersey January 22, 1749. Married April 23, 1715 to Jacomyntje DuBois, born October 30, 1693, daughter of Solomon DuBois and Tryntje Focken. Eight children, the first three born in Ulster County, New York, and the last five in Salem County, New Jersey.

c. Louis DuBois, born January 6, 1695; died 1784 in Pittsgrove in Salem County. Married June 21, 1720 Margaret Jansen, baptized at Kingston June 4, 1699, daughter of Matthys Jansen and Aaltje Elmendorf. Eleven children, born in Salem County, New Jersey.

d. Gieltjie DuBois, baptized May 13, 1697; died young

e. Gerret DuBois, baptized March 20, 1700; died young

f. Isaac DuBois, baptized February 1, 1702 and died before September 21, 1773 at Greenkill, Ulster County, New York, where he owned and operated a mill. Married first August 5, 1731 to Neeltje Roosa, baptized April 5, 1713, daughter of Albert Roosa and Aagje Krom. Married second October 5, 1760 Jannette Roosa. Seven children born to his first marriage in Ulster County, New York.

g. Gerret DuBois, baptized February 13, 1704; died at Marbletown, New York. Married there July 18, 1730 to Margaret Elmendorf, baptized June 20, 1708, daughter of Coenradt and Blandina Kierstede Elmendorf. He moved with some of his brothers to Pittsgrove, Salem County, New Jersey, where most of his eight children were born.

h. Catharine DuBois, baptized March 24, 1706. Married February 12, 1724 to Petrus Smedes who was baptized at Kingston December 7, 1701, a son of Benjamin and

Magdalena Louw Smedes. Eleven children born in Ulster County.

i. Rebecca DuBois, baptized October 31, 1708. Married September 15, 1726 to Petrus Bogardus baptized December 3, 1699, son of Evert and Tjaetjen Hoffman Bogardus. They had eight children.

j. Johannes DuBois, baptized November 10, 1710; lived at Hurley in Ulster County, New York. Married December 11, 1736 to Judike Wynkoop, baptized August 31, 1712, a daughter of Cornelius (1688) and Hendrikje Newkirk (1692) Wynkoop, and granddaughter of Arie (1663) and Lysbeth Lambertse Brink (1666) Newkirk. Eleven children born in Ulster County. One of their children was:

(1) Hendrica DuBois, baptized December 28, 1746; married May 4, 1771 her cousin, Jacob Newkirk, baptized August 26, 1744. They had four children, all of whom died unmarried:

(a) Judeke Newkirk, baptized August 30, 1771

(b) Nelly Newkirk, baptized November 22, 1777

(c) Johannes Newkirk, baptized November 22, 1777

(d) Judice Newkirk, baptized December 22, 1787

k. Sarah DuBois, baptized December 20, 1713. Married June 21, 1734 to Conrad Elmendorf, baptized October 10, 1710, son of Coenradt and Blandina Kierstede Elmendorf. Eight children, born in Ulster County, New York.

l. Neeltjen DuBois, baptized May 27, 1716. Married September 9, 1737 to Cornelius Newkirk, baptized May 1, 1715, son of Gerrit Nieuwkercke (1684) and Grietje or Grietjen Ten Eyck (1689). At least nine children, named in his will.

7. Ginitje Van Nieuwkercke, reported from another source, married to Solomon DuBois, brother of Jacob, who married her sister.

CHAPTER 2

Cornelis Gerretse Van Nieuwkercke
1662-1695/96

This son of Gerrit Cornelisse Van Nieuwkercke (1635), was born c.1662, probably on Long Island, New York. His will was dated February 7, 1695/96 and probated March 4, 1695/96, so he died between those dates. There was a survey of 86 acres of land laid out for him on April 5, 1686, on the north side of the Esopus Kill in Ulster County, New York. He served as a private under Captain Hendrickus Beekman, Kingston Troop of Horse in 1686 to 1687. He was married in Ulster County on September 16, 1683 to Jennetje Jansz Kunst, who was baptized February 24, 1664 at Kingston Church. She was a daughter of Jan Barentsen Kunst and his second wife, Jacomyntje Cornelis Slecht Kunst. Jan Barentsen Kunst was a house carpenter and came to America from Alckmaer, Holland, in May, 1658 aboard the *Gilded Beaver*. Another daughter of his by his first wife, Jennette Ariens, was Hillitje Jans Kunst, who married Nicholas Roosevelt, and they are the ancestors of President Theodore Roosevelt. Jennetje survived her husband and was living as late as August 2, 1729, at which time she was mentioned in a deed as the widow of Cornelis Newkirk, late of Hurley. Cornelis Gerretse had seven children, all of them baptized at Kingston, Ulster County, New York:

1. Gerrit Van Nieuwkercke, baptized July 28, 1684, and of whom more following
2. Jan Van Nieuwkercke, born November 29, 1685, and of whom more following
3. Adrian Van Nieuwkercke, baptized February 27, 1687, and of whom more following
4. Barent Van Nieuwkercke, born October 13, 1689, of whom more in Chapter 3.
5. Gilles Van Nieuwkercke (Gieletjen), baptized November 5, 1691 and died after June 13, 1749. Married October 5, 1714 to Jacobus Swartwout, born February 13, 1692 and died April 5, 1749, son of Thomas and Lysbeth Gardenier Swartwout.

They lived at Fishkill, New York, and had nine children, the first three baptized at Kingston, and the rest born in Dutchess County, New York:

a. Thomas Swartwout, born October 2, 1715; married Mary Garsling. Six children.

b. Elizabeth Swartwout, baptized May 26, 1717, married to Jacob DePeyster of Fishkill.

c. Jannetjen Swartwout, baptized October 11, 1719, and married Maes (or Moses) Ostrander. Three children, born at Fishkill.

d. Cornelius Swartwout, born January 21, 1722; married June 19, 1746 Elizabeth daughter of Henry and Catharine Ter Bosch. Seven children, born at Fishkill.

e. Rudolphus Swartwout, born May 6, 1724; married first October 1, 1749 to Gerardina Brinkerhoff, daughter of Abraham and Femmetje Remsen Vanderbeek Brinkerhoff; and second October 14, 1762 to Sarah Polhemus, who died March 5, 1820 at the age of 94 years, 2 months and 12 days. He had four children.

f. Samuel Swartwout, baptized January 23, 1726; married April 16, 1749 Phebe Pudney, a daughter of John Pudney of Rombouts. Eight children, born there.

g. Jacomyntje Swartwout, born October 14, 1728; married September 19, 1748 to Hendricus Rosecrans, Jr. and had six children.

h. Catharine Swartwout, baptized September 3, 1732; married Joseph Dorland, and had a son.

i. Jacobus Swartwout, baptized November 5, 1734; married March 9, 1760 to Aeltje Brinkerhoff, born September 23, 1740, a daughter of Isaac and Sarah Rapelje Brinkerhoff. He lived at Fishfill, and was Colonel in the Revolutionary War. He had eight children.

6. Jacomyntje Van Nieuwkercke, baptized June 8, 1694. Married first September 28, 1715 to Hendrick Kip, who was baptized July 7, 1688 and died between December 12, 1751 and December 14, 1754, the date of the making and probate of his will. There, he left property to his wife, with the remainder to Cornelius Newkirk, eldest son of Gerret, and to cousin

Cornelius Newkirk, son of Jan. Jacomyntje married second August 25, 1755 to Captain Peter DuBois. One child, born to the first marriage:

    a.   Jannetjen Kip, baptized September 23, 1716; died single before December 12, 1751.

7.   Cornelius Van Nieuwkercke, born August 30, 1696, and of whom more following

Gerrit Nieuwkercke
1684-1724

This son of Cornelis Gerretse Van Nieuwkercke (1662), was baptized July 28, 1684 in the Dutch Church at Kingston, Ulster County, New York, and died c.1724 in Hurley. Some records tend to indicate that he dropped the Van from the family name. He was married in Ulster County about 1708 to Grietje or Grietjen Ten Eyck, who was baptized February 10, 1689, daughter of Mathys and Jenneken Roosa Ten Eyck. His will, executed July 25, 1724, and probated September 3, 1724, provided for his wife, five living children, and one to be born in November, 1724. After his death, his wife married secondly June 22, 1731 to William Burhans or Willem Borhans. His children, all baptized in Kingston, were:

1.   Cornelius Van Nieuwkercke, baptized September 28, 1711; died young

2.   Jannetjen Van Nieuwkercke, baptized October 12, 1712. Married January 15, 1730 Gerrit Elmendorf, baptized January 26, 1696, son of Coenrad Elmendorf. They had four children.

    a.   Conrad Elmendorf, baptized August 14, 1734
    b.   Garret Elmendorf, baptized March 14, 1736; died young
    c.   Margrietje Elmendorf, baptized April 3, 1737
    d.   Garret Elmendorf, baptized January 16, 1743

3.   Cornelius Van Nieuwkercke, the second use of the name after the infant death of the earlier child, baptized May 1, 1715, and of whom more.

4.   Matthew Van Nieuwkercke, or Matheus, baptized January 13, 1717 in Ulster County, New York, and of whom more.

5.   Benjamin Van Nieuwkercke, baptized October 30, 1720, of whom more

6. Coenradt Van Nieuwkercke, baptized May 14, 1722, of whom more
7. Gerretjen Van Nieuwkercke, baptized November 22, 1724; married November 12, 1743 Abraham Van Keuren, baptized September 23, 1711, and died October 12, 1776. His parents were Tjerck Matthysen Van Keuren and Marytje Ten Eyck Van Keuren. Eight children:
    a. Garret Van Keuren, baptized November 9, 1746
    b. Margaret Van Keuren, baptized January 28, 1750; died young
    c. Abraham Van Keuren, baptized February 16, 1752
    d. Margaret Van Keuren, baptized February 9, 1755
    e. Marietje Van Keuren, baptized December 12, 1756
    f. Tjerck Van Keuren, baptized July 13, 1760
    g. Martin Van Keuren, baptized October 26, 1762
    h. Levi Van Keuren, baptized December 6, 1767

Cornelius Newkirk
1715-1783

This son of Gerrit Van Nieuwkercke (1684) was baptized May 1, 1715 and died before February 14, 1783, when his will was probated in Ulster County, New York. Married September 3, 1737 to Neeltjen DuBois, who was baptized May 27, 1716, a daughter of Jacob DuBois (1661) and Gerretje Newkirk DuBois (1665). Eleven children, born in Ulster County, New York:
1. Catharine Newkirk, baptized February 26, 1738; died after 1781. Married October 26, 1765 to Johannes or John E. DeWitt, baptized September 19, 1733, son of Egbert DeWitt (1699) and Mary Nottingham DeWitt; and had four children.
2. Garret C. Newkirk, (listed also as Gerrit in Mormon IGI records), baptized September 23, 1739, and died December 26, 1813. Married December 8, 1764 to his second cousin, Leah Nieuwkirk. She was baptized April 29, 1744, daughter of Cornelius Nieuwkirk (1710). Note that some members of the family had begun to anglicize the name even further than this group. He served as a private in the Revolution. Six children, all born in Ulster County, New York:

a. Diana Newkirk, or Dina, born October 20, 1765. Probably married 1793 to Jacobus DeWitt
b. Neeltje Newkirk, baptized May 14, 1769
c. Cornelius Newkirk, baptized December 6, 1772
d. Elizabeth Newkirk, born July 28, 1776, and died young
e. Eleanor Newkirk, baptized November 22, 1777, and died November 8, 1826. Married September 18, 1800 to Eli DeWitt
f. Elizabeth Newkirk, second of that name after the earlier infant death; baptized November 16, 1783
3. Margrietjen Newkirk, or Margretje, baptized on October 24, 1742, and died in February, 1783
4. Jacob Newkirk, baptized August 26, 1744, and married May 4, 1771 to Hendrica DuBois, who was baptized December 28, 1746, daughter of Johannes and Judike Wynkoop DuBois. Four children, born in Ulster County, New York, and all of whom died unmarried:
a. Judeke Newkirk, baptized August 30, 1771
b. Nelly Newkirk, baptized November 22, 1777
c. Johannes Newkirk, baptized November 22, 1777
d. Judice Newkirk, baptized December 22, 1787
5. Jannetjen Newkirk, baptized October 12, 1746; died young
6. Matthew Newkirk, or Matheus, baptized April 2, 1749, and died c.1781. Married December 9, 1774 to Cornelia Bevier, born January 21, 1755, daughter of Samuel Bevier and Sarah Le Fevre (or Zara Le Fevre, baptized February 3, 1717). No children.
7. Jannetjen Newkirk, the second to bear the name, baptized on August 5, 1750 and died October 19, 1833. Married Richard Broadhead, baptized December 3, 1749 and died October 17, 1824 in Ulster County. Five children.
8. Benjamin Newkirk, baptized October 15, 1752; died August 7, 1826. Married September 7, 1774 to Margaret, or Margritje, Broadhead, who was baptized December 3, 1749 and died October 17, 1824 at Ulster County. They had six children:
a. Benjamin Newkirk, Jr., baptized April 19, 1778
b. Anne Newkirk, or Ann, baptized February 2, 1780, and married to Stephen DeWitt

c. John Broadhead Newkirk, baptized November 17, 1781. He may be the same John Newkirk shown at the age of 70 in the 1850 census of Ulster County, a farmer, apparently widowed, with two children, perhaps his youngest:
    (1) William Newkirk, born c.1830
    (2) Margaret Newkirk, born c.1830
d. Cornelius B. Newkirk, baptized November 15, 1783; died October 23, 1853 at Saugerties, New York. Married to Elizabeth, born September, 1803 and died January 4, 1880. They are buried at Leurenkill Burial Ground near Ellenville, Warwarsing, New York. Perhaps the same Cornelius shown in the 1850 census of Ulster County at the age of 66, with wife Elizabeth at age 49, and two children:
    (1) Eleanor Newkirk, born c.1828 in New York
    (2) Ann Newkirk, born c.1834 in New York
e. William Henry Newkirk, baptized November 14, 1795
f. Mary Newkirk, born June 21, 1798

9. Isaac Newkirk, baptized April 7, 1754 and died December 24, 1825. Married Anna Jane Broadhead, who was born July 30, 1737 and died March 3, 1830. Private during Revolution. Twelve children, all born in Ulster County, New York:
a. Neeltje Newkirk, baptized May 18, 1783, and died 1847. Married Peter LeFever
b. Matthew Newkirk, or Matheus, baptized August 14, 1784; died November 5, 1784
c. Anna Newkirk, born December 13, 1785, and christened January 7, 1786. Married John B. Newkirk. Probably a cousin, and perhaps the same individual born c.1782, who died at Lurenkill, New York February 26, 1858. According to Mormon IGI records, they had children, born in Ulster County, including:
    (1) Nellie Maria Newkirk, born August 12, 1810
    (2) William Newkirk, born July 10, 1814
d. William Broadhead Newkirk, baptized January 25, 1788, and died February 25, 1872 in Venango County, Pennsylvania. Married to Alida Freer, born April 26, 1796 in Dutchess County, New York. The family appears

14

in the 1850 census of the county, although there, the wife's first name is misspelled Olliday. Their children included, at least:

(1) Moses Newkirk, born March 1, 1822 and died 1887. Moses appears to have remained in Ulster County, New York, where he appeared in the census of 1850, with a wife, Mary, born c.1818, and children:
   (a) William Newkirk, born c.1845 in New York
   (b) John Gray Newkirk, born c.1847, and of whom more
(2) Edgar Newkirk, born c.1824 in New York
(3) William Newkirk, born c.1827 in New York
(4) Elizabeth Newkirk, born c.1830 in New York
(5) Cornelius H. Newkirk, born 1834 in Pennsylvania
(6) Caroline M. Newkirk, born 1837 in Pennsylvania

e. Rachel Newkirk born July 10, 1790, died June 13, 1797
f. Margaarita Newkirk, born January 29, 1793; died May 19, 1793
g. Cornelius Newkirk, born 1794; an infant death
h. Wyntje Newkirk, born September 4, 1795; died September 10, 1888; and married April 5, 1823 to Henry Broadhead
i. John I. Newkirk, born August 1, 1797 and died April 11, 1873 in Chemung County, New York. Married February 9, 1823 to Amy Burhans, born c.1807 in Connecticut. The family appears in the 1850 census of the county, although the name is listed as John J. Newkirk, a farmer. There was also in the household one James Slauson, born c.1826 in New York. Children included:
(1) Milton Newkirk, perhaps a twin, born c.1826 in New York
(2) Nelly Newkirk, perhaps a twin, born c.1826 in New York
(3) Isaac Newkirk, born c.1828 in New York
(4) Ann Newkirk, born c.1837 in Pennsylvania
(5) Rachel Newkirk, born c.1842 in New York

j. Rachel Newkirk, second child of this name, born June 4, 1799; died May 4, 1875. Married August 11, 1826 to Abram Devens

k. Margaret Newkirk, born August 22, 1801; died July 13, 1837

l. Matilda Newkirk, born 1803; married George Peterson

10. Jacomyntje Newkirk, baptized June 8, 1755; died young

11. Jacomyntje Newkirk, the second child of this name, born October 29, 1758 and died April 12, 1805. Married January 24, 1778 to Henry Broadhead, born October 15, 1752 and died January 15, 1820. Children unknown.

John Gray Newkirk
1847-1907

This son of Moses Nieuwkercke (1822), was born c.1847 in Ulster County, New York, and died 1907. He was married to Lemira Susanna Bailey and had two sons who, it appears, began using the more familiar spelling, Newkirk:

1. Harris D. Newkirk, a doctor, born 1878 and died 1938. At least a son:
    a. Dana Shelton Newkirk, born 1906 and died 1962. A son:
        (1) Joel H. Newkirk, in 1983 living in Santa Monica, California
    b. Burt Leroy Newkirk, of whom more

Burt Leroy Newkirk

This son of John Gray Newkirk (1847), was married in 1910 to Mary Louise Leavenworth in Minneapolis, where he was a member of the faculty of the University of Minnesota, in astronomy. In 1902, Burt Leroy Newkirk earned his Ph.D. from the University of Munich, and was the first American to be awarded a summa cum laude degree from that University at the time. There were four children:

1. Horace Leavenworth Newkirk, born 1911. Married to Eileen, who died in 1989, and had one daughter:
    a. Nadenia Newkirk

2. Virginia Bailey Newkirk, born c.1914 and married to Bernard M. Cain. Four children:
   a. Emily Cain
   b. Richard Cain
   c. Barbara Cain
   d. Elizabeth Cain
3. Muriel Louise Newkirk, born c.1917 and died February, 1991. Married Dr. Douglas V. Frost, who predeceased her, and had four children, all living in 1991:
   a. Ray Frost
   b. Melodie Frost
   c. Nancy Frost
   d. Constance Frost
4. John Burt Newkirk, my correspondent for this family, born 1920, and married to Carolyn Mae Jordan in 1951. He holds a Doctor of Science degree, and was Phillipson Professor Emeritus of the University of Denver, in Colorado. In his retirement, he is president of Colorado Biomedical, Inc., and he and Carol run the business, travel, ski, cycle and keep bees. Four children:
   a. Jeffrey Burt Newkirk, born 1959 and died 1980
   b. John Jordan Newkirk, born 1961
   c. Victoria Louise Newkirk, born 1964
   d. Christina Brooks Newkirk, born 1968

Matthew Newkirk
1717-1791

This son of Gerrit Nieuwkercke (1684) was baptized January 13, 1717 in Ulster County, New York, and died between June 1, 1789, the date of his will, and March 28, 1791, the date of probate. He served in the Foot Company of Militia at Hurley under command of Captain Cornelius Wynkoop in 1738. Married November 8, 1740 to Annetje or Annaatjen Kool. She was baptized April 20, 1713, daughter of Jacob and Sarah Legg Kool. Matthew's will is summarized in *Ulster County, New York Probate Records, Volume II*, by Gustave Anjou, originally published in 1906, and reprinted 1992 by Heritage Books, Inc., Bowie, Maryland. The book is a must addition to the library of anyone who has ancestors in Ulster County during the seventeen and eighteenth centuries. In his will, Matthew mentions only two of his sons, Garret M. and Jacobus, and his daughter Margaretta, as well as his grandson, Matthew Oliver. Matthew was apparently fairly well-to-do, listing ten slaves in various bequests to his children. Seven children have been reported, however, all born in New York, probably Marbletown:

1. Garrett M. Newkirk, baptized October 25, 1741 (or October 16, 1740), and married June 15, 1765 to Batah de Lamater, baptized April 18, 1742
2. Jenneke Newkirk, baptized November 7, 1746
3. Benjamin Newkirk, baptized February 14, 1748
4. Catharina Newkirk, baptized August 5, 1750
5. Margaretta Newkirk, baptized June 6, 1755; married February 15, 1778 to Dr. James Oliver, and had at least one son:
   a. Matthew Oliver.
6. Jacobus Newkirk, baptized March 5, 1758; married June 19, 1788 to Elizabeth Cantine (or Contyne) born April 20, 1762. They had a daughter, born in New York:
   a. Mary Newkirk, born 1798 and died 1851; married to Peter Jacob Cantine
7. Peter Newkirk, baptized March 5, 1758 and married January 19, 1787 to Jane Cantine, born December 2, 1766 in Ulster County. Children, all born there:
   a. Peter Newkirk, Jr., baptized August 4, 1799
   b. Aaron Newkirk, baptized November 29, 1801; died at Kingston June 27, 1867. Probably the same person who appears as a painter in the 1850 census of Ulster County, New York, with a wife, Catherine, and several children, including:
      (1) Gap A. Newkirk, a clerk, born c.1828
      (2) Cornelius Newkirk, a tin-man, born c.1832
      (3) Lisly Newkirk (or Delilah), born c.1837
      (4) Moses Newkirk, born c.1840
      (5) John Newkirk, born c.1846

Benjamin Newkirk
1720-

This son of Gerrit Nieuwkercke (1684) was baptized October 30, 1720. He served in Captain Cornelius Wynkoop's Company of Foot at Hurley in 1738. Married May 19, 1767 Catherine Rutsen; at least one son:

1. Gerrit Benjamin Newkirk, baptized November 12, 1769 at Kingston, New York, and died October 8, 1808. Married November 3, 1793 to Maria Roosa, born June 16, 1773 and died August 8, 1884. They had children, born in New York:
   a. Caty Rusten Newkirk, born May 10, 1795, and died November 22, 1797
   b. Benjamin Garret Newkirk, baptized January 28, 1800, and died January 15, 1869 at Hurley, Ulster County. Married February 13, 1822 Blandina DeWitt, born June 17, 1800; died October 22, 1862. They appear in the 1850 census for Ulster County. In 1991, I received information on this family from Stanley Clifton Newkirk (1932), of Ulster Park, New York, indicating there were nine children:
      (1) Elizabeth Newkirk, born c.1822
      (2) Catharine Newkirk, born January 30, 1823 married January 12, 1842 to Bogardus Newkirk, born March 27, 1815, a son of Cornelius Newkirk (1780). This may be Cornelius S. Newkirk, Jr., born November, 1780; died October 20, 1867. Married Magdalena, born June, 1782; died November 3, 1815. Both buried at Hurley, New York; not otherwise now identified in the study.
      (3) Cornelia Newkirk, born July 4, 1825, died October 23, 1849
      (4) Maria DeWitt Newkirk, born October 26, 1828, and died January 13, 1882
      (5) Margaret Ann Newkirk, born January 17, 1830
      (6) Sarah Newkirk, born February 14, 1832 and died November 16, 1918

(7) Garret Newkirk, born March 14, 1834, of whom more

(8) Charles DeWitt Newkirk, born November 15, 1836 and died March 9, 1916

(9) Ten Eyck Newkirk, born December 6, 1839

Garret Newkirk
1834-1912

This son of Benjamin Garret Newkirk, or Nieuwkercke, (1800) was born in Ulster County, New York, March 5, 1834, and died in 1912. He was married to Cornelia DeWitt November 18, 1857, who was born May 12, 1837 and died June 22, 1901. They had a Negro servant, Nancy Cole, from the Virgin Islands, who first served his parents. She died March 28, 1893 at 72 years, and is buried with the family in the New Hurley Cemetery. On her stone is inscribed "All Done, Good and Faithful Servant." Six children:

1. Benjamin Garret Newkirk, born September 3, 1858 and died November 14, 1939

2. Ann DeWitt Newkirk, baptized October 4, 1861; died October 21, 1878

3. Maria Newkirk, born 1864

4. John Ten Eyck Newkirk, born July 6, 1866; died 1944

5. Abe Gasbeck Newkirk

6. Frank Newkirk, born May 21, 1871; died July 29, 1954. Married September 4, 1894 to Rachel Ann Tappen, who was born September 2, 1868 and died December 31, 1938. Six children:

   a. Gertrude Newkirk, born June 10, 1895; died March 12, 1982

   b. Garret Newkirk, born 1898; died 1946

   c. Stanley Tappen Newkirk, born May 7, 1900 and died April 25, 1958. His first marriage to Mildred Morehouse ended in divorce. Married second April 18, 1932 to Lena Mertine, born September 24, 1912; at least one son:

      (1) Stanley Clifton Newkirk, born July 20, 1932. Married March 18, 1953 to Joyce Seymour, who was born October 15, 1934. Four children:

(a) Joseph Lester Newkirk, born June 10, 1955
(b) Susan Patricia Newkirk, born April 17, 1957
(c) Daniel Thomas Newkirk, born November 13, 1959
(d) Trisha Lynn Newkirk, born March 11, 1963
d. Frank Newkirk, an infant death
e. Ruth B. Newkirk, born October 14, 1903
f. Rachel Ann Newkirk, born 1911; lived seven months

Coenradt Newkirk
1722-1805

This son of Gerrit Nieuwkercke (1684) was baptized May 14, 1722 in Ulster County, New York, and died in Hurley, January 25, 1805. Married May 13, 1747 (or 1749) to Anne DeWitt, baptized March 23, 1725 in Ulster County; died October 12, 1805, daughter of Johannes and Mary Broadhead DeWitt. His will, dated April 26, 1796, probated April 4, 1806, is reported in *Ulster County, New York Probate Records*, Volume 1, by Gustave Anjou. He reports Coenradt's mother as Lysbeth Lambertsen, daughter of Lambert Huybertsen, which does not check with other information, reporting Lysbeth as wife of Arien Gerritsen Newkirk (1661); see Chapter 9 of this study. On page 48 of his study (will of Coenrad Elmendorf), and page 184 (Cornelius Newkirk will), Anjou correctly identifies Lysbeth as the wife of Arien Gerritsen Newkirk. The will names nine children; there were perhaps twelve, born in Ulster County:
1. Andrew Newkirk, baptized April 3, 1748
2. Benjamin Newkirk, baptized August 26, 1750; died single
3. Johannes Newkirk, baptized November 3, 1751; died January 14, 1818 in Fairfield County, Connecticut. Married December 30, 1779 to Margaret Harsin (Aarsen), born c.1759 and died September 27, 1817 in Fairfield County. Her name has been variously reported as Balli or Maria. They had six children, born either in New York or Connecticut:
   a. Sarah Newkirk, baptized November 26, 1780, and married to Thomas Campbell
   b. Ann Newkirk, or Anna, baptized August 25, 1781 or 1782

c. Conrad Newkirk, born 1783; married Lucretia Jennings. Mormon IGI records report his birth July 17, 1791.

d. Maria Harsin Newkirk, baptized June 20, 1784; married to Thomas Edgerly

e. Garret Harsin Newkirk, born April 26, 1787; died February 1, 1831. Married to Amelia Cannon, born February 6, 1788; died November 8, 1874; both in Fairfield County.

f. Blandina Newkirk, baptized July 29, 1789, and married Colonel Segar

g. Charles Newkirk, born September 2, 1793, or November 28, 1796 in New York

h. Peggy Newkirk, baptized November 29, 1794

i. John Newkirk, baptized June 24, 1798 in New York

j. DeWitt Newkirk, born May 30, 1799 in New York.

4. Charles Newkirk, baptized April 22, 1753

5. Margaret Newkirk, baptized August 27, 1754; died January 28, 1839

6. Mary Newkirk, or Maria, baptized June 7, 1756

7. Gerretje Newkirk, or Geertjen, baptized March 5, 1758; died November, 1833. Married 1783 to Caleb Sweat

8. Anna Newkirk, baptized November 22, 1759

9. Jannette Newkirk, or Jennetje, baptized June 20, 1762, and died November 10, 1782, single.

10. Blandina Newkirk, baptized May 20, 1764; probably married August 5, 1692 to Elisha Southworth in Kingston, New York.

11. Coenradt Newkirk, (perhaps Coenradt C.) baptized June 5, 1766, died December, 1850. Married Neeltje Heermaantsen, born September, 1767; died January 15, 1846. They are buried in Katsbaan Cemetery at Saugerties, New York. He appears in the 1850 census of Ulster County, New York, at the age of 85, in the household of one of his sons, Henry H. Mormon IGI records supply the names of other children:

a. Annatje Newkirk, baptized April 11, 1790 at Red Hook, Dutchess County, New York.

b. Margaretha Newkirk, christened March 4, 1791

c. Charles Newkirk, baptized May 6, 1792

d. Cornelia Newkirk, baptized June 15, 1794

e. Catharina Dorothea Newkirk, born March 15, 1799
f. Jane Juliane Newkirk, born June 1, 1801
g. Hendrick Hermance Newkirk, born October, 1802 in New York, christened December 31, 1802 at Katsbaan, Ulster County, New York; and a blacksmith. He died November 18, 1875, and was married to Laura Sherman, born April, 1802 in New York, and died December 15, 1882. The census included four children, all born in New York:
    (1) Mary Newkirk, born c.1833
    (2) Gertrude Newkirk, born c.1837
    (3) James Newkirk, born c.1842
    (4) George Newkirk, born c.1847
h. Neeltje Meyer Newkirk, christened October 28, 1804
i. Geertrude Lansing Newkirk, baptized November 19, 1809
12. Andreas Newkirk, born c.1768; perhaps married June 27, 1793 to Janneke Louw, as shown in Mormon IGI records. They had children, according to those records, including:
    a. Benjamin Newkirk, born May 11, 1794
    b. Anna De Witt Newkirk, born February 21, 1796
    c. Maria Newkirk, born October 28, 1798

Jan Nieuwkercke
1685-

This son of Cornelis Gerretse Van Nieuwkercke (1662) and Jennetje Jansz Kunst (1664), was baptized November 29, 1685 in Kingston, Ulster County, New York. He was married November 6, 1708 in the New York Dutch Reformed Church to Jenneke Van Brestede, who was baptized September 12, 1683, a daughter of Andries and Annetje Van Borsum Brestede. They perhaps spent most of their lives in Dutchess County, New York, and had eleven children, all baptized in New York, probably Dutchess County:
1. Cornelius Nieuwkercke, a twin, baptized March 19, 1710; died young
2. Annatje Nieuwkercke, a twin, baptized March 19, 1710, and married three times. First in July, 1727 to William Miller;

23

second April 6, 1733 to John J. Dobbs; third to Cutler. She had one child from her first marriage, four from the second; none from the third:
   a.   John Miller, baptized July 3, 1728
   b.   John Dobbs, baptized January 15, 1734
   c.   Anna Dobbs, baptized October 13, 1736
   d.   Jenneke Dobbs, baptized November 26, 1738
   e.   Isaac Dobbs, baptized April 17, 1743
3. Andries Nieuwkercke, a twin, baptized January 23, 1712; and died before November 13, 1763, without children
4. Cornelius Nieuwkercke, a twin, second to bear the name, baptized January 23, 1712; died young
5. Jannetje Nieuwkercke, baptized February 21, 1714, married first to Jan Hermance, and second to Jacobus Van Etten. She had five children by Hermance and one by Van Etten, the first two born in Ulster County, New York, the others in Dutchess County:
   a.   Jan Hermance, baptized January 24, 1738
   b.   Abraham Hermance, baptized April 14, 1740
   c.   Jacomyntje Hermance, baptized May 8, 1743
   d.   Goozen Hermance, baptized December 15, 1745
   e.   Jacob Hermance
   f.   Jenneke Van Etten, baptized September 14, 1754
6. Engeltje Nieuwkercke, baptized April 8, 1716. Married Isaac Ryckman and lived in New York City. Three children:
   a.   Johannes Ryckman, baptized January 4, 1741, and died young
   b.   Isaac Ryckman, baptized April 17, 1743
   c.   Johannes Ryckman, baptized November 9, 1746
7. Cornelia Nieuwkercke, baptized January 14, 1719. Married first October 20, 1738 Philipus Hoff; and second October 14, 1748 Cornelius Van Keuren, widower of Kezia Hoogteeling. Three children from her first marriage; two from the second:
   a.   Catharine Hoff, baptized October 7, 1739
   b.   John Hoff, baptized September 6, 1741
   c.   Andries Hoff, baptized July 31, 1743
   d.   Cornelius Van Keuren, baptized January 14, 1750
   e.   Thomas Van Keuren, baptized July 12, 1752

8. Jacomyntje Nieuwkercke, baptized March 14, 1722; died young
9. Cornelius Nieuwkercke, the third child to bear this name, baptized May 8, 1723 and married May 17, 1749 to Maria Cooper. Lived at Fishkill, Dutchess County, New York. His will of November 13, 1763 suggests no surviving children.
10. Jacomyntje Nieuwkercke, the second use of the name, baptized June 21, 1727 and died November 13, 1763

Adrian Nieuwkercke
1687-

This son of Cornelis Gerretse Van Nieuwkercke (1662) and Jennetje Jansz Kunst (1664), was baptized February 27, 1687 in Ulster County, New York. In Mormon IGI records, his name appears as Ariaan Nieuwkerk. Married April 27, 1711 to Aaltjen Bogaard, who was baptized February 26, 1688, the daughter of Hendrick and Jennette Martens Bogaard. Eight children, all born in Ulster County:
1. Jannetjen Nieuwkercke, baptized March 15, 1713. Married September 14, 1731 to Johannes Burhans, who was baptized February 18, 1709 and died c.1804. Eleven children, born in Ulster County, the first two of whom died young:
    a. Johannes Burhans, baptized November 18, 1733
    b. Hendricus Burhans, baptized January 25, 1735
    c. Saartje Burhans.
    d. Aaltje Burhans, baptized September 9, 1739; married November 26, 1761 to Jan Schoonmaker. He was baptized May 18, 1740, the son of Tyrrick Schoonmaker (1699) and Theodotia Wittaker (1710).
    e. Johannes Burhans, baptized June 7, 1742
    f. Margriet Burhans, baptized September 7, 1744
    g. Cornelius Burhans, baptized August 15, 1746
    h. Hendricus Burhans, baptized August 1, 1748
    i. Helena Burhans, baptized October 18, 1750
    j. Jannetje Burhans, baptized January 28, 1753
    k. Jacomyntje Burhans, baptized December 27, 1755

2. Sarah Nieuwkercke, baptized October 16, 1715 and died June 19, 1788. Married September 30, 1737 John William Meyer, born February 13, 1714 in Ulster County, and died September 12, 1794, son of Christian and Ann Geertruyd Theunyes Meyer. Eleven children, born in Ulster County, New York:
   a. Christian Meyer, baptized October 24, 1738; died young
   b. Christian Meyer, baptized August 24, 1739
   c. Aaltjen Meyer, baptized March 11, 1741
   d. Hendricus Meyer, baptized December 26, 1742
   e. Maria Meyer, baptized November 2, 1743
   f. Johannes Meyer, baptized February 19, 1746
   g. Petrus Meyer, baptized June 25, 1750
   h. Tobias Meyer, baptized December 26, 1751
   i. Leah Meyer, baptized January 2, 1754
   j. Benjamin Meyer, baptized November 11, 1755
   k. Samuel Meyer, baptized February 6, 1757
3. Cornelius Nieuwkercke, baptized July 14, 1717; died young
4. Hendricus Nieuwkercke, baptized September 9, 1722
5. Cornelius Nieuwkercke (second use of this name), baptized February 28, 1725 and married May 28, 1752 to Lea Van Etten. Seven children, born in Ulster County, New York:
   a. Arie Nieuwkercke, baptized February 16, 1753. Married about 1785 in Ulster County, to Maria Reislie and had children, born in Ulster County:
      (1) Andrea Nieuwkercke or Andreas, according to some reports, but listed as Andrew A. in the 1850 census of Ulster County. Baptized May 14, 1786; married to Elizabeth, born c.1787 in New York. No children listed.
      (2) Lea Nieuwkercke, baptized July 10, 1791
      (3) Elisabet Nieuwkercke, baptized July 29, 1793
      (4) Annatje Nieuwkercke, christened March 26, 1795
   b. Jacobus Nieuwkercke, baptized February 27, 1755
   c. Catharina Nieuwkercke, baptized August 14, 1757; and perhaps married February 2, 1778 to Benjamin Van Ette in Dutchess County, New York. At least one daughter;
      (1) Catharina Van Ette, baptized May 29, 1785 at Kingston.

d. Johannes Nieuwkercke, baptized April 7, 1760. May be the same who married Elisabet Reisle. At least one son:
    (1) Aaron Nieuwkercke, baptized February 20, 1794
e. Maria Nieuwkercke, baptized February 7, 1763
f. Petrus Nieuwkercke, baptized October 6, 1765. Perhaps the same Petrus who married Catharina Reisle and had children, among whom were these four, born at Kingston, New York:
    (1) Andreas Nieuwkercke, baptized November 1, 1790
    (2) Levi Nieuwkercke, baptized May 28, 1800. This could possibly be the same Levi shown in the 1850 census of Ulster County, with a wife, Maria, born c.1805, and a daughter. Also in the household was one Peter Hearder, born c.1826. The daughter was:
         (a) Catherine Nieuwkercke, born c.1831
    (3) Neltje Nieuwkercke, baptized May 6, 1802
    (4) John Nieuwkercke, baptized July 9, 1804
g. Benjamin Nieuwkercke, baptized February 4, 1776. Married Catherine Van Keuren, and had a daughter:
    (1) Leah Nieuwkercke, baptized May 6, 1800 in New York
6. Rachel Nieuwkercke, baptized January 21, 1728; married May 15, 1748 to Hezekiah DuBois, baptized February 25, 1727, a son of Hezekiah and Ann Person DuBois. They had three children:
    a. Maria DuBois, baptized September 12, 1756
    b. Aleda DuBois, baptized April 19, 1763
    c. Hendricus DuBois, baptized April 24, 1765
7. Jacomyntje Nieuwkercke, baptized May 18, 1729 and married November 22, 1749 Johannes Van Etten, baptized December 26, 1721 and died October 22, 1803, son of Jacobus and Catharine Kool Van Etten. His will was made at Shawangunk May 11, 1802 and probated October 22, 1803. Three children;
    a. Jacobus Van Etten, baptized October 8, 1750
    b. Catharine Van Etten, baptized January 15, 1758, and married to Wilhelmus Row.
    c. Maria Van Etten, baptized August 9, 1774; married Elias Van Etten

8. Gerret Nieuwkercke, baptized November 25, 1732. Married November 22, 1749 to Cornelia Wells, baptized May 29, 1737, a daughter of Samuel and Marytjen Oosterhout Wells. Lived in Saugerties, New York; nine children, born in Ulster County:

a. Aaltjen Nieuwkercke, baptized December 26, 1758. Perhaps the same who was married September 6, 1783 in Greene County to Mattheus Lehman (Mormon church IGI records)

b. Samuel Nieuwkercke, baptized June 4, 1760/61

c. Trintje Nieuwkercke, baptized December 11, 1763. Married in Ulster County, November 27, 1783, Martinus Snyder, baptized February 22, 1748, his first wife; son of Martinus Snyder (1698) and Annah Deamute Backer Snyder, both born in Hackenberg, Germany, and immigrated to America.

d. Marytje Nieuwkercke, baptized May 12, 1765; died young

e. Hendricus Nieuwkercke, born August 17, 1767. This may be the same individual shown as Henry, born c.1765 in New York, with a wife Mary, born c.1775 in Ireland, who appears in the household of John Newkirk in the 1850 census for Steuben County, New York, probably their son:

(1) John Nieuwkercke, born c.1800, and married to Magdelin, born c.1804. At least five children:

(a) Elizabeth Nieuwkercke, born c.1827

(b) Sylvanus Nieuwkercke, born c.1829

(c) Sarah Nieuwkercke, born c.1833

(d) Martha Nieuwkercke, born c.1836

(e) William Nieuwkercke, born c.1840

f. Margrietje Nieuwkercke, baptized September 17, 1769

g. Petrus Nieuwkercke, baptized January 13, 1772

h. Johannes Nieuwkercke, baptized June 30, 1774

i. Annatje Nieuwkercke, baptized February 4, 1776

Cornelius Nieuwkercke
1696-1744

This son of Cornelis Gerretse Van Nieuwkercke (1662) and Jennetje Jansz Kunst (1664), was baptized August 30, 1696 at Kingston, Ulster County, New York, and died August 17, 1744 at Pittsgrove, Salem County, New Jersey. He was married March 17, 1721 to Rachel Ten Eyck, who was baptized November 5, 1699 at Kingston, daughter of Mathys Ten Eyck and Jannetje Roosa Ten Eyck. The will of Rachel, dated July 5, 1762 at Pittsgrove, New Jersey, was probated October 29, 1771. In 1715, Cornelius was listed as a soldier in Captain Johannes Schepmoe's Hurley Company of Foot, under command of Colonel Jacob Rutsen. He was a millwright, and in 1718 purchased a tract of 380 acres in Salem County, along the Morris River, but does not appear to have moved there until about 1721. He, his wife, and eldest son, Abraham, were instrumental in establishing the Presbyterian Church of Pittsgrove, April 30, 1741. He and his wife are buried there, each with a stone inscribed with a lovely verse. The children, all born in Salem County, New Jersey, were:

1. Abraham Nieuwkercke, born June 8, 1722, of whom more.
2. Matthew Nieuwkercke, born September 17, 1724; died single April 17, 1797. His will is reported to be of record at Trenton, in which valuable genealogical data can be found. He was probably a wagon master in the Revolutionary War.
3. Garret Nieuwkercke, born March 23, 1726, of whom more.
4. Jannetjen Nieuwkercke, (or Yonika), born August 6, 1728. Married June 3, 1747 to Jacob DuBois, born February 19, 1719 and died September 28, 1794, son of Barent DuBois. Jacob was Captain of the Pittsgrove Minute Men, and his Muster Roll contains the name of seven members of his family, the earliest record of the Revolution in Salem County. Six children, born in Salem County, New Jersey:
   a. Rachel DuBois, born September 21, 1749, and died October 15, 1811. Married May 3, 1768 to John Hayman Krom, born March 20, 1741, son of John and Elizabeth Hayman Krom. He died of smallpox December, 1776,

while he was in service during the Revolution. Four children.

b. Catherine DuBois, born October 15, 1751; married Joel Garrison, who died c.1798. Six children.

c. Sarah DuBois, born September 23, 1754; married John DuBois, born August 12, 1752, son of Reverend Jacob DuBois and Mary Allegar DuBois. Six children.

d. Jonathan DuBois, born October 2, 1757; died February 21, 1838, unmarried.

e. David DuBois, a twin, born September 19, 1761, and died in May, 1837. Married first Elizabeth Burroughs, daughter of Joseph F. and Eleanor DuBois Burroughs. She died September 23, 1803 and he married second April 23, 1804 to Freelove Whitaker, born March 29, 1778; died January 1, 1842, daughter of Ambrose and Rachel Leake Whitaker. He had a total of eight children; two by the first, and six by the second marriage.

f. Lydia DuBois, a twin, born September 19, 1761; died February 29, 1848. Married to Andrew DuBois; one child.

5. Jacomyntje Nieuwkercke, born June 9, 1731. Married May 21, 1751 to Matthew DuBois, born May 8, 1722 and died 1773. Married second in 1779 to Allen Delaps. Seven children, born in Salem County, New Jersey, all to the first marriage:

a. Sarah DuBois, born February 24, 1753

b. Lewis DuBois, born December 25, 1755; married December 22, 1777 to Rebecca Craig. He had at least five children:

(1) Samuel DuBois.

(2) Sarah DuBois, married Dickenson.

(3) Rebecca DuBois.

(4) Elizabeth DuBois, married Nicholas.

(5) John DuBois, married Sarah Newkirk, born May 29, 1786, a daughter of Jacob Newkirk.

c. Anna DuBois, born August 23, 1757

d. Rachel DuBois, born November 24, 1759

e. Cornelius DuBois, born January 2, 1762

f. Matthew DuBois, born September 5, 1765
g. Benjamin DuBois, born December 30, 1767
6. Cornelius Nieuwkercke, born September 2, 1733, of whom more.
7. Elizabeth Nieuwkercke, born May 8, 1735 and died January 12, 1802. Married c.1752 to David DuBois, born November 18, 1724 and died November 12, 1801. They had twelve children, born in Salem County, New Jersey.
8. Catherine Nieuwkercke, born November 5, 1737; married January 16, 1758 to William Garrison
9. Mary Nieuwkercke, born August 19, 1740; married Aaron Brown, born August 1, 1737 at Daretown. Four children.
10. Sarah Nieuwkercke, born April 25, 1742; died January 28, 1813. Married first about 1760 to Joseph DuBois, born April 6, 1737; and second April 20, 1782 to Judge Henry Wynkoop, born March 2, 1737 in Bucks County, Pennsylvania, and died March 25, 1816. Reportedly she had one child from each marriage. Her children were:
a. Benjamin DuBois, born c.1770
b. Susannah Wynkoop, born April 11, 1784, died March 2, 1849. Married October 13, 1808 John Lefferts, born c.1779, died January 14, 1859. They had children:
(1) Sarah W. Lefferts, born August 19, 1809
(2) Elizabeth V. Lefferts, born February 20, 1811
(3) Henry Wynkoop Lefferts, born February 16, 1813
(4) Edward V. Lefferts, born September 8, 1815
(5) James L. Lefferts, born April 27, 1818
(6) Reading Beatty Lefferts, born March 10, 1822
(7) Mary Helen Wynkoop Lefferts, born February 2, 1825
(8) Worth Lefferts, born February 25, 1828

Abraham Nieuwkercke
1722-1765

This son of Cornelius Nieuwkercke (1696), was born June 8, 1722 in Salem County, New Jersey, and died there in June, 1765. Buried in the Pittsgrove Presbyterian Church cemetery. He married

31

first December 23, 1745 to Ann Richman, born c.1728 and died before June, 1762. He married second June 23, 1762 to Sarah S. Van Meter. He spelled his name as Nieukirk, but most of his descendants adopted the more common form of Newkirk. He had six children, all born Salem County, New Jersey:

1. Elizabeth Nieuwkercke, born November 3, 1746 and died there December 9, 1794. Married February 22, 1769 to Ezekial Rose, who was born December 9, 1745 and died December 5, 1824 in Union County, Indiana; son of John and Mary Rose. He was a Revolutionary soldier in Captain Jacob DuBois Company of Salem County Militia. After the death of Elizabeth, he married second a widow, Charlotte Moore, by whom he had two more daughters. Elizabeth's children were:

   a. Uriah Rose, born January 18, 1770; died October 18, 1839 in Union County, Indiana. Married first Rachel DuBois, born October 22, 1765 and died January 12, 1802, daughter of David DuBois (1724) and Elizabeth Newkirk (1735) DuBois. Married second April 9, 1804 Tamson Garrison. He had four children from his first marriage, and ten from the second.

   b. Isaac Rose, born January 29, 1771; died as a young man

   c. John Rose, born August 28, 1774; was a teacher and author of a small arithmetic textbook. Married first Ann Richman and second Elizabeth Rose Harker, born April 6, 1798, daughter of Abraham and Catherine Robinson Rose. He had three children by his first marriage; one by second.

2. Mary Nieuwkercke, born August 3, 1748. Married January 2, 1772 William Thompson

3. Rebecca Nieuwkercke, born March 17, 1750; died 1803. Married to Uriah Mayhew, born July 27, 1746 and died 1803. Nine children.

4. Isaac Nieuwkercke, born November 29, 1753, of whom more.

5. Jacob Nieuwkercke, born April 27, 1763, of whom more.

6. Ann Nieuwkercke, born November 28, 1764, died December 31, 1854 in Union County (or Franklin County), Indiana. Married about 1787 to her cousin, Josiah DuBois, born July 18, 1762 and died 1813 in Salem County, New Jersey; son of

Reverend Jacob DuBois and Mary Allegar DuBois. They had ten children, born in Salem County; most of whom located in Fairfield, Franklin County, Indiana with their mother after the father's death:

a. Sarah DuBois, born May 8, 1788
b. Mary DuBois, born December 16, 1790
c. Abraham DuBois, born January 9, 1792
d. Ann DuBois, born August 1, 1793
e. Abigail DuBois, born May 15, 1795
f. Rebecca DuBois, born March 6, 1796 and died February 4, 1880. Married William S. Rose, born November 25, 1791 in Salem County, New Jersey, and died February 1, 1876. Ten children.
g. Elizabeth DuBois, born April 16, 1804
h. Phebe DuBois, born May 8, 1807
i. Josiah DuBois, died young
j. Eleazer DuBois, died young

Isaac Nieuwkercke
1753- 1802

This son of Abraham Nieuwkercke (1722) was born November 29, 1753 in Salem County, New Jersey, and died June 2, 1802. Married Ann Curry, born May 5, 1753 and died 1802. Twelve children, born in Salem County, New Jersey, most of whom apparently adopted the simplified spelling of Newkirk:

1. Elizabeth Newkirk, born February 17, 1776
2. Abraham Newkirk, born June 17, 1777 and died August 14, 1850 in Tazewell County, Illinois. Married January 22, 1798 in Salem County, New Jersey to Elizabeth Hewyard, who died February 2, 1848 in Tazewell County, Illinois. There is a deed dated February 8, 1831 and recorded in Liber L.B. of Deeds, folio 361 in the Clerk's Office at Salem, New Jersey. It is from Abram Newkirk and Elizabeth, his wife, of Tazewell County, Illinois; to Joseph, Abram, Benjamin, and John Newkirk, "*sons of the said Abram Newkirk and Elizabeth, his wife*" whereby they convey to their sons, "*in consideration of natural love and affection*" all that parcel of land in Salem

County, Pittsgrove Township, New Jersey, described as the plantation whereon Elizabeth formerly lived, which were specified in the last will and testament of Joseph Hewyard (or Howard). It appears that the parents, having moved to Illinois, are there conveying to their four sons property back in New Jersey, which their mother had inherited from her father. There may have been daughters, unknown at this time, but they had at least four sons:

a. Joseph Newkirk, born about 1799, married about 1830 to Susan, born c.1812, and had children:
    (1) Charlotte Newkirk, born c.1831
    (2) Isaac R. Newkirk, born c.1833
    (3) Louisa Newkirk, born c.1835
    (4) Joseph Newkirk, born c.1837
    (5) Hetty Newkirk, born c.1840
b. Abraham Newkirk, Jr., born October 19, 1801 in New Jersey, who adopted the spelling Nieukirk. His descendants, in order for several generations include: Appollis McHenry Nieukirk, born March 29, 1835; Henry Allen Nieukirk, born June 27, 1869; Marion Ivan Nieukirk, born May 26, 1900; and Donald Nieukirk.
c. Benjamin Newkirk, born c.1808; married Nancy.
d. John H. Newkirk, born c.1810 in Salem County, New Jersey, and found in the 1850 census of Tazewell County, Illinois, with his wife, Ruth (Ruth Dillon, born c.1813 in Clinton County, Ohio); and a number of children. Also in the household is his father, at the age of 74. She was the daughter of Nathan Dillon, reportedly born January 7, 1790 in New Garden, Guilford County, North Carolina; and Mary Hoskins, born there February 2, 1796. The children of John H., all born in Illinois, included:
    (1) Isaac Newkirk, or Isaiah, born c.1832; married c.1855 to Rebecca Israel, and had children:
        (a) Birdie Newkirk, born c.1886; married c.1908 to Henry Harter, born c.1883, and had at least one son:
            1. William Harter, born c.1910.

        (b)   Eva Newkirk, born c.1888; married John Neal, and had at least one daughter:
            1.   Eva Neal, born c.1902

    (2)   Nathan Newkirk, born c.1833

    (3)   Oliver Newkirk, born June 15, 1834, of whom more.

    (4)   Sarah Ann Newkirk, born c.1837, of whom more.

    (5)   Rilla Newkirk (or Arrilla), born c.1840, and married R. V. Probasco.

    (6)   Ellis Newkirk, born c.1841

    (7)   Lewis Newkirk, born c.1843, of whom more.

    (8)   Adella Newkirk, born March 28, 1845. Married August 22, 1861 to Carr Dudley, and had children:
        (a) William N. Dudley
        (b) John T. Dudley
        (c) Rosanna B. Dudley
        (d) Charles E. Dudley
        (e) Frederick A. Dudley
        (f) Lulu F. Dudley
        (g) Lewis H. Dudley
        (h) Bessie O. Dudley

3.   Martha Newkirk, born December 9, 1778

4.   Sarah Newkirk, born October 18, 1780

5.   Robinson Newkirk, born August 29, 1782

6.   William Newkirk, born April 29, 1784

7.   Isaac Newkirk, born September 9, 1785; married 1807 Eunice Garrison

8.   Jacob Newkirk, born December 6, 1788. Could this be the same Jacob who is found in the 1850 census of Union County, Indiana? If so, he is listed at 60 years of age, with wife Mary, born c.1800 in New Jersey. Three children, born in Indiana:
    a.   Isaac Newkirk, born 1825
    b.   Jacob Newkirk, born 1829
    c.   Louise Newkirk, born 1826.

9.   Rebecca Newkirk, born September 10, 1789

10. Benjamin Newkirk, born September 20, 1791; married 1796 to Rebecca Van Meter, born May 8, 1796, daughter of David Van Meter (1761) and Sarah Newkirk (1765).

11. Ann Newkirk, born June 6, 1793; married Nealy Van Meter
12. Mary Newkirk, born January 6, 1797

Oliver Newkirk
1834-1907

This son of John H. Newkirk (1810) was born June 15, 1834 and died November 22, 1907. Married February 6, 1856 to Eliza Bennett, born January 9, 1840, died November 22, 1907. They had children:

1. John E. Newkirk, born c.1857; married November 5, 1889 first to Rosa J. Powers, and had two children. Married second April 8, 1901 to Frances E. Brock. His two children were:
   a. Walter L. Newkirk, born October 17, 1891
   b. Jessie A. Newkirk, born July 23, 1861; died November, 1904
2. Martha A. Newkirk, born April 30, 1868; married c.1890 to Vincent Comfort, and had children:
   a. Elroy Comfort, born c.1892
   b. Sadie M. Comfort, born c.1894
   c. Robert L. Comfort, born c.1896
   d. Claude E. Comfort, born c.1898
3. Rosanna Newkirk, born April 25, 1865; married c.1889 to H. Gardner, and had children:
   a. Kingsley E. Gardner, born c.1890
   b. Berney Gardner, born c.1892
   c. Stanley Gardner, born c.1893
   d. Martha Gardner, born c.1895
   e. Sarah Gardner, born c.1897
   f. Henry B. Gardner, born c.1899
   g. Charles H. Gardner, born c.1901
4. Emma R. Newkirk, born c.1863
5. Lillie L. Newkirk, born June 4, 1878; married c.1900 Orlando Dillon, and had at least one child. Married second to c.1905 Oliver B. Muggles, and had at least a son:
   a. Edna Dillon, born c.1901
   b. Oliver B. Muggles, born c.1908

6. Sarah A. Newkirk, born c.1870; married c.1900 William Izatt, and had children:
   a. Anna Izatt, born c.1901
   b. Ida J. Izatt, born c.1903
   c. William A. Izatt, born c.1905
   d. Mary F. Izatt, born c.1907
   e. Russell A. Izatt, born c.1910
   f. Ralph E. Izatt, born c.1912

Sarah Ann Newkirk
1837-

This daughter of John H. Newkirk (1810) was born c.1837 and married to Cyrus Dillon. They had children:
1. Ella Dillon, born c.1854; married Clinton Trollop and had at least one daughter:
   a. Gertrude A. Trollop, married 1890 to Charles H. Burlingame, born c.1853, and had a number of children:
      (1) Vera Gertrude Burlingame, born October 16, 1892 and died 1977. Married September 29, 1910 to her cousin, Rudolph Frederick Maurer, born December 20, 1888 and died April 29, 1949, which see following
      (2) Jane Evans Burlingame.
      (3) Robert C. Burlingame.
      (4) Clifford Burlingame.
      (5) Henry Burlingame.
      (6) Franklin Burlingame.
      (7) Mildred Burlingame.
      (8) Elizabeth Burlingame.
2. Lewis Dillon, born c.1855; married Ollie Miars.
3. Ellis Dillon, born c.1857
4. Walter Dillon, born c.1859

37

Lewis Newkirk
1843-1909

This son of John H. Newkirk (1810) was born c.1842 in Tazewell County, Illinois, and died about 1909 in Logan County, Illinois. Married June 5, 1862 in Tazewell County to Armintha M. Hight, born October 6, 1842 in Middletown, Ohio, and died 1914 in Logan County, Illinois. She was the daughter of Stewart Hight, born August 16, 1809 in Middletown, Ohio, and Mary Proctor, born c.1810. Lewis had six children:

1. Rolla Newkirk, a son, born 1863, died 1896. Married August 1, 1886 to Anna Spence, and had children:
   a. Lewis Newkirk, born c.1887
   b. Henry Newkirk, born c.1889
   c. Ida Newkirk, born c.1891
   d. Roy Newkirk, born c.1892
   e. Floyd Newkirk, born c.1894
2. Florence Mildred Newkirk, born May 2, 1867, and died May 4, 1903. Married October 22, 1888 in Lincoln, Illinois, Samuel Henry Maurer, born May 30, 1868 at Attelwil, Aargau, Switzerland, son of Jakob Maurer, born there June 17, 1833. They had six children:
   a. Rudolph Frederick Maurer, born December 20, 1888 and died April 29, 1949. Married September 29, 1910 his cousin, Vera Gertrude Burlingame, born October 16, 1892, which see above.
   b. Pansy Mae Maurer, born April 20, 1890; died April 11, 1953
   c. Rolla Maurer, born September 15, 1891, died October 31, 1975. Married c.1919 Anna Maurer, born c.1900; died c.1955
   d. Hazel Anna Maurer, born February 26, 1893, died August 3, 1971. Married Robert Phillips, and had two children. She married second Lester Miner. Her two children were:
      (1) Marjorie Phillips.
      (2) Robert Phillips.

e.   Nelson Edward Maurer, born December 3, 1894, died March 25, 1971. Married first to Leone, and second Mamie Foules.

f.   Clark Lewis James Maurer, born August 8, 1897 at Bushnell, Illinois, died May 21, 1954 at Jamaica Plain, MA. Married June 21, 1923 Margaret Agnes Carmody, born June 27, 1898 in Harlem, died May, 1978 at Natick, MA. Children:

    (1)   Margaret Ann Maurer (Peggy), born August 8, 1927 on Webb Avenue, in the Bronx, New York, who is correspondent for this large family group. Married June 18, 1949 Andre Jacques de Bethune, born August 20, 1919.

    (2)   Clark James Bernard Maurer, born August 20, 1935, and married September 19, 1964 to Beatrice Marple Etheridge, born April 18, 1941

3.   Lawrence Newkirk, born 1870

4.   May E. Newkirk, born 1872, died after 1928. Married March 5, 1891 to Charles Seacrist, and had children:

a.   Harry Seacrist.

b.   Delphia Seacrist.

c.   Edna Seacrist.

d.   Ruby Seacrist.

e.   Kenneth Seacrist.

5.   Clarke Newkirk, born August, 1876, died 1961. Married c.1900 Tully Barkmeier, born 1878, died 1900.

6.   Lee Newkirk, born January 30, 1879, died January 28, 1913. Married c.1905 Virgie Watts, born c.1885, and had children:

a.   Thelma A. Newkirk, born c.1906

b.   Thirsa Newkirk, born c.1906; married Harry Gehagen, born 1890

Jacob Nieuwkercke
1763-1826

This son of Abraham Nieuwkercke (1722) was born April 27, 1763 in Salem County, New Jersey, and died there November 19, 1826. Married first to Whitaker, who died in childbirth, and second

to Phebe Thompson, daughter of John and Mary Thompson. He had children, born in Salem County:
1. Catherine Nieuwkercke, born January 17, 1783
2. Sarah Nieuwkercke, born May 29, 1786; died August 19, 1811. Married November 23, 1808 to John DuBois, born November 21, 1780 and died February 27, 1814
3. John Nieuwkercke, born March 2, 1789; died 1826. Married December 11, 1811 to Ruth Sayre
4. William Nieuwkercke, born July 21, 1791, and died 1854. Married May 2, 1816 to Harriet Johnson, born January 3, 1796 and died August 28, 1828
5. Mary Nieuwkercke, born September 26, 1793
6. Rebecca Nieuwkercke, born November 11, 1795; married Garret Groff
7. Abraham Nieuwkercke, born April 19, 1798
8. Isaac Nieuwkercke, born July 27, 1801; married to Julia Ann Burt
9. Jacob Nieuwkercke, born September 11, 1803
10. Phebe Nieuwkercke, born December 22, 1805
11. Thompson Nieuwkercke, born April 14, 1806
12. Victor M. Nieuwkercke, born September 3, 1811. This may be the same person listed in the 1850 census of Philadelphia County, Pennsylvania, as a tailor, with a wife, Eliza, born c.1805 in Delaware, and children, all born in Pennsylvania, including:
    a. Margaret Nieuwkercke, born 1824; perhaps married to Alfred Lykens, a clerk, born c.1825 in Philadelphia, and had a child:
       (1) Edwin Lykens, born c.1843
    b. Mary A. Nieuwkercke, born c.1834
    c. Josephine V. Nieuwkercke, born c.1838
    d. Edward Nieuwkercke, born c.1840
    e. Clementine H. Nieuwkercke, born c.1843
    f. Victor M. Nieuwkercke, Jr., born c.1847

Garret Nieuwkircke
1726-1786

This son of Cornelius Nieuwkercke (1696), was born March 23, 1726 in Salem County, New Jersey, and died there September 9, 1786. Buried in the Churchyard at Daretown. Married May 10, 1753 to Elizabeth DuBois, born April 10, 1730 and died January 6, 1785; buried with her husband. She was a daughter of Louis DuBois and Margaret Jansen DuBois. Like other members of his family, Garret served in the Revolution, for a time in the Commissary General's Department. Six children, born in Salem County, New Jersey:

1. Elizabeth Nieuwkercke, born May 1, 1754. Married August 8, 1774 Robert Patterson.
2. Cornelius Nieuwkercke, born November 24, 1756 and died November 16, 1823 at Pittsgrove, in Salem County. Married March 19, 1776 to Abigail Hanna, born March 3, 1757 and died November 20, 1802. He enlisted September 10, 1775 as a private in Captain Jacob DuBois Company of Minute Men, and appears on muster rolls of the company. His children, all born in Salem County, New Jersey, were:
   a. Ann Nieuwkercke, born October 24, 1777; married to William Wallace
   b. Elizabeth Nieuwkercke, born August 8, 1779, married to Constant Woodman
   c. Margaret Nieuwkercke, born August 25, 1781; married to Hoshell Shull
   d. Garret Nieuwkercke, born August 10, 1783, and married December 4, 1803 to Catherine Elwell, and had five children, three of whom died young. The other two were:
      (1) Caroline E. Nieuwkercke, married June 15, 1837 Isaac R. Smith of Philadelphia
      (2) Margaret S. Nieuwkercke, married Samuel Hibler.
   e. Mary H. Nieuwkercke, born November 24, 1786 married John M. Taber, born March 28, 1791, died September 2, 1828
   f. Samuel Nieuwkercke, born January 12, 1788 died August 26, 1822. Married May 3, 1809 to his second cousin

Rachel Newkirk. She was born March 4, 1787 and died September 17, 1823. She was a daughter of Matthew Newkirk (1764). At least one son:

    (1)   Samuel Nieuwkercke, Jr., born 1820, of whom more.

g.   Sarah Nieuwkercke, born June 25, 1791; died November 9, 1868. Married May 23, 1816 to James Van Meter. He was born July, 1789 and died July 23, 1858.

h.   Matthew Nieuwkercke, born May 31, 1794, of whom more.

i.   Hannah Nieuwkercke, born February 17, 1798: married June 6, 1816 to Peter DuBois, born July 24, 1789, died March 14, 1876, son of Thomas and Sarah Foster DuBois.

3.   John Nieuwkercke, born July 18, 1759; died in Salem County between February and June, 1784. He was a Revolutionary soldier, in Captain Cornelius Nieukirk's company. Married Susanna Hurst, named in his will, dated February 23, 1784 and proven June 2, 1784. Two children, born in New Jersey:

a.   Mary Nieuwkercke, born c.1780, died young

b.   John Nieuwkercke, born c.1782, died single

4.   Margaret Nieuwkercke, born February 17, 1762; married August 31, 1780 to Jesse Rambo and had a daughter:

a.   Catherine Rambo.

5.   Sarah Nieuwkercke, born June 21, 1765, died December 7, 1828. Married David Van Meter, born July 17, 1761 and died November 25, 1816. Five children:

a.   Amy Van Meter, born February 16, 1785

b.   Elizabeth Van Meter, born July 16, 1788

c.   Ephraim Van Meter, born May 16, 1791

d.   Rebecca Van Meter, born May 8, 1796, and married Benjamin Newkirk.

e.   Margaret Van Meter, born June 4, 1801

6.   Matthew Nieuwkercke, or Matheus, born March 22, 1769, of whom more.

Samuel Newkirk, Jr.
1820-1879

This son of Samuel Newkirk (1788) was born 1820 and died 1879. He married Sarah U. Dawson, born 1820 and died 1885. They had a daughter: Sarah C., born in Forest County, Pennsylvania; married James L. Wick. However, listing No. 128567 of the Daughters of the American Revolution Lineage Book, gives the lineage of Mrs. Sarah C. Carson Wick as follows: it is stated there that the early ancestor was Cornelius Newkirk (1733-1795), who commanded a company in the 2nd Battalion, New Jersey Militia, and was married to Mary Miller (1739-1806). He is said to be the father of Matthew Newkirk (1764-1823), who married Catherine Burroughs (1767-1828); and they, in turn, were parents of Samuel Newkirk (1788-1822). It appears to me that the researcher making that report made one basic mistake. Matthew Newkirk and his wife Catherine Burroughs were the parents of four children, as reported elsewhere in this text, including: Rachel, 1787; Hannah, 1789; Christiana, 1791; and Benjamin, 1794. Their daughter, Rachel (1787) married Samuel Newkirk (1788), her second cousin. Samuel was the son-in-law of Matthew Newkirk, not his son. If my information is correct as to the lines of descent to Mrs. Sarah C. Carson Wick, she still qualifies under the rules of the DAR, in that Garret Nieuwkircke (1726-1786), who appears to be her direct ancestor, served in the Revolution as reported above.

Matthew Newkirk
1794-1868

This son of Cornelius Newkirk (1756) was born May 31, 1794 at Pittsgrove, New Jersey, and died May 31, 1868 in Philadelphia, Pennsylvania. As a young man, he went to Philadelphia about 1810, where he met and married on May 1, 1817 his first wife, Jane Reese Stroud, who died in 1819. She was said to be a lady of great beauty. He married second July 2, 1821 to Margaret Heberton, born January 15, 1799 and died September 28, 1841, daughter of George Heberton, Esquire. He was married third July, 1846 to Hattie M. Smith, who died 1868. Matthew was at one time minister of the Broad Street Presbyterian Church in the city, and it is said that Neukirk Street there was named for him. He served in the War of 1812 in First Company Washington Guards, First Brigade, First Division, Pennsylvania Militia. He was a partner in the firm of Newkirk and Heberton, a director of The United States Bank, and otherwise prominent in business and social affairs of the city of Philadelphia. A detailed account of his life and activities appears in the writings of Dr. Adamson Bentley Newkirk, as they appeared in Volume II, *Genealogies of Pennsylvania Families From The Pennsylvania Genealogical Magazine*, Hinman-Sotcher, published by Genealogical Publishing Company, Inc., 1982. The family appears in the 1850 census for Philadelphia County. There, his wife is listed as Kitty, born c.1800 in New Jersey, suggesting that perhaps the second wife was Margaret Catherine Heberton. Also in the household is Mary Heberton, born c.1766 in New Jersey, apparently mother of the wife. There are several other individuals in the household, not carrying the Newkirk name: Jane Hughes, born c.1810 in Delaware; John Simpson, a waiter, born c.1822 in New York; Sarah Armstrong, born 1805 in Delaware; Charlotte Hunter, born c.1810 in Delaware; and Anne Rogers, born c.1833 in Pennsylvania. Four children died young; four others survived:

1. George Heberton Newkirk, born c.1825, died September 22, 1861.
2. Mary Jane Newkirk, married William Henry Oliver.
3. William Henry Newkirk, born c.1834; died March 11, 1864
4. Matthew Newkirk, Jr., minister of the Presbyterian Church, and the author of *A Memorial of Matthew Newkirk*, printed privately 1869, born September 23, 1838. He was probably married at Lancaster, June 7, 1865 to Eliza Hayes Jacobus and had at least one daughter, according to IGI records of the Mormon church:
    a. Margaret Heberton Newkirk, born October 11, 1867 at Philadelphia, and named for her grandmother; married October 25, 1888 to Henry Clark Boden at Philadelphia (or Lancaster)

Matthew Newkirk
1769-1820

This son of Garret Nieuwkircke (1726) was born March 22, 1769 and died January 7, 1820. Married first June 24, 1789 to Mary Van Meter, born 1770 and died July 7, 1802, daughter of Benjamin and Bathsheba Dunlap Van Meter. Married second March 5, 1803 to Rebecca Mayhew, born c.1784 and died September 11, 1809; and married third to Elizabeth Foster, daughter of Jonathan Foster. Children, four from the first marriage and three from the third, born in Salem County, New Jersey:

1. Elizabeth Newkirk, born September 9, 1789, and married to Essinger. Moved to Pennsylvania, and had children.
2. Bathsheba Newkirk, born November 25, 1792 and died June 1, 1865. Married Judge Jeremiah Stull, born November 6, 1791 and died October 19, 1854. Four children, born in Salem County, New Jersey.
3. Ann Newkirk, born March 7, 1795 and died March 16, 1831. Married twice: first Henry Van Meter; second James S. Caruthers, born March 20, 1782, died January 17, 1840. One child from the first marriage; six from the second.
4. Sarah Newkirk, born May 14, 1800; married November 3, 1821 to Nicholas Olmstead. Eight children, born in Salem County
5. Matthew Newkirk, born March 8, 1814; died December 22, 1887 in Licking County, Ohio. He married first March 2, 1837 in Hamilton County, Ohio, Nancy Miller, born 1815 and died November 3, 1874. They had six children, three of whom died young. Married second April 3, 1878 in Hamilton County, Ohio, to Mary E. Fleek. His family appears in the census of 1850 for Licking County. In the household are Eliza Jackson, born c.1834 in Ohio; and Hiram Branch, a clerk, born c.1830 in Vermont. Matthew is a merchant, and the children, born in Ohio, included:
   a. Edward Newkirk, born c.1841
   b. Charles Newkirk, born c.1846
   c. William Newkirk, born c.1848

6. Nathaniel Reeve Newkirk, a doctor, born July 22, 1817 and died November 11, 1866 at Bridgeton, New Jersey. Married twice: first to Mary; second on December 5, 1856 to Martha Reeve Bacon. She was born January 29, 1826, and died July 22, 1909. They appear alone in the census of 1850 for Salem County, New Jersey. He had six children, born in Cumberland County. The children were:

    a. Elizabeth Thompson Newkirk, born September 25, 1857
    b. John Bacon Newkirk, born March 6, 1859, and married December 1, 1915 to Mary Chapman Borton of Moorestown, New Jersey. No children.
    c. Matthew Newkirk, born July 16, 1860; died young
    d. Anna Bacon Newkirk, born January 7, 1862; died young
    e. Horatio Wood Newkirk, born February 4, 1863; died young
    f. Isaac Roberts Newkirk, born March 22, 1866; married March 12, 1899 to Mary Louisa Maris, born April 11, 1866; died October 14, 1924. Seven children.

7. Mary Elizabeth Newkirk, born August 26, 1819; died July 6, 1884

Cornelius Newkirk
1733-1795

This son of Cornelius Nieukerke (1696), was born September 2, 1733 in Pillsgrove, (later called Pittsgrove), Salem County, New Jersey, and died there November 8, 1795. His will was dated October 16, 1795 and probated June 17, 1796, describing a rather substantial estate. Buried at the Presbyterian church cemetery in Daretown. Married October 19, 1758 to Mary Miller (1739), daughter of Joast and Christiana Miller. Mary died August 6, 1806 and is buried with her husband. Cornelius was a Captain in the 2nd Regiment, Salem County Militia, prior to December 13, 1776. He was with other troops at Mt. Holly at the time of the battle of Princeton; served at Gloucester under Colonel Benjamin Holme in May, 1777; commanded a company of forty men at Gillingsport; served under Lt. Colonel Josiah Hamilton in July and August, 1777; at Haddonfield under Colonel Jacob Ellis February 4 to

March 9, 1778; in service during the invasion of the enemy at Swedesboro; commanded company acting as guard over effects of Tories at Pittsgrove April 13 to 21, 1778; commissioned Lt. Colonel of 2nd Battalion November 7, 1786; commanded 1st Regiment June 5, 1794; resigned as Lt. Colonel of the 4th Salem Regiment November 6, 1794. He and his brother Matthew (1724) signed the Salem County petition of 1787, favoring ratification of the Federal Constitution of the State of New Jersey. He had thirteen children, born in Salem County, New Jersey:

1. Garret Newkirk, born c.1758. He is thought to have married Catherine Elwell of Pittsgrove, December 4, 1802.
2. Rachel Newkirk, born August 4, 1759. She was married first December 24, 1778 to William Elwell, who died April 14, 1788, leaving one son. Married second to Levi Elwell before October 16, 1795, and he died about November, 1807. They had five children:
   a. Samuel Elwell, named in his grandfather's will in 1795
   b. Isaac Elwell, married Elizabeth Rose in Salem County April 6, 1811.
   c. Joast Elwell
   d. Matthew Elwell
   e. Dorothy Elwell, married March 19, 1822 David DuBois and lived in Franklin County, Ohio.
3. Joast Newkirk, born March 6, 1761, of whom more.
4. Matthew Newkirk, born February 7, 1764; died September 27, 1823. Commissioned Second Lieutenant in Salem County Militia on October 11, 1799, promoted September 13, 1800 to First Lieutenant. Married December 18, 1785 to Catherine Burroughs, born November 26, 1767 and died April 28, 1828. Children, born in New Jersey:
   a. Rachel Newkirk, born March 4, 1787; died September 17, 1823. Married May 3, 1809 to her cousin, Samuel Newkirk, born January 12, 1788, and died August 26, 1822; a son of Cornelius Newkirk (1756). Her children are treated under the section devoted to her husband's family, which see.
   b. Hannah Newkirk, born August 22, 1789
   c. Christiana Newkirk, born August 17, 1791

d. Benjamin Newkirk, born December, 1794. Married to Rebecca Van Meter, born May 8, 1796. This may be the Benjamin A. Newkirk who appears as head of household in the 1850 census of Ulster County, New York, born c.1794; no wife listed, four children:
   (1) Jane E. Newkirk, born c.1833
   (2) Peter L. Newkirk, born c.1836
   (3) Andrew Newkirk, born c.1838
   (4) Bowman Newkirk, born c.1841
5. Christiana Newkirk, born January 21, 1765; died January 1, 1833. Buried at Daretown. Married April 16, 1809 to William Lippincott
6. Abraham Newkirk, born June 4, 1768, of whom more.
7. Rebecca Newkirk, born August 3, 1771; died August 23, 1779
8. Andrew Newkirk, born August 2, 1773, of whom more.
9. Cornelius Newkirk, born September 13, 1775, of whom more.
10. Elizabeth Newkirk, born March 21, 1777. Married November 8, 1796 John Cade, who died 1850 in Gloucester County, New Jersey. They had no children.
11. Benjamin Newkirk, born October 4, 1780; died November 15, 1827. Married November 14, 1806 to Elizabeth Elwell, born October 15, 1783 and died September 7, 1868. Both are buried at Daretown, New Jersey. No children.
12. Mary Newkirk, born January 1, 1783; died June 8, 1786
13. John Newkirk, born August 28, 1785; died July 8, 1806

Joast Newkirk
1761-1825

This son of Cornelius Newkirk (1733) was born March 6, 1761 in Salem County, New Jersey, and died August 22, 1825. Married Sarah Ayers, born January 9, 1762; died November 1, 1821. He was a private in Captain Cornelius Niuekirk's company from October 20, 1777 to March 9, 1778. Commissioned Lieutenant in Salem County Militia May 20, 1800. Children, all born in Salem County, New Jersey:
1. Jacob Newkirk, born December 13, 1781, and died September 12, 1848. Married Mary, who died July 20, 1859

2. Joseph Newkirk, born August 20, 1783; died November 1, 1852. Married twice: first November 12, 1807 to Rebecca DuBois, born c.1786 and died December 27, 1844. Married second to Susannah, born c.1813 in New Jersey. He appears in the 1850 census for Salem County, New Jersey, as a farmer, with his second wife, and two other persons in his household: Sarah DuBois, born c.1833 in New Jersey; and Samuel Arle, born c.1837 in Pennsylvania

3. Susannah Newkirk, born September 13, 1785, and married to Michael Swing

4. Rebecca Newkirk, born June 14, 1788; died October 28, 1813

5. Sarah Newkirk, born March 30, 1790; died c.1874

6. Cornelius M. Newkirk, born June 26, 1792, and died May 4, 1874. Married February 11, 1815 to Michele DuBois, born April 20, 1789 and died June 30, 1864. She was a daughter of Isaac and Elizabeth Burroughs DuBois, and the granddaughter of Elizabeth Newkirk (1735) and David DuBois (1724). Cornelius M. Newkirk is mentioned on page 3 of the June, 1985 issue of *Newkirk Notes* by Gil and Mary Alford, in an exchange note with Frances A. Pericone, then living in Vineland, New Jersey. They report that he had at least a son, Clement Newkirk, born 1815 in Pittsgrove, New Jersey. Clement was the father of Lorenzo Newkirk, born 1841 in Elmer, New Jersey. Lorenzo was the father of B. Hayes Newkirk, born 1879 in Morris County, Kansas. His daughter was Verna Mae Newkirk, born 1914 in Monroeville, New Jersey, and she was the mother of Frances A. Pericone, our correspondent. The family of Cornelius M. Newkirk (1792) appears in the 1850 census of Salem County, New Jersey, with his wife listed as Minche, born in New Jersey. Also in the household is Enoch Price, born c.1834; and Sarah Moore, born c.1828; both in New Jersey. There is one child bearing the surname Newkirk, who may be a daughter. Numerous references to this family, and important genealogical information, were also found in *The American Descendants of Chretien DuBois of Wicres, France,* Part Nineteen, 1983, which I discovered in the public library at Hagerstown, Maryland. The children included:

a. Clement Newkirk, born c.1815, of whom more.

b. Joseph Newkirk, of whom more.
c. Cornelius Newkirk, born c.1817, of whom more.
d. Matilda Newkirk, perhaps, born c.1831
7. Mary Newkirk, born May 1, 1793; died June 9, 1794

Clement Newkirk
1815-

This son of Cornelius M. Newkirk (1792) and his wife, Michele DuBois Newkirk (1789) was born c.1815, and appeared in the 1850 census of Salem County, New Jersey, in his own household, with a wife Mariah, born c.1813 in New Jersey, and children, born in New Jersey. From various sources, his children included:
1. Isaiah W. Newkirk, born c.1833; married Sarah E. Elwell. Six children:
   a. David E. Newkirk, born September 17, 1862; died February 20, 1864. Buried at Bible & Friendship cemetery, Monroeville, New Jersey, as was most of this family.
   b. Gille B. Newkirk, born January 30, 1865; died January 9, 1942. Married August 3, 1882 to Henry Howard Prickett, born April 12, 1858; died May 21, 1932. Six children:
      (1) Clara Ray Prickett, born February 8, 1883 and married October 14, 1903 to Chester Pedrick, born April 3, 1881; died May 21, 1917. Four children:
         (a) Anna F. Pedrick, born 1905
         (b) Joseph N. Pedrick, born 1907
         (c) Verna E. Pedrick, born 1908
         (d) Evan C. Pedrick, born 1910
      (2) Newkirk Prickett, born 1884; died 1885 at Monroeville, New Jersey
      (3) Isaiah Prickett; married Bessie.
      (4) Evan S. Prickett, born September 1, 1886; died December 28, 1955. Married Laura Lesch, who died 1954. A daughter:
         (a) Gladys R. Prickett
      (5) Ray Prickett.

      (6)   Verna Prickett; married Louis Johnson.
- c. Clement H. Newkirk, born November 18, 1867; died March 30, 1958. Married January 14, 1891 Mary E. Hurst, and had four children:
  - (1) Mabel Newkirk, born 1891; died November 20, 1972 and is buried in Cold Springs Cemetery, Cape May, New Jersey. Married 1918 John Speck.
  - (2) Alice Newkirk.
  - (3) Alberta Newkirk, born 1897; married Eldridge.
  - (4) Rhoda Newkirk, born 1900; died 1906
- d. Wilbert E. Newkirk, born April 4, 1870; died November 16, 1938. Married September, 1894 Anna Eliza Newkirk, born August 12, 1873; died June 22, 1903, his first cousin, and daughter of Lorenzo Newkirk (1841) and his wife, Ruth Thomas. They had a daughter:
  - (1) Mildred Elizabeth Newkirk, born January 20, 1899; died August 31, 1939.
- e. Maria Newkirk, born May 18, 1874, and died August 1, 1956. Married February 15, 1892 Harry Cassady, and had at least three children:
  - (1) Florence Cassady.
  - (2) Mary Lizzie Cassady.
  - (3) Sarah Cassady.
- f. George D. Newkirk, born February 4, 1876, and died December 28, 1954. Married November 4, 1893 to Phebe K. Frazer.
2. Charles F. Newkirk, born c.1839; married Lydia Denelsbeck and had six children:
   - a. Tamson B. Newkirk, born 1862, married William Bishop
   - b. Martha D. Newkirk, born 1866, married William Strang.
   - c. Elverta Newkirk, married Albert Coombs.
   - d. Seymore Newkirk, born c.1869; died October 14, 1881
   - e. William Beckett Newkirk, born c.1871; died January 26, 1952. Married January 27, 1891 to Ray Ella Overs, died 1906; a daughter of William Overs of Elmer, New Jersey. He married second in 1908 to Elizabeth DuBois of Daretown who died in April, 1943. Five children:
     - (1) Helen Newkirk, married Mulford Bishop.

(2)   Iva Newkirk, married Frank Woolman.

(3)   Margaret Newkirk, married Dayton R. Gibson.

(4)   Bella Newkirk, married Moore.

(5)   Hannah Newkirk, married Joseph M. Holt or Hart.

f.   David Newkirk, born c.1872; died October 29, 1892

3.   Lorenzo Newkirk, born 1841; married Ruth R. Thomas. Four children:

    a.   Anna Eliza Newkirk, born August 12, 1873; died June 22, 1903. Married her first cousin, Wilbert E. Newkirk, born April 4, 1870; died November 16, 1938, son of Isaiah W. Newkirk (1833). They had a daughter:

        (1)   Mildred Elizabeth Newkirk, born January 20, 1899; died August 31, 1939.

    b.   Albertus Newkirk, born February 5, 1876; died February 25, 1937 and married October 9, 1902 to Anna Lorena Garton. She was born c.1883; died December 11, 1969, daughter of Oliver Garton and Amy Sithins Garton. Six children:

        (1)   Lorenzo Newkirk, born April 28, 1904; married July 20, 1937 to Margaret Joy McCool, born January 31, 1902. One daughter:

        (a) Elizabeth Ann Newkirk, born July 24, 1942

        (2)   Cortlyn Garton Newkirk, born November 23, 1906, and married February 24, 1936 to Dorothy Zimmerman, who was born November 26, 1913. Two daughters:

        (a) Lois Caroyl Newkirk, born October 9, 1936; married June 17, 1961 to Donald Malcolm McCallum. At least one son:

        1.   Donald Malcolm McCallum, Jr.; 1963.

        (b) Joyce Anna Newkirk, born August 27, 1947; married Robert Calsam and had a daughter:

        1.   Diane J. Calsam, born 1965.

        (3)   Cleora McFarland Newkirk, born June 22, 1908; married July 29, 1933 Peter Paul Rogalsy, died February 2, 1959. A daughter:

(a) Carol Ann Rogalsy, born October 18, 1937; married May 9, 1959 Richard Shumway. They had at least one son:
   1.   Scott W. Shumway, born 1964
(4) Alda Newkirk, twin, born May 4, 1911; died May 5, 1911
(5) Carolyn Newkirk, twin, born May 4, 1911, died September 6, 1911.
(6) Audrey Anna Newkirk, born February 20, 1920; married June 8, 1940 Charles Levi Humphreys, born October 25, 1912. Two sons:
   (a) Charles William Humphreys, born January 12, 1949
   (b) John Albertus Humphreys; February 3, 1952

c.   Birchard Hayes Newkirk, born November 29, 1879; died November 23, 1954. Married November 29, 1900 to Bertha Reed Graf, born February 8, 1879; died May 12, 1965. Six children:
(1) Beatrice Graf Newkirk, born August 8, 1902, and married November 25, 1925 to Bartlett Marion Mathews, born February 11, 1903. Three children:
   (a) Glen Alfred Mathews, born May 9, 1926
   (b) Marion Wayne Mathews; August 9, 1928
   (c) Donald Reuben Mathews; February 18, 1932
(2) George Harold Newkirk, born August 9, 1905; died July 21, 1953. Married first April 17, 1927 Minne Vera Hughes, divorced. Married second July 9, 1938 Emily Louella Ruhl, born September 28, 1916.
(3) Dudley Richman Newkirk, born May 15, 1907; died August 30, 1972. Married June 17, 1933 to Anna Frances Fithian, born November 30, 1907; daughter of George Fithian and Christine Staub. A son:
   (a) Richard Dudley Newkirk; April 14, 1942
(4) Lester Hayes Newkirk, born May 30, 1909; married October 12, 1940 Hester Mae Johnson,

born August 30, 1906, daughter of Rev. Henry Johnson.

(5) Verna Mae Newkirk, born February 19, 1914, died Elmer, New Jersey, September 14, 1979. Married November 5, 1936 George Richard Hemple, born June 4, 1908; died August 24, 1941. They had a son, and she married second July 24, 1945 Clyde Benjamin Corathers, born October 20, 1920, and had a daughter:

    (a) Erwin Newkirk Hemple, born May 5, 1939

    (b) Frances Ann Corathers, born February 15, 1947, and married to Perricone.

(6) Kenneth Franklin Newkirk, born November 26, 1915, and married June 5, 1937 to Helene Vivian Dare, born April 1, 1916. Four children:

    (a) Janice Eileen Newkirk: December 9, 1938

    (b) Kenneth Franklin Newkirk: March 12, 1940

    (c) Alan Wayne Newkirk, born July 14, 1943

    (d) Patricia Lynn Newkirk: September 14, 1950

d. Nellie Graff Newkirk, born September 27, 1881; died 1911.

4. Cornelius M. Newkirk, married Adelaide S.; three children:

a. Lille Newkirk, born 1883

b. Frances Newkirk, born 1885

c. Laura Newkirk, born 1885

5. Elizabeth Newkirk, born c.1843

6. John Newkirk, born c.1845

7. Hannah Newkirk, born July 2, 1846

8. Harriett Newkirk, perhaps, born March 13, 1853

9. Laura Newkirk, perhaps, born June 30, 1860

Joseph Newkirk

This son of Cornelius M. Newkirk (1792) and his wife, Michele DuBois (1789), had several children, including:

1. Benjamin Newkirk, married Annie Elwell and had a son:

a. Hayes Newkirk, married and had a son:

    (1) Earl Newkirk.

2. Edward Newkirk, married Mary and had a son:
   a. William Newkirk.
3. Rebecca V. Newkirk, married William H. Thomas; a son:
   a. Howard M. Thomas, who died August 4, 1953. Married Elizabeth D. Bill, who died May 15, 1955, and had seven children:
      (1) William Thomas, born April 12, 1899. Married Marguerite Fithian, born 1894; daughter of George O. Fithian and Christine Staub. Two children:
         (a) Howard H. Thomas
         (b) Doris Thomas, married Connahey
      (2) Joseph Hill Thomas, born May 3, 1901
      (3) Velma Thomas, born December 20, 1902
      (4) Loretta Thomas, born January 14, 1905
      (5) Ralph H. Thomas, born 1908, and married Laura Frances Elwell, born June 11, 1909, daughter of Otis H. and Laura Hitchner Elwell. A son:
         (a) Ralph H. Thomas, born 1932
      (6) Hazel Thomas, born March 12, 1912; married November 12, 1930 Norman J. Dilks, born May 24, 1910.
      (7) Samuel Thomas, married Pauline Sparks.

Cornelius Newkirk
1817-

This son of Cornelius M. Newkirk (1792) and Michele DuBois Newkirk (1789) was born c.1817, and appears in his own household, near that of his father, in the 1850 census for Salem County, New Jersey. No wife is listed, but there are four children, born in New Jersey. Two more children appear in other records:
1. Thomas W. Newkirk, born c.1840; perhaps, as listed in IGI records, married Henrietta, and father of, at least:
   a. Henry R. Newkirk, born Salem County March 5, 1865.
   b. Cornelius D. Newkirk, born c.1865
   c. Oley O. Newkirk, born c.1868
   d. Sallie D. Newkirk, born c.1869
2. Harriet W. Newkirk, born c.1841

3. Minche Newkirk, born c.1843
4. Hannah A. Newkirk, born c.1846
5. Anne E. Newkirk, married Benjamin Elwell. Four children:
   a. Elizabeth Elwell, married Harry Pauldin Gray. Children:
      (1) Henrietta Gray
      (2) Josephine Gray.
   b. Minnie Elwell, married John M. Woolman. A son:
      (1) Ralph Woolman.
   c. Otis H. Elwell, married Leola Evans, daughter of Frank Evans and Laura Hitchner. A daughter:
      (1) Laura Frances Elwell
   d. Lydia V. Elwell, born June 21, 1921, and married to Howard L. Zimmers.
6. Omar H. Newkirk, married Phebe Hitchner; three children:
   a. Elizabeth Newkirk, born 1888, and died June 25, 1967. Married Oscar Gaunt, born October 11, 1884; died April 13, 1969. Two children:
      (1) Stanley Gaunt, a doctor.
      (2) Dorothy R. Gaunt
   b. Robert Newkirk, died age 79; married Bertha Richman, born at Harrisonville, New Jersey and died July 30, 1956. She was a daughter of Linnboyd Richman and Anna Elizabeth Coles Richman. Three children:
      (1) Warren B. Newkirk, married June 26, 1949 to Mrs. Helen Cassady, daughter of Ora Wentzell.
      (2) Carolyn Newkirk, married November 13, 1937 to Reverend Ulysses Grant Hagaman, born August 1, 1868.
      (3) Marian Alberta Newkirk, married June 25, 1949 to Walter Postell.
   c. Olive Bilderbeck Newkirk, born 1891; died December 8, 1971. Married Warren S. Barth, and had a son:
      (1) Omar Barth; as of 1973, the pastor of the First Baptist Church of Paterson, New Jersey.

Abraham Newkirk
1768-

This son of Cornelius Newkirk (1733) was born June 4, 1768 in Salem County, New Jersey. A report by Charles E. Munat, in 1983 living in Middletown, Connecticut, states that Abraham died in 1817 in Muskingum County, Ohio. Dr. Adamson Bentley Newkirk dates his death there at 1843. Married October 5, 1807 to Grace Loper. She was born January 28, 1788 in New Jersey and, after her husband's death, married second Dr. Nathan Sears. The two of them died at Mt. Carmel, Illinois. Abraham's children, all born in Salem County, New Jersey; and all died in Wabash County, Illinois; were:

1. William Newkirk, a doctor, born August 21, 1809; died June 4, 1877. Married March 11, 1832 in Muskingum County, Ohio to Sarah Crooks, who was born c.1811 in Maryland or Ohio. The 1850 census of Muskingum County, Ohio carries a family headed by William Newkirk and wife, Sarah, born in the proper time frame, with four children, all listed as born in Maryland, which may be this family. Children were:
    a. Mary Jane Newkirk, born c.1831
    b. Clarinda Newkirk, born c.1833
    c. Nathan Newkirk, born c.1835
    d. Clarissa Newkirk, born c.1841
    e. Rufus Marion Newkirk, born c.1849 in Ohio. This individual has been reported as being a son of this family, although it seems more likely that he belongs to the family of another William Newkirk, reported following.
2. Hugh Newkirk, born May 25, 1813; died June 6, 1846. Married c.1834 to Theresa Herr, born August, 1813 in Germany; died c.1887 in Pike County, Illinois. Five children, two of whom were:
    a. Amanda Carolina Newkirk
    b. William Newkirk, born in Illinois. His descendants have been reported as including, at least: Rufus Marion Newkirk, born 1849 in Ohio; Allen H. Newkirk, born 1888; Ivan Newkirk, in 1983 living in Mt. Carmel,

Illinois and the correspondent for this family. See William (1809) above for comment as to this family grouping.

3. Zachariah Newkirk, born June 15, 1816, and died November 6, 1863. Married twice; first to Covilla Heggens, and second to Eliza Ann Greathouse. He had two children from his first marriage, and seven from the second, all born in Wabash County, Illinois. He appears in the 1850 census of that county, with his second wife and several children. In the same 1850 census, in the nearby household of Robert and Eliza Hayes, was Jane Newkirk, born c.1842. In the household of Alfred Fanguery were found five Newkirk children, all born in Illinois: Caroline A., 1838; Clarissa, 1839; Mary J., 1840; Martha H., 1841; and William, 1844. We can not now identify these children, but they may belong to the family of Zachariah. Perhaps either Eliza Hayes or the wife of Alfred Fanguery was an early daughter of Zachariah, and has the young children (her brothers and sisters?) in her household. Those listed in the household of Zachariah in 1850 were:
   a. Martha H. Newkirk, born 1843
   b. Mary E. Newkirk, born 1846
   c. William H. Newkirk, born 1849

Andrew Newkirk
1773-1850

This son of Cornelius Newkirk (1733) was born August 2, 1773 in Salem County, New Jersey, and died January 2, 1850. Married May 3, 1795 to Tryphenia Fish, born April 11, 1776 and died September 10, 1848. Their children were born in Salem County, New Jersey:

1. William Newkirk, born January 29, 1797, and died on November 4, 1874. Married twice; first March 20, 1824 to Christianna Hitchner, born March 30, 1802 and died October 11, 1851; second to Rebecca Miller. He and Christiana appear in the 1850 census of Cumberland County, New Jersey. He had no children.
2. Enoch Newkirk, born June 21, 1799; died October 27, 1871. Married three times: first April 5, 1823 to Lydia Hutchinson,

58

born July 2, 1798 and died February 3, 1828; second April 12, 1830 to Susannah Ayars, born September 11, 1797 and died October 26, 1851; third March 25, 1852 to Ann Abbott, born September 24, 1816 and died April 3, 1902. He had six children, two by the first marriage, one by the second, and three by the third. Probably the same head of household in 1850 census of Salem County, New Jersey, with his wife Susannah, and several children. Also in the household is Amanda Clark, born c.1839 in New Jersey. There is also Rebecca Newkirk at age 45, born c.1805, who is his sister. The children, born in New Jersey, were:

a. Andrew Newkirk, born c.1827
b. John Newkirk, born c.1832
c. Enoch Newkirk, Jr., born June 28, 1853
d. Triphenia Newkirk, perhaps, born March 20, 1855
e. Firman H. Newkirk, born January 1, 1857

3. Lydia Newkirk, born October 11, 1801, died January 28, 1802
4. John Newkirk, born December 26, 1802, and died September 28, 1882. Married twice: first January 12, 1826 to Sarah Ann Elwell, born August 17, 1805, died February, 1857; second to Hannah Moore, born c.1808. John is head of household in the 1850 census of Salem County, New Jersey, with Sarah Ann, and several children. The household also includes Albert Dare, born 1840; and Zaccheus Carson, born 1813. The children, born to the first marriage, in New Jersey, included:

a. Lydia Newkirk, born c.1828
b. Ann Newkirk, born c.1835

5. Rebecca Newkirk, born June 3, 1805; died December 29, 1874
6. Edmund Newkirk, born September 23, 1807, and died October 12, 1885. Married October 11, 1834 to Lydia Elwell, born February 13, 1816 and died February 6, 1871. The 1850 census for Cumberland County, New Jersey, includes the family, with Elizabeth Bates, born c.1833, living with them, and one son, the only survivor of their five children:

a. William A. Newkirk, born March 19, 1839; died June 28, 1898. Married Hannah J. Cassidy and raised a large family in Salem County, New Jersey.

7. Eliza Newkirk, born August 11, 1812; died April 20, 1832
8. Israel F. Newkirk, born August 13, 1815; died May 22, 1847. Married Temperson Anderson, born February 6, 1818 and died June 28, 1851. One child:
   a. Andrew A. Newkirk, born December 9, 1835, and died March 1, 1883.

Cornelius Newkirk
1775-1826

This son of Cornelius Newkirk (1733) was born September 13, 1775 in Salem County, New Jersey, and died March 9, 1826. Married August 14, 1797 to Mary Reed, born April 29, 1779 and died September 23, 1823. Children, born Salem County:
1. James E. Newkirk, born May 23, 1800 and died October 15, 1878. Married Maria Vansant, and second to Sarah Thomas. This may be the same James Newkirk who appears alone in the 1850 census of Newcastle, Delaware, listed as a blacksmith. Eight children.
2. Emily Newkirk, born May 23, 1800; died March 6, 1876. Married February 1, 1821 to William Conklyn, born March 21, 1797 and died August 6, 1868. Six children.
3. Alexander Newkirk, born August 23, 1802, and died December 29, 1823. No children.
4. Furman Newkirk, born November 25, 1805; died June 28, 1806
5. Reed Newkirk, born June 5, 1810. Married March 22, 1834 to Jane S. Young, born January 13, 1815 and died September 28, 1872. They appear in the 1850 census of Salem County, New Jersey. Five children, of whom two were:
   a. John Newkirk, born c.1843
   b. Aaron Newkirk, born c.1850
6. Furman Newkirk, the second child of this name, born December 8, 1813 and died September 8, 1825
7. Lambert Newkirk, born November 26, 1815. Married September 23, 1836 to Ann Mitchell, born c.1820. The family appears in the 1850 census of Salem County, New Jersey, with

Annette Simpkins, born c.1833, in the household, and five children; born New Jersey; they had nine:

a. George M. Newkirk, born December 18, 1837
b. Joseph H. Newkirk, born December 14, 1839
c. John P. Newkirk, born August 17, 1843
d. Mary Newkirk, born June 3, 1844
e. Samuel C. Newkirk, born November 12, 1846
f. Caroline E. Newkirk, born July 26, 1851
g. Quinton K. Newkirk, born January 19, 1856
h. Charles R. Newkirk or Charles Henry Newkirk, born January 14, 1858/59
i. Lambert Newkirk, Jr., born October 14, 1860

8. Elbert Newkirk, born September 23, 1818; died June 10, 1893 in Cumberland County, New Jersey. Married March 11, 1841 to Hannah Brooks, born June 23, 1820 and died September 26, 1890. Five children:

a. William Brooks Newkirk, born December 6, 1841 in Cumberland County, New Jersey; died June 21, 1918. Served in the Navy during the Civil War. Married January 21, 1867 Mary F. Glasbey, born June 17, 1839; died May 29, 1924. Two children.

b. John Brooks Newkirk, born February 17, 1843; died April 20, 1920. Served in Company H, 24th Regiment, New Jersey Volunteers, Civil War. Married May 28, 1864 Mary Ann Ireland, born October 18, 1845; died May 23, 1932. Four children.

c. James Polk Newkirk, born March 16, 1845 at Bridgeton, New Jersey; died April 4, 1916 at Camden, New Jersey. At sixteen, he enlisted for three years in Union forces in Company H, 10th Regiment, New Jersey Volunteers, ending his service as First Lieutenant, Company C. Participated in the battles of the Wilderness, Spottsylvania Courthouse, Cold Harbor and Winchester. Taken prisoner May 8, 1864 at Spottsylvania; recaptured by Custer's Cavalry May 9 at Beaver Dam; again captured at Winchester August 16, 1864; and spent six months in Confederate prisons at Lynchburg, Danville and Libby.

Married January 2, 1867 Rachel Rice Ford, born April 7, 1850 and died May 23, 1937. Seven children.

d.   Adeline Brooks Newkirk, born June 14, 1846; died May 18, 1893. Married January 3, 1864 Joseph L. Mulford, born September 24, 1844; died July 5, 1912. Served in the Navy during the Civil War. They had two children.

e.   Mary Reed Newkirk, born December 6, 1852, and died December 18, 1914. Married March 23, 1869 to Joseph Atwood Fisler, born October 23, 1843 and died May 10, 1913. Four children.

CHAPTER 3

Barent Nieuwkercke
1689-1765

This son of Cornelis Gerretse Van Nieuwkercke (1662) and his wife, Jennetje Jansz Kunst (1664), was baptized October 13, 1689 in Kingston, Ulster County, New York. At the time of his marriage, he lived "under the jurisdiction of Hurley." He was married May 23, 1713 to Rebecca Van Buntschooten at the Old Dutch Church at Kingston. She was one of the daughters of Teunis Elias Van Buntschooten and Gerretje Van Buntschooten, from Holland. After marriage, the couple lived in New York until about 1723, when they relocated to New Jersey. Barent was a millwright and a carpenter, and worked at his trade until about September, 1737, when he purchased a large farm of about 535 acres from his brother-in-law, John Hood, about eight miles north of the present city of Martinsburg, West Virginia, where he died in 1765. At the time, of course, his farm was located in the Virginia Colony.

According to court orders of Frederick County, Virginia, permission was granted August 7, 1759 to Barent Newkirk and John Hoagland to build a mill on Tulisse Run. In addition to the mill, he built a large house, some of which is reportedly still standing. Frederick County, Virginia Order Book 4, at page 225, dated August 4, 1752, states: "*On Motion of Peter Newkirk, Henry Hogland, John Hogland, Jacobus Hogland, Henry Newkirk, Barron Newkirk and Tunis Hood, ordered that their names be added to the list of tithables.*" Obviously, some of the names are spelled phonetically. Henry and John Hoagland were reportedly sons of Jacobus Hoagland, and they were married to daughters of Barent Newkirk. It should be remembered that, while we associate Barent with Berkeley County, Virginia (later West Virginia), it was first part of Frederick County, with Berkeley being established in 1772, and West Virginia not until the Civil War period.

Barent Newkirk appears in at least one deed in the records of Frederick County, Virginia. On September 3, 1764, as recorded in Deed Book 10 at page 93, he conveyed a tract of 130 acres to

63

Henry Newkirk, apparently his son. This deed was after the making of his will, as mentioned following. The land was part of the tract Barent had earlier acquired from John Hood, who had obtained a total of 1,175 acres by King's Patent dated November 12, 1735.

Barent left a will, dated February 18, 1764, and entered in Frederick County, Virginia, Will Book 3 at page 294, on August 6, 1765. He first leaves to his wife, Rebecca, one third part of all his land and the whole benefit of the dwelling house, during her natural life; together with her selection of a horse and two cows, and her bed furniture. He leaves to Barent Newkirk (1736/55), son of Cornelius Newkirk (1716), deceased, a tract of land containing 103 acres as his full share "and he not to claim more." It appears that during his lifetime, Barent gave farms to most of his sons, which he confirms under his will, referring to each tract mentioned in the will as "commonly called Henry Newkirk's plantation" (or Cornelius or Teunis).

He left son Henry Newkirk a tract of 104 acres; son Teunis received 106 acres which he had in possession; and son Peter received all the remainder of the original tract of land of Barent. Son Henry was to pay 20 pounds to son Elias Newkirk as his share. To his daughter, Jean Hoagland, he left the sum of 20 shillings; as he did to his daughter Jemima Hoagland. (The will did, in fact, spell Hogland and Hougland, although the girls were married to brothers, and neither spelling appears to have been correct!). He also left the sum of 20 shillings to a grand daughter, Martha Boon, whom we have not identified. His son, Tobias, was not mentioned in the will; it was written in 1764 and Tobias was living in North Carolina prior to 1750, not to return to Virginia. Son Abraham was not mentioned, either, although he was still living in Virginia at the time of the will. Sons Henry and Teunis were the Executors.

Following are the children of Barent Nieuwkercke, as we now know them. Here, we have assigned a son Christopher Cornelius Newkirk (1760), as a son of Teunis (1718), as found in other records. Later in the study, we will report another Cornelius, born c.1770, the son of Elias Newkirk (1722), as suggested by other researchers. The truth is, we simply can not now prove either assumption at this point, and we may well have reversed the two Cornelius Newkirks in this report. In any case, the children of

Barent Nieuwkercke, all apparently born at Kingston, Ulster County, New York, appear to have included:

1. Gerretjen Newkirk, or Jean, baptized April 14, 1714 and died c.1798 in Allegheny County, Pennsylvania. Married John Hoagland.

2. Cornelius Newkirk, baptized August 12, 1716; died before 1764, the date of his father's will. Apparently he was married twice, although we have neither name. At least one son, as mentioned in his father's will:

   a. Barent Newkirk, born between 1736 and 1755 in New York or in Virginia. This Barent appears in a number of records of Frederick County, Virginia. Under his grandfather's will, he inherited a tract of land of 103 acres, on which his father Cornelius had lived during his lifetime. By deed dated October 29, 1768 and recorded in Deed Book 12 at page 559, in Frederick County, Virginia, Barent and his wife Rachel Newkirk conveyed 101 acres of land to Van Swearington. The deed clearly refers to Barent as "grandson and heir at law of Barent Newkirk, deceased." The description of the land states that it joins the lands of Cornelius Newkirk and Tobias Newkirk, and includes rights to a water course that flows through the lands of Peter Newkirk. By deed dated August 1, 1769, recorded in Deed Book 13 at page 57, Barent and his wife Rachel convey the 103 acres he had inherited to John Hood, Jr. I have found no record of children from this Barent, although his descendants are said to have lived in Switzerland County, Indiana.

3. Teunis Newkirk, baptized July 13, 1718, and died in Fairfield, Ohio. By deed dated August 1, 1769 and recorded in Deed Book 13 at page 59 in Frederick County, Virginia, Teunis and his wife Mary conveyed 106 acres of land willed to him by his father, to his cousin, John Hood, Jr. Teunis, Barent and Peter Newkirk were reported in Bedford County, Pennsylvania, in 1773. In 1783, Teunis was in Westmoreland County, and in 1787 in Fayette County, Pennsylvania, where he was a small land holder. He later removed to Fairfield County, Ohio, where he died. Married to Mary, and had at least one child:

a. Christopher Cornelius Newkirk, born c.1760 (Mary and Gil Alford reported his birth as 1739); his descendants were in Indiana. Christopher is apparently the grandfather of James E. Newkirk (1921), who has contacted me.

4. Henry Newkirk, baptized January 1, 1721, and appointed constable in 1746 in Berkeley County, Virginia (now in West Virginia). Listed in court records at Winchester, Virginia, and later moved to Westmoreland County, Pennsylvania, and finally to Fairfield County, Ohio, where he died. It appears more than likely that he had a family, although we have not yet identified the children. As will be explained by reference to various records and time periods in Chapter 11, it is reasonable to conclude that one of his sons was:

a. Henry Newkirk, Jr., born c.1740, of whom more in Chapter 11.

5. Elias Newkirk, baptized October 21, 1722, and died after 1800 in Montgomery County, Kentucky. It has been reported that he married and located near Louisville, Kentucky, and that he had descendants there, and in Ohio. He is thought to be the father of Cornelius Newkirk, who married Elizabeth Powell, and the progenitor of what Mary and Gil Alford refer to as the "dozens cousins" although that has not been proven. He was on the tax lists of Kentucky, and apparently died about 1797. Elias also served in the Revolutionary War; a report dated October 4, 1775, headed as Captain Henry Hoagland's Roll, lists Henry Hoagland, Captain; William Hoagland, Lieutenant; James Hoagland, Ensign; and Elias Newkirk, Sergeant. He was perhaps married September 6, 1746 to Sarah Lounsberri, who was born in Dutchess County, New York. An unproved report says that he had eight children; I can now list only five:

a. Cornelius Newkirk, born c.1770 in Berkeley County, Virginia (later West Virginia); married May 19, 1794 in Clark County, Kentucky, to Elizabeth Powell, born c.1770 in Virginia, and of whom more

b. Mary Newkirk, born c.1775 in Washington County, Pennsylvania; died March 20, 1855 in Owen County, Kentucky. Married in Clark County, Kentucky, June 22,

1796 to Uriah Wilson. Uriah was sworn as an officer of the Kentucky Militia in Montgomery County, in 1798. He was born c.1767 in Virginia, and died October 11, 1852 in Owen County.

    c.   Henry Newkirk, born c.1781, probably in an area of Virginia that later became Kentucky, which was formed in 1792 (after his birth), and died c.1864 in Pendleton County, Kentucky, and of whom more

    d.   John Newkirk, born c.1782 in Pennsylvania or Kentucky

    e.   Elias Newkirk, Jr., born c.1785 in Kentucky; died 1849 in Ohio. Married Rebecca Parker (or perhaps Lydia Parker) in Mason County, Kentucky, January 7, 1805

6.   Tobias Newkirk, born c.1723, of whom more

7.   Abraham Newkirk, born October 19, 1724, of whom more in Chapter 4

8.   Peter Newkirk, born c.1727; died c.1804 in Bullitt County, Kentucky. Married c.1754 to Cornelia Sousley, and of whom more in Chapter 8.

9.   Jemima Newkirk, born c.1726/30, named in her father's will. Married Henry Hoagland about 1750 in Frederick County, Virginia. They settled in southwestern Pennsylvania and later moved to Shelby County, Kentucky, where she died about 1790.

Cornelius Newkirk
1770-1839

Cornelius, thought to be a son of Elias Newkirk (1722), but possibly Christopher Cornelius Newkirk, son of Teunis Newkirk (1718), was born about 1770 in Berkeley County, Virginia (later West Virginia, and died 1839 in Crawford County, Indiana. Cornelius moved with his father and family to Kentucky, who appear to have left Virginia about 1774, migrating first to southwest Pennsylvania, where they remained for about six years, before moving on to Kentucky, where they settled in Clark County (later Estill County), probably between 1790 and 1793. Cornelius was married May 19, 1794 to Elizabeth Powell, probably in Clark County. She was born c.1770, probably in Orange County, Virginia, a daughter

67

of Thomas and Ann Powell. References to the family appearing in tax records of Clark County from 1797 to 1818, and records of the Primitive Baptist Church in the area are recounted in the June, 1985 issue of *Newkirk Notes* by Mary and Gil Alford, adding more color to this family.

Cornelius appears to have also been a preacher in the Primitive Baptist Church. There is no record of his having been in military service, but he did serve in 1825 as a Judge; or perhaps Justice of the Peace; in English, Crawford County, Indiana. His will was probated there May 11, 1839. The children, mentioned in his will, all born in Clark County, Kentucky (or in Estill County, formed from Clark in 1808), included:

1. Nancy Newkirk, born c.1796 and died c.1870. Married January 11, 1813 Joseph Snowden, born June 9, 1791 in Washington County, Pennsylvania, and died March 29, 1856 in Crawford County, Indiana
2. Mary Newkirk, born December 31, 1797; died April 15, 1876. Buried in Orange County, Indiana. Married April 15, 1819 to Garrett Hall, born February 13, 1792 and died August 17, 1880 in Indiana. She was his second wife; at least one son:
   a. Martin Hall, born November 16, 1821; the great grandfather of Mrs. Edna L. Miller, in 1983 living in Grand Junction, Colorado
3. Barent Newkirk, (Barnet) born 1799, of whom more.
4. Malinda Newkirk, born c.1801, and married February 24, 1820 to James Briley, in Crawford County, Indiana. He was born c.1798 in North Carolina
5. Thomas Newkirk, born c.1802, of whom more.
6. Margaret Newkirk, born c.1803, and married July 19, 1822 to James McDonald
7. Elizabeth Newkirk, born March 16, 1805; died October 29, 1856 and buried in Orange County, Indiana. Married there March 15, 1825 to Abner McDonald, Jr., born September 4, 1805 in Virginia, and died February 13, 1880 in Indiana
8. John Newkirk, born c.1808, of whom more
9. Elias Newkirk, born c.1809, of whom more
10. Benjamin Newkirk, born c.1810, of whom more

11. James Henry Newkirk, born 1812 in Estill County, Kentucky, and married December 8, 1830 to Frances E. Tillman in Crawford County, Indiana. Listed in the 1850 census of that county, with his wife and children, including:
   a. Thomas Newkirk, born c.1832
   b. Louisa Newkirk, born c.1834
   c. Willshire Newkirk, born c.1835
   d. Telitha Newkirk, born c.1837
   e. George Newkirk, born c.1839
   f. Marshall Newkirk, born c.1841
   g. Ermin Newkirk, a daughter, born c.1843
   h. Harvey Newkirk, born c.1845
   i. Lucinda Frances Newkirk, born c.1848, who married Thomas Smith. They were the great grandparents of Ethel B. Johnson (Mrs. Edward Johnson), in 1983 living at Southgate, Michigan
12. Jane Newkirk, born c.1814 in Estill County. Married August 16, 1838 to James Ray in Crawford County, Indiana

Barent Newkirk
1799-1870

This son of Cornelius Newkirk (1770) was born about August 13, 1799 and died September 1, 1870 in Red Bluff, California. Married February 12, 1821 (or April 15, 1819) Martha Dawson, born c.1797 in Virginia, and died c.1861 in Missouri. The family appears in the 1850 census for Audrain County, Missouri, with Barent listed simply as B. Newkirk, and several of his children listed by initials also. There are also two other Newkirk households listed in that census, who may be married sons of Barent and Martha. They are C. C. Newkirk, born c.1824 in Kentucky, with a wife and one child; and Joseph Newkirk, born c.1823 in Kentucky, with a wife and one son. The children of Barent included, at least:
1. Richard Newkirk, born c.1829, perhaps in Kentucky, and had at least a son:
   a. John Barnett Newkirk, born September 7, 1852; at least one son:

      (1)   John Irvin Newkirk, born February 2, 1897, who was the first husband of Myrtle N. Davis, in 1983 living at Ceres, California
2.   Catharine Newkirk, born c.1831 in Kentucky
3.   Isaac N. Newkirk, born 1833 in Missouri, who had a son:
    a.   Isaac N. Newkirk, Jr., born 1874, who had a son:
        (1)   Elbert L. Newkirk, who had a daughter:
            (a)   Kathie Newkirk, married Graham
4.   S. A. Newkirk, a son, born c.1835 in Missouri
5.   Silas J. Newkirk, born 1837 in Missouri and had a son:
    a.   Osborne Newkirk, born 1860 in Missouri; a son:
        (1)   Clyde F. Newkirk, born 1889 in Iowa; a son:
            (a)   Charley L. Newkirk
6.   L. Newkirk, a son, born c.1839 in Missouri

Thomas Newkirk
1802-1849

This son of Cornelius Newkirk (1770), was born c.1802 and died 1849. Married December 11, 1824 to Lucinda Dawson in Crawford County, Kentucky. She was born c.1795 and died c.1830 in Clark County. He married second December 18, 1831 Permelia Ringo, born 1815 and died 1832. Married third April 12, 1835 in Orange County, Indiana, to Rachel Snowden, who was born c.1814 and died c.1849. The December, 1986, issue of *Newkirk Notes* carries further information relative to the family of Thomas Newkirk and his three wives. Some of the information came from Edythe S. Hobson, derived from cemetery records of Furnace, in Estill County, Kentucky; some of it is supposition based on census and other supporting data. It appears that Thomas had several children, including:
1.   Cynthia Dial Newkirk, appearing in the 1850 census as Sythia, born 1826; died 1925, single
2.   Benjamin W. Newkirk, born c.1830 in Kentucky; married to Mary Everman. The 1850 census for Clark County, Kentucky carries the family, with one child listed, perhaps his son:
    a.   John W. Newkirk, born July 21, 1848 in Kentucky, and died December 23, 1922 in Estill County. Married

Margaret, born November 17, 1852 and died September 20, 1943 in Estill County. Their children included:
    (1)   Clarence A Newkirk., born July 21, 1875, and died February 12, 1893
    (2)   Claude Newkirk
    (3)   Alma Newkirk
    (4)   Roscoe Newkirk
    (5)   Myrtle Newkirk
    (6)   Mable Newkirk
    (7)   John W. Newkirk, perhaps the same John W. Newkirk who was born April 14, 1891 and died July 21, 1925, who may have been the father of:
        (a)   John W. Newkirk, Jr., born June 3, 1919 and died April 21, 1920
    (8)   Lilly H. Newkirk, born August 28, 1895
3.   Jonas Newkirk, born c.1836 in Fayette County, Kentucky
4.   Cyrus Napoleon Newkirk, born November 23, 1840 in Kentucky, and died February 18, 1886. Married in 1865 to Sarah F. Berkley in Fayette County, Kentucky. She was born August 22, 1848 and died May 15, 1932. They are buried in Bush Graveyard on the Iron Works Road, near Graham Farm in Clark County, Kentucky. At least one son:
    a.   Victor Lee Newkirk, born c.1870 in Kentucky; at least one son:
        (1)   Clay McTyre Newkirk, born c.1903 in Kentucky, and died November 30, 1987. Married in 1926 to Florence Roberts of Owsley County, Kentucky, who died in 1977. Clay had at least two daughters:
        (a)   Rozena Newkirk, who married Marvin Lee Reams; in 1983, lived in Nashville, Tennessee
        (b)   Betty Jane N. Newkirk, married to Massey

John Newkirk
1808-1866

This son of Cornelius Newkirk (1770), was born c.1808 and died c.1866, probably in Crawford County, Indiana. Married March 15, 1825 to Nancy Snowden; and second February 11, 1855 to Mrs. Elizabeth Landiss. He appears in the 1850 census of Crawford County, with several of his children, but with no wife listed. The children, all born in Indiana, were:

1. Harrison Newkirk, born 1831, and had a son:
    a. John Newkirk, born 1859 in Indiana. Two children:
        (1) Laura Newkirk, born 1880; married Jones; at least one son:
            (a) Richard Jones, married Frances
        (2) Edgar Newkirk, born 1888. At least one daughter:
            (a) Mary Newkirk, married Hays; and lived at Tarzania, California in 1983
2. Mary Newkirk, born c.1834
3. Charles Newkirk, born c.1836
4. Cornelius Newkirk, born c.1840
5. Hester Ann Newkirk, perhaps a twin, born c.1840

Elias Newkirk
1809-

This son of Cornelius Newkirk (1770), was born c.1809 and married twice; first January 1, 1829 to Nancy Tillman, and second October 1, 1849 to Mrs. Mary Rice, both in Crawford County, Indiana. He appears in the 1850 census of the county with his second wife, and several of his children. There were eleven children, according to reports of Mack Tucker and James E. Newkirk; seven born to the first marriage and four to the second, including:

1. Mary F. Newkirk, born c.1830; married June 21, 1855 to George W. Sinclair and had two daughters:
    a. Jane Sinclair, married a doctor in French Lick, Indiana
    b. Elizabeth Sinclair, married McDonald and died at French Lick, Indiana, the mother of several children, including at least:
        (1) David McDonald
        (2) Eli McDonald
        (3) Mary McDonald
        (4) Jane McDonald
        (5) Susie McDonald

Cornelius P. Newkirk
1831-1926
Seated, wearing cap: other family members not identified.

2. Cornelius P. Newkirk, born February 2, 1831; died January 27, 1926. Married March 13, 1856 Anna Wellman; married second January 9, 1866 Sarah Giles. Three children born to each marriage:
a. Ellen Newkirk, born c.1857; married Lafe Willard
b. Frank Newkirk, born c.1859; married October 16, 1879 to Nancy J. Tillery, and had children:
    (1) Thomas Newkirk, born 1880
    (2) Charles Newkirk, born 1882
    (3) Ethel Newkirk, born 1884
    (4) Alice Newkirk, born 1886
c. James Newkirk, born c.1865; single

d. Mary Newkirk, born November 11, 1870; married December 2, 1888 to J. Hence Walls

e. Emma Newkirk, born c.1872; married January 31, 1900 to Lafayette Willard

f. Anna Newkirk, born 1874, married December 30, 1891 to James Willard.

3. Nancy Jane Newkirk, born 1833; married March 15, 1878 to Charles Conner

4. Benjamin Newkirk, born c.1835

5. Elizabeth Hannah Newkirk, born January 11, 1837; died April 7, 1901. Married May 31, 1860 to Hugh McDonald

6. John Morrison Newkirk, born c.1836, of whom more.

7. James Edward Newkirk, born January 3, 1841. Perhaps served in the Civil War, possibly wounded; mentioned a visit to him by John Newkirk in 1862, who was probably his uncle. James Edward was in the "Louisville Legion" and died April 16, 1928; buried at Frankfort, Kentucky. Married in 1876 to Katherine Montfort and had children, all born in Kentucky:

a. Martha Florence Newkirk, born February 18, 1869; died August, 1908. Married Charles Samples

b. Henry Warren Newkirk, born on August 15, 1870 in Shelby County; died January, 1896

c. Otis Edward Newkirk, born on December 1, 1872 in Henry County; died April, 1915. Married Mamie Chilton

d. Mary Louise Newkirk, born August 16, 1874; died December 28, 1932. Married twice: first to Victor Black and second to Graves

e. Julia Isabel Newkirk, born November 14, 1876; died August 13, 1972. Married November 15, 1893 to Horace R. Kesler

f. Marcus T. Newkirk, born June 11, 1879; died May 10, 1963

g. Nannie Victoria Newkirk, born November 11, 1882; died January 21, 1977 Dallas, Texas. Married October, 1909 to Charles E. Oliver

h. Lester Smoot Newkirk, born February 6, 1884; died February 8, 1936. Married twice: Pauline Boyer, and Elisie

i. Katie Ethel Newkirk, born February 9, 1889; died August, 1919. Married Morse.
8. David Newkirk, born c.1851
9. Samuel P. Newkirk, born c.1851
10. William M. Newkirk, born c.1852
11. Elizabeth N. Newkirk, born c.1859

Martha Florence Newkirk
1869-1908

Katie Ethel Newkirk
1889-1919

Nannie Victoria Newkirk
1882-1977

James Morrison Newkirk
1836-

This son of Elias Newkirk (1809) was born c.1836, probably in Crawford County, Indiana; married November 20, 1860 to Margaret Hall. It was reported in *Newkirk Notes* that John Morrison left his family in about 1876 to 1878 and went to live in either Poplar Bluff, Missouri, or Pine Bluff, Arkansas (although note the date of birth of Martha E. in 1888, which may be an error). He died some years later of what was called swamp fever. There are apparently Newkirks living around Poplar Bluff, but none in the Pine Bluff, Arkansas area. He had at least two children:
1.   George Albert Newkirk, born February 18, 1864 in Orange County, Indiana; died June 4, 1940. Married May, 1910 Susan Jane Hardy in Crawford County; at least one son:
   a.   John Benjamin Newkirk, born August 27, 1927 in Crawford County, Indiana, and died February 15, 1983 in Arizona. Married December 28, 1945 to Lela Ruth Johnson, and had children:
      (1)   Charles Virgil Newkirk, born October 4, 1946; married February 21, 1970 to Marvie Pegram, and had children, born in Arizona:
         (a)   Clinton Newkirk, born 1971
         (b)   Christie Newkirk, born 1973
         (c)   Tanya Newkirk, born 1975
      (2)   Janis Newkirk, born September 19, 1948; married December 11, 1970 to John Everett
      (3)   Anita Newkirk, born October 29, 1950; married July 11, 1968 to Bob Guyll
      (4)   Marilyn Newkirk, born January 27, 1953; married March 20, 1976 to Jack Brewer
      (5)   Linda Newkirk, born May 10, 1955, and married August 18, 1977 to Wendell Rinehart
      (6)   George Jay Newkirk, born April 18, 1960
      (7)   James Vaughn Newkirk, born February 4, 1963; married March 4, 1981 to Mary Reynolds
2.   Martha E. Newkirk, born May 28, 1888 Indiana; died young

Benjamin Newkirk
1810-1876

This son of Cornelius Newkirk (1770), was born c.1810 and died c.1876. Married July 5, 1828 to Milly Brown in Crawford County, Indiana, who was born c.1805 and died between 1880 and 1890. The children, born in Indiana, were:

1. James B. Newkirk, perhaps James Benjamin, born c.1829, who married Martha and had children:
   a. Elizabeth Newkirk, born 1862
   b. William Newkirk, born 1866
   c. Mary Newkirk, born 1867
   d. Joel Newkirk, born 1869
2. Susannah C. Newkirk, born c.1830
3. Elizabeth Newkirk, born January 9, 1831 in Orange County; died April 13, 1904, and married January 1, 1855 to John Cunningham
4. Benjamin William L. Newkirk, born c.1833, of whom more.
5. Francis M. Newkirk, born July, 1835; died May 9, 1901
6. Zachariah Elias Newkirk, born July 21, 1837; died April 9, 1909 in Parke County, Indiana. Married August 12, 1860 in Crawford County to Olive Cunningham, and had children born in Orange County, Indiana:
   a. Mary Elizabeth Newkirk, born March 11, 1862, and died February 2, 1922 Montgomery County, Indiana. Married William Akins October 3, 1881
   b. Thomas Joel Newkirk, born August, 1865
   c. Benjamin Franklin Newkirk, born February, 1870
   d. Ida A. Newkirk, born 1876
   e. Tresse E. Newkirk (Teresa), born 1878
   f. William E. Newkirk, born April, 1880
   g. John Newkirk, born June, 1882
   h. Harry Newkirk, born February, 1888
7. Benton Newkirk, born c.1840; married Catherine
8. Jonathan D. Newkirk, born August 9, 1843, of whom more.
9. Joel Rice Newkirk, born January 31, 1847, of whom more.

10. Sarah J. Newkirk, the tenth and last child of Benjamin Newkirk (1810), and his wife, Milly Brown Newkirk (1805), born c.1851

Benjamin William L. Newkirk
1833-1872

This son of Benjamin Newkirk (1810) was born c.1833, and died October 18, 1872 in Crawford County, Indiana. Married January 6, 1855 to Nancy Cunningham and had children, all born in Indiana:
1. Thomas B. Newkirk, born April 2, 1859
2. John Newkirk, born March 21, 1860. Married first January 3, 1884 to Goodson; second to Eva Estelle Linton; and third to Jane Lowe. Six children from the first, one from the second, and none from the third marriage:
   a. Hershell Newkirk
   b. Earl Newkirk; married Edith Totten
   c. Virgil Newkirk
   d. Walter Newkirk, married Nellie Keeling; at least one daughter:
      (1) Fredia Newkirk; married Cameron
   e. Martha Newkirk, married Chauncey Goldman
   f. Dora Newkirk, married Harry Woods
   g. Stella Newkirk, who was married seven times: to Chester Odle, Wilbur Gregory, John Sinclair, Roy Denbo, Logan Wisemen, Onstott, and White
3. Jesse Barnett Newkirk, born February 6, 1862; died February 25, 1942. Married first October 14, 1888 to Mary Linton; and second in 1899 to Martha Hotten. Two children from the first marriage, eight from the second, born in Indiana:
   a. Omer Newkirk, born June, 1891; died 1978. Married twice in Crawford County, Indiana; first to Dora Goff and second to Velma E. Scott; and had children:
      (1) Ileene Newkirk, married James E. Atz
      (2) Aleene Newkirk, married Jack Gibbs
      (3) Vincent J. Newkirk, married Marion; two children:

(a) Marilyn Kay Newkirk, born 1946; married September 28, 1968 to Noel Pickett

(b) Ronnie Newkirk, born 1948; married Gloria Richenbaugh and had a daughter:

    1. Melissa Kay, born May 2, 1968

b. Henry Herbert Newkirk, born 1893; died 1963. Married Esther L. Gregory and had children:

    (1) J. Herbert Newkirk

    (2) Douglas Newkirk

c. Walter Newkirk, born 1899, and died February 13, 1982. Married Lena Edwards and had a son:

    (1) Franklin Newkirk

d. Dora Newkirk, born 1903; married Harry Goss

e. Cloyd A. Newkirk, born May 10, 1905; died August 17, 1983. Married November 5, 1927 Alberta McIntosh, and had at least one son:

    (1) Ralph Newkirk

f. Archie Newkirk, born 1908; died January 20, 1948

g. Dana Newkirk, born October 9, 1912; married October 10, 1931 to Gilbert Denton

h. Albert Newkirk, born 1914; died 1954

i. Ernest Newkirk, born after 1914

j. Elwood Newkirk, born after 1914

4. Millie M. Newkirk, born April 18, 1865

5. Mary Ellen Newkirk, born October 13, 1868

6. William C. Newkirk, born May 17, 1869

7. Simeon Newkirk, born c.1875

Jonathan D. Newkirk
1843-1917

This son of Benjamin Newkirk (1810) was born August 9, 1843, and died May 11, 1917. Married first March 28, 1867 to Elizabeth Hull; second December 23, 1888 to Mariah Jane Cope. At least five children, probably born in Crawford County, Indiana:

1. Millie Newkirk, born 1866; married 1910 to Nathan Hollen

2. Demaris Ellen Newkirk, born January 6, 1868; died March 27, 1930. Married August 29, 1889 in Orange County to Billy Hammond
3. Lucy Newkirk, born September 5, 1872; died August 14, 1946. Married July 2, 1897 to George D. King
4. Jonathan Benton Newkirk, born January 27, 1889; died 1970. Married February 18, 1915 to Bessie Dendall
5. George W. Newkirk, born March 5, 1892; married December 14, 1915 to Minnie B. Denton. First two children were born in Crawford County, and the third in Orange County, Indiana:
    a. Chester L. Newkirk, born September 17, 1917; married first to Thelma Apple, second Dolly Mix. At least a son:
        (1) Chester L. Newkirk, Jr., born February 22, 1953; married Mrs. Sherry Schooler
    b. Velma June Newkirk, born June 15, 1921; married first in Muscogee County, Georgia, May 23, 1942 Joe Lowe, and second August 7, 1971 to Maurice A. McGlasson
    c. Helen Ruth Newkirk, born January 18, 1925; married to William Howard Wolfe.

Joel Rice Newkirk
1847-1917

This son of Benjamin Newkirk (1810) was born January 31, 1847, and died February 18, 1917. Married March 10, 1868 to Lydia Margaret Sowers. Children, born in Parke County, Indiana:
1. Benjamin Phillip Newkirk, born March 4, 1869; died June 12, 1944 in Orange County, California. Married August 12, 1894 in Henry County, Missouri to Jessie Smith and had children:
    a. Benjamin Oral Newkirk, born October 10, 1900 in Missouri; married June 12, 1923 to Beulah Bell Pugh in Orange County, California, and had children, born in Kern County, California:
        (1) Joel Glen Newkirk, born January 23, 1924, and married November 26, 1944 to Louise Fox
        (2) Benjamin Leroy Newkirk, born November 2, 1925 and married 1951 to Judy Ann Jamison

b. Jessie Ruth Newkirk, born May 14, 1902 in Kingfisher County, Oklahoma; married June 15, 1920 in Kern County, California to Evan Preston Pugh

2. James Henry Newkirk, born May 25, 1871; died November 20, 1949, single

3. Daughter, a twin, stillbirth October 12, 1873

4. Joel Rice Newkirk, Jr., a twin, born October 12, 1873; died June 14, 1955 in Buchanan County, Missouri. Married December 20, 1898 in St. Clair County, Missouri to Mary Elizabeth Hopper and had children, the first two born in St. Clair County; the last two in Parke County, Indiana:

   a. Samuel Floyd Newkirk, born May 31, 1900; died June 10, 1954. Married January 24, 1923 to Bessie Roach

   b. James Sylvester Newkirk, born December 7, 1901; died March 24, 1960 in Polk County, Iowa. Married first February 19, 1922 to Sarah Wright, and second March 12, 1943 to Emma Veach

   c. Essie May Newkirk, born March 14, 1903; died June 5, 1934 in Buchanan County, Missouri. Married December 24, 1925 in DeKalb County, Missouri, Floyd W. Mason

   d. Marcus Joel Newkirk, born June 4, 1905; died November 26, 1971 in DeKalb County, Missouri. Married there December 31, 1928 to Lula Evelyn West, and had at least one son:

      (1) Marcus Eugene Newkirk, born January 20, 1930 in DeKalb County, Missouri. Married November 9, 1956 to Emma L. Guess; two daughters, both born in DeKalb County, Missouri:

         (a) Marcia Jean Newkirk, born April 8, 1958, and married to Harry K. Hopper

         (b) Alice Marie Newkirk, born May 17, 1959; married March 12, 1979 to Bruce D. McKee

Henry Newkirk
1781-1864

This son of Elias Newkirk (1722) was born c.1781, probably in an area of Virginia that later became Kentucky, which was formed in 1792 (after his birth). Henry was married to Phoebe about 1801 in Montgomery County, Kentucky. It appears that this family, or at least several of his sons, made their way to Tennessee, and then to Alabama, where they are found with their families in the 1850 census. It has been suggested to me by Aileen M. Whitt of New Richmond, Ohio, that this Henry was not a son of Elias, at all, but was, rather, the same Henry Newkirk, Jr. reported in Chapter 11 of this study as a son of Henry Newkirk, born c.1740. She reports, of course, that Pendleton County, Kentucky is separated from Clermont County, Ohio, only by the Ohio River, and that there has been confusion in sorting out this particular individual. The reader is cautioned to review carefully both family listings in this study. His children included:

1. James Newkirk, born c.1803 in Kentucky, a farmer. He is listed as head of household in the 1850 census for DeKalb County, Alabama, apparently widowed, with several children, all born in Tennessee:
    a. Henry Newkirk, born c.1833
    b. Finey Newkirk, a daughter, born c.1836
    c. Samuel H. Newkirk, born c.1838
    d. James L. Newkirk, born c.1840
    e. Martha Newkirk, born c.1845
2. Hiram Newkirk, born c.1810 in Kentucky; married February 12, 1831 to Malinda Barndon (or Brandon), born c.1812. He is listed in the 1850 census of DeKalb County, Alabama, with his wife, and children. There is also one Phoebe Newkirk at the age of 70, who is his mother. The first of his children was born in Tennessee, and the remainder in Alabama, including:
    a. Jemima Newkirk, born c.1833. She is known to be the great grandmother of Mrs. Bessie Wyatt Oliver, according to the September, 1984 issue of *Newkirk Notes*
    b. Margaret P. Newkirk, born c.1835
    c. John S. Newkirk, born c.1838. It is possible, not proven, and now only suggested, that this could be the same individual listed in Mormon IGI records for Missouri as John Smith Newkirk, married May 26, 1861 in Miller County, Missouri, to Margaret Ann Brandon. His date of birth will fit nicely, and the name Brandon appears

associated with the family (his mother's name). John Smith Newkirk and Margaret Ann Brandon Newkirk had at least three children, born in Missouri:
- (1) William Hurrick Newkirk, born December 2, 1866
- (2) James H. Newkirk, born c.1869
- (3) Armanda Newkirk, born November 3, 1871
  - d. Hugh R. Newkirk, born c.1840
  - e. James L. Newkirk, born c.1842
  - f. Mary Ann Newkirk, born c.1844
  - g. Martha C. Newkirk, born c.1847
  - h. Alley E. Newkirk, a daughter, born c.1849
3. Henry Newkirk, born c.1811 in Kentucky, a farmer. Listed as head of household in the 1850 census of DeKalb County, Alabama, with his wife, Lucy, born c.1807 in Tennessee, and several children; the first born in Tennessee, the rest in Alabama:
   - a. Phereby F. Newkirk, as it appears in the census, but probably Phoebe F., for her grandmother, born c.1836
   - b. Hogan Newkirk, born c.1838
   - c. Solomon Newkirk, born c.1840
   - d. Malinda J. Newkirk, born c.1842
   - e. William B. Newkirk, born c.1844
   - f. Elizabeth Ann Newkirk, born c.1846
4. John L. Newkirk (according to census interpretation), born c.1812 in Montgomery County, Kentucky, a farmer. He has been identified as John Wesley Newkirk by Mrs. Elizabeth P. Rohrer, granddaughter of Lydia Ellen Newkirk (1888), listed following. Mrs. Rohrer lived in Fremont, California in 1984. He is listed in the 1850 census for DeKalb County, Alabama, with his wife, Nancy Farris, born c.1811 in Tennessee, and their five children. The first three were born in Tennessee, and the last two in Alabama. A sixth child was reported in the December, 1984 issue of *Newkirk Notes*:
   - a. Hiram Crabtree Newkirk, born May 11, 1837, of whom more.
   - b. Louisa J. Newkirk, born c.1841
   - c. Diatha Newkirk, born c.1844
   - d. Mary E. Newkirk, born c.1845; married Ray

e. Harriett Newkirk, born c.1847
f. Phoebe Newkirk, married Gerin.

Hiram Crabtree Newkirk
1837-1921

This son of John L. Newkirk (1812) was born May 11, 1837 in Meigs County, Tennessee and died May 9, 1921 (or 1931) in Jessieville, Garland County, Arkansas, and buried there in Green Cemetery. He was a sergeant in Co. H, 1st Regiment, Volunteer Arkansas Cavalry during the Civil War. Married four times: first c.1858 to Martha Jane Ray, born January 4, 1840 in Tennessee and died November 14, 1880 at Jessieville. Married second to Missouri Merriott, and third to her sister, Arkansas Merriott. He was probably married a fourth time to Mary A., who lived from 1853 until some time in the 1900s. His children included:

1. John Wesley Newkirk, born January 29, 1859 in Arkansas and died February 32, 1923. He was married to Sallie Glenn, born June 29, 1869, died February 19, 1933; daughter of C. T. and Amanda Howard Glenn. Four children:
    a. Calvin C. Newkirk; married Minnie Banks
    b. Martha Newkirk, who died young
    c. A. Forest Newkirk, married Eula Ward
    d. Minnie Newkirk, born September 19, 1892, and died September 15, 1920. Married first to Cotnam, and second to Steve Clare
2. E. Hogan Newkirk, born November 29, 1863 in Arkansas, and died June 9, 1940. Married c.1883 Lucy Ellen Smith, daughter of the Reverend David Smith
3. George Enos Newkirk, born March 9, 1866 in Texas; died of tuberculosis November 7, 1931 in Vilonia, Faulkner County, Alabama, where he had served as the County Registrar during 1921. Married c.1885 to Martha Isobel Oates, born November, 1869 in Marble Township, Saline County, Arkansas, the daughter of John Wesley Oates and Mary Jane Green. Children, born in Jessieville, Garland County, Arkansas:
    a. James Wesley Newkirk, born September 19, 1886, and died May 8, 1917

b. Lydia Ellen Newkirk, born August 17, 1888 and died September 28, 1972 in Mountain View, California, and was buried at sea. Married about 1906 to Marcus Lonzo Dickson; also married to Thomas Carrigan and Robert Lawrence

c. Enos Edward Newkirk, born November 22, 1890, and died September, 1980. Married January 16, 1912 to Edna Kilgore

d. Ophelia Newkirk, born December 8, 1892 and died 1971. Married David Akin; Walker J. Merriott; and Edward Sugar

e. Mary Jane Newkirk, born April 15, 1895; died December, 1976. Married Leon Buyce

f. Pearl Newkirk, born July 2, 1898. Married to J. Vander Merriott

g. Orpha Newkirk, born March 4, 1901; married Barnes

h. William Newkirk, born May 11, 1903

i. Roy C. Newkirk, born October 16, 1905; died in 1980

4. Thomas Newkirk, born c.1871 in Arkansas and married to Alice Terry

5. Joseph Newkirk, born c.1874 in Garland County, Arkansas, and died in the 1890s

Tobias Newkirk
1723-

This son of Barent Nieukerke (1689) and Rebecca Van Buntschooten, was born c.1723 in Kingston, Ulster County, New York, and died in Duplin County, North Carolina. His family presumably moved from New York, first to New Jersey when Tobias was an infant, and then about 1737 to Frederick County, Virginia. One story has it that, at one time, Tobias went to England and, while there, was asked to make obeisance to the King. He refused and was given the preference of leaving the Kingdom, or submitting. He returned to America. He appears also to have lived for a time in Jefferson County, Kentucky, near Louisville, where a reference was found in Minute Book A, dated December 3, 1781, which stated that Tobias Newkirk, Peter Newkirk, Jemima

Hoagland and Elias Newkirk were entitled to four hundred acres of land. The others named were three of his brothers and a sister; all of them known to have lived in the area mentioned. It is also said that, in their first home in North Carolina, one of the boys fought with an Indian lad and bloodied his nose. The next morning, Tobias found a mark in blood on his doorstep, and this was a sign that the Indians intended to make war. He gathered his family together and left that night. The other settlers, who did not heed the warning, were killed. He was an extensive farmer and slave holder in Duplin County, and was the progenitor of the North Carolina Newkirks. Tobias married Penelope Brosard about 1748, perhaps in Frederick County, Virginia, although he may have gone to North Carolina as a single young man, and met her there. They had children, all born in Duplin County:

1. Henry Newkirk, born January 10, 1750. He was married to Nancy Southerland, and apparently second Catherine, whose name appears in an 1818 deed of the county (unless, of course, his wife's name was Nancy Catherine). His children are listed following as they were found in various reports of others, although date comparisons cause me to question the accuracy. I suspect that Henry may have had other children, not listed here, and that one or more of these might possibly be a grandchild. As an example, the last listed child here would have been born when Henry was 86 years old! Not impossible, but unlikely. And, there appears to be a rather large time gap between the birth of the earliest child and the others. The birth of Cornelius in 1775 (when Henry was 25, appears quite logical). They were all born in Duplin County, North Carolina:

   a. Cornelius Newkirk (Killis), born c.1775; married to Lena Williams Davis, a widow; no children.

   b. Alexander Newkirk, born April 4, 1787; died March 1, 1870. Married June 29, 1811 Mrs. Rachel Wells Basden

   c. Catherine Newkirk, born c.1789/1800; married to Jesse Brown

   d. Dorcas Newkirk; reportedly, but questionable when the date is considered; born c.1836; married November 6, 1856 to Thomas Brickle and moved to Alabama

2. Abraham Newkirk, born June 15, 1754, of whom more following.
3. Rachel Newkirk, born c.1758; married to Daniel Southerland, born c.1749 and died June, 1831. He served in the Revolution, and, in 1802, he was a Warden of St. Gabriel's Parish. Children:
   a. Jeremiah Southerland, born March 8, 1782, and died September 6, 1845. Married Catherine Wells, and had thirteen children.
   b. Samuel Southerland.
   c. Rhoda Southerland.
   d. Solomon Southerland, married Rilley Kennedy, daughter of Thomas Kennedy, and had at least one child.
4. Jemima Newkirk, born c.1759
5. Peter Newkirk, born c.1760

Abraham Newkirk
1754-1823

This son of Tobias Newkirk (1723) was born June 15, 1754 in Duplin County, North Carolina, and died there July 19, 1823. Married first 1789 to Mrs. Mary Ann Brosard Brockne, born November 21, 1749, widow of Lieutenant Barent Brockne of the Revolution. She was a daughter of Peter Androus Brosard and Ann Penny. Married second Rachel Rhodes, born July 30, 1767. Rachel was the daughter of Benjamin Rhodes (1720) and Rachel Thomas (1730). Abraham enlisted as a private in Colonel James Moore's 3rd North Carolina Regiment in the Revolution. At the battle of Moore's Creek Bridge, on February 27, 1776, the commander of the regiment was standing near young Abraham and a young man named Ben Lanier, who were fighting side by side. He saw them both fire at the same time at the British officer, Captain MacLeod, and saw him fall. Later, the commander told the two young men they must run a foot race and that the winner would claim the honor of killing the British officer, and fall heir to his watch. Abraham won the race. Abraham reportedly brought home several relics of the war, including a cannon ball weighing twenty-four pounds, and a sword measuring nearly four feet, with bone handle, which has been passed down for several generations in the family.

There is some difference of opinion as to the true origin of the sword. Perhaps it, too, was the property of the British officer that Abraham was credited with killing at the battle of Moore's Bridge. However, at one time, Mary Newkirk Davis, born May 28, 1897, (widow of Professor John B. Davis) stated positively that the sword had belonged to Colonel Joe Rhodes, who never married. It was his sister, Rachel, who became the second wife of Abraham Newkirk, and she had apparently acquired the sword from her brother. There was a Lieutenant Joseph Rhodes who took part in the battle of Moore's Bridge, and that may well have been the same individual, known in later years as Colonel Rhodes. In any case, the sword remained in the Newkirk family for several generations. At some point, the owner of the sword cut off about eight and a half inches of the sword to make a kitchen knife. Fortunately, all the parts were kept together, and the sword was donated by Dr. and Mrs. William B. Herring c.1994 to the Moore's Creek National Battlefield Monument near Currie, North Carolina, who have certified to its authenticity as an American copy of a British Horseman's sabre from the 1760s. According to the Park Ranger, Linda L. Brown, the sword was sent to the restoration department at Harper's Ferry, and both pieces have been reserved. It is now on display at the battlefield.

Abraham left a will, which is of some historical interest, and is repeated here for that purpose:

I, Abraham Newkirk, of the State of North Carolina, County of New Hanover, considering the uncertainty of this mortal life and certainty of death, do make and publish this, my last will and testament in manner and form following; - viz -

First, I give and bequeath unto my beloved wife Rachel Newkirk the following negroes, viz:, Tyge, Stillar, Kate, George, Nimrod, Charlotte, Hannah, Dover, Sam, Charlie, Keezy, April, Mingo, Daniel. Also my manor plantation, five hundred and thirty acres with all appurtenances to the same belonging. Also all my household and kitchen furniture, stock of every kind, plantation and blacksmith tools. And my wife Rachel is to support and school all my children which may not be schooled at my decease. All the above property my wife shall hold during her natural life and after her decease the said lands and all other property and lands of which I am possessed at my decease and not hereafter willed in this will to be equally divided between my sons Joseph Newkirk, Timothy Newkirk and Henry J. T. Newkirk and after my wife's decease all the above negroes, together with their increase and the balance of my wife's legacy to be equally divided between my sons Joseph, Timothy, Bryan, Benjamin R., Henry J. T. and Jacob F. Newkirk.

I do also lend unto my daughter Penny Newkirk during her natural life, the following negroes; viz: Dolly and Dinah and Dinah's children, viz: John, Bill, Caeser, Gilford, Peyton and Sam. Also one bed and furniture and at her decease to the lawful heirs of her body, if any such there be and if none, to return to the lawful heirs of my body and to be equally divided among them.

I also give and bequeath unto my son Bryan Newkirk three negroes; Bob, Ben and Crease and their increases, one bed and furniture.

I also give and bequeath unto my daughter, Ann J. Williams, the following negroes, Juda, Zilph, Saffo and Isaac and their increase also one bed and furniture.

I also give and bequeath unto my son Henry J. T. Newkirk the following negroes, Virgil, young Stella, Chloe and Rosetta and their increase, one bed and furniture.

I also give and bequeath unto my son Jacob F. Newkirk my lower plantation by the name of "New Ground" containing three hundred and twenty acres, also the following negroes, viz: Else and Snooy and their increase, one bed and furniture.

All of the above legacies to remain in the possession of the said wife, Rachel Newkirk, until the heirs become of age or marry and if there be any disorderly, disobedient negroes, I desire that such be leased out to the best advantage until the owners are capable of taking them into possession.

And I, the said Abraham Newkirk do hereby appoint my beloved wife Rachel Newkirk, Executrix and my sons Joseph Newkirk and Timothy Newkirk, Executors to this my last will and testament, hereby revoking all former wills by me made, do ordain and establish this my last will and testament.

In testimony thereof I have hereunto set my hand and seal this nineteenth day of July in the year of our Lord one thousand eight hundred and twenty three.

Abraham Newkirk

Witnesses:
Wm. W. Rivenbark
Charley H. Rivenbark
Henry J. T. Newkirk
New Hanover County Court August Term, 1823

Two children were born to the first marriage of Abraham Newkirk, and eight to the second:

1. Penelope Newkirk, born June 30, 1785; married Enoch Hawes
2. Mary Ann Newkirk, born October 22, 1787, and died August, 1864. Married 1809 to Major James Matthis, born 1764, son of Edmond Matthis; his second wife.
3. Joseph Newkirk, born November 20, 1791, a twin; died August 1, 1856 (or August 22, 1886). Married first to Catharine Mills, who died January 20, 1836, and second July 26, 1844 to Elizabeth A. Hawes Jones, who was born c.1801 and died April 7, 1871. She was the daughter of John Hawes, Esquire, and Hannah Anderson, and had been twice married before her marriage to Joseph Newkirk. Joseph appears as head of household in the 1850 census of Hanover County, North Carolina, with his second wife, listed there as Eliza. There are several children, although this may not be a complete list:
   a. James Leonard Newkirk, born September 14, 1822, died January 20, 1874. Married Ann Huffman, born c.1822; died 1865, and had three children.
   b. Timothy Henry Rhodes Newkirk, born May 19, 1829, died 1891. Married Elizabeth Haywood Hall, born 1836 and died 1917. Ten children.
   c. Rachel Catherine Newkirk, a twin, born January 14, 1830 and died c.1836 (not appearing in the 1850 census)
   d. Charles Henry Newkirk, a twin, born January 14, 1830; died c.1836 (not appearing in the 1850 census)

e. Franklin Newkirk, born c.1830, appearing in the census, but not otherwise known as a child of Joseph. Could be a child of his wife, Elizabeth, from a first marriage

f. Mary L. Newkirk, born c.1831, appearing in the census, but not otherwise known as a child of Joseph. Could be a child of his wife, Elizabeth, from a first marriage

g. Thankful Jane Newkirk, born January 11, 1832; married Nathaniel Bonham, born 1814, died 1871. Thankful could also be a child of Joseph's wife, Elizabeth, from one of her earlier marriages. They had five children.

h. Bryant Benjamin Newkirk, born February 5, 1834 and died February 22, 1913. Married Mary Ann Gufford Bonham, born 1832, died 1914. Thirteen children:

(1) Joseph Hezekiah Newkirk, born November 8, 1853 and married first to Eva St. Clair Wendley, born February 14, 1853, by whom he had seven children. Married second to Charity Priscilla Code.

(2) Sarah Elizabeth Newkirk, born April 12, 1855 and died 1923. Married to Alfred Taylor Herring in Pender County, North Carolina. Six children.

(3) James Buchanan Newkirk, born August 29, 1856 and died 1924. Married to Anne Elizabeth Taylor, and had six children.

(4) Katherine Brosard Newkirk, born January 16, 1858; died 1928, single.

(5) Henry Franklin Newkirk, born July 27, 1859, and died January 18, 1953. Married Ida Bell Currie, born December 25, 1872; died May 3, 1957. Five children.

(6) Susan Hill Newkirk, born February 21, 1861, and died 1939, single.

(7) Hattie Carey Newkirk, born March 4, 1863; died 1943. Married to William Cannady of Scotts Hill, North Carolina.

(8) Mary Bryant Newkirk, born October 19, 1864 and died 1960, single.

(9)   Attelia Whitted Newkirk, born March 11, 1867; died 1949. Married Festus Arthur Mason and had two children.

(10)   David Harvey Newkirk, born September 15, 1868, and married Lucy Ellen Wells of Rose Hill, North Carolina. Four children.

(11)   Benjamin Newkirk, born March 11, 1870, died 1961. Married to Ella King Herring of Tomahawk, North Carolina. Six children.

(12)   Harriet Rachel Gufford Newkirk, born February 23, 1872, died 1964, single.

(13)   Timothy Rhodes Newkirk, born March 19, 1874, died 1954. Married to Ada Gore of New Hanover County, North Carolina. Two children.

i.   Abraham Newkirk, born 1835; died in infancy

j.   Mary Ann Newkirk, born January 3, 1836; married to Chester Rockwall, born 1829; died 1864.

4.   Timothy H. Newkirk, born November 20, 1791, a twin; died October 2, 1859 at Rose Hill, North Carolina. Married April 19, 1836 to Elizabeth Stallings, who was born August 12, 1785 and died October 21, 1857, daughter of Major Shadrack Stallings and Jane Wells. Timothy and his wife and children are buried in the old Newkirk cemetery near Rose Hill, North Carolina. The will of Timothy filed in book WB-3 at folio 5, Duplin County, North Carolina, listed a total of seventy-one slaves by name, and others not named. He left his plantation to his nephew, Timothy Henry Rhodes Newkirk (1829), son of his twin brother, Joseph. The children were:

a.   Timothy H. Newkirk, Jr., born May 10, 1828, and died October 20, 1835.

b.   C. B. Newkirk, born August 2, 1826; died same day.

c.   Penelope Newkirk, born January 20, 1823, and died September 12, 1828.

5.   Bryan Newkirk, or Bryant, born June 5, 1794, of whom more.

6.   Ann Jane Newkirk, born May 5, 1796, and died June 18, 1875. Married May 20, 1815 to Captain Stephen Williams, born May 31, 1791 and died June 18, 1849. He was the son of David Williams and Elizabeth Anderson. Children:

a. Bryan Newkirk Williams, born July 13, 1818, and died December 11, 1879. Married to Nancy Wells, and had seven children.

b. Mary Ann Williams, born June 20, 1820; married first James Huffman and second Alfred Hall.

c. Catherine Williams, born June 11, 1816 and died 1840. Married Stephen Herring.

d. Joseph T. Williams, born March 16, 1825, died October 25, 1891, single.

e. David Henry Williams, born June 23, 1828, died August 4, 1898. Married October 7, 1851 Asah Feison Colwell.

f. Samuel A. Williams, born November 14, 1830, and died February 14, 1898. Married September 23, 1852 to Lucinda Wells.

g. Harriett A. Williams, twin, born February 16, 1836, and married February 13, 1852 to James E. Wells.

h. Rachel Caroline Williams, twin, born February 16, 1836, and died December 3, 1893. Married to Stokes Wells.

i. Elizabeth Williams, born April 25, 1833; married February 13, 1852 to James Alderman.

7. Abraham Newkirk, Jr., born February 20, 1798; died young

8. Benjamin Rhodes Newkirk, born April 3, 1801; died March, 1872. Married first Lavinia Huffman; second March, 1825, to Harriet Huffman, perhaps her sister. The entire family is buried in the Newkirk Cemetery in Duplin County, North Carolina. Children born to the second marriage were:

a. Rachel Ann Newkirk, born December 7, 1826, died November 21, 1891. Married Albert G. Hall.

b. Francenia Caroline Newkirk, born December 14, 1827, died October 30, 1883. Married March 30, 1852 to Colonel John D. Powers. Six children.

c. Margarete Huffman Newkirk, born July 25, 1829, died May 22, 1844, single.

d. Mary Eliza Newkirk, born May 14, 1830, and died July 17, 1845, single.

e. Helen C. Newkirk, born July 13, 1832, died June 1, 1890. Married January 20, 1848 to the Reverend Julien Poydras Faison, a Baptist minister, and Chaplain in the

Confederate Army. See also *Heritage of Sampson County, North Carolina* for information relative to their descendants. In the 1870 census, she and her husband are living in her father's home and she is there listed as Ellen.

9. Henry John Thomas Newkirk, born June 12, 1804; died 1858. Never married.

10. Jacob Felix Newkirk, born August (or April) 26, 1807; died December 10, 1842. Jacob was married January 26, 1830 to Mary Huffman, born c.1813. She may be the same Mary Newkirk who appears as head of household in the 1850 census of New Hanover County, North Carolina, perhaps as a widow. She has in her household the following children, apparently hers, all born in North Carolina; their full names and pertinent dates come from Bill Powers of Griffin, Georgia, who has graciously provided large amounts of the information relative to the descendants of Abraham Newkirk (1754) and Rachel Rhodes. Children were:

a. John Abram Newkirk, born December 14, 1830, and died June 7, 1867. Married December 9, 1852 to Nancy Southerland.

b. Ann Rachel Newkirk, born October 1, 1831, died January 10, 1885. Married October 9, 1851 to Joseph Ward.

c. Harriet Adelaida Newkirk, born February 27, 1835; married May 2, 1854 to William W. Wayne.

d. Benjamin Henry Newkirk, born 1837, died August 7, 1863, single. Enlisted in New Hanover County, North Carolina, November 8, 1861 as private, Company A, 41st Regt, North Carolina Troops, 3rd Regt, North Carolina Cavalry. Died in hospital August 7, 1863, at Petersburg, Virginia, of typhoid fever.

e. George Bryan Newkirk, born 1839, died 1864. Enlisted in Duplin County, August 28, 1861, as private, Co. E, 30th Regt, North Carolina Troops. Promoted to sergeant on October 24, 1862. Killed at or near Charlestown, West Virginia, August 21, 1864.

Bryan Newkirk
1794-1863

This son of Abraham Newkirk (1754) and Rachel Rhodes (1767), was born June 5, 1794 in Duplin County, North Carolina, and died July 8, 1863 in Sampson County, North Carolina. He owned a large plantation on Black River and built a handsome home on the west side of the river near Newkirk's Bridge, and is buried there. The site is located on the south side of the road leading from Harrells to Kerr. He was a wealthy man for the period; his will lists at least ninety-five negro slaves by name in various bequests to his children, all of whom are named there. In some records, he appears as Bryant Newkirk, but verbal family history reports him as Bryan. Married c.1820 to Mary Catherine Hawes in Duplin County, North Carolina. She was born July 4, 1803 and died March 26, 1888 in Sampson County, North Carolina. Her parents were Edmond Alexander Hawes, II, and Elizabeth Ann Robinson. Bryan, or Bryant, appears in the 1850 census of New Hanover, with a number of children, all born in North Carolina:

1.   Abram Francis Newkirk, born May 21, 1821, died January 25, 1891 at Wilmington, North Carolina. He was a doctor, and a graduate of Jefferson Medical College in Philadelphia. He was enlisted in New Hanover County, October 1, 1861 as Captain, 22nd Regiment, North Carolina Militia. Appointed Captain, Co. A, 41st Regiment, North Carolina Troops (3rd Regiment, North Carolina Cavalry), CSA, to rank from October 18, 1861. Resigned September 12, 1863 by reason of his having been placed under arrest under charges which he felt were invalid; his efforts to have the charges investigated having failed. Company A, originally known as the "Rebel Rangers", was enlisted at Scott's Hill in New Hanover. The company was ordered to special service to guard the coast-line, and became known as *Newkirk's Coast Guard*, after its first captain. Mormon IGI records carry several references to Abram F. Newkirk, probably this individual, being in New Hanover County, North Carolina, in the proper time frame. He married February 11, 1850 in Wilmington, to Mary Isabella

Willkings, born March 20, 1828 at Wilmington, and died there December 8, 1885; the daughter of Winslow S. Willkings and Sophia W. Larkins. Children:

a. Bryan Winslow Newkirk, born February 10, 1853, died June 18, 1938. Married first February 23, 1882 Florence Mercer and had six children. She was a daughter of John W. Mercer (1812), and Anna Jane Evans (1822), and was born March 6, 1863, died December 13, 1896. Bryan Winslow married second April 20, 1898 to Mary Kate Roberts, no children. He and Florence are buried in Oakdale cemetery, Wilmington, North Carolina.

b. William Seavey Newkirk, born January 11, 1854, died February 7, 1913. Married to Caroline Virginia Whitney. Four children.

c. Sophie Wilkings Newkirk, born September 6, 1855, died October 29, 1942, single.

c. Anne Julia Newkirk, born August 7, 1857, died July 29, 1929. She married the Reverend Thomas Bradford, a Methodist minister, and had two children.

d. Robert Newkirk, born September 1, 1859, and died 1956. Married August 6, 1905 to Mattie Lee Stephens. Three children.

e. Mary Newkirk, born March 16, 1862, died October 1, 1937. Married Horace T. Charles and had five children.

f. Haywood Francis Newkirk, born January 8, 1865, died August 25, 1941. Married August 30, 1896 to Catherine Vose.

g. Abraham Francis Newkirk, II, born May 21, 1867, died October 24, 1873, single.

h. John Newkirk, born c.1869, died young, single

i. Charles Newkirk, of whom nothing is known.

2. Ann Julia Newkirk, born June 23, 1826, died March 10, 1900. Married November 9, 1843 Jeremiah Berry Seavey, a doctor. He was born June 21, 1815 in New Hampshire and educated at Bowden College in Maine. On a sea voyage to South America, he was shipwrecked off North Carolina and made his way to Wilmington. He became a teacher to the numerous children of Bryan Newkirk and finally married one of his

charges, who was eleven years his junior. He built his three-story home in 1843 on a hill near Wildcat, a tributary to Black River, which still stands. He died 1881 and is buried in the family cemetery near the home. They had children:

a. Mary B. Seavey, born January 8, 1845
b. Eugenia F. Seavey, born September 26, 1847, and died 1905. Married February 7, 1871 to J. A. Moore, born August 18, 1845, died August 18, 1904. Children:
    (1) Mary S. Moore, born November 4, 1872
    (2) James Upham Moore, born April 21, 1874, died April 19, 1918. Married Mollie Coston of South Carolina.
    (3) Julian Harrison Moore, born October 22, 1882, died 1896
    (4) Joel J. Moore, born July 29, 1884, died January 11, 1935. Married Alice Barker.
    (5) Eugenia Estelle Moore, born September 29, 1884. There is an obvious discrepancy between the date of birth of this child, and her brother just above; these are the dates reported in *Genealogies, The Newkirk and Allied Families*, pages of which have come into the author's possession. Eugenia was married January 19, 1910 to Charles Sprunt Corbett.
    (6) George Leighton Moore, born September 26, 1887
    (7) Martha Hawes Moore, born October 30, 1891; married 1929 to Randolph Merriweather.
c. Hannah Seavey, born September 22, 1848, and died August 18, 1914.
d. Jeremiah Berry Seavey, II, born January 5, 1867, and died June 16, 1933.
3. Madley Newkirk, perhaps, a girl, born c.1828; died November 27, 1919. She does not appear in the will of Bryan, but has been reported as a child in the family.
4. Bryan Benjamin Rhodes Newkirk, born 1829, died September 20, 1844, single.
5. William Usher Newkirk, born April 15, 1831, died May 17, 1910. He was married c.1860 to Jane Madeline Devane, born

April 15, 1843 and died December 9, 1899. They lived on a plantation on the west side of Black River near Ivanhoe, in Sampson County, North Carolina, and had children:

a. Mary Elizabeth Newkirk, born June 14, 1862, died 1940. Married David Carey Fennell, born January 16, 1884. Children:

(1) Margaret Howey Fennell.

(2) Jane Newkirk Fennell, married Dr. J. J. Dobbie; children:

(a) John Graham Dobbie.

(b) Jane Stewart Dobbie.

(3) Annie Thomas Fennell, who married Starkey S. Shubrick.

(4) Nell Stewart Fennell, married Dr. John Eugene Wine.

(5) Mary Madeline Fennell, married Dudley Graham Shaw, and had children:

(a) Dudley Graham Shaw, II, born August 2, 1907, and married Roslin Shaw.

(b) William Graham Shaw, born December 26, 1936

(c) Mary Nell Shaw, born June 30, 1941

(d) Colin Stewart Shaw, born May 9, 1944

(e) Roberta Shaw, born October 11, 1946

(f) Robinson McGregor Shaw, born February 20, 1952

(6) David Carey Fennell, born March 24, 1911. Married 1939 Beryl Brinkman, and had children:

(a) Madeline Beryl Fennell, born September 10, 1940

(b) Lois Guenn Fennell, born February 23, 1945

(c) Susan Christine Fennell, born May 9, 1948

(d) Robin Elizabeth Fennell, born January 17, 1951

(7) Madeline J. Fennell, born December 1, 1913, and married 1941 to Ivey Mathews. Children:

(a) Carey Beryl Mathews, born July 2, 1942

(b) John Dudley Mathews, born May 31, 1944

(2) William Francis Gilbert, born July 24, 1911; died May 15, 1941. Lieutenant in Navy; lost at sea.

(3) Sarah Evans Gilbert, born August 7, 1918. Married in June, 1941 Melvin Pruitt; children:

  (a) Francis Pruitt, born June, 1942

  (b) Jane Elizabeth Pruitt, born August 2, 1946

6. James Richard Newkirk, born November 16, 1832, died July 27, 1897 in Sampson County, North Carolina. In the original edition of this study, we had listed this son as being James Rhodes Newkirk, based primarily on reports of an individual of that name, who served as 3rd Lieutenant, Co. A, 41st Regt, North Carolina State Troops (3rd Regt, North Carolina Cavalry), CSA, in the Civil War, appearing in Volume II, *North Carolina Troops, 1861-1865*, by Manarin, for North Carolina Archives. We are apparently incorrect, and regret the error. We have since received massive amounts of data on these families from Bill Powers of Griffin, Georgia. Based on his analysis of the census data, family oral history, and other reports, it now appears clear that the James Richard Newkirk listed here is correct in this family, and that James Rhodes Newkirk reported in military records is, at best, a relative, and probably so, considering the use of the name, Rhodes, and his presence in Sampson County. James Richard was married May 23, 1859 to Mary Theresa Usher, born October 24, 1841, and died December 30, 1895. Her father, William Usher, with his family, lived near the Newkirk plantation, and it was for him that William Usher Newkirk (above) was named. Her mother was Eliza M. Love. Family oral history reports that when Sherman's army marched through North Carolina, burning the plantations, James Richard gave him the secret Masonic sign, and Sherman left the Newkirk plantation. Nine children, all born North Carolina:

a. Katherine Fulton Newkirk, born June 18, 1860, died March 5, 1954 Andalusia, Alabama. Married Benjamin Hamilton Zeagler, born May 4, 1860 at Zeagler Station, Scribben County, Georgia, and died December 29, 1957, son of George Mindolf Zeagler. They owned the Dixie Hotel in Andalusia, Alabama, and had children:

(1) Mary Esther Zeagler, born August 7, 1898, died August 15, 1945. Married James Wilford Shreve, and had children:
  (a) James Wilford Shreve, II.
  (b) Robert Fulton Shreve.
(2) Lois Zeagler, born April 12, 1900, and died June, 1989. Married to Oscar Page Banks, born April 2, 1900. They had children:
  (a) Zeagler Newkirk Banks, born December 18, 1922. Married Elizabeth Fleming and had children:
    1. Gayle Banks, born September 11, 1948
    2. Elizabeth Banks, born May 24, 1952
  (b) Arthur Waddell Banks, who married Dorothy Bryant and had at least one child:
    1. Walter Page Banks, born June 3, 1953
(3) Katie Connor Zeagler, born November 5, 1901, died April 23, 1901.
(4) Paul Crestwell Zeagler, born April 10, 1903 and married to Clarabell Ott, and had children:
  (a) Eleanor Catherine Zeagler.
  (b) Paul Zeagler.
  (c) Edward Zeagler.
b. William Bryan Newkirk, born April 6, 1861, died November 8, 1928 at Tampa, Florida, where he operated a furniture store, reportedly with a partner who was from Australia. Married there October 9, 1907 to Geraldine L. Carty. Children, perhaps born in Florida:
(1) Geraldine Aletta Newkirk, born December 6, 1908; married Lowell B. Sapp, and divorced.
(2) Marie Thersa Newkirk, born December 19, 1910 and later changed the spelling of her second name to Tersa. Married F. Burton Stanford.
(3) William Brian Van Ryan Newkirk, born November 15, 1912, died July 27, 1980. Dropped the Van Ryan part of his name late in life. Married Jane Louise Epple.

(4)   Julia Fulton Newkirk, born December 24, 1915, died May 9, 1984. Married to Gus Pelaz.

(5)   Mary Imelda Newkirk, born June 28, 1918, died November 5, 1988. Married William Bailey.

(6)   John Carty Newkirk, born December 15, 1922.

(7)   Ralph Leon Newkirk, born August 28, 1924; married Helen.

c. Maria Love Newkirk, born c.1866, died before 1907, single.

d. James Richard Newkirk, Jr., born c.1870 and died in Tampa, or in Missouri.

e. Jeremiah Seavey Newkirk, born January 23, 1871, died March 26, 1936 in Brunswick, Georgia, where he was a grocer. Married there December 13, 1919 Cora Rosalee Clark, born March 2, 1882 in Georgia, died November 25, 1965. She was a daughter of William Arward Clark and Virginia Barber. Children, the first three and last three born in Brunswick, Georgia; the middle three in St. Augustine, Florida:

(1)   Leona Theresa Newkirk, born November 30, 1905, died October 7, 1969 at Miami, Florida. Married Albert Jack Gieger in Wichita, Kansas, and had three children.

(2)   Arward Theodore Newkirk, born August 29, 1906, died July 13, 1975 in Cochran, Georgia; single.

(3)   Bernard Fulton Newkirk, born January 17, 1909 and died August 24, 1985 in Brunswick, Georgia. Married there August 19, 1944 to Nonene Purvis, born May 12, 1917 at Dublin, Georgia. They had two children; one adopted and one natural born.

(4)   Esther Virginia Newkirk, born December 30, 1910. Married August 19, 1950 in Hartford, Kansas, to Reginald Devaux; one child.

(5)   Annie Agnes Newkirk, born May 30, 1913, died May 9, 1982 at Bremerton, Washington. Married Glynn County, Georgia to Norman Greig; a child.

(6)   Roy James Newkirk, born August 19, 1914, died April 24, 1992 in Portland, Oregon. Married in

Rincon, Georgia to Louise Helmy. Married second July 8, 1966 in Reno, Nevada, Phyllis J. Sheridan.

(7) Irving John Richard Newkirk, twin, born September 2, 1918 and married in 1944 to Sarah Hires. Married second to Audry Sheridan. Two children.

(8) Joseph Seavey Newkirk, twin, born September 2, 1918, died March 20, 1966 at La Grange, Georgia. Married at Brunswick, September 30, 1946 to Edith Hazel Windsor, born August 4, 1922, died May 24, 1980. Five children.

(9) Robert Aloysius Newkirk, born May 31, 1921, died 1988 in Portland, Oregon. Married three times; first June 18, 1943 in Duluth, Minnesota, to Phyllis J. Sheridan and divorced, after which she married second his brother, Roy James, which see above. Robert was married second in the late 1970s to Cleone Gonya, and in 1986 to Darlene Olsen. Five children from his first marriage.

f. Gustavus R. Newkirk, born c.1876, died at Asheville, North Carolina. Married Laura.

g. Walker Newkirk, born c.1878, died in Tampa, Florida. Married Rosa, and had children:

(1) Francis W. Newkirk; in 1995 in a nursing home due to a stroke. One adopted child.

(2) James Richard Newkirk, died January 16, 1991

(3) Richard Newkirk, died young by drowning

h. Josephine Cecilia Newkirk, born 1880, died before 1907

i. Charles W. Newkirk, perhaps died young.

7. Henry Haywood Newkirk, born July 2, 1834, died April 28, 1875 in Texas. Married c.1851 to Mary E. Henry. In the 1860 census, they were found in Leon County, Texas; in 1870 in Anderson County, Texas. They had children:

a. Quessie Newkirk, a male, born c.1851; a school teacher

b. Henry Newkirk, born c.1854; married Mamie Long.

c. Mary B. Newkirk, born c.1864; married Shaw or Edward Howell.

8. Rachel Emma Newkirk, born c.1836, and married to Erskine Alexander McKoy. They had children:

a. Carrie McKoy, born October 15, 1855; married December 23, 1875 to Jacob Giles.
b. Usher McKoy, married Sallie Ingram.
c. Josephine McKoy, born c.1863; married Giles Lucas.
d. Margaret McKoy, born November 14, 1865, and married May 2, 1888 to Elijah B. Parker. They had children:
   (1) Irene McKoy Parker married Parley B. Rasmussen and had children:
      (a) Parley B. Rasmussen, II, born November 2, 1924
      (b) John Parker Rasmussen, born November 24, 1932, died January 27, 1946
   (2) Annie Laurie Parker, married September 20, 1920 Julius Hansen, and had children:
      (a) Thomas Julius Hansen.
      (b) Annie Joyce Hansen, married July 6, 1952 to Vitto Royynto.
   (3) Emma Pearle Parker, married December 22, 1926 Frank B. Meacham, and had children:
      (a) Frank Parker Meacham, born September 2, 1927, married to Eloise Carmichel, December 23, 1951. At least one son:
         1. Frank Richard Meacham, born December 10, 1952
      (b) Jo Ann Meacham, born January 11, 1934
   (4) Sarah Ethel Parker, married November 27, 1930 to David W. Wray. At least one son:
      (a) John David Wray, born November 14, 1933
   (5) John W. Parker, married Millie Biggs.
   (6) Edward B. Parker, of whom nothing more
   (7) Oda Lee Parker, of whom nothing more is known.
   (8) Josephine Parker, married Lester Maxwell Green, and had at least one son:
      (a) Lester Maxwell Green, II, married December 15, 1953 to Ruth Atkinson, and had a son:
         1. Lester Maxwell Green, III, born March 8, 1954
e. Edward B. McKoy, no further information

f.   Willie McKoy, no further information
g.   Annie McKoy, no further information
9.   Laura E. Newkirk, born c.1839, and perhaps died in Texas. Married December 23, 1856 in New Hanover County, North Carolina, C. Thomas Henry, born c.1826. At least one child:
     a.   C. Thomas Henry, II, of Waco, Texas
10. Evelyn Caledonia Newkirk, born February 3, 1841, died May 6, 1912. Married November 2, 1856 John Archibald Corbett on a plantation on Black River near Ivanhoe, North Carolina. He was born November 28, 1841 and died May 22, 1913, son of John Corbett (1798), and Jeannette Sellers (1794). They had children:
     a.   Mary Jeannette Corbett, born November 26, 1865, and married April 22, 1885 to John Winfield Scott Robinson, and had six children.
     b.   Archibald Haywood Corbett, born June 16, 1869. Married first June 14, 1899 Mary Berkeley Murphy May; and second in 1903 to Alberta Williams.
11. Josephine Newkirk, born October 6, 1844, died April 20, 1910. She was married November 23, 1867 in New Hanover County to Gustavus Adolphus Bronson, born February 6, 1837 and died April 21, 1899. They had children:
     a.   Callie Bronson, born 1870, and married to Thomas A. Wortham.
     b.   Mamie Bryan Bronson, born 1871, and died 1916. Married James Gillis.
     c.   Lillie Bronson, born 1876, and died 1951. Married Henry Cabbell Bentley.
     d.   Laura Bronson, born 1879, and died 1904. Married John Stedman Collins.
12. Mary Bryan Newkirk, born December 11, 1849, and died November 27, 1919 at Wilmington, North Carolina. Married William Francis Alexander, born January 20, 1855, died May 4, 1916; buried in Bellevac cemetery, Wilmington, North Carolina. He was a son of Obediah Francis Alexander and Hester Ann Pateway. They had children:
     a.   Caledonia Frances Alexander, married George Shepherd.

b. Charles Obediah Alexander, born June 3, 1877, and died November 23, 1911. Married Ivey Moore.
c. Bryan Newkirk Alexander, born September 13, 1879, died April 5, 1892; single.
d. Josephine Alexander, married G. A. Meacham.
e. Eugenia Alexander, born September 4, 1885, a twin; married Charles Lerrquine Jones.
f. William Francis Alexander, born September 4, 1885, a twin, married first Violet Davey and second her niece, Marjorie Davey.
g. Mary Esther Alexander, born c.1888; married Delbert Palmer.

CHAPTER 4

Abraham Newkirk
1724-1790

This son of Barent Newkirk (1689) and Rebecca Van Buntschooten Newkirk, was born October 19, 1724 near Princeton, New Jersey, and died c.1790. One report states that he was born in Ulster County, New York, which may be correct, although the reported movements of his parents puts them in New Jersey about 1723, prior to his birth. Mormon IGI records report his birth as being in Fairfield County, Ohio. He went with his father to Virginia about 1737, and lived in Berkeley County until about 1770, when he moved to Washington County, Pennsylvania. He was married to Kezia Shipman about 1749, a daughter of Teunis Shipman, probably in Frederick County, Virginia. He is buried a short distance north of the town of Bentleyville, in Washington County, Pennsylvania, on the Warner farm, with his wife. Abraham was a Revolutionary War soldier, as reported on page 136, Volume Two, *Pennsylvania Archives, Sixth Series*, where it is reported: *"Harrisburg, Pennsylvania, USA. January 11, 1915, To Whom It May Concern: I hereby certify that one Abraham Newkirk was a private in Captain John Craven's Company, Fifth Battalion, Washington County Militia."* They had eight children, all born in Berkeley County, Virginia:

1. Teunis Newkirk, born July 20, 1750, of whom more
2. Drusilla Newkirk, born about 1752 and died young
3. Isaac Newkirk, born 1754, of whom more
4. Elizabeth Newkirk, born about 1757; married Hull, or Hall
5. Sophia Newkirk, born c.1761; died March 17, 1854 in Mercer County, Pennsylvania. Married first to John Knox, by whom she had a son; second to James Rice, by whom she had four children.
6. Abraham Newkirk, Jr., born 1764; please see Chapter 5
7. Henry Newkirk, born 1768; please see Chapter 6
8. Reuben Newkirk, born about 1769, of whom more

Teunis Newkirk
1750-1823

This son of Abraham Newkirk (1724) and Kezia Shipman Newkirk, was born July 20, 1750, apparently in Frederick County, Virginia, and died May 1, 1823 near Lancaster, Fairfield County, Ohio. He was married first about 1779 to Margaret Miles, who was born April 13, 1759 and died June 11, 1798, a daughter of George Miles. It appears that she had a brother, George Miles, Jr., who died before 1813, with no issue, leaving his sister as his legal heir. She had predeceased her brother, however, leaving her children as surviving heirs of the estate. In 1813, by deed entered March 14, 1814 in Deed Book 25 at page 397, in Berkeley County, West Virginia, it appears that "*James Newkirk and Joseph Newkirk, children and heirs of Margaret Newkirk, late Margaret Miles, sister and legal representative of George Miles, deceased*" convey to their brother George Newkirk all their right, title and interest in the estate of Margaret Newkirk, in particular as to a tract of land of which George Miles died seized, containing about 346 acres and 3 roods of land. There is a similar deed, dated March 26, 1816, recorded in Deed Book 34 at page 147, from Reuben Newkirk and Isaac Newkirk, with the same explanation of family relationships, to George Newkirk, relinquishing their interests as well.

Teunis married secondly on April 9, 1801 to Susannah Hay, born July 6, 1781 in Berkeley County, and died July 4, 1842 in Fairfield County, Ohio; daughter of William Hay, who was a great uncle of the Honorable John Hay, once Secretary of State. Teunis acquired several tracts of land in Berkeley County between 1779 and 1796, including: 195 acres from Daniel Williamson, September 20, 1779, Deed Book 5, page 364; 242 and 3/4 acres from Edward Davis, May 9, 1780, Deed Book 6, page 126; 110 acres from John Shaver, November 23, 1790, Deed Book 9, page 439; 50 and 1/2 acres from Michael Miller and his wife Mary, April 29, 1790, Deed Book 12, page 139; and two tracts of 257 acres and 106 acres from George Miles, December 6, 1796, Deed Book 13, page 154. The various deeds referred to total 961 and 1/4 acres of land.

The property was generally located on North Mountain, and along the Potomac River, and part of it was said to be of the original 1,175 acres that John Hood obtained by King's Patent on November 12, 1735; some of which Hood had earlier conveyed to Barent Newkirk (1689), Teunis' grandfather. By deed dated April 22, 1799, recorded in Deed Book 15, page 216, Berkeley County, Virginia (later West Virginia), Teunis sold five parcels of his land, containing a total of 653 and 1/2 acres to his son, George Newkirk (1780). On August 29, 1800, Deed Book 20 at page 418, he conveyed to his son George a 546 acre farm "during the lifetime of Teunis Newkirk only." Presumably, that farm would be disposed of by the will of Teunis, which I have not seen.

Soon after, Teunis moved to Fairfield County, Ohio, with his brother, Reuben (1769), leaving sons George, James, Isaac and Joseph in Virginia. Nine children were born to his first marriage in Berkeley County, Virginia; and five to the second marriage, the first probably in Berkeley County, and the last four in Fairfield County, Ohio. They were:

1.   George Newkirk, born March 12, 1780 and died August 18, 1822, of whom more in Chapter 7
2.   Henry Newkirk, born October 10, 1781; died March 21, 1800
3.   John Newkirk, born August 25, 1783; died July 1, 1787
4.   Anna Newkirk, born January 25, 1786; died July 1, 1787
5.   James Newkirk, born December 11, 1788; died 1817. Married January 10, 1815 to Mary Porterfield. Two daughters.
6.   Joseph Newkirk, born January 18, 1791; died March 5, 1869 at Big Prairie, Wayne County, Ohio. Married first August 8, 1816 to Eveline Kemp, born c.1798 and died August 24, 1823. Married second in 1824 to Frances Stuart, born c.1803, and died June 17, 1871. Reportedly, there were as many as fourteen children. Although the listed age is a bit off, which is not unusual, this is probably the same Joseph Newkirk listed in the 1850 census of Wayne County, with a wife, Frances, born c.1803 in Pennsylvania. At the time, there are five children, born in Ohio. Joseph appears to have had the first three children listed following from his first marriage, and the last eleven from his second, all born in Wayne County, Ohio:
     a.   Tunis Newkirk, born October 17, 1817; married July 26, 1848 to Lucy A. Wallace.

b. Sarah Ann Newkirk, born May 19, 1820; died June 29, 1836

c. Joseph Newkirk, born September 18, 1822; died January 24, 1823

d. Darius Histaspus Newkirk, born February 20, 1826, and died May 2, 1847.

e. Isaac James Newkirk, born October 11, 1826. Married March 8, 1867 Susan M. Lived in St. Helena, California.

f. Eliza Maria Newkirk, born February 23, 1828; married January, 1847 to Almon Aylesworth. Lived in Columbus, Ohio.

g. Martha Newkirk, born October 10, 1829, and married January, 1852 to Ransom Bartle. Lived in Independence, Iowa.

h. Mary Jane Newkirk, born October 19, 1831; married May 8, 1861 Dr. George Leggett.

i. Caroline Newkirk, born December 4, 1833; married April 15, 1861 to Sanford S. Clark. Lived in Independence, Iowa.

j. Robert Stewart Newkirk, or Stuart, born November 10, 1835, and died March 24, 1889. Married October 14, 1868 to Flora C. Aylesworth, born March 15, 1844 in Wayne County, Ohio; died July 13, 1905. They had children, the first born at Lincoln, Illinois, and the rest in Wayne County:

    (1) Glenn Stuart Newkirk, born April 1870 and died November 2, 1870

    (2) James A. Newkirk, born September 11, 1874 and married to Lottie W. Bixler.

    (3) Joseph H. Newkirk, born January 2, 1876, and died August 7, 1876.

    (4) George R. Newkirk, born December 24, 1880.

k. Joseph Newkirk, born September 27, 1838; died January 24, 1839

l. Henry Clay Newkirk, born August 4, 1840; died August 23, 1871

m. David Bonnett Newkirk, born September 12, 1843; died October 26, 1844.

n. Albert Newkirk, born February 8, 1848; died October 14, 1849

7. Reuben Newkirk, born March 5, 1793; died October 7, 1819

8. Isaac Newkirk, born June 5, 1795; died August 29, 1873. Married first September 29, 1836 at Indianapolis, Indiana, to Ellen Foote; and second October 24, 1844 Ellen Ellis Seibert in Berkeley County, Virginia. Reportedly, there were four children. The 1850 census of Washington County, Maryland, lists Isaac, a chairmaker, and his second wife, Ellen, born c.1806 in Virginia. They had two children in the household, and we believe there was at least one other son born to that marriage (Tunis Ellis) after the taking of the census. There may have been more children born to the first marriage, in 1850 living in their own households. Three children were:

a. Mary M. Newkirk, born c.1846

b. Sarah P. Newkirk, born c.1848

c. Tunis Ellis Newkirk, born 1853 and died c.1938, deriving his name from the given name of his grandfather, and the last name of his mother, although his first name more often appears with this variant spelling. This individual was found in records of Washington County, Maryland, with the spelling of the name as Tunis, used here. He was married twice, first on January 4, 1883 to Virginia Tice, born c.1858. After her death, he married secondly February 11, 1904 to Jane L. Rubeck, born c.1879 (he was then twice her age!). He may actually have been married three times, perhaps first on December 26, 1878 to Ann Elizabeth Hassett. She was born c.1855 and died January 29, 1880 at the age of 25 years, 5 months and 22 days, with no reported children from that marriage. There appear to have been children from the other marriages, and quite a few, considering the terms of his will. It is found in Book 18 at page 371, dated February 22, 1928 and entered for record November 25, 1938. In his will, he leaves one third to his wife, Jane L. Neikirk (the spelling found there). He then leaves 8/39 of his estate to be divided equally between the children of his marriage to Jane L. Neikirk; and the remaining 6/13 of the estate to be divided equally between the children born to his first wife Virginia. No children are listed by name. Accounts of his estate are also found in the records, and there, all of his children are listed;, there having been six born to each of his marriages. The widow received $939.55 as her one-third dower right; the children from the second marriage received $96.37; those from the first $216.83. Children of the marriage to Virginia are listed first following:

    (1)   Harry E. Newkirk, perhaps the eldest, named as the co-administrator

    (2)   Ralph T. Newkirk, co-administrator of the estate

    (3)   Clarence T. Newkirk

    (4)   Nellie K. Newkirk

    (5)   Noah E. Newkirk

    (6)   Fred T. Newkirk

    (7)   Mabel Newkirk, married to Faith

    (8)   Madge Newkirk, married to Corbett

    (9)   Sarah Newkirk, married to Faith

    (10)   John Newkirk

    (11)   Clyde Newkirk

    (12)   Evelyn Newkirk, married to Ervin

9. An infant, stillbirth August 28, 1797

10. Anna Newkirk, first child of the marriage to Susannah Hay (1781), born November 3, 1802 and died May 23, 1882 at Perryville, Ohio. Married March 26, 1818 to John Comer at Lancaster, Ohio, who died February 25, 1872. They had twelve children.

11. Jeptha Newkirk, born May 11, 1807 and died July 14, 1881 in Fairfield County, Ohio; of which he had been elected Treasurer some years earlier. He was married July 25, 1830 to Nancy Ann Michaels, born August 14, 1806 in Pennsylvania, and died April 9, 1880 in Fairfield County, Ohio. Nine children were reported, seven of whom appear in the 1850 census of Fairfield County, Ohio, all of them being born there:

a.   John Newkirk, born c.1832

b.   Samuel T. Newkirk, born c.1838

c.   Susanna L. Newkirk, born c.1838

d.   Elvira V. Newkirk, born c.1840

e.   Anne Newkirk, born c.1842
f.   Louisa I. Newkirk, born c.1844
g.   Laura Elizabeth Newkirk, born December 29, 1848
12. John W. Newkirk, born January 22, 1813 and died December 26, 1864. Married March 3, 1836 to Julia Ann Stansberry, born c.1820 in Ohio. Seven children were reported, five of whom appear in the 1850 census of Fairfield County, Ohio, all born there:
    a.   William Newkirk, born c.1839
    b.   Jeptha Newkirk, born c.1842
    c.   Thomas B. Newkirk, born c.1846
    d.   Jared H. Newkirk, born c.1846
    e.   Stansberry Newkirk, born c.1850
13. Virginia Newkirk, born October 17, 1817 and died April 16, 1902 at Reading, Michigan. Married February 4, 1835 to John Lamb. Nine children.
14. Jane Perty Newkirk, born January 5, 1821; died February 22, 1889 at Hillsdale, Michigan. Married October 25, 1844 to Daniel Lincoln Pratt. He was born June 24, 1820 in Plainfield, Massachusetts, and died November 7, 1902 at Hillsdale, Michigan. His parents were William Pratt (1793) and Lovina Colson or Coliton. He was a well-known attorney and a Judge of the Circuit Court. They had nine children.

Isaac Newkirk
1754-1823

This son of Abraham Newkirk (1724) was born March 23, 1754 in Berkeley County, Virginia, and died January 31, 1823 in Washington County, Pennsylvania. His will dated April 27, 1822 was probated February 13, 1823, and he is buried in the Pigeon Creek Churchyard at Bentleyville. He was married to Rhoda Carroll, who was born c.1765 and died February 18, 1825; buried with her husband. Minutes of the Court of Yohogania County, Virginia (later West Virginia) of March 25, 1778 ordered a Bill of Indictment be referred to the Grand Jury against Henry Newkirk, Isaac Newkirk and others for refusing to help the constable in execution of his office. (Henry is apparently Isaac's brother, born c.1721). In *The History of Washington County, Pennsylvania*, it is reported that the Newkirks were early settlers in the county, and that the land they owned was located in both Fallowfield and Somerset Townships. In the section on Somerset Township it is reported that the first persons to make their way into the wilderness of Somerset Township were the Newkirk family and the William Colvey family. Further, the Newkirks were reported as having come from Maryland or Virginia prior to 1777. Isaac served in the Revolution with Pennsylvania troops from Washington County, and in 1782 accompanied Captain William Crawford on the ill-fated expedition against the Wyandot and Delaware Indians on the Muskingum. He bought lands at Big Prairie, Ohio, on which some of his children later settled. On February 27, 1786, he obtained a warrant for 300 acres on Pigeon Creek, in Washington County, Pennsylvania, called *Agricultura*. The property was also claimed by William Colvin, who had a warrant dated February 13, 1786, but was returned to Isaac Newkirk by warrant dated November 3, 1807. On September 26, 1816, according to county records, Isaac laid out a town, which he called *Perriopolis*, either partly on or adjacent to his farm. However, no lots were sold, and no buildings were erected. His children, born in Washington County, were:

1. John Newkirk, born August 7, 1786, of whom more.
2. Henry Newkirk, born September 25, 1789, of whom more.
3. Reuben Newkirk, born February 29, 1792, of whom more.
4. Teunis Newkirk, appearing also as Tunis, born November 26, 1794 and died October 7, 1866 in Bentleyville, Pennsylvania. Married first on January 7, 1820 to Jane Rainey, born c.1798 and died 1840. Married second October 20, 1840 to Amanda F. Niblick, born c.1822. He reportedly had as many as thirteen children. The census of Washington County, Pennsylvania, for 1850, includes the family, with six of the children:
   a. John R. Newkirk, born c.1828
   b. Caroline Newkirk, born c.1833
   c. William A. Newkirk, born c.1835
   d. Harriet Newkirk, born c.1843
   e. Mary E. Newkirk, born c.1846
   f. George Newkirk, born c.1848

5. Jane Newkirk, born April 13, 1795 and died November 14, 1840 at Bentleyville, Pennsylvania. Married February, 1810 to John G. Springer, who died January 11, 1869 and is buried with his wife at Bentleyville. Eight children.

6. George William Newkirk, born January 18, 1797 and died June 5, 1846. Married Maria Bennett, and of whom more

7. Cyrus Newkirk, born May 5, 1799 and died November 17, 1850. Married November 29, 1825 Sarah Herron Alexander, who was born March 28, 1803 and died May 19, 1893. The family appears in the 1850 census of Washington County, Pennsylvania, with six children, all born in Pennsylvania; there was a total of nine:

a. Joseph Alexander Newkirk, born September 24, 1826; died November 23, 1886. Married November 15, 1848 to Nancy W. Hopkins, born June 24, 1829. Five children, born in Washington County, Pennsylvania:

(1) Thomas Hopkins Newkirk, born August 11, 1849

(2) Harriet O'Ella Newkirk, born November 29, 1850; married February 27, 1873 Mortimer Richardson.

(3) Charles D. Newkirk, born September, 1855.

(4) Nora Newkirk, born November 15, 1868; married May 29, 1889 to John B. Myers.

(5) Clyde Newton Newkirk, born August 29, 1870. As a young man, he became known nationwide as Newton Newkirk, creator and writer of a humorous newspaper page known as *Bingville Bugle*. The column was syndicated and ran in numerous papers from 1903 to 1919; a satire of rural press and country life in general. It is said that Bing Crosby related that he took his stage name from a character in the column, known as *Bingo*, simply dropping the last letter of the name.

b. Isaac Newkirk, born July 7, 1828; married January 3, 1855 to Amanda Bentley.

c. James Samson Newkirk, born May 13, 1830. Married March 16, 1859 to Louisa Richardson.

d. Henry Newkirk, born February 24, 1832; died October 24, 1874 at Pittsburgh. Married September 26, 1854 to Olive Jane Richardson.
e. Harriet Emeline Newkirk, born June 15, 1834; died October 21, 1837.
f. Permelia Jane Newkirk, born August 18, 1836 and died October 21, 1837.
g. Rhoda C. Newkirk, born August 24, 1838; died January 27, 1860
h. Harriet Jane Newkirk, born February 8, 1841, and died February 28, 1870 at New Brighton, Beaver County, Pennsylvania. Married March 13, 1860 to Howden.
i. Emily Josephine Newkirk, born April 13, 1843; died June 30, 1876 Bentleyville, Washington County, Pennsylvania.

8. Louisiana Newkirk, born November 5, 1803; died January 27, 1868. Married George Leyda about 1823. He was born November 24, 1794 and died March 17, 1864. They lived in Washington County, Pennsylvania, and had three children.

9. Luzerba Newkirk, born May 27, 1806 and died September 16, 1864. Married November, 1824 John Rainey, born November 5, 1799 in Washington County, Pennsylvania, and died September 29, 1882. Both are buried in the Newkirk cemetery at Big Prairie, Ohio. They had eight children and, after her death, John was married secondly to Elizabeth Wells on May 18, 1868. He was a farmer, and a Presbyterian.

10. Susannah Newkirk, born February 18, 1807; died February 18, 1830. Married James Leyda, born July 17, 1801. They lived at Big Prairie, Ohio, and had one child, died young.

John Newkirk
1786-1827

This son of Isaac Newkirk (1754) was born August 7, 1786 in Washington County, Maryland, and died October 2, 1827 in Wayne County, Ohio. Married to Christena Clouse, who was born c.1781/91; died September 17, 1827 in Wayne County. A biography of his life appears in *History of Wayne County, Ohio, From the Days of the Pioneers and First Settlers to the Present Time*, by

Ben Douglass, Wooster, Ohio, 1878. He was one of the earliest settlers of the area, moving to Clinton Township about 1814, where he purchased a farm from Joshua Oram. He was known as Captain John Newkirk; kept a stage-office; was among the first Justices of the Township; and taught the first school in Lake Township. His name appears frequently in the county records, and he was the father of at least seven children, born in Wayne County, Ohio, except the second child:

1. Elizabeth Newkirk, born June 3, 1812; died December 9, 1845. Married January 24, 1830 to Benjamin Leyda.
2. Milton Newkirk, born August 28, 1814 Washington County, Pennsylvania; died April 19, 1884 in Ashland County, Ohio. Married Wayne County, Ohio February 15, 1838 to Catharine Motz, born September 16, 1815 in Franklin County, Pennsylvania; died September 24, 1906 Wayne County, Ohio. Seven children, born in Ohio:
   a. Emaline Newkirk, born January 15, 1839, and married October 12, 1859 William Dilgard.
   b. Ruphina Newkirk, born May 4, 1841, and married April 7, 1859 to Peter Howsen.
   c. Delphina Newkirk, born January 20, 1843; married April 12, 1877 to John Kick.
   d. Newton M. Newkirk, born September 12, 1843; died June 19, 1926 in Wayne County, Ohio. Married there March 14, 1867 to Martha Rickabaugh, born December, 1844; died May 10, 1916 in Wayne County, Ohio. One infant death.
   e. Adaline Newkirk, born November 20, 1849 at McZena, in Ashland County, Ohio; married February 13, 1873 Henry Walters
   f. Philo H. Newkirk, born September 12, 1852 at McZena; died September 8, 1855.
   g. John Rainey Newkirk, born November 13, 1856 at McZena; died 1924. Married September 18, 1877 to Lydia E. Huckendublen, born February 20, 1856 at Big Prairie, Ohio; died March 14, 1934. One son:
      (1) Charles H. Newkirk, born March 24, 1881 at McZena, Ohio, and died January 31, 1905.

3. Newton Newkirk, born January 14, 1816; died September 21, 1839; a cabinetmaker, single.
4. Ursula Newkirk, born March 9, 1818; died 1892. Married June 22, 1837 in Wayne County to Tobias M. Gibbon.
5. Cyrus Newkirk, born April 14, 1821; died January 3, 1890 at Nokomis, Illinois. Married 1847 Sarah Evers.
6. Rhoda Newkirk, born November, 1825. Married March 9, 1848 to John Brown.
7. George Washington Newkirk, born March 12, 1827; died June 15, 1861. Married to Leah Foster.

Henry Newkirk
1789-1847

This son of Isaac Newkirk (1754) was born September 25, 1789 in Washington County, Maryland, and died August 21, 1847 at Big Prairie, Wayne County, Ohio. His biography also appears in the Wayne County history referred to above. He also arrived in Wayne County as early as 1814, where he settled on a farm purchased by his father, and by the following year, had apparently obtained his own farm near Big Spring, on which he erected a frame home for himself. He appears to have returned for a short time to Pennsylvania, where he was married March 19, 1818 to Jane Hart, and returned with his bride to the farm in Ohio. She was born January 26, 1801 and died February 21, 1854 in Wayne County, daughter of David and Sarah Hart. Together, they joined the Methodist Church and deeded the grounds on which it was built, with the cemetery grounds as a public place of burial. It was incorporated and named Newkirk Cemetery Association in their honor. In 1827, he joined with General Thomas McMillen, and constructed the first carding factory in the township. The widow, Jane, appears in the 1850 census of Wayne County. Included in the household is one P. H. Newkirk, a farmer, born c.1807, not otherwise identified, but may possibly be the son listed below as Paxton. Henry had a number of children, born in Wayne County, Ohio, including:

1. Sarah P. Newkirk, born April 18, 1819; died February 1, 1841 at Ft. Madison, Iowa of pneumonia. Married February 13, 1837 to George P. Bell or Beall.
2. Isaac Newkirk, born June 5, 1821 in Clinton Township; died December 22, 1870 at Big Prairie in Wayne County, Ohio, of pneumonia. His biography also appears in the Wayne County history mentioned earlier. Married March 25, 1847 to Sarah O. Gibbon and joined the Methodist church in the winter of 1856, serving as Sunday school Superintendent and Steward. While serving on a grand jury in Wooster, he suddenly became violently ill, and died December 22, 1870. His obituary stated that he was *"known and beloved by his neighbors, for his lofty spirit of honor, spotless integrity, delicacy of conscience, kindness of heart, and promptness of decision."* He had nine children, born in Wayne County, Ohio:
   a. Henry M. Newkirk, born August 9, 1848; died April 4, 1895. Married October 26, 1876 to Anna B. Linn, born 1854 in Pennsylvania; died 1930 in Wayne County. They had seven children, born in Wayne County:
      (1) George Clyde Newkirk, born August 18, 1877, and died November 1, 1877.
      (2) Effie Dale Newkirk, born October 2, 1879; died 1962
      (3) John Linn Newkirk, born August, 1883
      (4) Mary Helen Newkirk, born August 5, 1885
      (5) Edith Blanche Newkirk, born April, 1888
      (6) Myra Irine Newkirk, born September 1, 1891 and married to Donald Weimer.
      (7) Henry M. Newkirk, born February 18, 1895; died October, 1967. Married Mary M. Potts.
   b. Mary K. Newkirk, born December 20, 1851; married May 26, 1868 to Joseph D. Peters.
   c. Ida W. Newkirk, born September 24, 1853; died March 2, 1922. Married Dr. Robert A. Baldwin and lived at Wooster
   d. John Gibbon Newkirk, born March 21, 1855; died November 18, 1868 at Big Prairie, Ohio
   e. Leslie Victor Newkirk, born March 27, 1857

f. Eugene Wade Newkirk, born August 23, 1859; died January 18, 1937 at Wooster, Ohio
g. Robert O. Newkirk, an infant death in 1862
h. George Grant Newkirk, born c.1862; died February 27, 1864
i. Thomas Isaac Newkirk, born May 30, 1866. Lived and worked for the railroads in Illinois.
3. David H. Newkirk, born May 7, 1825; died July 2, 1826. He was the first person buried in the cemetery of the Methodist church built on his father's property.
4. Paxton H. Newkirk, born April 27, 1827; died May 3, 1861 of pneumonia. Married January 1, 1850 (or April 15, 1852, according to IGI records) to Sarah Ellen Pocock, born about 1830 in Maryland. They had three children, all born at Big Prairie, in Wayne County, Ohio:
    a. Emma Jane Newkirk, born October 9, 1853
    b. Paxton H. Newkirk, Jr.; married December 20, 1885 to Annie Campbell. He died November 21, 1890.
    c. Arthur Clinton Newkirk, born November 21, 1856; died December 18, 1925. Married November 4, 1891 Lydia A. Bruce.
5. Rhoda Maria Newkirk, born October 12, 1829; died April 7, 1891 at West Bridgewater, Pennsylvania. Married October 29, 1850 Adam P. Hopkins of Washington County, Pennsylvania. At least two children:
    a. Henry Hopkins
    b. Mary Hopkins
6. Emily J. Newkirk, born August 14, 1833; graduated from Washington Seminary in Pennsylvania. Married March 27, 1865 to Wilson N. Paxton, a prominent attorney of Pittsburgh, Pennsylvania
7. Nercissa L. Newkirk, born February 15, 1834; graduated from Urbana Seminary, Ohio, and was married June 20, 1861 to Ben Douglass, the author of the Wayne County, Ohio history referred to earlier. They had children:
    a. J. Mabel Douglas
    b. Anna D. Douglas

Reuben Newkirk
1792-1863

This son of Isaac Newkirk (1754) was born February 29, 1792 in Washington County, Maryland, and died September 14, 1863 in Wayne County, Ohio. Married March 1, 1817 to Margaret Leyda, born October 20, 1793 and died August 19, 1855 in Fairfield County, Ohio. A sketch of Reuben appears in *History of Wayne County, Ohio.* According to that sketch, Reuben and his brother John built a saw-mill soon after arriving in Wayne County about 1814, the first one in the township. He apparently returned to Washington County, Maryland soon after that, where he married Margaret Leyda. They returned to Ohio by wagons, crossing the Killbuck stream near what was known as Sharp's Bridge, with the horses forced to swim the deep stream. The wagons were reportedly drawn across with vines. Reuben had built his home the year before, to which he brought his bride. The report states that: "Physically he was a fine specimen of manhood. He was a man of strictest integrity, rigid morality and unimpeachable private character." While preparing this study early in 1995, I received a packet of information from Greg Edward Leimeister (1965), a descendant of this individual, with numerous papers and group sheets, which forms the basis for much of this report. Reuben had five children, all born in Wayne County, Ohio:

1.   Helen Leyda Newkirk, born February 22, 1818; died October 10, 1842
2.   Rhoda Carroll Newkirk, born June 12, 1821; died January 25, 1831
3.   Ohio State Newkirk, born December 10, 1824; died December 25, 1893 and married January 1, 1850 to Emily Barber.
4.   John Washington Newkirk, born July 4, 1826; died 1907. Married March 1, 1849 to Rebecca Wells, born March, 1830; died 1902, daughter of William Wells of Holmes County, Ohio. Politically active, he served three years as Commissioner of Wayne County. According to Warren W. Roberts of Fridley, Minnesota, they had as many as nine children:
     a.   Marian Ethel Newkirk, born December 19, 1849, and of whom more following

b. Germiah Newkirk, a female, born c.1852 according to the census of 1860 and 1870. Also found as Zeriah; could be the same M. Z. Newkirk who was married to Leslie Norman Aylesworth on March 14, 1871. In *Wayne County Burial Records*, by the Wayne County Historical Society his wife is listed as Margaret Zuie Aylesworth, born 1852 and died in 1923.

c. An unnamed infant death, October 15, 1853

d. Reuben Franklin Newkirk, born January 31, 1854; died 1913. He was married in Holmes County, Ohio, January 18, 1877 to Laura Alice Hostetler, born April 26, 1858; died 1931, daughter of Jonathan Hostetler (1819) and Susan Emaline Alleman Hostetler. Seven children, all born in Wayne County, Ohio:

    (1) Onida Newkirk, born October 27, 1879; died August 2, 1903. Married September 14, 1902 John Thomas.

    (2) John M. Newkirk, born August 21, 1880, of whom more.

    (3) Bessie Newkirk, born February 24, 1883; died September 14, 1883.

    (4) Mable Newkirk, born July 22, 1885; married June 8, 1905 to Reno C. Moore.

    (5) Susie Fay Newkirk, born July 22, 1885

    (6) Lulu Newkirk, born June 17, 1889; died November 8, 1962. Married to Karl Denver Boling.

    (7) Neta Newkirk, born April 23, 1894; died August 16, 1895

e. John Lyman Newkirk, born c.1857; married May 11, 1879 Martha Jordan.

f. An unnamed infant death, October 21, 1861

g. Minnie Newkirk, born c.1864, according to 1870 and 1880 census. Married April 13, 1884 to Henry Clinton Daugherty.

h. Esila Newkirk or Esta or Ella, born c.1868; see 1870 and 1880 census

i. Elsa Ora Newkirk, born October 31, 1873; lived less than a year.

5. Mina Carroll Newkirk, perhaps. This may be a child of this family, but not now proven. She was born August 12, 1834, and married January 2, 1853 to Wilbur Robert Smith. She married second February 22, 1869 to J. G. Parsons.

Marian Ethel Newkirk
1849-1930

This daughter of John Washington Newkirk (1826) was born December 19, 1849 near Big Prairie, Wayne County, Ohio; the first of their nine children. She died May 1, 1930 at Fremont, in Dodge County, Nebraska. Married November 28, 1867 to Jacob Jackson Kelser, born March 13, 1842 on a farm in Holmes County, near Loudonville, Ohio, and died October 24, 1924 at North Bend, Dodge County, Nebraska, son of Lewis Kelser and Magdalena Spreng. Lewis Kelser was born Friedrich Ludwig Goelzer at or near Mimbach, about three miles west of Zweibrucken and about seven miles east of Saarbrucken, in the western part of what was in the early eighteenth century the Bavarian Pfalz or Palatinate. He and his wife immigrated to America, where his name was anglicized to Lewis Kelser.

Jacob was mustered into the Union Army at Nashville, Ohio, on May 30, 1861 as a private, Co. H, 23rd Ohio Regt. Also in the company was his brother, Chris Kelser; and in the same regiment, two individuals who would attain high positions after the Civil War. They were Lt. Col. Rutherford B. Hayes, 19th President of the United States, wounded at the Battle of South Mountain; and Sgt. William McKinley, 25th President of the United States. During November to December of 1861, Jacob was absent on sick leave at Camp Ewing, West Virginia, suffering from chronic diarrhea, typhoid fever, and loss of eyesight. He returned to duty and took part in the battles of South Mountain and Antietam. His mustering out papers of June 30, 1864 indicate that he was a teacher. About 1869 or 1870, he moved to North Bend, Dodge County, Nebraska, to take part in a land drawing for veterans of the Civil War. He won a drawing for good farmland, occupied it long enough to perfect the title, and sold it, moving into North Bend, where he sold milk, cream, butter and eggs. He and Marian Ethel had children:

Marian Ethel Newkirk
1849-1930

Jacob Jackson Kelser
1824-1924

1. Grant Kelser, born October 28, 1868, died October 11, 1869
2. Emma Kelser, born and died October 4, 1870
3. Bessie Kelser, born October 5, 1871; married 1888 William Warren Roberts, a pharmacist, the son of Thomas Roberts and Mary Myrick of Greene County, Iowa. Three children:
   a. Harold Harrison Roberts, who had a son:
      (1) Richard Harold Roberts.
   b. Reno Eli Roberts, who had a daughter:
      (1) Marian Esther Roberts.
   c. Warren Thomas Roberts, who had children:
      (1) Warren Wilcox Roberts, my correspondent for this family.
      (2) Carolyn Roberts, married to Smith, and second to Abbott.
      (3) Thomas Dabney Roberts.
4. John N. Kelser, born December 2, 1872
5. Chancey Kelser, born April 4, 1875, died June 20, 1875
6. Marian Ethel Kelser, born January 16, 1882

John M. Newkirk
1880-1909

This son of Reuben Franklin Newkirk (1854) was born August 21, 1880 in Wayne County, Ohio; died September 5, 1909 at Barberton, Ohio. Married March 24, 1906 to Nellie Grace Taylor, born March 22, 1889 in Wayne County, Ohio; died September 10, 1937 at Akron, Ohio, daughter of James B. Taylor and Elizabeth Mary Lytle Taylor. Two children:
1. Karl Ford Newkirk, born August 23, 1906 at Shreve, Wayne County, Ohio; died July 18, 1968 at Akron, Ohio. Married there September 10, 1930 to Maude Evelyn Matti, born December 7, 1906, daughter of Henry Louis Matti (1881) and Fannie Bird Ladd Matti (1879). Two children, born at Akron, Summit County, Ohio:
   a. Nola Jeanne Newkirk, born August 27, 1932 at Akron. Married there June 22, 1957 to Paul Anthony Leimeister, born April 28, 1932 at Akron, son of Anton Leimeister

and Rozalia Wismek Leimeister. Three children were born there:

(1) Mark Andrew Leimeister, born April 14, 1958. Married June 9, 1984 to Susan Diane McKnight, born October 11, 1958, daughter of Thomas Fred and Joann McKnight. Two children born at Akron:
(a) Kelsey Lynn Leimeister; March 26, 1989
(b) Ryan Thomas Leimeister November 11, 1991

(2) Kurt Alan Leimeister, born July 19, 1961

(3) Greg Edward Leimeister, born March 31, 1965. Greg is the contributor of much of the information found in this chapter.

b. Karl Edward Newkirk, born February 26, 1941 at Akron, Ohio. Married September 29, 1962 at Cleveland to Charlotte Teresa Price, born June 18, 1941, the daughter of Alfred Price and Roxanne McKenzie Price. Three children and divorced. Married second March 25, 1987 at Lime Tree Beach, St. Thomas, Virgin Islands, to Sharon Kay Risner Scheidler; daughter of Johnson Emerson Risner and Clarice Aileen Beck Risner; and had a son and daughter from a first marriage. They had no children. His three children were:

(1) Karl Alfred Newkirk, born April 18, 1963 at Cleveland, Ohio and married January 11, 1990 at Hamilton, Ohio, Karen Louise Lorenz, born April 19, 1965 at Cincinnati, daughter of James Edward and Patricia Jean Perry Lorenz. Three children, born at Hamilton, Butler County, Ohio:
(a) Alexandra Elle Newkirk; August 17, 1990
(b) Ellery Lynn Newkirk; August 13, 1992
(c) Anissa James Newkirk; November 11, 1993

(2) Laura Marie Newkirk, born August 16, 1966 at Pittsburgh, Pennsylvania.

(3) Lisa Christine Newkirk, born June 23, 1969 at Cleveland and married August 15, 1992 Matthew Scott Lauffer.

2. Besse Mabel Newkirk; died October 5, 1933 at Akron, Ohio.

George William Newkirk
1797-1846

This son of Isaac Newkirk (1754) and Rhoda Carroll, was born January 18, 1797 in Washington County, Pennsylvania, and died June 5, 1846. Married Maria Bennett, who was born March 11, 1797 in Washington County, and died there March 28, 1879. She appears as head of household in the 1850 census of the county, apparently a widow, with her name spelled Mariah. Also in the household is one Otto Baumgarner, age 7, born c.1843, not otherwise identified. The children, all born in Washington County, included:

1. Isaac Newton Newkirk, born September 15, 1824 and died November 13, 1894; buried in Beebe, Arkansas. His stone reads that it was erected by his sister, Mary E. Newkirk. He was married in Washington County March 25, 1859 to Emma Allen, who was born September 8, 1833 in Fayette County, Pennsylvania, and died September 25, 1908 in Laclede County, Missouri. They appear to have moved several times. Seven children, three born in Washington County, Pennsylvania and the last four in Sumner County, Tennessee:
   a. Frank E. Newkirk, born November 24, 1861 and died September 28, 1930, single, in Jasper County, Missouri
   b. Clara Estelle Newkirk, born April, 1864, died September 30, 1930, perhaps Oklahoma. Married Martin Hubbard
   c. Edgar A. Newkirk, born July 13, 1866 and died July 30, 1935 at Leavenworth, Kansas. Married February 10, 1910 in Sumner County, Tennessee to Laura West
   d. Cora Louise Newkirk, born February 12, 1869, and died September 5, 1935 in Okmulgee County, Oklahoma. Married 1905 in Missouri to Jehu West
   e. Laura Newkirk, born August, 1871; married April 10, 1910 in Laclede County, Missouri, to William Shawn
   f. William Newkirk, born August 19, 1875; died June 14, 1961 in Laclede County, Missouri. Married April 29, 1918 to Minnie Froelich
   g. Walter Laurie Newkirk, born November 21, 1879, and died September 26, 1959. Married in Laclede County,

Missouri, November 23, 1909 to Katherine Kuhn. She was born April 28, 1886 in Laclede and died August 29, 1964 in Adams County, Illinois. They had nine children, all born in Adams County:

(1)   Mary Emma Newkirk, born December 4, 1910; married June 28, 1940 to William D. Barnes

(2)   Mitchell Joseph Newkirk, born March 12, 1913; married December 31, 1937 Marie Bernice Collard

(3)   William Daniel Newkirk, born June 16, 1916; married in Covenston, Indiana, September 13, 1936 Margaret E. Selsor, born January 15, 1915 in Indian Creek, Missouri; died July 16, 1983 at Denver, Colorado. Three sons and a daughter:

    (a)   John W. Newkirk; Arlington Heights, Illinois

    (b)   James D. Newkirk of Hopkins, Minnesota

    (c)   Robert S. Newkirk of Broomfield, Colorado

    (d)   Daughter, who was married to Mitch Wagers of Englewood, California

(4)   George Francis Newkirk, born August 12, 1918; married January 8, 1943 to Emma Winkelman

(5)   Charles Newkirk, born July 19, 1920; married February 8, 1953 to Polly Affre

(6)   Henriette Louise Newkirk, born June 14, 1922; became a nun and is known as Sister Maria

(7)   Walter Eugene Newkirk, born September 1, 1924, and married March 16, 1957 Merley Miller Moody

(8)   Robert Allen Newkirk, born December 19, 1925; married February 25, 1950 in Germany to Martha

(9)   Richard Albert Newkirk, born December 19, 1925, and married first February 22, 1953 Helen Rilly; second November 29, 1968 to Patricia Noe Carter

2.   Harvey N. Newkirk, born April 23, 1827; died May 10, 1832

3.   Cynthia H. Newkirk, born October 9, 1829. Married March 13, 1847 to Dr. John M. Keys

4.   Mariah Louisa Newkirk, born August 9, 1832, and married November 6, 1856 to Andrew Howden

5.   Rhoda J. Newkirk, born April 27, 1835

6.   Mary E. Newkirk, born 1837

Reuben Newkirk
1769-1855

This son of Abraham Newkirk (1724) and his wife, Kezia Shipman Newkirk, was born c.1769 in Berkeley County, Virginia (later West Virginia), and died April 29, 1855 in Fairfield County, Ohio. He is buried there at Lewis Center. He was married September 24, 1797 in Berkeley County to Mary Kemp. For a period of time, he was a merchant in the town of Sheperdsville, Virginia, but about 1803, joined his brother Tunis (1750), in Fairfield County, Ohio. He and his wife, Mary, are listed alone in the 1850 census of Delaware County, Ohio. Their first two children were born in Virginia; the rest in Ohio:

1. Delilah Newkirk, born August 11, 1798; married Andrew Ramsey, and had eight children in Fairfield County, Ohio.
2. Cyrus Newkirk, born May 27, 1800. In 1819, he was married to Catherine Wildermuth, lived in Ohio and Wisconsin, and reportedly had nine children, born in Fairfield County, Ohio. The family appears in the 1850 census of Lafayette County, Wisconsin, with six of their children. There is also one David Newkirk, listed as a miner, born c.1829 in Ohio, not listed in normal birth order with the other children, and not otherwise identified. Children were:
    a. William Newkirk, born c.1831 in Ohio
    b. Isaac Newkirk, born c.1835 in Ohio
    c. Catherine Newkirk, born c.1837 in Illinois
    d. George W. Newkirk, born c.1839 in Illinois
    e. Elizabeth J. Newkirk, born c.1841 in Illinois
    f. Tunis Newkirk, born c.1843 in Wisconsin
3. Zelu Newkirk, born October 27, 1804, and died April 28, 1861 in Marshall, Illinois. Married first December 26, 1819 to Asa Phelps or Philips; and second April 18, 1841 Horatio Evans, her sister's widower. Four children were born to her first marriage; two from the second.
4. Permelia Newkirk, born December 23, 1805 and died before April 18, 1841. Married August 11, 1822 to Horatio Evans; lived in Fairfield County, Ohio, and had six children.

5. Shipman Newkirk, born June 18, 1807 and died October 11, 1852 in Fairfield County, Ohio. Married January 21, 1830 to Elizabeth Rice, born c.1807. Seven children have been reported to me, although only six appear in the 1850 census of the county:
   a. Rachel Newkirk, born c.1831
   b. Mary Newkirk, born c.1833
   c. Hannah Newkirk, born c.1836
   d. Margaret Newkirk, born c.1839
   e. George W. Newkirk, born c.1843
   f. Reuben Newkirk, born c.1845
6. Missouri Newkirk, born October 17, 1809 and died November 26, 1856. Married October 12, 1826 to William Henry Cooper of Fairfield, Ohio. Two children.
7. Henry Newkirk, born January 14, 1812 and died November 23, 1881 in Richland County, Wisconsin. Married November 18, 1832 to Elizabeth Hempy, who was born c.1812 and died April 2, 1844 in Fairfield County, Ohio. He married second June 1, 1844 Mary Ann Barfeld, born January 20, 1828; died January 31, 1905; and moved to Henry County, Iowa, and moved later to Richland County, Wisconsin, where he died. He had a total of eleven children. This is the same Henry Newkirk who appears in the 1850 census of Fairfield County, Ohio, with a wife Mary, born c.1824, his second wife. There were four children, all born in Ohio. In 1995, I received information from Dan Newkirk of Aliso Viejo, California, a descendant of this family, providing names of the eleven children, first four born to the first marriage, and the last seven to the second:
   a. John Newkirk, born c.1833
   b. America Newkirk, born c.1834
   c. William Newkirk, born c.1837
   d. Mary Ann Newkirk, born c.1842
   e. Henry Clay Newkirk, born c.1845
   f. Catherine G. Newkirk, born c.1846
   g. Martha V. A. Newkirk, or Martha Jane, born c.1848
   h. Edwin Lewis Newkirk, born April 26, 1852, and of whom more
   i. Sharon S. Newkirk, born c.1856

131

j.   Francis Marion Newkirk, born c.1858

k.   George W. Newkirk, born c.1863

8.   Anna Newkirk, born March 13, 1814 and died January 2, 1907 in Richland County, Wisconsin. Married May 15, 1831 to David C. Wildermuth, who died April 6, 1890. Ten children.

9.   John C. Newkirk, born March 14, 1817 and died December 24, 1881 in Delaware County, Ohio. Married October 20, 1836 to Sarah Walters in Fairfield County, Ohio. She was born c.1817 and died c.1905. They appear in the 1850 census for Delaware County, Ohio, not far from his father and mother. Three children listed, born in Ohio; reportedly there was a fourth child:

a.   Missouri Newkirk, born 1837

b.   Cyrus Newkirk, born 1838

c.   Alice A. Newkirk, born 1850

10.   Olivia Newkirk, born October 20, 1820 and died December 17, 1900 in Kosciusko County, Indiana. Married October 31, 1836 Peter Bolenbaugh, born March 6, 1816 and died March 6, 1887. Nine children.

Edwin Lewis Newkirk
1852-

This son of Henry Newkirk (1812) and his second wife, Mary Ann Barfeld (1828), was born April 26, 1852 and married to Julia S. Rosenbaum, born August 18, 1857. They had eleven children:

1.   Loren Grant Newkirk, born 1872; died 1960

2.   Frederick Herbert Newkirk, born August 13, 1874; married 1897 Sinai Pearl Miller, born March 25, 1880 and had three children:

a.   Loren Miller Newkirk, born April 12, 1898; married 1925 to Marjorie Fassett, born June 12, 1897; three children:

(1)   Nell Patricia Newkirk, born July 19, 1927; married Robert H. Schwichtenberg, born 1928, and had two children:

        (a) John Michael Schwichtenberg, born August, 1948

        (b) Susan Schwichtenberg born November, 1949, and married to Randolph Harrison.

    (2) Loren Fassett Newkirk, born September 24, 1930; married Marjorie Lou Bouchie, born December 23, 1933, and had four children:

        (a) Sharon Newkirk, born February 17, 1955, and married to Allen Lohse.

        (b) Loren Newkirk, born April 26, 1956, and married to Christine Marie Smith.

        (c) Betsy Ann Newkirk, born September 19, 1957, and married to Steven Thompson.

        (d) Sandra Kay Newkirk, born January 10, 1969; married Steven Keith Lovfald.

    (3) Carol Dawn Newkirk, born June 20, 1936

b. Irene May Newkirk, born March 9, 1900; married 1916 to Albert Silcox, and had three children:

    (1) Loren Miller Silcox, born August 18, 1918

    (2) Elmer Lee Silcox, born March 8, 1921

    (3) Pearl Olive Silcox, born June 11, 1922

c. Warren Webber Newkirk, born May 18, 1913; married 1940 to Frances Loretta Curl, born January 17, 1914, and had two children:

    (1) Dan Allen Newkirk, born February 10, 1945, my correspondent for this branch of the family. Married 1990 to Barbara Marie Czerniel, born May 5, 1956, and had a son:

        (a) Joseph Tyler Newkirk, born March 11, 1993

    (2) Mary Jane Newkirk, born June 25, 1947; married 1969 to Arthur Patrick Keogh, born October 15, 1945, and had two children:

        (a) Kimberly Anne Keogh; October 31, 1973

        (b) Michael Patrick Keogh; September 15, 1975

3. Myrtle L. Newkirk, born 1876; died 1882

4. Daisy B. Newkirk, born 1878; died 1889

5. Lulu May Newkirk, born 1883; married 1900 Adolph D. Carrol and had four children:

      a.   Walter E. Carroll, born 1901

      b.   Lurene V. Carroll, born 1902

      c.   Violet M. Carroll, born 1905

      d.   Grace D. Carroll, born 1915

6. Walter Edwin Newkirk, born 1885; died 1918

7. Mildred L. Newkirk, born 1888; and married 1907 to Clifford McIntyre and had two children:

      a.   Leona McIntyre.

      b.   Agnes McIntyre.

8. Pearl C. Newkirk, born 1890; married Paul Funk, and had a daughter:

      a.   Mildred Funk, born 1912

9. Leo G. Newkirk, born 1892; married Cora Hayford.

10. Vernon L. Newkirk, born 1895; married Eleanor Swanson and had four children:

      a.   Marion Newkirk

      b.   Lucille Newkirk

      c.   Evelyn Newkirk

      d.   Shirley Newkirk

11. Gracie Darling Newkirk, born 1897

CHAPTER 5

Abraham Newkirk, Jr.
1764-1840

This son of Abraham Newkirk (1724) and Kezia Shipman, was born March 10, 1764 in Berkeley County, Virginia, and died October 5, 1840 in Adams County, Ohio. He is buried in the Hull Church cemetery, on land which he donated to the church. Married first about 1785 to Margaret Knox, who died July 8, 1823, after which he was married second to Marcia Stewart. He first moved to Washington County, Pennsylvania with his father and other family members. There, in 1781, there was surveyed for him, as assignee of Henry Newkirk (1740), his cousin, a farm known as *The Legacy*, containing a little over 413 acres. On December 16, 1797, there is a deed in the records of Washington County, Pennsylvania, in which Abraham and his wife Margaret convey the property to Henry Newkirk, for the sum of One Dollar. It had been believed that the couple gave the land to their son, but at the time of the conveyance, he would have been only about eight years old. Perhaps he reconveyed the property to his cousin, it appearing that he had obtained it by assignment, perhaps under a bond or indebtedness. On March 28, 1816, Abraham sold the last of his holdings and moved to Adams County, Ohio, where, on April 15, 1817, he purchased a farm of 110 acres on Brush Creek, a few miles west of Dunkinsville, where he lived until his death. The town of Dunkinsville has been reported to me from several sources, but it does not appear on my maps of Ohio, nor in the Postal Service Zip Code Directory. Presumably, it existed at one time in Adams County, Ohio. Abraham's children, all born in Washington County, Pennsylvania, on *The Legacy* farm to his first marriage, were:

1. Hannah Newkirk, born May 6, 1787; died September 18, 1864 and buried at Hull Church cemetery. Married John Hull as his second wife. He was born November 17, 1782; died November 17, 1865. The first six children were born in Washington County, Pennsylvania; last two at Dunkinsville:

a. Newkirk Hull, born November 24, 1806; died September 21, 1884. Married Miriam Freeland. No children.
b. Abraham Hull, born August 3, 1809; died December 3, 1868. Married May 15, 1830 to Eliza Gilpin. Nine children.
c. Cyrus Hull, born October 6, 1811; died November, 1894 in Grant County, Indiana. Married to Anna Jones; five children
d. Josiah Hull, born August 6, 1813; died October 6, 1875 in Adams County, Ohio. Married in 1835 to Charlotte Jones, born September 19, 1816; died February 17, 1874. Five children.
e. Lorinda Hull, born November 12, 1815; married December 9, 1834 to John Kees. Lived in Adams County, Ohio, and in Brown County, Illinois. Five children.
f. Margaret Hull, born January 10, 1817; died August 11, 1863. Married Andrew Mahaffy.
g. Orpha Hull, born November 26, 1819; died June 15, 1888 in Brown County, Illinois. Married August 17, 1840 Arthur Smith, born January 3, 1817 in Brown County, and died November 15, 1885. Seven children.
h. George Washington Hull, born January 3, 1823; died April 13, 1893 in Ashland, Kentucky. Married to Frances Dale Russell, born June 14, 1817 in Stouts, Ohio, and died August 4, 1886. One daughter.
2. Henry Newkirk, born December 25, 1789; died October 21, 1821 in Brown County, Ohio. He owned the land and laid out the town of Georgetown, county seat of Brown County. He was married February 20, 1816 in Pennsylvania to Hannah Bentley, born November 27, 1792 and died May 5, 1856 in Brown County, Ohio. He had three children:
a. Lorinda Newkirk, born June 7, 1817; married July 19, 1837 Dr. James Sidwell, born September 6, 1814; died October 7, 1866. Only one of their seven children lived to maturity.
b. Adamson Bentley Newkirk, born March 12, 1819; died December 18, 1883 at Falls City, Nebraska. A medical doctor, with an outstanding record of private and public

service, he was married September 4, 1844 to Lucy Mary Taliaferro Barker, born August 18, 1826 in Bracken County, Kentucky. Eight children, the fifth of whom was:

    (1)   Adamson Bentley Newkirk, Jr., born March 12, 1858 in Chicago and being the Dr. A. B. Newkirk whose writings have been referred to in this work.

  c. Cyrus Newkirk, born March 12, 1821 in Brown County, Ohio, and married December 3, 1849 Rebecca Isaminger, born June 29, 1828 at Franklin Furnace, Ohio. Five children, one of whom is shown with the parents in the 1850 census for Gallia County, Ohio:

    (1)   Antoinette Newkirk, born 1849

3.   Reuben Newkirk, perhaps, born c.1791. Moved to Wayne County, Ohio. He is probably the same Reuben found in the 1850 census of Wayne County, Ohio, at the age of 59, with a wife, Mary, born c.1793, both born in Pennsylvania. There are no children listed.

4.   Anna Newkirk, born June 1, 1792; died August 29, 1839 in Cass County, Indiana. Married John B. Clary. Five children, the first born in Darke County, Ohio, the rest in Rush County, Indiana:

  a. Isaac N. Clary, born January 28, 1819, and married December 7, 1843 Rebecca Remley. Lived in Cass County, Indiana, where he died October 5, 1899. Five children.

  b. Margaret Clary, born August 17, 1820; married William Michael. Lived at Logansport, Indiana; two children.

  c. John C. Clary, born September 18, 1826; married first October 8, 1847 to Susannah Foy, who died February 24, 1863. Married second July 14, 1863 to Narcissa W. Dunham, who died March 17, 1898. Married third Susannah Ballenger and lived at Logansport, Indiana. Nine children.

  d. Rachel A. Clary, born January 18, 1826, and married September, 1846 to Thornley Michael. Lived in Cass County where she died March 6, 1905. Five children.

e. William D. Clary, born May 12, 1828, and married December 2, 1852 Elizabeth J. Worl. Lived in Lucerne, Indiana, and had nine children.

5. Orpha Newkirk, born July 15, 1794; died October, 1851 in Memphis, Scotland County, Missouri. Married John Dunkin and had six children, born in Adams County, Ohio:

   a. Harkless Dunkin, born May 9, 1816; married Lydia Matthews and had five children.

   b. Henry Dunkin, born January 8, 1818; died May 6, 1882 in Lee County, Iowa. Married Virginia Sproule; eight children.

   c. Margaret Dunkin, born August 1, 1820; married William Wittenmeyer; buried with her three children Jacksonburg, Ohio.

   d. John Dunkin, born April 30, 1825; died February 15, 1884 at Browing, Missouri. Married first on September 7, 1847 Esther Jones; second October 30, 1858 to Elizabeth Hilt. Ten children.

   e. Sarah J. Dunkin, born August 20, 1832; died July 2, 1911 at Pueblo, California. Married first March 5, 1851 Dr. George William Mason, born July 16, 1824; died April 10, 1865 at Tipton, Missouri. Married second September 15, 1868 Reverend E. J. Keplinger, who died November 17, 1898. Two children survived infancy.

   f. Joshua Dunkin, born October 5, 1835 and died at Powersville, Missouri. Married November 16, 1853 his first cousin, Anna Fear, born December 21, 1833. Eight children, three of whom died young.

6. Nancy Newkirk, born October 3, 1796; died October 24, 1850 in Adams County, Ohio. Married June 10, 1819 Dr. Peter Fear, who was born September 29, 1795 and died June 7, 1855. They had nine children:

   a. Maria Fear, born February 22, 1820; married September 23, 1837 to Charles Thurman, born February 22, 1812; died in 1890. Lived in Adams County, Ohio; nine children.

   b. Margaret Fear, born August 2, 1822; died March 4, 1882 at Bahalia, Ohio. Married George Phillips, born February

138

16, 1818; died March 15, 1874 at West Union, Ohio. They had seven children.

- c. Francis Fear, born December 11, 1824; died April 28, 1902 at Waverly, Kansas. Married first January 29, 1851 Mary Ellen Sparks at Winchester, Ohio; and second October 31, 1865 Martha Rawlings. Seven children from first marriage; two from the second.
- d. Orpha Fear, born February 11, 1827, and married to Samuel Mahaffey; moved to a northwestern state.
- e. Cyrus Fear, born September 26, 1829; died young.
- f. John F. Fear, born October 7, 1831; died young.
- g. Anna Fear, born December 21, 1833; married her first cousin, Joshua Dunkin, born October 5, 1835. Eight children.
- h. Matilda Fear, born January 6, 1836; married May 27, 1857 to Samuel H. Beard. Lived at West Union, Ohio, and had six children.
- i. William Fear, born March 18, 1838; died young.

7. John Newkirk, born March 17, 1799; died March 31, 1867 in Tipton County, Indiana. Married Sarah Walmsley, born December 16, 1804 and died May 20, 1875. The family appears in the 1850 census of Rush County, Indiana, with a number of children. Nine children, born in Rush County, Indiana:

- a. Elizabeth Newkirk, born May 30, 1825; died March 30, 1895. Married first October 31, 1839 Wesley P. David; married second August 24, 1874 James Morris. Ten children, all born to the first marriage.
- b. Emily A. Newkirk, born October 1, 1827; died June 3, 1870 in Tipton County, Indiana. Married December 21, 1844 to John P. Simmonds. Six children.
- c. Leah Newkirk, born May 6, 1831; died August 8, 1905 in Tipton County. Married Thomas Cochran, and had eight children.
- d. James Ross Newkirk, born March 5, 1832; married March 19, 1856 to Melissa A. Hasket. Ten children.
- e. Margaret A. Newkirk, born June 3, 1837, and married February 17, 1859 John Wesley Tichenor. Five children.

f. Christopher C. Newkirk, born September 24, 1838; died February 10, 1904. Married first November 2, 1865 to Sarah Walmsley; married second 1872 to Susan C. Eiler. Two children to first marriage; one to the second.

g. John W. Newkirk, born April 5, 1840; killed in the Civil War 1862

h. Jonathan H. Newkirk, born March 2, 1843; married October 6, 1867 Nancy A. Moody; three children.

i. Holliday S. Newkirk, born January 25, 1847; married July 3, 1869 Frances Houchins. Lived Mapleton, Iowa; four children

8. Keziah Newkirk, born August 8, 1801; died February, 1884 in Adams County, Ohio (probably). Married Amos Dunkin, and had seven children:

a. Abraham Dunkin, born September 26, 1824; died April 23, 1898 at Bentonville, Ohio. Married February 3, 1853 Martha Ann Downing. Eight children.

b. Hercules Dunkin, born April 11, 1826; married Damaris Sample and had five children at Bentonville, Ohio.

c. Sarah Dunkin, born March 11, 1828; married first March, 1849 Benjamin F. Howell; second December 28, 1858 John Lawill. Lived at Cherry Fork, Ohio; two children from her first marriage.

d. Emma Dunkin, born April 11, 1830 and died August 6, 1855. Married Myers. No children.

e. Jane Dunkin, born February 7, 1832; died March 30, 1901 at West Union, Ohio. Married December 31, 1854 George H. Darling, born May 7, 1833 at West Liberty, West Virginia; died January 10, 1895. Five children.

f. Margaret Dunkin, born April 24, 1834; married first 1859 to Marcus Hawk, who died October 29, 1884. She married second George Roush. Lived in Brown County, Ohio, and had four children, surnamed Hawk.

g. Reason Dunkin, born July 31, 1836; married in 1857 to Frances Lawill. No children.

9. Teunis Shipman Newkirk, born April 25, 1805, of whom more

10. William Newkirk, born August 1, 1806; died April 19, 1887 at Bellfast, Highland County, Ohio. Married Rebecca Storer.

The 1850 census of the county includes the family, with his wife born c.1807 in Pennsylvania. Also in the household is Mary or Macy (probably Marcia) Newkirk, at age 84, born c.1766 in Maryland, who is probably his mother. The children, born in Ohio, were:

a. Abraham Newkirk, born November 7, 1827 at Bellfast, Ohio. Married first November 10, 1853 Martha Ann Lovett, and second February 14, 1867 Eliza Ann Grimes. Five children from first marriage; three from second.

b. Macy S. Newkirk, born April 3, 1833; married September 30, 1847 John Williamson. In the census, her name appears as Nancy. Lived at Ripley, Oklahoma, and had eleven children.

11. Cyrus Newkirk, born May 16, 1810; died October 2, 1855 in Grant County, Indiana. Married, perhaps in Adams County, Ohio, to Cassa Ann Phillips, who was born November 6, 1814 in Virginia. Many of their descendants lived in Howard and Grand Counties, Indiana. Nine children:

a. Abraham Newkirk, born August 17, 1834; died July 11, 1871 in Grant County, Indiana, where his two children were born. Married December 27, 1867 Rebecca J. Gray, born May 12, 1849 in Randolph County, Indiana.

b. William Newkirk, born May 1, 1836; died June 10, 1907 in Grant County, Indiana. Married first November 6, 1861 Sarah S. Nesbit, who died September 17, 1900. Married second Anna Nesbit. Three children lived past infancy.

c. Margaret Jane Newkirk, born February 1, 1840 in Adams County, Ohio; married June 9, 1861 Hercules S. Kilgore. Lived at Swayze, in Grant County, Indiana. Six children.

d. George Newkirk, born November 5, 1842; married first January 9, 1867 Martha Ann Floyd, who died March 30, 1874 at the age of twenty-seven. Married second July 18, 1875 to Virginia Frances Fellows Kingery. Only one of his five children survived. In August, 1862, George enlisted in Company H, 101st Indiana Volunteers of the Union army and served until June 21, 1865. He lived in

Howard County, Indiana; was twice elected County Commissioner by large Republican majorities.

e. Mary A. Newkirk, born November 27, 1844; died July 28, 1908. Married April 16, 1864 to Hamilton Bishop, born July 4, 1839; died September 23, 1909. Lived in Howard County and had seven children.

f. Sarah K. Newkirk, born September 10, 1846 died young.

g. John Francis Newkirk, born March 2, 1850; married March 29, 1877 to Margaret Jane Warwick. They lived at Swazey, Indiana and had three children. According to *Newkirk Notes*, he was father of at least one son:

   (1) John William Newkirk (Herk), the father of:

      (a) Larry W. Newkirk; in 1983 living in Santa Rosa, California

h. Emma Elizabeth Ellen Newkirk, born August 8, 1852; married October 5, 1870 to John Wesley Bishop. Six children.

i. Louisa Adaline Newkirk, born October 7, 1854; married January 14, 1875 Milton Stout. Four children.

12. Emily Newkirk, born June 10, 1813. Married Charles Osman; two daughters, who died young. Married second Abraham Hawk.

Teunis Shipman Newkirk
1805-1874

This son of Abraham Newkirk, Jr. (1764) was born April 25, 1805 in Washington County, Pennsylvania. He moved to Adams County, Ohio with his parents in 1816, where he was married to Mary Bayless, who was born June 15, 1808 and died March 5, 1873; daughter of Daniel Bayless. Some entries in the Morman IGI index lists the wife's name as Mary J. Walker, married c.1829, which appears to be an error. About 1827, the family moved to Rush County, Indiana, where they lived until the death of Teunis Shipman on August 31, 1874, and where they were found in the 1850 census, listed under the name of Shipman Newkirk. He owned a large, productive farm about eight miles north of Rushville.

Teunis Shipman Newkirk
1805-1874

Teunis Shipman Newkirk and his wife were parents of eight children, the first being born in Adams County, Ohio, and the rest in Rush County, Indiana:
1. Daniel Bayless Newkirk, born January 1, 1825, of whom more
2. Mary J. Newkirk, born June 12, 1829, of whom more

3. Sarah Jane Newkirk, born December 11, 1830, of whom more
4. Eliza J. Newkirk, born c.1834; died in infancy
5. William Riley Newkirk, born January 1, 1837, of whom more
6. Malinda J. Newkirk, born August 14, 1840, of whom more
7. Margaret A. Newkirk, born July 21, 1845; died December, 1913. Married February 1, 1866 to George W. Hendrix, born May 15, 1837 in North Carolina. They had children, born in Rush County:
   a. Mary Etta Hendrix, born October 26, 1866
   b. William A. Hendrix, born May 20, 1871. Married June 29, 1902 to Ernest Crawford and lived at Connersville, Indiana. Two children, born in Rush County:
      (1) Robert E. Hendrix, born December 31, 1904
      (2) Kendall E. Hendrix, born December 26, 1908
   c. Dora A. Hendrix, born January 5, 1878
   d. Charles L. Hendrix, born December 20, 1879
   e. Laura A. Hendrix, born March 31, 1882
8. George Marshall Newkirk, born August 11, 1849; died July 22, 1899. Married first Malinda J. Cross and second on April 27, 1881 to Mary M. Fry. He had children, born in Rush County:
   a. Carey F. Newkirk, born May 18, 1868, and died October 26, 1870
   b. Albert H. Newkirk, born May 29, 1871, and married February 22, 1897 to Minnie K. Mattingley. Lived at Connersville, Rush County, Indiana. Four children, born there:
      (1) Ruby A. Newkirk, an infant death, December 12, 1897
      (2) George M. Newkirk, born February 27, 1900
      (3) Flossie M. Newkirk, born February 12, 1904
      (4) Frank A. Newkirk, born May 24, 1914
   c. Charles Gilbert Newkirk, born August 25, 1882, and married April 24, 1912 to Edith Elmetta Long. One son, born in Rush County, Indiana:
      (1) Kenneth Charles Newkirk, born January 4, 1913
   d. Glenn E. Newkirk, born March 25, 1887

e.   Noley G. Newkirk, born September 25, 1888. Married
     December 25, 1909 to Anna Marie Locke
f.   Murle M. Newkirk, born November 20, 1896

Daniel Bayless Newkirk
1825-1903
Polly Hamilton Newkirk
1829-1911

Daniel Bayless Newkirk
1825-1903

This son of Teunis Shipman Newkirk (1805) was born
January 1, 1825 in Adams County, Ohio, and died December 3,
1903. Married August 3, 1845 in Rush County, Indiana to Polly
(or Mary) Hamilton, born January 1, 1829, and died April 27,
1911; buried at East Hill cemetery in Rushville, Indiana. They
moved to what was known as the Indian Reserve on the north line
of Madison County, Indiana, near what is now known as Independ-

ence. He was of medium height, but weighed about two hundred pounds, and was a leading citizen of his community, being named Justice of the Peace on November 1, 1855, and for a time, operating a mercantile business in the small town that grew up on part of his land. On July 18, 1854, he was commissioned Captain, Company M, 2nd Regiment, 11th Military District of Indiana. In the fall of 1869, he moved back to Rush County, and in a short time, became the largest land-owner in the county. They appear in the census of 1850 for Madison County, Indiana, with children, all born there:

1. Eliza J. Newkirk, born October 1, 1846; died the next day
2. Sarah Jane Newkirk, born May 28, 1848. Married first to William Shields, son of Thomas Shields. He was born November 10, 1845 and died January 16, 1869. Married secondly to Richard Benson, and third to Daniel O'Keefe. There was one child born in Madison County, Indiana to the first marriage; two to the second in Rush County; and none to the third:
    a. Daniel T. Shields, born September 6, 1867, and married February 11, 1891 to Maude Mason. Lived in Chicago
    b. Herbert E. Benson, born March 13, 1874; married September 15, 1902 to Minnie E. Wilson, daughter of William E. Wilson; lived in Indianapolis. They had six children; the first born in Rush County, the second and third born in Fayette County; and the last three in Marion County, Indiana:
        (1) Pearl M. Benson, born October 29, 1904
        (2) Loter D. Benson, born March 13, 1906
        (3) Gertrude L. Benson, born August 27, 1908
        (4) Florence L. Benson, born August 16, 1910
        (5) Eugene W. Benson, born November 8, 1911
        (6) Harley Allen Benson, born September 9, 1913
    c. Albert L. Benson, born March 31, 1877; married October 26, 1898 to Ethel May Clifton. Lived at Mays, Rush County, Indiana, where the children were born:
        (1) Lenna P. Benson, born September 28, 1904
        (2) Albert B. Benson, born December 15, 1907

3. James L. J. Newkirk, born August 20, 1852; married September 10, 1873 to Rebecca Behymer, a daughter of William Behymer. Children, all born in Rush County, Indiana:

a. Robert L. Newkirk, born July 22, 1874. Married August 30, 1905 to Priscilla Bitner, and lived at Sexton, in Rush County. One child, born there:
    (1) Rolla Elbert Newkirk, born June 20, 1910

b. Daniel B. Newkirk, born March 10, 1876. Married November 5, 1890 to Vista M. Carson and lived at Falmouth, in Rush County. Four children, born there:
    (1) Laverne Newkirk, born April 29, 1901
    (2) William J. Newkirk, born December 18, 1904
    (3) Daniel B. Newkirk, Jr., born January 1, 1906
    (4) Helen M. Newkirk, born November 7, 1908; died April 29, 1913

c. Fanny L. Newkirk, born November 14, 1879. Married Ozro Kirkham, who was born April 8, 1879, and lived at Sexton, Indiana

d. Emma Pearl Newkirk, born April 9, 1881. Married October 21, 1900 to Fred Neuman, who was born September 26, 1876, and lived at Beesons, Indiana. Children:
    (1) Robert M. Neuman, born March 20, 1902; infant death
    (2) John J. Neuman, born April 17, 1911

e. Lillie M. Newkirk, born February 13, 1883. Married December 20, 1901 to Virgil T. Longfellow, who was born October 15, 1876. Lived at Sexton.

f. Mira J. Newkirk, born September 16, 1890. Married in 1914 to Court F. Oldham and lived at Sexton, Indiana

g. James Garland Newkirk, born March 20, 1892. Lived at Sexton, Indiana. Married September 25, 1915 to Alta Stevens.

Thomas Jefferson Newkirk
1854-1919

4. Thomas Jefferson Newkirk, born October 30, 1854, and lived the latter part of his life at Evanston, Illinois; died December 27, 1919 at Daytona, Florida. Married twice; first on November 8, 1877 to Kate Fayhe, a daughter of Michael Fayhe. She was born October 18, 1857 and died November 9, 1878. Married second November 27, 1879 to Emma A. Warren, daughter of Zina Warren. She was born July 18, 1859 at Carmel, Indiana. There was one child born to the first

marriage and four to the second, all in Rush County, Indiana. Thomas J. was a lawyer, and the author of *Genealogy and History of the Newkirk, Hamilton and Bayless Families*, apparently a private printing, but found in some major libraries. His biography appears in *History of Rush County, Indiana*, Brant and Fuller, Chicago, 1888. That publication reports his birth date as October 31, 1855, contrary to other reports. He was a prominent young member of the Rushville Bar; and a surveyor for Rush County until the spring of 1887. In 1883, he formed a law partnership with Claude Cambern. He was an unsuccessful candidate for State Senator in 1880, and a Democratic alternate to the Chicago Convention of 1884. His children were:

a.   Jesse Newkirk; November 1, 1878 to February 9, 1879
b.   Claude Newkirk, born October 11, 1880; died September 28, 1891
c.   Warren T. Newkirk, born January 22, 1883. Married December 29, 1903 to Anna M. Stephens; lived in Chicago, Illinois
d.   Josephine Newkirk, born August 24, 1890. Married June 10, 1912 to Napoleon B. McKay, DDS, and lived at Forest City, Iowa. A daughter:
   (1)   Alice Newkirk McKay, born November 29, 1915 at Evanston, Illinois
e.   Carlisle R. Newkirk, born September 17, 1892. Married January 27, 1912 to Eloise Patterson; and they lived at Hartshorne, Oklahoma. One child:
   (1)   Catherine Alice Newkirk, born November 17, 1912 in Evanston, Illinois
5.   Rebecca L. Newkirk, born April 4, 1860. Married January 9, 1884 to Joseph Vandament; children, born in Rush County, Indiana:
a.   Mary Della Vandament, born September 2, 1885, and married November 28, 1906 to Jesse B. Gilson. One son:
   (1)   William J. Gilson, born April 29, 1910 in Rush
b.   Walter T. Vandament, born April 17, 1887, a doctor. Married July 16, 1910 to Gretta Pearl Kirkpatrick. A daughter, born in Rush County, Indiana:

(1)   Laura Geneva Vandament, born June 12, 1911
- c.   Millie E. Vandament, born January 30, 1892
- d.   Mina Pearl Vandament, born April 12, 1894; lived five months
6.   Millie Newkirk, born June 27, 1868. Married November 30, 1893 to Rollie E. Zorne. No children.

Mary J. Newkirk
1829-1912

This daughter of Teunis Shipman Newkirk (1805), was born June 12, 1829 in Rush County, Indiana, and died November 16, 1912. Married February 14, 1850 to Joseph Kiser, a farmer. They lived at Sexton, and had children, born in Rush County, including:

1.   William F. Kiser, born November 19, 1854, a twin; died March 28, 1898. Married to Sarah O. Berry, daughter of James Berry. She died October 21, 1903. Children, born in Rush County:
- a.   Omar M. Kiser; September 8, 1880 to July 24, 1894
- b.   Elsie D. Kiser, born November 13, 1883; infant death
- c.   Derby Ross Kiser, born January 20, 1892
2.   James F. Kiser, born November 19, 1854, a twin; infant death
3.   Rebecca Jane Kiser, died in infancy
4.   George Milton Kiser, died in infancy
5.   Jefferson Kiser, died in infancy
6.   Sarah Emeline Kiser, born June 1, 1865, and died November 16, 1900. Married Lawrence G. Porter, who died March 22, 1902. Children, all born in Rush County, Indiana:
- a.   Elmer Porter, born May 22, 1886; married February 15, 1908 to Maude Bowne and lived at Rushville
- b.   Orval Porter, born May 25, 1889
- c.   Kellis Porter, born November 23, 1894
7.   Elsworth W. Kiser, born October 19, 1869, a twin. Married August 25, 1889 Emma Ova Berry, daughter of James Berry, and had children, born in Rush County:
- a.   Chester R. Kiser: December 10, 1890 to January 1, 1891
- b.   Sophia H. Kiser, born May 26, 1896
- c.   Roxy V. Kiser, born December 19, 1897

d.   William F. Kiser, born February 26, 1902
8.   Elmer Kiser, born October 19, 1869, a twin; lived at Dunrieth, Indiana. Married February 18, 1891 to Joalta Lindamood and had children, born in Henry County, Indiana:
a.   Minnie Kiser, born September 27, 1893
b.   Flossie Kiser, born January 23, 1894

Sarah Jane Newkirk
1830-1848

This daughter of Teunis Shipman Newkirk (1805) was born December 11, 1830, and died about 1848. Married July 3, 1845 to Aaron Walker and had two children, born in Rush County, Indiana:
1.   Mary C. Walker, born April 2, 1846 and died October 20, 1889. Married April 7, 1862 to Samuel J. Bell, son of John Bell. He was born October 11, 1839 and died February 7, 1905. Eight children, born in Rush County, Indiana:
a.   Safrona P. Bell, born November 27, 1863; infant death
b.   Julius E. Bell, born February 8, 1867; married December 25, 1895 to Eva Newhouse. They lived at Kennedy, Alabama
c.   Corena J. Bell, born April 6, 1870; infant death
d.   Ida J. Bell, born December 27, 1872; married January 17, 1889 to Orno H. McBride. He died February 19, 1913, and they lived at Indianapolis. Three children, born in Rush County, Indiana:
(1)   Ethel J. McBride, born May 18, 1890; married December 24, 1912 to Raymond A. Reinhard.
(2)   Verna B. McBride, born May 19, 1892; married June 4, 1911 Robert G. Ward.
(3)   William C. McBride, born July 11, 1894
e.   Margaret Bell, born May 11, 1879; married December 15, 1897 to Lennie Winkler. Four children, born in Rush County, Indiana:
(1)   Herald L. Winkler, born February 24, 1899
(2)   Carl E. Winkler, born March 14, 1901
(3)   Mamie B. Winkler, born July 22, 1903

151

  (4) Herman L. Winkler, born December 24, 1908
 f. Walter Bell, born October 12, 1882
 g. Josie M. Bell, born December 6, 1884; married November 5, 1902 to Alva Eakins. Lived at Mays, Indiana
 h. LeRoy Bell, born August 21, 1886; infant death
2. Lucy Ann Walker; February 2, 1847 to March 11, 1848

William Riley Newkirk
1837-1911

  This son of Teunis Shipman Newkirk (1805) was born January 1, 1837 and died July 11, 1911. Married August 20, 1855 to Polly Ann Cross and, after her death, married second October 21, 1875 to Rebecca Dougherty. He had children, born in Rush County, Indiana:

1. Melvina J. Newkirk, born February 10, 1860, and married twice. Married first September 10, 1873 Elbert O. Newhouse, and lived at Connersville, Indiana. He was born July 5, 1855 and, after his death, she was married second August 23, 1908 to Asbury J. Harrison. Three children to the first marriage; none to the second, all born in Rush County, Indiana:
 a. Daisy M. Newhouse, born March 27, 1878. Married December 29, 1894 to John P. Carpenter and lived at Elwood, Indiana. Two children:
  (1) Ruby L. Carpenter, born August 9, 1896; an infant death
  (2) Lillian A. Carpenter, born November 27, 1897
 b. Iva A. Newhouse, born September 25, 1879
 c. Anna B. Newhouse, born October 28, 1884
2. Clara Newkirk, born May 10, 1870. Married October 20, 1887 to Omar Gartin. Two children, born in Rush County:
 a. William R. Gartin, born June 29, 1889
 b. Lowell C. Gartin, born May 17, 1891
3. Flossie Newkirk, born September 22, 1887. Married December 22, 1908 to William Winship. A daughter, born in Rush County, Indiana:
 a. Margaret R. Winship, born April 29, 1910

Malinda J. Newkirk
1840-

This daughter of Teunis Shipman Newkirk (1805) was born August 14, 1840. She was married November 14, 1861 to Joseph M. Bell, and had children, born in Rush County, Indiana:

1. Harvina J. Bell, born December 14, 1862; married February 13, 1884 John H. Gray. Two children, born in Rush County:
    a. Lena B. Gray, born July 21, 1886. Married September 11, 1907 Edwin C. Meyer. Children, born Rush County:
        (1) Robert E. Meyer, born October 9, 1909
        (2) William C. Meyer, born December 20, 1913
    b. Mary J. Gray, born May 12, 1893. Married September 14, 1911 to Lewis R. Bishop
2. Cora A. Bell, born March 26, 1865. Married October 14, 1885 to William H. McMillin. Three children, born in Rush County:
    a. Edith Belle McMillin, born July 12, 1886, and died April 12, 1915. Married Walter E. Smith.
    b. Nellie Josephine McMillin, born December 21, 1887. Married October 16, 1907 Frank L. Logan, and had two children, born in Rush County:
        (1) Russell W. Logan, born October 7, 1911
        (2) Frank W. Logan, born March 4, 1915
    c. Rubie Mae McMillin, born September 28, 1889. Married November 1, 1911 to Ross Logan. A son, born in Rush County, Indiana:
        (1) William John Logan, born August 14, 1913
3. William M. Bell, born November 12, 1868. Married April 8, 1894 to Nellie M. Clifton. Three children, Rush County:
    a. Edward C. Bell, born April 2, 1895
    b. Vern W. Bell, born April 10, 1897
    c. Maude E. Bell, born November 18, 1902
4. Almeta A. Bell, born August 11, 1870. Married February 8, 1887 to George J. Austin. Three children, Rush County:
    a. Jeannette Austin, born June 20, 1888. Married December 25, 1907 Roy Alexander. Children, born in Rush County:
        (1) Mariam Alexander, born September 16, 1908

        (2)   Russell Alexander, born August 18, 1910; died young

        (3)   Roland Alexander, born August 14, 1911 and died August 3, 1912

        (4)   Roland Alexander, born December 14, 1914

    b.   Gilbert Austin, born April 20, 1890. Married April 3, 1915 to Gladys Walker

    c.   Beatrice Austin, born February 17, 1893

5.   Edward E. Bell, born September 4, 1878. Married October 18, 1899 Pearl A. McCarty. A child, born Rush County, Indiana:

    a.   Cassett M. Bell, born August 24, 1902

6.   Lowell W. Bell, born December 27, 1883. Married December 31, 1903 to Nellie McMannis. Three children:

    a.   Gladys A. Bell, born November 23, 1904, Rush County

    b.   Otho Gano Bell, born September 28, 1907 Martinsville, Indiana

    c.   Mary M. Bell, born August 3, 1915 at Indianapolis

CHAPTER 6

Henry Newkirk
1768-1853

This son of Abraham Newkirk (1724) and his wife, Kezia Shipman Newkirk, was born February 2, 1768 in Berkeley County, Virginia (later West Virginia), and moved about 1770 to Washington County, Pennsylvania with his parents. He died December 13, 1853 in Beaver County, Pennsylvania. Married March 1, 1791 to Rebecca Davis in Maryland. She was born in Maryland March 25, 1771 and died in Beaver County about 1830. Henry moved about 1812 to Beaver County, Pennsylvania. His children, all born in Washington County, Pennsylvania, included:

1. Catherine Newkirk, born February 17, 1792; married to James Swasic
2. John Forest Newkirk, born July 22, 1794, and died May 5, 1857 in Beaver County. Married Elizabeth McBride, who was born March 6, 1794 and died April 26, 1868. They are probably the couple appearing in the census of 1850 for Mercer County, Pennsylvania. He is listed simply as John F., an inn-keeper. Both are shown there as born c.1796, with six children, the whole family born in Pennsylvania:
   a. Christiana Newkirk, born c.1824
   b. Matilda Newkirk, born c.1826
   c. John Newkirk, born c.1828; a carpenter
   d. Eliza Newkirk, born c.1833
   e. Henry Newkirk, born c.1836
   f. Minerva Newkirk, born c.1840
3. Rhoda Newkirk, born October 26, 1796. Married to James Ludlow
4. Bathsheba Newkirk, born September 6, 1799 and died June 2, 1845. Married Matthew Dillon, born January 19, 1795 and died May 31, 1854
5. Keziah Newkirk, born April 3, 1802 and died February 17, 1872. According to one report, she was married December 6, 1825 to Matthew Welsh, born January 5, 1794 and died

December 29, 1864. However, according to information received from Laurel Shanafelt Powell in 1985, then living at Pebble Beach, California, and according to IGI records of the Mormon church, Keziah's husband was Andrew John Welsh, not Matthew. Laurel has a copy of his will, and pictures of the couple with their son. Laurel Powell suggests that Andrew Welsh had a prior marriage and that the first child listed following is from that first marriage. She is descended from Seth McClure Welsh; therefore, if she is correct, she is not a lineal Newkirk descendant. Children, born in Beaver County, Pennsylvania:

a.   Seth McClure Welsh, born May 22, 1819
b.   James P. Welsh, born before 1839
c.   John Wesley Welsh, born before 1839
d.   Ira E. Welsh, born before 1839
e.   Andrew J. Welsh, born before 1839

6.   Shipman Newkirk, born October 17, 1804; of whom more
7.   Phebe Newkirk, born April 29, 1808 and died March 8, 1891. Married April 26, 1827 to Robert Douthitt, born September 19, 1802 in Beaver County, Pennsylvania; died there February 11, 1891
8.   Louisarba Newkirk, born February 11, 1810 and died 1835. Married Alexander Heights
9.   Louisiana Newkirk, born October 11, 1812 and died March 12, 1900. Married May 19, 1830 to William Hunt, who was born June 21, 1801 and died August 5, 1851

Shipman Newkirk
1804-1889

This son of Henry Newkirk (1768) was born October 17, 1804 in Ohio, and died March 10, 1889 in Poweshiek County, Iowa. He was married about 1824 to Jane Thompson, who was born December 16, 1804 and died September 3, 1869. Her parents were James Thompson and Sarah Gilliland Thompson. Their family appears in the 1850 census of Washington County, Pennsylvania, with several of their children. Also in the household at the time are Henry Newkirk, at the age of 92, born in Virginia; and Margaret Newkirk, aged 57, born in Pennsylvania. Henry (1768) is Shipman's father; Margaret is not identified. In 1994, I received a computer print-out of information on this family from Mark and Amy Gray (born Anne Marie Zalesky 1962) of Conifer, Colorado; she is a descendant. They very generously have permitted me to use their data, from which much of the following is derived. The children of Shipman Newkirk were born in Washington County, Pennsylvania:

1. Almaytron Newkirk, born April 14, 1828; married November 14, 1850 to Maria Barclay. They had children, some of whom are found in IGI records of Iowa, including:
   a. William B. Newkirk, born c.1852
   b. Albert S. Newkirk, born April 7, 1854. The Mormon IGI records of Iowa carry references to Albert Almarion Newkirk, who may be this individual, with a mistake in the middle initial, and the proper name of Albert Almaytron Newkirk (for his father). If so, he was married July 30, 1879 to Amanda Jane Bristow, and had at least one son, born at Taylor, Bedford County, Iowa:
      (1) Clyde Almaytron Newkirk, born October 10, 1883
   c. Laura E. Newkirk, born September 8, 1857
   d. Ida May Newkirk, born c.1864
   e. Isaac N. Newkirk, born about January, 1867
   f. Lillian L. Newkirk, born c.1869
2. Rebecca Jane Newkirk, born July 15, 1829
3. Sarah J. Newkirk, born May 6, 1831; died May 12, 1878. Married November 3, 1852 to John P. Barclay in Beaver, Pennsylvania
4. Henry Newkirk, born January 16, 1833
5. Rhoda Newkirk, born April 26, 1834; married September 15, 1854 to John Cochran
6. Eldridge Newkirk, born June 26, 1836; married November 15, 1857 to Mary E. Bross
7. Phallysta Newkirk, born May 10, 1838; married March 1, 1860 to William W. Leekins
8. Elmira Newkirk, born October 23, 1840; married June 16, 1857 to Walker Mayer
9. Matilda Newkirk, born May 18, 1842, and married August 23, 1860 to Michael Swagler Cunnings

10. Caroline Newkirk, born December 15, 1843; died May 15, 1884. Married February 27, 1867 to John W. Lantz
11. Keziah Newkirk, born c.1845; of whom more
12. Reuben Newkirk, born April 27, 1852; perhaps the Reuben reported in IGI records as married September 17, 1872 to Mary Jennie Scott in Poweshiek County, Iowa.

Keziah Newkirk
1845-1914

This daughter of Shipman Newkirk (1804), was born October 28, 1845 in Washington County, Pennsylvania, and died December 20, 1914 in Minnesota during a family outing. Returned to Elkton, South Dakota for burial. Married September 5, 1865 to James B. Cox, a doctor, born c.1842 and died December 20, 1914. His parents were the Reverend James C. W. Cox and Matilda Ellen Turner Cox. They had children, born at Belle Plaine, Benton County, Iowa:
1. Lena Winifred Cox, born March 5, 1867; died June 3, 1872
2. Ralph Newkirk Cox, born October 8, 1868, died July 9, 1946. Married October 8, 1889 Rozella Mae Kepner. Children:
   a. James Baker Cox, born September 5, 1905 and married March 17, 1938 to Heta Richards
   b. Ralph Earl Cox, born January 22, 1909; married March 7, 1947 to Kathryn Grubhoffer and had a son:
      (1) Thomas Earl Cox, born March 7, 1947. Married July 7, 1973 Delaine Kay Lewis, lived in Denver, and had two children:
         (a) Stephanie Nicole Cox, born April 22, 1976
         (b) Courtney Noelle Cox, born June 18, 1978
3. Leroy Eldridge Cox, born March 13, 1873; died September 22, 1955
4. James Earl Cox, born January 23, 1875 and died September 30, 1905. A doctor.
5. Ethel Kesiah Cox, born July 15, 1878, of whom more.

Ethel Kesiah Cox
1878-1056

This daughter of Keziah Newkirk (1845) and James B. Cox (1842) was born July 15, 1878 and died February 10, 1956; buried at Miami, Florida. Married October 14, 1903 to Emil R. Zalesky, born 1880 and died 1956; a son of Joseph and Amelia Zalesky. Children, born at Elkton, Brookings County, South Dakota.:

1. Richard Cox Zalesky, born February 10, 1906. Colonel, USA, retired. Married June 29, 1931 to Opheilia Gregoire, born November 29, 1902 at Salix, Woodbury County, Iowa, daughter of William Gregoire and AnnMarie Pulcherie Hubert Gregoire. His children were:
   a. Mariann Jean Zalesky, born October 1, 1935
   b. Dean Richard Zalesky, born June 25, 1938 at Sioux Falls, South Dakota. Married to Mary Cecily Whitteker, October 29, 1960 at Colchester, Connecticut; born October 27, 1939 at Brooklyn Navy Yard, New York, daughter of J. Kenneth Whitteker and Cecily Smith Whitteker. Divorced, and married second June 9, 1989, Barbara Jane Brickley at Lakewood, Jefferson County, Colorado. She was born March 12, 1949. Children, born at Denver:
      (1) Michael Dean Zalesky, born July 31, 1961. Married June 26, 1982 to Sherri Lynn Johnson, born April 2, 1960. They had children, born at Aurora, Arapahoe County, Colorado:
         (a) Jamie Lynn Zalesky, born September 5, 1985
         (b) Kellie Leigh Zalesky; December 27, 1988
      (2) Anne Marie Zalesky, born October 5, 1962. Married August 4, 1984 at Aurora, Arapahoe County, Colorado to Mark Everett Gray, born September 30, 1960 at Denver, Colorado, son of Kenneth Everett Gray and Beverly Ann Gibson.
      (3) Christine Courtney Zalesky; January 20, 1969
2. James E. Zalesky, born c.1908; died November 24, 1977
3. Marion M. Zalesky, born c.1911; in 1994 lives in Texas
4. Ann K. Zalesky, born June, 1917

CHAPTER 7

Newkirks of Berkeley County, West Virginia

Berkeley County, West Virginia, was one of the original areas of Virginia which became part of the new state formed as a result of the War Between The States. Berkeley was created as a Virginia county in 1772, from part of Frederick County. Frederick, in turn, was formed in 1738 from parts of Orange County. Orange had been created in 1720 from parts of Essex County (1694), King and Queen (1691), and King William (1701). It is necessary that the researcher follow the sequence of county formation in tracing ancestors, in order to know in which set of county records the information might be found.

In the case of the Newkirk families, Barent Newkirk (1689), arrived in what was then Frederick County, Virginia, about 1737, just about the time the county was formed. He remained there until his death in c.1768, just prior to the formation of Berkeley County. All records relative to Barent are therefore found in Frederick County, Virginia, at the courthouse in Winchester. But, the geographic location of his residence was in the area of Frederick which, in 1772, became Berkeley County, Virginia, about eight miles north of the present-day town of Martinsburg, West Virginia. Records of his children then, between 1737 and 1772, would be found in Frederick County and, thereafter, in Berkeley County, Virginia/West Virginia.

At the courthouse in Martinsburg can be found the wills of Berkeley County from 1772 to the present (even though those prior to 1865 were filed in Virginia). Birth and death records from 1865 to the present are also found in the Clerk's office. The courthouse, however, has a basement research room, below the office of the Registrar of Wills. It contains deeds and land grants beginning in 1772, and a set of Historic Records Books in about twenty-five volumes, with miscellaneous information. Any researcher should be aware that, in most courthouses, there are odd volumes of information that are not indexed and, often, are not known to exist by the clerks in the office! This writer searches the more obvious records,

160

and then wanders through the stacks, checking each set of books. It is amazing what is sometimes found in that way. As an example, in a courthouse in North Carolina, I was told that birth records were not kept prior to 1914. That appeared to be true, except that I just happened to find on the shelves a set of books entitled *Delayed Birth Records*. At the time of beginning to keep actual records in 1914, citizens were encouraged to record birth records that they could document by family Bibles, or personal knowledge. This set of books contained all those records, dating from the 1700s.

Numerous family groups of the Newkirk families are found in Berkeley County, West Virginia, principally in and near Martinsburg. It appears that they are primarily descended from some of the sons of Abraham Newkirk (1724) and his wife Kezia Shipman Newkirk. As previously reported in this study, Abraham was born near Princeton, New Jersey, one of the sons of Barent Newkirk (1689) and Rebecca Van Buntschooten Newkirk. He moved with his family to Virginia, living in Berkeley County until about 1770, when he moved to Washington County, Pennsylvania. Abraham and Kezia had eight children, all born in Berkeley County and, as reported elsewhere, one of them, Teunis (1750), was married to Margaret Miles (1759), and secondly to Susannah Hay (1781). He had nine children from his first marriage, all born in Berkeley County, and five from the second, the first of those born in Berkeley, and the remainder probably in Fairfield County, Ohio.

Teunis apparently moved to Ohio about 1800, leaving sons George (1780), James (1788), Joseph (1791) and Isaac (1795) in Berkeley County. Of these, Joseph moved to Wayne County, Ohio, where he died in 1869. James reportedly had only two daughters, and died in 1817. Isaac apparently remained for a time in Berkeley County, later moving to Washington County, Maryland, and had at least three, or perhaps four, children.

The remaining son, George, born in 1780, appears to be the progenitor of most of the Newkirk family members that we can now identify in Berkeley County, West Virginia.

161

George Newkirk
1780-1822

George, son of Teunis Newkirk (1750) was born March 12, 1780 in Berkeley County, Virginia (later West Virginia), and died there c.1822. As discussed in Chapter 4, George obtained large tracts of land from his father. The land records of Berkeley County contain records to deeds from a number of individuals to George Newkirk in the years from 1802 forward. On September 9, 1816, in Deed Book 30, page 428, one James Bowman assigned a Power of Attorney to Captain George Newkirk, Esquire. One can assume that George was a member of the local Militia, and a well known, well to do, respected member of his community. By deed recorded January 25, 1802 in Deed Book 17, page 304, George conveyed a tract of 32 acres and 32 poles to John Newkirk, who is not there identified. The land is identified as being part of the five tracts that George obtained from his father, Teunis, in 1799.

George was married September 9, 1802 to Mary or Martha Mason. She is apparently the M. Martha Newkirk buried at Falling Water Presbyterian Church cemetery, which suggests that her name may have been Mary Martha Mason. Her stone states that she was born October 8, 1781 and died December 10, 1857. What is believed to be his will is filed in Will Book 6 at page 522 in Berkeley County. It is dated August 25, 1814 and entered for record January 13, 1823. He mentions his wife, there appearing as Martha, and three children. His son, James, is to receive "my mills and real estate" with the stipulation that James pay certain amounts of money over time to his sisters. He names his wife and his brother, James Newkirk (1788), as Executors. The Will contains an interesting bit of history, explaining why a man of only 34 years of age would write a will. George states: *Having been lately detailed for a tour of Militia duty, do hereby make this instrument wrote with my own hand and signed my last will and testament.* Certain of his lands were said to adjoin the lands of James and Joseph Newkirk, two of his brothers. His children, named in the will, were:
1.   Margaret Newkirk
2.   James Mason Newkirk, born July 20, 1806, of whom more
3.   Mary Newkirk

James Mason Newkirk
1806-1873

This son of George Newkirk (1780) was born July 20, 1806 in Berkeley County, Virginia (later West Virginia), and died June 4, 1873 of consumption. He is buried with other family members in the cemetery of the Falling Waters Presbyterian church. He was married January 28, 1833 to Mary Ford, born c.1811; died July 12, 1892, aged 81 years, 4 months and 23 days. James Mason appears in several deeds in Berkeley County as a grantee, between 1841 and 1873, and was a prosperous farmer, as were many others of the family. His family appears in the 1850 and 1860 census reports for the county. In the 1850 census, Martha Newkirk is included at the age of 60, who is probably his mother, although the listed age is somewhat low. He died without a will, and his estate was settled by his two sons. Papers appear in Deed Book 71, page 139, in Berkeley County, dated March, 1874. There is a plat of the lands of James M. Newkirk, deceased, divided into two parcels. As an interesting aside here, the plat shows the names of adjoining property owners, and one of them is W. M. Hurley. That is, of course, the author's surname, although I can not identify that particular individual. In the division of estate, it is stated that he left only two children as his heirs. They were:

1. James Mason Newkirk, Jr., born c.1837, of whom more
2. George Newkirk, born c.1839, of whom more

James Mason Newkirk, Jr.
1837-1902

This son of James Mason Newkirk (1806), was born on March 19, 1837 in Berkeley County, Virginia and died June 23, 1902 of cancer. Buried at Falling Waters Presbyterian church cemetery. The 1860 census of the county lists his family, with a wife, Virginia, born c.1840 in Ohio. The family next appears in the 1870 and 1880 census, and in 1880, his wife Virginia does not appear, having died October 6, 1878 at age 38 years, 11 months and 3 days. The marriage record of his son, James Clifford (1869) states that the mother of James Clifford was Elvira Virginia

Newkirk. The 1870 census includes Isaac Newkirk in the household at the age of 75 (born c.1795), who is apparently a great uncle, as discussed earlier in Chapter 4. There is a reported death from typhoid of one Isaac Newkirk, a cabinetmaker, in Berkeley County, Virginia, on March 24, 1870 at the age of 74 years, 4 months and 20 days, which would calculate as a birth date of November 5, 1795. As previously reported, those dates are close within a year of the dates reported for Isaac Newkirk, son of Teunis Newkirk (1750), but not nearly as close as should be expected. We may well have another Isaac Newkirk, not yet identified! In the 1880 census, Mary, born c.1811, the mother of James Mason Newkirk, Jr., is in his household.

He was a farmer, and was a member of the Virginia Legislature prior to statehood of West Virginia. In the division of his father's estate, he received a tract of 305 acres and 23 perches as his share. On May 12, 1874, by deed recorded in Deed Book 71, page 163, he and his wife, Virginia, conveyed 24 and 1/4 acres of the land he had received from his father's estate, to his brother George Newkirk (1839), apparently in final settlement of the estate. His children included:

1. Charles F. Newkirk, born September 28, 1865 at Falling Water, and died March 5, 1930. He is buried at the Hedgesville cemetery in Berkeley County, West Virginia. He is perhaps the same Charles F. who was married to Rosa, as they appear in several records of the births of their children. There is also a listing of the estate of C. F. Newkirk in the courthouse at Martinsburg, dated March 25, 1930, which lists the widow, Rosa, one daughter and two sons, all living at Hedgesville, including:
   a. Virginia Belle Newkirk, born January 7, 1906. Married December 23, 1928 to Leslie C. Grubbs, born c.1900 in Virginia, a son of Asa and Nannie Grubbs
   b. Charles Hamilton Newkirk, born October 19, 1907
   c. Roy Mason Newkirk, born May 11, 1909. Married March 11, 1929 Helen F. Hess, born c.1910, a daughter of Claude and Esther Hess
2. Jeptha M. Newkirk, died January 28, 1868 at age of 15 days.

3. James Clifford Newkirk, born October 2, 1869 and died October 1, 1934. Buried at Falling Water Presbyterian cemetery. Married January 10, 1900 to Nellie V. Ellis, born March 19, 1878 in Berkeley County, daughter of George and Nannie Ellis. She died June 26, 1947 and is buried with her husband. His will, dated December 7, 1932 and filed for record November 1, 1934, is found in Will Book 28 at page 62, Berkeley County courthouse. It is quite straight forward, simply leaving everything he owns to his wife, Nellie V., *"to do with as she pleases."* At least the following children:
   a. Ellis M. Newkirk, born c.1903. Married February 24, 1927 Nina Virginia Crim, born 1905; daughter of A. M. Crim
   b. Nannie V. Newkirk, born c.1904; married February 24, 1926 to Wilmer Dunham, born c.1893, son of William C. and Elizabeth Dunham
   c. Daughter, still-birth July 20, 1915
   d. Laura F. Newkirk, born c.1916; married November 13, 1937 to Winter N. Speck, born c.1916, a son of Benjamin S. and Lillian Speck
   e. Ruth Ellis Newkirk, born June 3, 1917
4. Annie M. Newkirk, born August 12, 1872 and died November 16, 1881 from fever. Buried at Falling Water
5. George Newkirk, born August 17, 1875 and died July 26, 1954. Buried at Falling Water with other family members. Married Washington County, Maryland, September 22, 1898 to Hezzie L. McKitchen (or Hezzie L. M. Kitchen as reported on their marriage license), born January 23, 1881, died April 27, 1956; also buried at Falling Water. At least two sons:
   a. Claude Mason Newkirk, born June 10, 1899
   b. Raymond Newkirk, born March 7, 1902; died February 1, 1922

George Newkirk
1839-1928

This son of James Mason Newkirk (1806) and Mary Ford Newkirk (1811), was born May 25, 1839 in Berkeley County,

Virginia (later West Virginia), and died November 25, 1928. He is buried in the cemetery of Falling Waters Presbyterian church with other family members. He was married December 12, 1865 to Mary Elizabeth Anderson, born March 28, 1839 in Washington County, Maryland. She was a daughter of David and Mary Anderson; died August 28, 1920 and is buried in the cemetery of Falling Waters Presbyterian church with her husband and other Newkirk family members. Under the division of estate of his father, George received a tract of 223 acres, 3 roods and 28 perches. As mentioned above, his brother, James Mason Newkirk, Jr. (1837), later conveyed 24 and 1/4 acres to George, apparently to balance their inheritances.

George's will, dated October 7, 1920 and entered for record November 27, 1928 in Berkeley County, West Virginia, in Will Book 27 at page 161, is quite simple. It leaves his estate to his children, to share and share alike, but does not include any names. Apparently his wife was deceased prior to 1920, when he wrote his will. The family appears in the 1870 and 1880 census for Berkeley County. In 1870, his parents, James M. Newkirk (1806) and Mary Ford Newkirk (1811) are found in his household. There is also what appears to be a family of negroes in the household, born in Virginia, named Broadus, including Adam (1813), a laborer; Jane (1820), a servant; Noah (1853), a servant; Henrietta (1856), a servant; and Emily (1861). That same year Adam Broadus (1851) was found in the household of James Mason Newkirk, Jr. (1837), brother of George. In the 1870 census, George is listed as having wealth of $ 1,617; his father James Mason Newkirk, Sr., was shown in the 1850 census with wealth of $ 14,880; in 1860 he had $ 31,040; and in 1870, $ 39,100. The family is listed in a somewhat obscure book entitled *Statement of Heirs*, found at the courthouse in Martinsburg, dated November 27, 1928. Children of George and Mary Elizabeth, all born in Berkeley County, were:

1. Anna Mary Newkirk, born c.1867. She is discussed in the book *History of Frederick County, Md.*, by T. J. C. Williams. It is reported there that she was a daughter of this family. She was married in January 7, 1887 to Louis Orndorf Willis, son of William and Frances Willis. Through his grandmother, he was related to Elizabeth Orndorf, for whom the town of

Hagerstown, Maryland, was first named, as Elizabethtown. He was also a descendant of Jonathan Hager, for whom the town was later named. In 1928, the family was living at New Market, Maryland. At least nine children:

a. Hugh Finley Willis
b. Elizabeth Newkirk Willis
c. William Brand Willis
d. Christopher Hampton Willis
e. Frances Finley Willis
f. Louis Orndorf Willis, Jr.
g. George Newkirk Willis
h. Mary Anderson Willis
i. Levin Charles Willis

2. David H. Newkirk, born 1868 and died 1936; buried at Falling Water cemetery. In 1928, he lived at Hedgesville, West Virginia. Married December 31, 1889 to Mary Susan Ellis, born 1871 and died 1952. His will was dated March 29, 1935 and entered for record February 19, 1936 in Will Book 28 at page 145 in Berkeley County, West Virginia. It mentions only his wife. After his death, she married at the age of 70, on November 20, 1941, Robert E. Snyder, a widower, born c.1876 in Virginia. There were at least eight children:

a. Mary A. Newkirk, born February 17, 1891
b. James Ellis Newkirk, born c.1891 and married June 21, 1916 to Martha Virginia Dodd, who was born August 22, 1894 and died October 10, 1918; a daughter of Samuel L. and Sarah Dodd. Also buried at Falling Water. They had at least one child:
(1) Maurice Dodd Newkirk, born June 14, 1917. Married April 29, 1936 to Louise Arnold, born c.1916, daughter of David A. and Sallie R. Arnold. He died in 1950 and is buried at Falling Water.
c. George H. Newkirk, styled Jr. in the birth records, but also clearly naming his parents and listing him as the third of their children, born March 26, 1896. He may be the same George H. Newkirk who is buried at Falling Water, although the stone indicates birth date of January 7, 1896; he died November 28, 1970 and was a war

veteran. Married January 29, 1931 to Eva Thomas, born c.1906, a daughter of Howard and B. Triggs Thomas

d. John David Newkirk, born February 8, 1898 and died May 18, 1957; buried at Falling Water. Married March 24, 1917 Mary Belle Everhart, born August 2, 1900, daughter of C. E. and Annie V. Everhart. At least two children:

    (1) Frances Virginia Newkirk, born August 25, 1917

    (2) Charles David Newkirk, born December 6, 1918

e. Anna Mary Newkirk, born August 15, 1905

f. A son, twin, born April 16, 1909

g. A son, twin, stillbirth April 16, 1909

h. Donald E. Newkirk, died May 16, 1910 at one month

3. Jeptha Newkirk, born c.1871 and in 1928, lived at Pittsburgh

4. George Newkirk, died September 4, 1873 at fourteen days old

5. Eva Newkirk, born c.1875, according to the 1880 census, and died December 28, 1885 aged 11 years, 4 months and 19 days.

6. Theodore Newkirk, born June 29, 1877 and died January 27, 1948 and buried at Falling Water Presbyterian. In 1928, lived at Martinsburg, West Virginia. Married November 18, 1908 to Savilla T. Wood, daughter of I. J. Wood. She was born April 16, 1883 and died April 15, 1968; buried at Tomahawk Presbyterian cemetery in Berkeley County, West Virginia. They had at least one daughter:

a. Martha Jane Newkirk, born July 31, 1916

7. Nellie Mason Newkirk, listed in the *Statement of Heirs* referred to above as a daughter. Married February 25, 1906 to Lee Curtis Harwood; in 1928 lived at Keedysville, Maryland. He was born c.1881 in Frederick County, Virginia, son of Thomas and Mary Harwood. Report of their marriage includes the name of her parents also.

CHAPTER 8

Peter Newkirk
1727-1804

This son of Barent Nieukerke (1689) and Rebecca Van Buntschooten, was born about 1727 at the old Newkirk settlement near Martinsburg, in Berkeley County, Virginia (later West Virginia), and died intestate in Bullitt County, Kentucky in 1804. Married before 1754 to Cornelia Sousley in Virginia. She was born c.1730 in Virginia and died c.1805 in Bullitt County. Peter was raised on a farm near North Mountain and Martinsburg, where he farmed and helped his father with carpentry and operation of the family mill. He also served in the Revolutionary War. In 1765, Barent Newkirk's will in Frederick County, Virginia, gave 106 acres of land to Peter, which he and his wife, Cornelia, conveyed to Jacob Koofman, by deed dated September 19, 1771, recorded in Deed Book 15 at page 210 in Frederick County, Virginia, perhaps in preparation for leaving the county. In 1773, his name appears with other Newkirks in Bedford County, Pennsylvania. He was in the area of Louisville, Kentucky, as early as 1781, when an entry of December 3 of that year, in Minute Book A, for Jefferson County, Kentucky, states that Peter Newkirk, Jemima Hoagland, Elias Newkirk and Tobias Newkirk are entitled to four hundred acres of land. Jemima was Peter's sister; Elias and Tobias his brothers. Peter had as many as ten children, all born in what was then Virginia, but probably in an area that later was to become West Virginia:

1. Benjamin Franklin Newkirk, born 1754, of whom more
2. William Newkirk, born c.1758, of whom more
3. Richard Newkirk, born c.1760 in Virginia, according to the family chart in *Newkirk Notes,* by Mary and Gil Alford, where they reported that Richard was married twice: first in 1807 to Elizabeth Martin, and secondly to Ruth Inscoll. With the dates of birth of the children listed there, I believe that Richard, born 1760 in Virginia, was probably the father of a second Richard

(Jr.), and perhaps other children, but not the husband of either of the ladies mentioned, who were perhaps wives of his son:

    a.   Richard Newkirk, Jr., born c.1784, of whom more

4.   Isaac Newkirk, born c.1762, of whom more
5.   Peter Newkirk, II, born c.1765, of whom more
6.   Tobias Newkirk, born c.1767 in Virginia, and died after 1790 in Jefferson County, Kentucky. It is said that he was killed by Indians along with one of the Hoagland boys, while they were fishing on the Floyd Forks. Married Esther and had two sons, born in Kentucky:

    a.   Peter Newkirk, born April, 1783
    b.   Henry Newkirk, born c.1784

7.   Teunis Newkirk, born 1768, of whom more
8.   Charles Newkirk, born c.1771 in Virginia; died after 1828. Married to Camilla Wells.
9.   Louisa Newkirk, born c.1773 in Virginia; died after 1808. Married March 28, 1790 in Bullitt County, Kentucky, Matthew Rose.
10. A daughter, married Elias

Benjamin Franklin Newkirk
1754-1840

This son of Peter Newkirk (1727) was born December 25, 1754 and died May 17, 1840 in Jackson County, Indiana. Married first August 26, 1787 to Elizabeth; second on December 20, 1789 in Jefferson County, Kentucky to Mary Hawkins; and third March 3, 1801 in Jefferson County to Alice Sparks. She was born March 11, 1777 in Lancaster County, Pennsylvania, and died 1857 in Indiana. Benjamin had children; none born to the first marriage; one to the second, and the rest to the third:

1.   Henry Newkirk, born c.1795, of whom more
2.   Jemima Newkirk, born August 16, 1801 in Jefferson County, Kentucky, and died July 18, 1862. Married December 3, 1817 in Jackson County, Indiana, to William Henderson, born December 22, 1794 in Virginia, and died July 4, 1863. He was a son of Joseph Henderson (1770) and Jane McGee Henderson (1780)

170

3. Permelia Newkirk, born February 29, 1806, of whom more.
4. Moses Kirkendoll Newkirk, born December 6, 1806 and died January 28, 1881 Lawrence County, Indiana. Married August 27, 1833 in Jackson County, Indiana to Eleanor Fountain, born January 3, 1814 in Stokes County, North Carolina, and died January 3, 1896 in Lawrence County, Indiana. Moses K. appears in the 1850 census for the county as a carpenter, with five children, born in Indiana:
   a. Burilla Newkirk, born c.1835 or 1837
   b. Jeptha Newkirk, born c.1836; perhaps married Anne and was the father of:
      (1) Clarence L. Newkirk, born 1871 Lawrence County
   c. Lemuel Newkirk, born c.1838
   d. James F. Newkirk, born c.1842
   e. William L. Newkirk, born c.1849; perhaps the same individual reported in Mormon IGI records as married c.1873 to Martha, born c.1856 and had children:
      (1) Edith Newkirk, born c.1874
      (2) Nora Newkirk, born c.1876
      (3) Ella Newkirk, born c.1878
5. James Leonard Newkirk, born March 3, 1809, of whom more
6. Benjamin Richard Newkirk, born 1810 and died September 24, 1857 in Indiana. Married June 19, 1828 in Lawrence County, Indiana, Lucinda Beezly; married second in Washington County, Indiana, to Amanda Carothers; married third September 30, 1840 to Nancy Owens; and married fourth October 15, 1846 in Jackson County to Mary Mills, born 1815. He appears in a brief comment in the June 1, 1983 issue of *Newkirk Notes*, as submitted by Mary Ann Banks, then living at Winterset, Iowa. She provided some information, including a few dates that conflict with earlier data. First of all, Benjamin Richard (called only Richard in the referenced report), died September 24, 1857 as previously stated, and is buried in the Shields Cemetery at Leesville, in Lawrence County, Indiana. His third marriage to Nancy Owens, is reported as being August 3, 1840, and his fourth marriage is reported as being October 15, 1845. He is probably the Richard Newkirk listed in the 1850 census of Jackson County,

Indiana, born 1810, with a wife Mary A., born c.1816, and seven children. There is also one Margaret Renner in the household, born c.1832 in Indiana. If these are the children of Benjamin Richard, then it appears he must have had one child from the first marriage; three from the second; two from the third; and at least three from the fourth. There may have been other children, born in Indiana:

a. Lemuel Newkirk, born c.1831
b. Jacob Newkirk, born c.1836
c. Elsie Newkirk, born November 3, 1837 in Indiana, the maternal grandmother of Mary Ann Banks.
d. William C. Newkirk, born c.1839
e. Nancy A. Newkirk, born c.1842
f. Lucinda Newkirk, born c.1844
g. Amanda Newkirk, born c.1848
h. James Newkirk, born c.1849
i. Mary Richard Newkirk, born May 20, 1855; died May 20, 1900 Leesville, Lawrence County. Married Thomas Jefferson Hook. One of her descendants is said to be Mrs. E. Gertrude Silver, in 1983 living at Bedford, Indiana

7. Benjamin Franklin Newkirk, Jr., born January 29, 1812 and died March 5, 1887 in Indiana. Married October 16, 1834 in Lawrence County to Euphenia White. She was born July 28, 1818 and died June 11, 1863, in Indiana. In the 1850 census of Lawrence county, he is listed as a cabinetmaker and they have a second Benjamin Newkirk living in the household, also a cabinetmaker, born c.1829, too early to be a son, unless the elder Benjamin was first married very young, and this is a son of that marriage. Both children also appear in the Mormon IGI records of the state, born in Lawrence County, Indiana. The two children in the census were:

a. Nancy Newkirk, born c.1838
b. David Newkirk, born c.1843 (1841 according to the IGI)

8. Isaac B. Newkirk, born 1814 and married April 18, 1838 in Lawrence County, Indiana, to Mary Ann Critchlow, who was born October 5, 1815 in Kentucky, and died June 23, 1880 in Pike County, Indiana. The family appears in the 1850 census

for Lawrence County, with several children, born in Lawrence County, Indiana. Mormon IGI records supply other children:
a. William T. Newkirk, born c.1839
b. Nancy A. Newkirk, born c.1841, and perhaps married September 9, 1858 to Franklin McDade.
c. Elonson Newkirk, a son, born c.1843
d. Margaret E. Newkirk, born c.1845
e. Josiah Newkirk, born c.1847
f Benjamin Newkirk, born c.1849
g. Mary C. Newkirk, born c.1855
9. Polly Newkirk, born c.1816; died 1837, single

Henry Newkirk
1795-1846

This son of Benjamin Franklin Newkirk (1754), was born c.1795 in Jefferson County, Kentucky, and died 1846 in Brown County, Indiana. Married February 20, 1819 in Jackson County, Indiana to Polly Henderson, who was born c.1797 in Montgomery County, Virginia, and died c.1838. Two of her brothers were married to two of Henry's sisters, as earlier reported. He was married second May 24, 1840 in Brown County, Indiana, to Hannah Waggoner, born 1822 and died after 1856. He appears in the 1820 census of Jackson County with a wife and a daughter under ten years of age. By 1830, the family was found in Bartholomew County, Indiana, where they were listed with the first three children: Harriet, Delila and Isaiah. In 1836, Brown County was formed from part of Bartholomew, and Henry Newkirk was listed as one of the first landowners in that county. As an aside here, it is of interest to the author to recall that a large population of members of the Hines family lived in this area during this period, and to the present day. Hines is the maiden name of my wife.

In April of 1837, Henry served on a grand jury and in 1840, he was a road supervisor. See *The History of Brown County,* 1884. The probate records of Brown County contain over thirty pages devoted to the estate of Henry Newkirk. His widow, Hannah, was married March 4, 1847 to James Weddle Taggart, and he became

Guardian for Isaiah, Mary and James Newkirk. Henry was the father of five children from his first marriage, two from the second:

1.   Harriet L. Newkirk, born 1820, probably in Jackson County, Indiana. Married first June 21, 1840 in Brown County to Henry H. Porter, by whom she had four children. She was married second January 1, 1854 to Joseph Fox in Brown County. He was a son of Jonathan Fox and Fanny Clark Fox, and the brother of Isaac Fox, who married her sister, Delila C. Newkirk. The children of Harriet from her two marriages were:
     a.   Mary G., or Martha J. Porter, born c.1841, and married October 5, 1861 Henry Smith in Brown County, Indiana
     b.   John Hutson Porter, born c.1848; died while serving in Union forces in the 145th Infantry
     c.   William H. Porter, born c.1849
     d.   Armenus Benjamin Porter, born c.1851, and married December 14, 1876 to Matilda J. McCarty in Brown County, Indiana
     e.   William A. Fox, born c.1856
     f.   Richard M. Fox, born c.1859

2.   Delila C. Newkirk, born 1825 and married March 13, 1841 in Brown County, Indiana, to Isaac Fox. He died between 1850 and 1860, and they had at least the following children, according to the 1850 and 1860 census of the county:
     a.   Nancy J. Fox, born c.1842
     b.   Hannah Etta Fox, or Henrietta, born c.1844
     c.   William W. Fox, born c.1849
     d.   Joseph Fox, born c.1853
     e.   Armenis B. Fox, born c.1856

3.   Isaiah McCallen Newkirk, born c.1829. In the 1850 census, he is shown in the household of his stepmother, Hannah, and her second husband James W. Taggart, and is there listed at the age of 21, and classified as an "idiot"

4.   Eliza Jane Newkirk, born October 30, 1830 and married to John Howard Colvin on February 17, 1848 in Brown County, Indiana. She died in the spring of 1875 in Washington Territory

174

5. Armenis Benjamin Newkirk, born June 18, 1834. As a young man, he moved to Iowa, where he was married in 1855 to Cordelia Hudson. In 1865, Benjamin and his family, with his sister Eliza Jane Colvin and her family, traveled the Oregon Trail, and settled in Oakland, Douglas County, Oregon. It was there that Cordelia died and in 1868, Armenis Benjamin moved on with his daughter to Lewis River in the Reno District, near Woodland, Washington Territory. He had four children, but only one daughter lived to be an adult:
   a. Melissa J. Newkirk, born c.1858 in Iowa and married there January 23, 1878 to George W. Davis, who was killed in a shooting match when a bullet ricocheted off a target. They had a daughter:
      (1) Lela Davis, born c.1878
6. Mary Eliza Newkirk, born c.1842 to Henry's second marriage
7. James Samuel Newkirk, born October 17, 1845

Permelia Newkirk
1806-1865

This daughter of Benjamin Franklin Newkirk (1754) was born February 29, 1806, probably in Kentucky, and died January 17, 1865 in Brown County, Indiana. Married August 20, 1826 in Lawrence County, Indiana to Robert Henderson, brother of William, who married her sister, Jemima Newkirk (1801). Note, however, that either the two were not brothers, or that the dates of their births as reported from tombstone information is inaccurate. William was reportedly born December 22, 1794, just three months prior to the reported birth of his brother. It is entirely possible that the two boys were cousins, not brothers, and that they traveled in the same family group first to Kentucky, and then to Indiana Territory. However, in a transfer of the property of Joseph Henderson, the following entered into the division of the property: William and Jemima Henderson; Robert and Permelia Henderson; Henry and Polly Newkirk; Joseph and Delilah White; Hiram C. and Sarah Weddle; Alexander and Elizabeth Hanson. William, Robert, Polly, Delilah, Sarah and Elizabeth are known to be six of the eleven children of Joseph Henderson, so we conclude here that the date of birth of one of these boys in incorrect and that, they are in fact, brothers. Robert was reportedly born February 14, 1795 in Montgomery County, Virginia, son of Joseph Henderson (1770) and Jane McGee Henderson (1780). He was first married to Elizabeth Taggert. Robert and Permelia had at least one son:

1. Robert Henderson, Jr., born September 28, 1827 in Jackson County, Indiana; died August 10, 1910 in Brown County, Indiana. Married there December 13, 1849 to Mary Ann Davis, born August 27, 1830 in Jennings County, Indiana, daughter of Joe Davis (1805) and Sarah (1813) Davis. They had children, born in Brown County, Indiana:

   a. Emaline Henderson, born December 28, 1850; died January 2, 1942. Married January 23, 1872 to Logan Ping, born August 9, 1830, son of Job Ping and Christina Niece Ping.

   b. James Henderson, born December 31, 1852; died January 30, 1920. Married November 8, 1871 to Eda A. Floyd, born July 7, 1850; died June 28, 1918, daughter of James Floyd and Louisa Anderson Floyd.

   c. Permelia Ann Henderson, born January 6, 1855; married September 6, 1874 to Joseph Benjamin Henderson, born January 28, 1854 in Jackson County, Indiana, son of Joseph Henderson, Jr. and Phobe White Henderson.

   d. Joseph Benjamin Henderson, born September 2, 1856, and died November 1, 1856.

   e. John C. Breckenridge Henderson, born October 6, 1857 in Brown County; died December 2, 1941 in Muscatine, Iowa. Married July 26, 1875 Nancy Ann Hubbard, born September 26, 1855; daughter of George and Mary Brown Hubbard. They had at least a son:

      (1) Elmer Le Roy Henderson, born January 13, 1887 in Jackson County, Indiana; died October 15, 1970 in Aledo, Illinois. Married December 8, 1916 Frances Eva Marple at Rock Island, Illinois, born September 16, 1894 in Illinois City, and died March 30, 1975 at Aledo, daughter of Mason and Louise Twigg Marple. Le Roy and Frances are

buried at Buffalo Prairie Cemetery. One of their children was:

(a) Marian Isabelle Henderson, my correspondent; married Kenneth Brumbaugh Lewars.

f. William Henderson, born July 16, 1859; died March 27, 1866

g. Robert Michael Henderson, born April 4, 1863; died January 27, 1942. Married February 27, 1885 to Louisa Ellen Foster, born June 2, 1863 in Jackson County, Indiana and died May 2, 1932, the daughter of William Foster and Sarah Jane Henderson Foster.

h. Benjamin Franklin Henderson, born November 4, 1865, and died November 11, 1950. Married October 1, 1893 to Ruey M. Brown, born November 11, 1871 in Brown County; died December 20, 1931 at Indianapolis, daughter of Elisha and Ella Noblitt Brown.

i. Jasper Henry Henderson, born February 6, 1867; died December 23, 1946. Married March 24, 1892 to Lydia Ellen Brown, born 1873; died October 30, 1959, the daughter of Sandy M. Brown (1828) and Nancy A. Brown (1840).

j. Freeman Henderson, born October 6, 1870; died January, 1954 at Indianapolis, Indiana. Married August 16, 1894 to Monta Tulkington.

James Leonard Newkirk
1809-1865

This son of Benjamin Franklin Newkirk (1754), was born March 3, 1809 and died September 22, 1865 in Lawrence County, Indiana. Married there December 14, 1834 to Elvira Critchlow, who was born July 23, 1816 in Kentucky, and died December 25, 1865 in Lawrence County. They appear in the 1850 census of the county, with eight children, all born in Indiana. Later information from Alice Newkirk Salisbury, one of his descendants, demonstrates that there was a total of fourteen children. Another contact with Howard Lester Jones, Jr., of Omaha, Nebraska (1992), provides more information, all of it combined following:

177

1. Lucinda Newkirk, born September 25, 1835; married January 1, 1862 to Wiley Jones. She is buried in Seymour, Indiana
2. Amanda Melvina Newkirk, born August 3, 1837, and died April, 1921; Buried at Overton, Indiana. Married April 9, 1863 to Ezekial Logan Caress
3. Lynn Malinda Newkirk, born July 7, 1839; married first to Elisha Reed, and second to David Sutherland
4. Benjamin Franklin Newkirk, born March 27, 1841, and died January 26, 1896. Married December 29, 1870 Mary Dixon
5. Mary Elizabeth Newkirk, born June 13, 1843 and died in 1871. Married December 11, 1866 to Benjamin Carter, Jr., son of Benjamin Carter and Nancy Reynolds Carter. He was born February 17, 1844, and after the death of his wife, Mary Elizabeth, he married secondly Emma Anderson of England.
6. Elsie I. Newkirk, a twin, born c.1846 and died 1863
7. Michael Newkirk, a twin, born 1846 and an infant death
8. Nancy A. Newkirk, born c.1848 and died 1861
9. Francis Marion Newkirk, born 1850 and died 1874
10. James Edward Newkirk, born February 24, 1852 and died July 16, 1906. Buried at Clarysville, Lawrence County, Indiana. Married September 25, 1875 Mary Catherine Bowers
11. Margaret Laura Newkirk, born February 27, 1854; died January 19, 1934. Married August 12, 1873 David Bostwick Loudon. Buried at Gandy, Nebraska.
12. A stillbirth, 1856
13. William Leonard Newkirk, born April 4, 1858 in Indiana, and died April 25, 1936 at Los Angeles, California; buried at Inglewood, California. Married April 7, 1886 at North Platte, Nebraska, to Mary Elizabeth Sullivan, who was born March 17, 1867 in Pike County, Indiana, daughter of David Sullivan, II and Adaline Orvanda Chappell Sullivan. She died April 19, 1946 at Hastings, Nebraska. They had eight children:
   a. Nora Pearl Newkirk, born January 30, 1887 at Gandy, Nebraska, and died April 11, 1969 at Newport Beach, California. Married 1907 to Edward Brook Newell, born September 26, 1885 and died November 17, 1959. A daughter:

(1) Ruby Mae Newell, born December 23, 1908; married August 12, 1929 to Ray Huckfeldt, born September 1, 1908. A daughter:
    (a) Betty Lou Huckfeldt, born May 15, 1930; married Ted Raubinger, born April 12, 1926. They had two children:
        1. David Raubinger, born December 12, 1951; married Donna Ornstein, born May 19, 1952
        2. Susan Kay Raubinger, born May 14, 1954, and married to John Bandel

b. Ethel Dee Newkirk, born November 17, 1888 at Gandy, and died there April 12, 1890

c. Ivan Earl Newkirk, born April 13, 1890, of whom more

d. Everett John Newkirk, born June 8, 1892, of whom more

e. Gladys Mae Newkirk, born 1894, of whom more

f. Stillbirth, 1896, at Gandy

g. Howard Raymond Newkirk, born December 16, 1899, of whom more

h. Lester Forest Newkirk, born December 15, 1907 at Juniata, Nebraska; died December 15, 1973 at Boulder, Colorado. Married c.1932 Ruby May Hilflicker, born May 14, 1903 and died June 22, 1990. A son:
    (1) Roger Sullivan Newkirk, born January 12, 1939. Married twice: first on May 30, 1976 to Barbara Watson, and second on June 2, 1984 to Josephine Tipka.

14. Isaac B. Newkirk, born January 23, 1863 and died May 18, 1863. Buried at Leesville, Indiana.

Ivan Earl Newkirk
1890-1961

This son of William Leonard Newkirk (1858) was born April 13, 1890 at Gandy, Nebraska, and died November 13, 1961 at Beaverton, Oregon. He was married first in March of 1911 to Bessie Mae Monger, from whom he was divorced April 28, 1934. She was born October 27, 1894 and died June 3, 1975; buried at

Verona, Missouri. She was married secondly to Earl Loyd. Ivan Earl was married second to Genevieve Churchill. Seven children were born to his first marriage, all at Hastings in Adams County, Nebraska; four were born to the second, for a total of eleven:

1. Raymond Earl Newkirk, born July 7, 1912 and died July 3, 1979 at Cypress, California. Married three times: first to Maxine Caldwell; second to Virgie; and third to Edith Cook, who was born August 14, 1916. Children not reported.

2. Donald William Newkirk, born September 2, 1913; died April 5, 1971 at San Pedro, California. Married Pauline Ralston

3. Cecil Edward Newkirk, born October 10, 1915; died January 13, 1976 at Omaha, Nebraska. Married three times, order not known, but included: Minnie; Loraine; and May 27, 1953 to Mary Jane Graves, born January 28, 1922

4. Kenneth Loyd Newkirk, born June 16, 1916; married September 7, 1940 to Margaret Elizabeth Cook, born March 14, 1918 and died December 30, 1983. Children:
   a. Kenneth Loyd Newkirk, Jr., born May 25, 1943
   b. Mary Lou Newkirk, born June 8, 1946; married David Griffis, born December 13, 1945

5. Virginia Mae Newkirk, born July 18, 1919, of whom more

6. Kathleen Irene Newkirk, born February 8, 1922; died October 27, 1991 at Washougal, Washington. Married three times: to Harold Williams; to Joseph Watson; and on April 11, 1958 to Carl Kelly, born 1923 and died May, 1982

7. Mary Elizabeth Newkirk, born April 4, 1928 and died April 5, 1974 at Washougal, Washington. Married three times: to Bob Zook, born April 23, 1926 and died April 5, 1974; June 4, 1956 Paul Pass, born April, 1931 and died August 31, 1963; in 1964 to Robert Bratton. Children from each marriage:
   a. Patsy Kay Zook, born January 7, 1949; married in 1970 to Joe Ed Ehrs, and had two children, following. Married also to Wayne Fizzetie, born December 11, 1929 and died May 9, 1988. The Ehrs children were:
      (1) Heather Lee Ehrs, born January 12, 1971
      (2) Bryan Edward Ehrs, born March 24, 1976
   b. Phillip Patrick Pass, born October 19, 1951; married twice: first June 4, 1969 to Lori McDonald, born March

4, 1952, and had two children; second July 24, 1982 to Karen Kinsman. The children were:
- (1) Paul Patrick Pass, born November 12, 1970
- (2) Darla Suzanne Pass, born September 7, 1973, and married to Brian Gary. A son:
  - (a) Anthony Patrick Gary; January 11, 1992
- c. Susan Marie Pass, born September 9, 1954; married December 15, 1972 Kenneth Woodridge. Two children:
  - (1) Melissa Sue Woodridge; July 4, 1975
  - (2) Brian Edward Woodridge; September 16, 1976
- d. George Pass, born April 7, 1956; married May 11, 1973 to Linda Brill, born March 28, 1954. Children:
  - (1) Clinton James Pass; January 14, 1975
  - (2) Katherine Lee Pass; April 12, 1980
  - (3) Elizabeth Ashley; February 22, 1983
- e. Jack Bratton, born June 5, 1965
8. Nora Ann Newkirk, born October 9, 1936; married June 8, 1952 to John Harris, born April 11, 1929 and died November 26, 1985. Three children:
  - a. Michelle Marie Harris, born March 26, 1954; married January 17, 1974 to David Meier, born May 27, 1950. Children:
    - (1) Lisa Kristine Meier, born November 25, 1976
    - (2) Sara Renee Meier, born August 30, 1978
  - b. George Daniel Harris, born March 24, 1956; married June 10, 1978 Susan Wilson, born May 11, 1955. Three children:
    - (1) Tori Wilson Harris, born January 5, 1983
    - (2) Taryn Danielle Harris, born September 28, 1988
    - (3) Trace Oliver Harris, born March 28, 1992
  - c. Rosalie Ann Harris, born January 19, 1957, and married October 15, 1976 to Daniel Sheldon, born January 22, 1950. Three children:
    - (1) Leslie Ann Sheldon; June 15, 1981
    - (2) Natalie Rose Sheldon; March 8, 1984
    - (3) Scott Daniel Sheldon; December 1, 1987

9. David Ivan Newkirk, born June 28, 1938; married September 5, 1957 to Lorelie Harris, born February 11, 1939, and had four children:
   a. Wade Lee Newkirk, born May 17, 1959, and married September 1, 1979 Linda Sue Boschma, born February 28, 1958. Two children:
      (1) Brockdon Newkirk; March 1, 1980
      (2) Garth Newkirk; September 19, 1981
   b. Danette Lynn Newkirk, born September 13, 1960
   c. Dawn Diane Newkirk, born May 16, 1964; married May 2, 1987 to Sean McBroom, born September 28, 1964. A son:
      (1) Austin Joshua McBroom, born March 21, 1992
   d. Zed Jeffrey Newkirk, born June 13, 1965; married Tracy
10. Leonard Earl Newkirk, born March 22, 1940; married twice: to Kathy Robinson, born February 28, 1940. Second March 30, 1964 Linda Allen, born October 29, 1943. Two children:
    a. Robyn Earl Newkirk; December 26, 1965
    b. Becki Lynn Newkirk; June 10, 1967
11. Thomas Newkirk, born April 2, 1942, and married to Darlene Garrison.

Virginia Mae Newkirk
1919-1984

This daughter of Ivan Earl Newkirk (1890), was born July 18, 1919 at Hastings, Nebraska, and died April 30, 1984 at Omaha, Nebraska, where she is buried in the Westlawn cemetery. Married September 7, 1941 in Omaha to Howard Lester Jones, born February 23, 1909 at Niobrara, Nebraska, and died September 16, 1969 at Omaha. He was a son of Charles Henry Jones and Georgia Ann Dewey Jones. They had two children:
1. Howard Lester Jones, Jr., my correspondent, born May 9, 1953 at Omaha, Nebraska, and married August 5, 1978 to Patricia Lee Myers Tyson in Council Bluffs, Iowa. They were divorced in July, 1981. She was a daughter of Kenneth Paul Myers and Zelma Elizabeth Myers, and had first been married to William Tyson. She had two children from her first

marriage who were adopted by Howard Lester; the adoption was terminated after their divorce. The children were:
   a. Patrick William, born May 20, 1969
   b. Shawn Michael, born July 17, 1970
2. Susan Mae Jones, born May 10, 1955 at Omaha, and married February 16, 1980 to Richard Rolling at Offutt Air Force Base in Bellevue, Nebraska. He was born June 6, 1940 at Dubuque, Iowa, son of Harry Leo Rolling and Adrienne Elizabeth Houlahan Rolling. They had three children, the first two born at Riverside, California, and the third at Offut Air Force base:
   a. Christopher Michael Rolling, born September 10, 1981
   b. Matthew Martin Rolling, born October 14, 1982
   c. Elizabeth Mae Rolling, born February 6, 1986

Everett John Newkirk
1892-1968

This son of William Leonard Newkirk (1858) was born June 8, 1892 at North Platte, Nebraska, and died January 30, 1968 at Hastings, Nebraska. Married August 11, 1915 to Lillian Lametha Mason, who was born January 29, 1889 and died May 14, 1957. They had children:
1. Alice Newkirk, born February 17, 1918 and married July 20, 1936 to Howard Salisbury, born July 8, 1913.
2. Lillian Newkirk, born March 7, 1925; married June 20, 1943 to William Russell, born January 23, 1924. Children:
   a. Ann Russell, born May 6, 1945. Married October 10, 1964 William Lamont, born January 23, 1924, and had a daughter:
       (1) Lara Lamont, born February 25, 1967
   b. Gary Dee Russell, born March 31, 1948, and married February 4, 1972 to Lynn Ovellette, born December 9, 1946. Children:
       (1) Casey Ann Russell, born December 9, 1972
       (2) Kelly Michelle Russell, born November 22, 1976
       (3) Michael Aaron Russell, born September 15, 1978

3. Mason Everett Newkirk, born December 15, 1928; married October 25, 1957 to Martha Ingeburg, born March 25, 1936. Children:
   a. Kristine Newkirk, born September 27, 1958. Married January 6, 1979 to Steven Moore. Children:
      (1) Marina Michelle Moore; January 19, 1986
      (2) Jonathan Moore; April 21, 1987
   b. William John Newkirk; May 17, 1960
   c. Susan Newkirk, born October 29, 1961, and married February 12, 1982 to Said Hamilton, born May 28, 1953. Six children:
      (1) Jennifer Michelle Hamilton; March 9, 1982
      (2) William John Hamilton; June 14, 1984
      (3) Linda Marie Hamilton; September 18, 1985
      (4) Jeff Patrick Hamilton, twin; May 20, 1987
      (5) Phillip Andrew Hamilton, twin; May 20, 1987
      (6) Kevin Edward Hamilton; March 18, 1981
   d. Jane Newkirk, born September 25, 1963

Gladys Mae Newkirk
1894-1980

This daughter of William Leonard Newkirk (1858) was born November 4, 1894 at Gandy, and died April 24, 1980. Married in 1911 to Charles Nelson Newell, born June 19, 1890 and died July 25, 1935. They had children:
1. Geraldine Mae Newell, born June 13, 1915; married January 16, 1941 to George Thomas Davis, born October 10, 1906 and died March 22, 1979. They had children:
   a. George Thomas Davis, Jr., born July 4, 1943; married January 15, 1965 to Clare Loughrey, born August 21, 1946, and had children:
      (1) Brenda Christine Davis, born July 6, 1965
      (2) William Lance Davis, born May 28, 1968
      (3) Cynthia Jane Davis, born July 29, 1969
   b. Charles Richard Davis, born February 7, 1946
   c. James Steven Davis, born May 13, 1953

2. Charles Richard Newell, born January 21, 1931, and married October 15, 1950 to Betty Lou Clark, born July 28, 1931. Children:
    a. Judy Ann Newell, born November 8, 1952, and married to Curtis Ballard. Two children:
        (1) Jeanette Elizabeth Ballard, born January 30, 1972; married December 7, 1991 to James Stewart Reed
        (2) Amy Christina Ballard, born August 23, 1974
    b. Jeff Allen Newell, born April 28, 1955
    c. Cheryl Lee Newell, born December 14, 1958
3. Carolyn Ann Newell, born July 17, 1932, and married June 24, 1951 to Richard Rowell Paddock, born July 5, 1929. Divorced January 12, 1974, after four children:
    a. Richard Rowell Paddock, Jr., born December 30, 1954 and married April 22, 1978 to Becky Lynn Meek. Three children:
        (1) Lindsay Ann Paddock, born October 31, 1981
        (2) William Jacob Paddock, born April 9, 1986
        (3) Emily Marie Paddock, born May 20, 1991
    b. Sandra Lea Paddock, born December 28, 1956
    c. Julie Ann Paddock, born March 31, 1958 and married November 1, 1976 to Dean Beaudet. Two children:
        (1) Kelley Ann Beaudet, born December 2, 1977
        (2) Amy Beaudet, born November 12, 1981
    d. Catherine Louise Paddock, born September 29, 1960 and married June 6, 1979 to Scott E. Steward

Howard Raymond Newkirk
1899-1968

This son of William Leonard Newkirk (1858) was born December 16, 1899 and died November 7, 1968 at Inglewood, California. Married in 1925 to Erma Irene Mills, born September 22, 1907. They had two children:
1. Richard James Newkirk, born November 6, 1926; married to Dorothy Louise Searing, born November 18, 1930. They had four children:

a. Marjorie Alicia Newkirk, born November 12, 1952; married June 13, 1981 Richard Gonzales, born November 6, 1941. Three children:
   (1) Lisa Louise Gonzales; December 18, 1981
   (2) Matthew Jason Gonzales; March 3, 1986
   (3) Joseph Earl Gonzales; November 11, 1989
b. Richard Brent Newkirk, born February 20, 1954; married Mary Ruth Winchester, born July 24, 1954. Children:
   (1) Jennifer Elizabeth Newkirk; November 5, 1976
   (2) Catherine Ann Newkirk; March 13, 1979
c. Dan Christopher Newkirk, born October 9, 1955 and married January 28, 1978 to Charlotte Picker, born May 12, 1958. Two children:
   (1) Daniel Aaron Newkirk; April 30, 1981
   (2) Charlotte Grace Newkirk; June 29, 1983
d. Laura Christine Newkirk, born October 22, 1961
2. Veral Anne Newkirk, born May 2, 1934; died February 17, 1992. Married twice: first Donn Thomas Mire, born January 23, 1934; and second to Gordon Patrick Curtis, by whom she had two children:
a. Mike Allen Curtis, born January 6, 1966
b. Steven Patrick Curtis, born March, 1969

Richard Newkirk, Jr.
1784-1831

This individual is believed to be a son of Richard Newkirk (1760). He was born c.1784 in Kentucky and died c.1831 in Lawrence County, Indiana. He was perhaps married twice; first on May 26, 1807 in Kentucky to Elizabeth Martin, and second to Ruth Inscoll, who was born c.1796 in Kentucky and died February 12, 1864. Like other members of the family, he lived for a time in Kentucky, and apparently moved on to Indiana. He had children:
1. Enoch Boone Newkirk, born 1813 in Indiana and died January 7, 1838 in Huron County, Ohio. Married October 2, 1834 in Lawrence County, Indiana, to Mary B. Roarback, who was born January 29, 1820 in Orange County, Indiana, and died August 26, 1905 in Huron County. At least one son:

a. Enoch Dexter Newkirk, born 1838; died 1904
2. Elizabeth Newkirk, born c.1817 in Indiana, and died after May, 1866. Married February 11, 1841 to James M. Williams in Washington County, Indiana.
3. Cyrus M. Newkirk, born c.1819 in Indiana; married October 6, 1842 in Washington County, Indiana, Margaret A. Venard, born 1820. The 1850 census of the county includes the family, with three children, born in Indiana:
   a. Martha A. Newkirk, born c.1845
   b. Enoch Newkirk, born c.1847
   c. Elijah Newkirk, born c.1849
4. Elijah Newkirk, born about 1823 in Indiana, and died between 1860 and 1870 in Missouri, probably in Dent County. Married in 1840 to Elizabeth, born c.1824 in Alabama. The 1850 census of Texas County, Missouri includes the family, with four of their children, out of at least seven:
   a. Nicholas C. Newkirk, born 1842 Texas County, Missouri
   b. John C. Newkirk, born 1844 in Texas County
   c. Elizabeth Newkirk, born 1846 in Texas County
   d. Rutha Catherine Newkirk, born Texas County, Missouri, May 7, 1850, and married about 1864 to James Jones Williamson in Phelps County, Missouri. In late 1991 I received a letter from Norma Musgrove Craig of Ada, Oklahoma, who is a descendant of these two
   e. William Newkirk, born 1852 in Dent County, Missouri
   f. Enoch Boone Newkirk, born 1854 in Dent County
   g. Thomas N. Newkirk, born 1856 in Dent County

William Newkirk
1758-1840

This son of Peter Newkirk (1727) was born c.1758 in Virginia, probably in Berkeley County, and died c.1840 in Bullitt County, Kentucky. Married there October 31, 1797 to Rebecca Hall, born 1779 in Virginia and died after 1850. His will, dated September 13, 1840, was probated in Bullitt County November 9, 1840. It seems likely that there could have been other children born between the first two listed here, but the family included at least the following:

1. Elizabeth Newkirk, born c.1798; married November 23, 1815 to Samuel C. Gentry in Bullitt County, Kentucky.
2. John H. Newkirk, born c.1807 and married in Bullitt County June 20, 1833 to Frances Harris, born 1809. They appear in the 1850 census of Jefferson County, Kentucky, with John listed as a carpenter, and his wife listed as Fanny. There are three children, all born in Kentucky:
   a. Elizabeth Newkirk, born c.1836
   b. William Newkirk, born c.1839
   c. Simeon Newkirk, born c.1841
3. Louisa Hall Newkirk, born c.1809 in Kentucky
4. Asa H. Newkirk, born 1811 in Kentucky and married three times in Bullitt County: first December 14, 1837 to America Ridgeway, born c.1819 in Kentucky. Married second on October 27, 1859 (or 1860) to Catherine Smith; and third September 24, 1878 to Catherine Settle. He appears in the 1850 census of the county with his first wife, and five children, all born in Kentucky (there were perhaps others born after that census):
   a. John Q. Newkirk, born c.1838
   b. Charles L. Newkirk, born c.1840
   c. R. F. Newkirk, a daughter, born c.1843
   d. Julia A. Newkirk, born c.1845
   e. William J. Newkirk, born c.1847
5. Mary Ann Newkirk, born c.1817; married November 10, 1837 to Austin Hough
6. Charles C. Newkirk, born c.1820 in Kentucky
7. Clifton H. Newkirk, born c.1823 in Kentucky. The 1850 census of Bullitt County included a household headed by Clifton, as a farmer. In the household are: his brother Charles C.; his sister Louisa; and his mother Rebecca at age 71.

Isaac Newkirk
1762-1828

This son of Peter Newkirk (1727) was born c.1762 in Virginia, and died before June 30, 1828 in Lawrence County, Indiana. Married June 18, 1799 in Bullitt County, Kentucky, to Elizabeth Hall, born 1780 and died 1846 in Indiana. Probably all of his children were born in Bullitt County; all but Lewis are buried in Dixon Cemetery in Lawrence County, Indiana:

1. Cornelia Newkirk, born February 28, 1800, and died September 24, 1842 in Indiana. Married May 30, 1816 in Bullitt County, Kentucky, to Jacob Hoopingarner, born c.1795 and died December 18, 1857
2. Abigail Newkirk, born March 1, 1800 (perhaps a delayed twin of Cornelia?); died July 19, 1874. Married Cyrus Briskell
3. John Newkirk, born December 7, 1803; died March 3, 1869. He was married April 24, 1823 to Mary S. Proctor, born in Kentucky, January 23, 1806, and died February 16, 1886 in Indiana. The family appears in the census of 1850 for Lawrence County, Indiana, with six children, born there. It seems more than likely that there were other children, born between the date of marriage; 1823; and the oldest child listed in the census; 1830; who may have been in their own household by 1850. The Mormon IGI index for Lawrence County, Indiana, provides additional information on a number of children, and their families, as well:
   a. James M. Newkirk, born April 15, 1825
   b. Angeline Newkirk, born April 5, 1827
   c. Martha A. Newkirk, born February 27, 1831
   d. George Rappeon Newkirk, born June 25, 1833; married August 31, 1856 to Sarah Jane Proctor, born c.1839. They had several children according to the Mormon IGI index, born in Lawrence County, including:
      (1) Nickson R. Newkirk, born c.1853 or perhaps 1858
      (2) Romeo Newkirk, born c.1859
      (3) Sarah Newkirk, born c.1865
      (4) William Henry Newkirk, born c.1867

(5) Stella Newkirk, born September 12, 1873 at Bedford

    e. Amanda Newkirk, born October 14, 1835

    f. Lucy H. Newkirk, born March 11, 1839; probably married October 9, 1857 in Lawrence County, Indiana, to James McCormick.

    g. William H. Newkirk, born January 1, 1842

    h. Lemuel C. Newkirk, born September 25, 1848; married c.1876 Tabitha, born c.1861, and had children, including:

        (1) William S. Newkirk, born c.1877

        (2) Charles Newkirk, born c.1879

4. Sarah Newkirk, born February 3, 1805 and died January 14, 1889. Married December 20, 1820 Jackson County, Indiana, to Thomas Dixon

5. Lewis Newkirk, born April 8, 1808, and died February 6, 1875. He was married twice: first January 9, 1832 to Elizabeth Critchlow, born December, 1802 in Kentucky, and died September 10, 1852. Married second to Julia A. Powell, who died May 30, 1895. He appears in the 1850 census of Jackson County, Indiana, with his first wife, and four children, all born in Indiana. Once again, there were possibly other children of this family:

    a. Amilda Newkirk, born c.1833

    b. William L. Newkirk, born c.1835. At least one son:

        (1) James Riley Newkirk, born c.1873 and the ancestor of Ada L. Krig of Omaha, Nebraska

    c. John W. Newkirk, born c.1840

    d. Cassilda Newkirk, born c.1842

6. Enoch Boone Newkirk, born December 19, 1809; died September 17, 1873. Married three times: first August 12, 1830 in Washington County, Indiana, to Margaret Brock, born March 2, 1811 and died December 11, 1844. Second on May 31, 1845 in Jackson County, Indiana, Alice Tender; and third Leanah Houston Day, born November 14, 1814 in Tennessee, and died August 17, 1893. Enoch perhaps lived for a time in Owen County, Kentucky; the IGI records of the Mormon church list his marriage there May 30, 1846 to Alice Tender, rather than as shown above. The 1850 census of Jackson

County includes the family, with the third wife and five children, all born in Indiana. Other children are found in the IGI records of the Mormon Church. It is possible there were more children born before the census and in their own household; or born after the census. At least some of the children appear to have been:

a. Clifton Newkirk, born c.1834
b. Margaret Newkirk, born c.1835
c. Mary A. Newkirk, born c.1840
d. Jane Newkirk, born c.1841
e. Marilla Newkirk, born c.1843
f. Catherine R. Newkirk, born February 17, 1851 Lawrence County
g. Eveline Newkirk, born c.1855
h. McCardle Newkirk, born c.1861

7. Elizabeth Newkirk, born June 24, 1812; died December 17, 1889. Married June 5, 1830 to James H. McKeaigg

8. William Newkirk, born c.1815 in Kentucky. Perhaps the same William in 1850 census of Lawrence County, Indiana, with Elizabeth, born c.1816 in Kentucky; and six children, all born in Indiana:

a. Margaret Newkirk, born c.1838
b. Josephine E. Newkirk, born c.1840
c. Jane R. Newkirk, born c.1843
d. Napoleon B. Newkirk, born c.1847
e. Mary M. Newkirk, perhaps a twin, born c.1848
f. Martha Newkirk, perhaps a twin, born c.1848

9. Isaac Newkirk, born c.1822, and died February 29, 1892 in Lawrence County, Indiana. Married April 23, 1845 to Elizabeth Jane Milligan, born 1821 and died September 26, 1878. The 1850 census of Lawrence County includes the family, with one Carolina Roberts living with them, at age 40, born c.1810 in Indiana; and Margaret Roberts at age 14, born c.1836 in Indiana; neither otherwise identified. The elder female could be a widowed sister of Isaac's wife, with a child. There is one child listed under the Newkirk name; two others are found in the Mormon IGI records:

a. Mary E. Newkirk, born c.1848 in Indiana

b.   Louisa C. Newkirk, born c.1853 in Lawrence County, Indiana

c.   Gilbert Newkirk, born November 18, 1857

Peter Newkirk, II
1765-1833

This son of Peter Newkirk (1727) was born c.1765 in Orange County, Virginia, and died December 6, 1833 in Jefferson County, Kentucky. Married January 2, 1792 to Mary Stafford, who died c.1849 in Bullitt County, Kentucky. Peter wrote a will, dated December 4, 1833, which was entered for record in Bullitt County, Kentucky on February 3, 1834. His wife, a daughter of Thomas Stafford, wrote a will dated October 2, 1848, entered for record May 9, 1849 in Bullitt County, Kentucky. They had at least ten children, born in Jefferson County, Kentucky:

1.   Cassandra Newkirk, born c.1793; married September 24, 1813 to Samuel Applegate.
2.   William Newkirk, born c.1796; married September 12, 1816 Sarah Applegate, born c.1795 in Kentucky. Probably the same William appearing in the 1850 census of Floyd County, Indiana, a carpenter, with wife, Sarah, and two children:
     a.   Jefsu H. Newkirk, born c.1828 in Kentucky; an engineer
     b.   Mary Ellen Newkirk, born c.1834 in Indiana
3.   Thomas Stafford Newkirk, born c.1798; died before 1852 in Jefferson County, Indiana; no children.
4.   Mary Newkirk, born c.1800; married June 25, 1820 Levy Asher. She is second great grandmother of Rachel Bryson, in 1983 living at Bertram, Texas
5.   Pearson Newkirk, born c.1802; died before 1852, Jefferson County, with no children.
6.   Linea Newkirk, born 1804; married March 24, 1824 Robert Scott. At least one daughter:
     a.   Martha Ann Scott.
7.   Elizabeth Newkirk, born c.1805; married June 4, 1829 John Kelly. At least one daughter:
     a.   Frankie Kelly.

8. Enoch Boone Newkirk, born c.1806; married November 27, 1831 to Frances Kelly, born c.1805 in Virginia. Listed in 1850 census of Jackson County, Kentucky, as a carpenter, with four children, born in Kentucky, the last four listed. They must have had an earlier daughter, named in her grandmother's will:
    a. Martha Ann Newkirk, married to Young.
    b. Handish Newkirk, a son, born c.1838
    c. Frances Newkirk, born c.1842
    d. Boone Newkirk, born c.1845
    e. Albert Newkirk, born c.1850
9. Keziah Newkirk, born c.1813; married March 11, 1834 to Jonathan Brentlinger. A daughter, named in her grandmother's will:
    a. Susannah Brentlinger.
10. Jemima Newkirk, born 1814; married December 18, 1834 Henry Bates. At least a daughter, named in her grandmother's will:
    a. Mary Katherine Bates.

Teunis Newkirk
1768-1843

This son of Peter Newkirk (1727) was born April 30, 1768 in Virginia, and died November 5, 1843 in Moniteau County, Missouri. Married April 24, 1794 in Jefferson County, Kentucky to Catharine Drake. License Number 39654, issued in Jefferson County on July 22, 1793, authorized the wedding, performed by Reverend John Whitaker several months later. She was born November 13, 1775 in Virginia, and died November 30, 1855 in Montgomery County, Missouri. By deed dated February 26, 1835, recorded in Howard County, Missouri, in Book V, page 941, Teunis acquired a tract of 160 acres from Samuel M. Hughes and his wife Nancy E. Hughes. There is a second deed dated November 5, 1844, recorded in Howard County, Missouri, in which every child of this couple, with their respective spouse, convey 160 acres on the Missouri River to Harrison S. Elliott for the sum of one thousand, six hundred dollars, which is presumably the family property after the death of their father. The family bible, containing names and dates of birth of family members was printed and published by M. Carey and Son, Philadelphia, in 1818. They had a number of children, the first one born in Jefferson County, Kentucky, and the rest in Bullit County, Kentucky:

1. Charles Newkirk, born February 5, 1795; died November 21, 1852 in Morgan County, Missouri. Married first May 15, 1818 (or 1828) in Bullitt County, Kentucky, to Camilla Wells; divorced July 5, 1832. Married second in Morgan County, May 30, 1839 to Dicie Bowen. She was born January 1, 1815 in Virginia and died December 3, 1858 in Morgan County, Missouri. He appears in the 1850 census of the county, with his wife and four children, born in Missouri:
    a. James Newkirk, born c.1841
    b. Malissa Newkirk, born c.1842
    c. William Newkirk, born c.1844
    d. Charles Newkirk, Jr., born c.1846

2. Jemima Newkirk, born March 3, 1797; died January 26, 1846 in Morgan County, Missouri. Married May 5, 1816 in Bullitt County, Kentucky, to Thomas Bowen, born 1786 in Oneida, New York, and died March 1, 1836 in Indiana

3. Elizabeth Newkirk, born August 3, 1799; died October 17, 1870 in Howard County, Missouri. Married May 4, 1817 in Bullitt County, Kentucky, Hugh Stewart, born December 11, 1784 in Pennsylvania; died July 11, 1853 in Howard County

4. Drake Newkirk, born April 4, 1802; died February 10, 1872 in Moniteau County, Missouri, as did the rest of these children. Married first November 8, 1827 in Bullitt County, Kentucky, to Mrs. Sarah Shockency (or Sarah Sousley), born July 20, 1801 in Kentucky, and died February 3, 1861. Married second September 19, 1865 in Morgan County, Missouri, Delila Maddle. He may be the same Drake Newkirk who was married October 28, 1880 in Moniteau County to Matilda S. Smith, perhaps a third marriage. The 1850 census of the county includes the family, with his first wife, and six children, the first born in Kentucky, and the rest born in Missouri. Perhaps other children as well:
    a. Jefferson Newkirk, born c.1829

b. Margaret C. Newkirk, born January 24, 1832; died July 16, 1839
c. Francis Newkirk, born c.1834
d. Mary Newkirk, born c.1835
e. Rosean Newkirk, born c.1838
f. David Newkirk, born c.1840
g. Emeline Newkirk, born 1844. Perhaps the same Emeline S. Newkirk who was married on September 19, 1867 to Benjamin B. Walter in Moniteau County, Missouri.
h. Jesse D. Newkirk, perhaps. The Mormon IGI records include the birth of this individual in Moniteau County, Missouri, on November 2, 1885, with parents listed as E. D. Newkirk and Matilda Newkirk, which could be Drake Newkirk and the possible third wife mentioned above.

5. Peter Newkirk, born September 28, 1805; died April 27, 1864 and buried in the Newkirk cemetery in Moniteau County, as are most of his brothers and sisters. Married February 12, 1835 in Bullitt County, Kentucky, Mary Brown, born March 22, 1813 and died October 2, 1877. The Moniteau County 1850 census includes Peter, with six children, first two born in Kentucky; last four in Missouri. There were perhaps others:
   a. Charles Newkirk, born c.1837
   b. Hugh Newkirk, born c.1839
   c. Tobias Newkirk, born c.1841
   d. Louisa Newkirk, born c.1844
   e. Malissa Newkirk, born c.1846
   f. Alonso Newkirk, born c.1848. This may more properly be Alonzo P. Newkirk, who married Cordelia A. Hughes February 18, 1869 in Morgan County, Missouri.

6. Sarah Cordelia A. Hughes, born November 15, 1808; died June 14, 1862. Married September 22, 1838 in Morgan County, Missouri, to John McPherson, born January 21, 1824 and died April 13, 1862

7. David Seaton Cordelia A. Hughes, born December 20, 1811; died April 2, 1877. Married first January 12, 1841 in Morgan County, Missouri, Mary McPherson, born January 21, 1824 and died April 13, 1862. Married second October 27, 1864 in Morgan County to Isabella J. Sousley, born March 8, 1824

and died December 27, 1882. David and his first wife appear in the 1850 census of Moniteau County, Missouri, with three children. Also in the household is Catharine Newkirk (1775) at the age of 74, his mother, and Thomas Newkirk at age 21, born c.1829 in Kentucky, not identified. Three children listed in the census; others are found in the Mormon IGI records, born in Moniteau County, Missouri, unless otherwise noted:

a. Thomas Benton Newkirk, born January 19, 1842 in Morgan County, Missouri. Perhaps the same who was married there December 23, 1879 to Alice Dorman.

b. Malinda Katherine Newkirk, born November 14, 1843

c. Charles Drake Newkirk, born August 28, 1845. This may be the same Charles D. Newkirk who was married in Moniteau County, December 26, 1867 to Docia Howard.

d. Sarah Elizabeth Newkirk, born March 20, 1847.

e. Rose Ann Newkirk, born April 27, 1849. Perhaps the same who was married in Moniteau County, December 1, 1870 to Benjamin F. Hays.

f. Dicey Jane Newkirk, born September 24, 1851. Perhaps the same who was married February 17, 1876 in the county to George L. Short.

g. Joseph Harrison Newkirk, born October 11, 1853.

8. Harrison R. Newkirk, born February 6, 1814; died January 23, 1884. Married December 24, 1840 in Cooper County, Missouri to Margaret Jane Renshaw, born c.1813 in Kentucky, and died November 27, 1886. The 1850 census of Moniteau County, Missouri include the family with three children, born in Missouri. There may have been others:

a. Absalom Newkirk, born c.1842

b. Mary Newkirk, born c.1846

c. Millard Newkirk, born c.1848

9. Rosean Newkirk, or Rose Ann, born November 4, 1820; died May 26, 1846. Married November 1, 1841 William G. Howard, born April 16, 1816 in Monroe County, Kentucky, and died July 15, 1892.

CHAPTER 9

Arien Gerritsen Nieuwkirk
1663-

This son of Gerrit Cornelisse Van Nieuwkircke (1631) and his wife Chieltje Cornelissen Slecht, was born c.1663 at Midwout, Flatbush, Long Island, New York. Married after October 17, 1686 to Lysbeth Lambertse Brink. She was baptized February 14, 1666, a daughter of Lambert Huybertse Brink and Hendricke Cornelisse Brink of Wageningen, Gelderland, Holland. The will of Lambert Huybertse, dated February 12, 1695/96 is excerpted in *Ulster County, New York Probate Records*, Volume 1, page 60, by Gustave Anjou. His family is named there, including the spouses of his various children, and the division of his estate. It is also stated there that he assumed the surname Brink, probably after arrival in America. He leaves one fifth to various family members, including his son-in-law Arien Gerritsen, with the provision that his portion be laid off next to Arien's own property. Arien lived for a time in Hurley, Ulster County, New York, and later at Saugerties. He was a Justice of the Peace in 1699, and the Judge of Ulster County Probate Court before 1725. They had eight children, all baptized at Kingston, Ulster County, New York:

1. Ghilje Nieuwkirk, baptized January 29, 1688
2. Jan Nieuwkirk, or Johannis Nieuwkirk, baptized August 24, 1690 at Kingston. Married May 18, 1719 at the First Dutch Reformed Church at Albany, to Dorothea Douw, who was baptized there March 23, 1701; the daughter of Kendrick and Neeltye Myndertse Douw of Hurley, Ulster County, New York. They had six children, all baptized at Kingston:
    a. Adrian Nieuwkirk, baptized November 12, 1720, of whom more
    b. Hendricus Nieuwkirk.
    c. Elizabeth Nieuwkirk, baptized March 24, 1723. Married October 4, 1741 (or September 5) to Peter Van Bergen, born 1721.

    d.   Gerret Nieuwkirk, baptized December 20, 1724. Married Elizabeth Van Bergen and had children. Served in Captain William McGinnis' Company, Ulster County, Militia, 1755

    e.   Meyndert Nieuwkirk, baptized April 17, 1726

    f.   Neeltje Nieuwkirk, baptized April 7, 1728

3. Hendrikje Nieuwkirk, baptized November 11, 1692. Married December 14, 1711 to Cornelius Wynkoop, baptized June 4, 1688, son of Johannes Wynkoop and his first wife, Judith Bloodgood. The will of Cornelius is found in Liber 16, page 322, will records of Ulster County, New York. It was dated September 19, 1739 (written in Dutch). The will is rather interesting: he states that: *I have given to my son Johannes a gun, my other three sons shall therefore also have an ordinary gun each, before the division of the estate, and a sword or cutlass; my son Cornelis shall have the gun on which my name is engraved, but as it may not be in good condition, it shall first be cleaned and put in proper order.* They had eleven children.

    a.   Judike Wyncoop, baptized August 31, 1712. Married December 11, 1736 Johannes Du Bois, who was baptized November 10, 1710.

    b.   Elizabeth Wyncoop, baptized January 9, 1715. Married December 15, 1739 to Philippus Dumond, baptized September 28, 1707, son of Walran Dumond and Catrina Ter Bosch Dumond. Eight children.

    c.   Cornelia Wyncoop, baptized March 17, 1717. Married July 4, 1741 to Jan Van Dusen, Jr. Four children.

    d.   Johannes Wyncoop, baptized August 15, 1719.

    e.   Catrina Wyncoop, baptized February 18, 1722. Married June 20, 1747 Lucas Elmendorf, baptized May 4, 1718, the son of Coenradt Elmendorf and Blandina Kierstede Elmendorf. No children.

    f.   Lea Wyncoop, baptized May 31, 1724; an infant death.

    g.   Adriaan Wyncoop, baptized August 21, 1726. Married October 25, 1754 to Catharine Louw. No children.

    h.   Lea Wyncoop, second use of the name, baptized January 7, 1728.

i. Cornelius C. Wyncoop, baptized November 5, 1732. Married April 24, 1760 Maria Catherine Ruhl, daughter of Gustav M. Ruhl. Cornelius practiced law in New York City, and had nine children, the first seven baptized there.

j. Petrus Wyncoop, baptized December 22, 1734. Married Janneke Hardenbergh. Three children, born Ulster County

k. Maria Wyncoop, baptized December 22, 1734.

4. Gerret Nieuwkirk, baptized baptized 1697, of whom more.

5. Ariaantje Nieuwkirk, born November 19, 1699, and died after July 8, 1776. Married December 1, 1722 Jacobus Elmendorf, baptized June 3, 1694 and died between 1776 and 1792. He was a son of Coenrad Elmendorf and Ariantje Gerritse Van den Berg. The will of Jacobus is found in Liber A, page 357, filed in the Surrogate's Office, City of Kingston. It is dated July 8, 1776 and entered for record November 3, 1792. He names his wife, his children, and several grandchildren, who are to share in the estate. Reportedly, there were nine children:

a. Elizabeth Elmendorf, baptized May 26, 1723; died before 1776 when her father wrote his will. Married May 9, 1746 to Johannes Slecht, baptized October 18, 1719, son of Jan and Elizabeth Smedes Slecht. They had children, who were mentioned in their grandfather's will:

(1) Arreantje Slecht, baptized April 16, 1740

(2) Elizabeth Slecht, married Oke Sudam

(3) Jan Slecht, or Johannes, baptized January 13, 1752

(4) Margaret Slecht, baptized September 8, 1752

b. Arriantje Elmendorf, baptized December 6, 1724, and married December 14, 1751 to Abraham Slecht, baptized May 24, 1724, brother of Johannes, above. Patricia Burgoon Wiggins, a descendant of this family, has furnished family data on several generations of descendants, which is not included here. In 1995, she lived at Palm Bay, Florida. Children, born in Ulster County, New York:

(1) Jacobus Slecht, born April 19, 1753, of whom more

(2) Abraham Slecht, born July 17, 1755; married May 16, 1782 to Mary Roe.

(3) Arriantje Slecht, baptized October 16, 1757

    (4)   Jan Slecht, baptized June 1, 1760

    (5)   Elizabeth Slecht, baptized August 15, 1762

    (6)   Petrus Slecht, born October 14, 1764.

    (7)   Margaret Slecht, born c.1768.

c.   Coenradt Jacobus Elmendorf, baptized November 27, 1726. Married November 17 1759 to Catrina Hardenbergh, baptized September 7, 1729, daughter of Gerardus Hardenbergh and Janneke Elmendorf. Three children:

    (1)   Coenrad Edmundus Elmendorf, baptized October 5, 1763

    (2)   Jacobus C. Elmendorf, baptized April 13, 1772

    (3)   Antje Elmendorf, baptized April 30, 1775

d.   Ariaan Gerritse Elmendorf, baptized December 29, 1728. In his will, Jacobus Elmendorf left to his son Coenradt J. (above) 560 pounds, in trust, for Ariaan, with the observation *"whose course of Life is at present deplorable!"* The will provided that the legacy was for the support of Ariaan, who died single, after July 8, 1776.

e.   Margaret Elmendorf, baptized at Kingston c.1732; married March 9, 1760 to Egbert Du Mont, son of John Du Mont and Rachel Schoonmaker. He practiced law at Kingston, and they had no children.

f.   Gerrit Elmendorf, baptized May 5, 1734

g.   Jacobus Elmendorf, baptized July 18, 1736 and died after January 11, 1795. Married October 2, 1770 Elizabeth Sammons and had ten children:

    (1)   Jacobus Elmendorf, baptized February 18, 1771; died young

    (2)   Elizabeth Elmendorf, baptized August 1, 1772

    (3)   Jacobus Elmendorf, baptized November 22, 1774

    (4)   Arriantje Elmendorf, baptized January 5, 1777

    (5)   Cornelius Elmendorf, baptized December 2, 1778; died young

    (6)   Maria Elmendorf, baptized March 5, 1780; died young

    (7)   Carlintje Elmendorf, baptized April 6, 1783

    (8)   Sarah Elmendorf, baptized November 6, 1785

    (9)   Cornelius Elmendorf, baptized April 8, 1787

(10)   Maria Elmendorf, baptized January 11, 1795
h.   Cornelius J. Elmendorf, baptized December 17, 1738 and died after November 13, 1792.
i.   Petrus Elmendorf, baptized February 18, 1742, and died before July 8, 1776.
6.   Lea Newkirk, baptized August 9, 1702; married December 9, 1720 to Jacob Rutsen, Jr., son of Jacob Rutsen and Marretjen Hansen Rutsen. There were five children:
a.   Marretjen Rutsen, baptized September 9, 1722, who married her first cousin, Adrian Newkirk (1720), son of her mother's brother, Jan Newkirk (1690). They had a large family, treated under the section devoted to her husband, which see.
b.   Elizabeth Rutsen, baptized November 15, 1724, and married to Abraham Roosa, who died at Shawangunk in 1788. They had six children:
(1)   Aldert Roosa, baptized April 7, 1745
(2)   Leah Roosa, baptized April 12, 1747
(3)   Jacob Roosa, baptized December 31, 1749
(4)   Isaac Roosa, baptized April 21, 1751
(5)   Rebecca Roosa, baptized March 18, 1755
(6)   Sarah Roosa, baptized January 22, 1757
c.   Catherine Rutsen, baptized September 3, 1729. Note the conflict between this date of birth and that of Sarah, following. It is as reported by Dr. Adamson Bentley Newkirk in his study of the families; it appears Catherine was probably born a year or so earlier.
d.   Sarah Rutsen (or Zara), baptized September 21, 1729. Married January 20, 1756 (his second wife), to Nathaniel Cantine of Marbletown, baptized October 25, 1724, son of Peter Cantine and Elizabeth Blanshan Cantine. Sarah died before May 20, 1765, when Nathaniel married third Dorothy Newkirk, baptized October 27, 1745, daughter of Adrian Newkirk (1720) and Marretjen Rutsen Newkirk (1722). Sarah had two children, born at Marbletown:
(1)   Leah Cantine, baptized May 15, 1758
(2)   Elizabeth Cantine, born April 20, 1762

7. Rachel Newkirk, baptized April 9, 1704; married Jan Cornelius Bogart, baptized March 30, 1702 at Hackensack, New Jersey, the son of Cornelius Bogart and Willemtje van Voorhees Bogart. Seven children, the first and the last four baptized at Hackensack:

   a. Cornelius Bogart, baptized August 1, 1736; married to Sietsye Demarest and lived in Bergen County, New Jersey. They had twelve children.
   b. Willemtje Bogart, baptized April 15, 1739 at Schaarlenburgh. Married Jacobus Peek, a son of Jacob Peek and Sarah Demarest Peek. Lived in Bergen County; eight children.
   c. Jacob Bogart, baptized November 8, 1741; died young
   d. Sarah Bogart, baptized June 3, 1744. Married Isaac Roos. Lived in Bergen County and had two children.
   e. Antjen Bogart, baptized December 26, 1746
   f. Jacob Bogart, baptized November 8, 1741. Married Margriette, lived in Bergen County and had three children.
   g. Rachel Bogart, baptized September 2, 1753, and married Jacob Dumont. Lived in Bergen County and had two children.

8. Cornelius Newkirk, baptized 1710, of whom more

Jacobus Slecht
1753-1833

This son of Abraham Slecht (1724) and Arriantje Elmendorf Slecht (1724) was born April 19, 1753 and died September 2, 1833 at La Grange, Dutchess County, New York. Married February 28, 1799 at Fishkill to Elsie De Reimer, born May 3, 1777 at Albany; died June 30, 1841 at La Grange, daughter of Petrus De Reimer, III and Elsie Babbington De Reimer. The name has been found spelled various ways, as were most of the early Dutch names in the family; as Sleight, Slecht, Sleigh and other variations. Slecht appears to be the more commonly found form, and will be used here. Jacob had children, born at La Grange, Dutchess County, New York:

1. Elsie De Reimer Slecht, born October 23, 1800; died January 15, 1883. Married October 28, 1818 Abraham B. Stockholm.
2. James Edwin Slecht, born 1803; died December 23, 1825.
3. Peter Roosevelt Slecht, born July 29, 1804; died March 15, 1888. Married October 3, 1827 to Sarah Keese Barnes, born January 1, 1810 at Poughkeepsie, New York; died October 20, 1829 at La Grange, daughter of David Barnes and Nancy Ann Thorn Barnes. Peter was Captain of a company of Militia, Assessor and Commissioner of Highways when the town was bonded. At the time of his death, he was President of the Dutchess County Mutual Insurance Co., and for several years had been a director of the First National Bank. He was married second December 18, 1832 to Cathrine Storm Barnes. He had at least one son, born to the first marriage:
   a. James Edwin Slecht, born September 20, 1829 at Poughkeepsie, New York; died March 16, 1868 at Titusville, New York. Married there March 9, 1853 to Frances Hoag Titus, born September 17, 1833 at Titusville, New York; died there January 24, 1887, daughter of Elias Titus and Mary Annette Hoag Titus. Children, born at Titusville:
      (1) Mary Kate Slecht, born January 5, 1852; died April 27, 1941/43. Married June 15, 1881 Eugene Ham.
      (2) Rhoda Slecht, born January 19, 1857, of whom more.
      (3) Sarah Slecht, born 1858 married Augustus Angell.
      (4) Frances Slecht, born 1864; married November 20, 1892 at Dutchess County, New York, to Henry Follett Winchester.
4. Harriet Elmendorf Slecht, born June 6, 1807; died March 18, 1886. Married December 22, 1825 to Ricketson Gidley.
5. Henry Augustus Slecht, born November 17, 1817; died March 17, 1879. Married October 23, 1847 to Mary A. Ward.

Rhoda Slecht
1857-1923

This daughter of James Edwin Slecht (1829) and Frances Hoag Titus Slecht (1833) was born January 19, 1857 at Titusville, Dutchess County, New York, and died there December 16, 1923. Married November 3, 1885 to John Milton Ham, born April 14, 1861 in Dutchess County; died June 21, 1935, son of Milton Conrad Ham and Phoebe Ferris Ham. John Milton served as a Commissioner of his town for several years; as Clerk of the County; and for eight years, as postmaster of Millbrook, New York. They had five children, born at Washington Hollow, Dutchess County, New York:

1. Mildred Ham, born July 19, 1886; died February 5, 1964. Before her marriage, she was a school teacher, holding several positions of importance. Married June 30, 1925 to Herman Jordan Richardson, born May 6, 1888 at Amherst, Hancock County, Maine; died September 16, 1962 at Arcadia, Florida, son of Charles Samuel Richardson and Ida Mae Philbrick Richardson. He had been married July 19, 1909 to Viola Henrietta Bell, and divorced. In 1935, he moved to Florida, finally settling in the North Ft. Myers area, where, over the years, he and his wife established the River's Edge Trailer Park. Two children, born at Boston, Massachusetts:

   a. Rhoda Richardson, born October 31, 1927; died December 18, 1990 at Melbourne, Florida. Married May 18, 1945 at Montgomery, Alabama to Ranaldo Orla Burgoon, born February 21, 1918 at Midland, Michigan, son of Franklin Wayne Burgoon and Cora Edith Bunts Gantz Burgoon. They had four children:

      (1) Patricia Jean Burgoon, born February 19, 1946 at Ft. Myers, Florida, my correspondent for this family. Married June 10, 1980 Daniel Richard Wiggins.

      (2) Kathleen Ann Burgoon, born December 28, 1948 at Ladd Air Force Base, Fairbanks, Alaska. Married December 16, 1967 at Manti, Sanpede County, Utah, to Robert Keith Berger.

     (3)   John Michael Burgoon, born July 2, 1951 at Eglin Air Force Base, Okalossa, Florida. Married May 12, 1977 at Kensington, Montgomery County, Maryland, to Nicki Burnett.

     (4)   Shannon Burgoon, born November 26, 1963 at Patrick Air Force Base, Brevard, Florida; married March 29, 1986 at Palm Bay, Florida, Eugene Gary Terkoski.

   b.   John Jordan Richardson, born February 21, 1932, and married July 21, 1958 at Ft. Myers, Florida, to Elizabeth Ann Applewhite.

2.   Milton Conrad Ham, born March 10, 1891; died August 5, 1950

3.   John Fredrick Ham, born June 29, 1896, and died March 30, 1957. Married March 10, 1926 Bernice M. Benham.

4.   Alice Titus Ham, born March 27, 1899; died September 16, 1955

Gerret Nieuwkirk
1697-

This son of Arien Gerritsen Nieuwkirk (1663) was baptized May 30, 1697 at Kingston. Married October 19, 1718, at Albany, to Anna Vischer, who was baptized September 6, 1696; daughter of Johannes and Elizabeth Nottingham Vischer. Seven children, all baptized at Kingston:

1.   Elizabeth Nieuwkirk, baptized November 1, 1719. Married October 31, 1738 to Isaac Wimple, baptized August 28, 1715, son of Johannes and Ariantje Swits Wimple. Four children:

   a.   Arriantje Wimple, born 1740

   b.   Catalina Wimple, born 1742

   c.   Annatje Wimple, baptized March 27, 1747

   d.   Johannes Wimple, born May, 1749

2.   Ary Nieuwkirk, baptized August 6, 1721

3.   Johannes Nieuwkirk, baptized January 12, 1724, and died January 15, 1793. His will, dated January 15, 1793, was probated in Montgomery County, New York several years later. DAR Patriot Index reports him as a Major during the Revolu-

tion, listing him there as John. Married January 9, 1759 to Rachel Clute, and had six children, born in Schenectady, New York:

   a. Garret L. Nieuwkirk, baptized February 4, 1760, of whom more
   b. Tanneke Nieuwkirk, baptized May 4, 1762
   c. William Nieuwkirk, baptized February 3, 1765
   d. John Nieuwkirk, baptized September 10, 1767. May be the same John Newkirk, Jr., born 1762; died August 2, 1839, and married to Nellie Collier.
   e. Arie Gerritsen Nieuwkirk, baptized June 12, 1773
   f. Annatje Nieuwkirk, baptized August 10, 1776
4. Anna Nieuwkirk, baptized January 23, 1726; died after 1755
5. Gerret Cornelius Nieuwkirk, baptized January 12, 1729, of whom more
6. Jacob Nieuwkirk, baptized September 10, 1732 (or 1723); died 1790; and married Peterje Phillips (or Pieterje Philipse). Reported in DAR Patriot Index as sergeant during the Revolution from Pennsylvania. Two daughters, born Schenectady, New York:
   a. Annatje Nieuwkirk, baptized August 23, 1763
   b. Sarah Nieuwkirk, baptized October 25, 1765
7. William Nieuwkirk, baptized October 12, 1735

Garret L. Nieuwkirk
1760-1819

This son of Johannes Nieuwkirk (1724) was born February 4, 1760; died December 24, 1819. The March, 1988 issue of *Newkirk Notes* carried an article purportedly about this individual, reporting Garret C. Newkirk as a son of Johannes Newkirk (1724) and his wife, Rachel Clute Newkirk. According to other records, they did, in fact, have a son named Garret, but his middle initial was "L" rather than "C." Note following the report of the family of Gerret C. Newkirk, born January, 1760, but a son of Gerret Cornelius Nieuwkirk (1729), with whom the records have probably become confused. We believe, however, that the Garret C. Newkirk referenced in that report was actually this individual. If we are here dealing with the proper individual, his middle initial was "L" rather than "C" and he married Maria Vedder. Served as a Lieutenant during the Revolution. They had children:

1. Matheus Nieuwkirk, perhaps, baptized August 11, 1782 at Kingston, Ulster County, New York.
2. Catherine Nieuwkirk, who was baptized December 29, 1782 in Montgomery, New York.
3. Rachel Nieuwkirk, who was christened December 29, 1782 at Montgomery.
4. Albert Nieuwkirk, born 1790 in Montgomery, New York and perhaps the same Albert shown in Mormon IGI records as married there October 7, 1820 to Nancy Rouwlen.
5. Nancy Nieuwkirk, born 1793 in Montgomery, New York.
6. Neeltje Nieuwkirk, born November 21, 1794 at Montgomery.
7. Johannes Nieuwkirk, born January 18, 1797 at Montgomery.
8. Francis Van DeBogart Nieuwkirk, born July 14, 1799 and married October 12, 1822 in Fonda, Montgomery County, New York, to Elizabeth Seaman Vedder, born September 1, 1801. They had at least four children:
   a. Garret Cornelius Nieuwkirk, born at Ashford, in Cattaraugus County, New York, May 3, 1826; ancestor of Barbara Shehan, correspondent to *Newkirk Notes*. The family appears in the 1850 census of the county, with his wife, Jane, born c.1828, and the first three of their children, born in New York:
      (1) Venila Nieuwkirk, born c.1847
      (2) Mary Nieuwkirk, born c.1849
      (3) John Nieuwkirk, born c.1850
   b. Albert Nieuwkirk, born c.1828. Apparently listed in the 1850 census of Cattaraugus County as a farmer. In the household is Maria, born c.1833, probably his sister; and William Newkirk, born c.1834, not identified as yet.
   c. Maria Ann Nieuwkirk, born c.1833
   d. Eva Allen Nieuwkirk
9. Maria Nieuwkirk, born February 2, 1802 at Montgomery, New York.

Gerret Cornelius Nieuwkirk
1729-1821

This son of Gerret Nieuwkirk (1697) and Anna Vischer (1696) was baptized January 12, 1729, and died before January 7, 1822, when his will, dated July 6, 1808, was probated in Montgomery County, New York, where he is buried. Married to Nellie Quackenbos, and lived for a time in Schenectady, New York, and later in Montgomery County. Private during Revolution. They had seven children, all born or baptized in Schenectady:

1. Gerret Cornelius Nieuwkirk, Junior, born January 22, 1760, and died at Florida, New York, November 12, 1839. There are several documents found in Revolutionary Pension Records for New York, number W24339, which appear to pertain to this individual. Within that file, there is a letter dated January 17, 1929, signed by Winfield Scott, Commissioner, which states that Garrett Newkirk, son of Garret C. Newkirk, was born c.1760 in Florida, Montgomery County, New York. He enlisted there in 1777 and served as private at various times in Captain William Snook's company, Colonel Frederick Fisher's New York Regiment, serving until 1782, amounting in all to one year, five months and nine days. His records do not indicate that he participated in any battles; he was stationed for three tours of duty at Fort Fisher, Lacondago, New York; a log fort which he helped to build. He also was part of the mission which marched, or boated, up the Mohawk River, for between seventy and eighty miles, with cattle and supplies for the garrison at Fort Stanwix. In his petition for pension, he also stated that while on the way to Fort Putnam, he was captured by two Indians and detained with them for two days, until he made his escape during the night, and returned to the fort. He was allowed pension dated September 17, 1832, while living at Florida, New York. Married June 2, 1787 at Caughnawaga, Tryon County, New York, to Rachel Gardinier, born c.1763. As his widow, she was allowed pension August 31, 1840, while living at Glen, Montgomery County, New York, aged seventy-seven years. Other papers in the file contain interesting information relative to Garret's service.

2. Abraham Nieuwkirk, baptized October 31, 1762; died March 25, 1830 at the age of 67 years, 5 months and 15 days. Married Maria Garritson, born c.1769; died April 17, 1835 at the age of 65 years and 8 months. Served as a private during the Revolution. Buried on the Rees farm at Montgomery, New York.

3. William C. Nieuwkirk; perhaps the same William Newkirk who appears in the pension records of his brother discussed above. If so, he was born January 25, 1765, and married January 2, 1788; wife's name not reported. Mormon IGI records report several children born to William C. Newkirk and Mary Milot or Millatt, all born at Fonda, Montgomery County, New York, and christened in the Protestant Dutch Church of Caughnawaga. That individual could well be this William C., who was the father of several children, his only son being named Gerret Cornelius, perhaps for his father. The children were:

   a. Neeltje Nieuwkirk, born December 2, 1796
   b. Annetje Nieuwkirk, baptized 1799
   c. Maryte Nieuwkirk, or Marigreta, baptized 1803
   d. Rachel Nieuwkirk, baptized 1805
   e. Gerret Cornelius Nieuwkirk, baptized 1807. Could this be the same person listed as Garret Newkirk in the 1850 census of Florida, Montgomery County, New York, there said to be 44 years old (born c.1806)? If so, he has a wife, Mary A., born c.1814 in New York, as were their four children:
      (1) Agenet Nieuwkirk, born c.1834
      (2) Catherine Nieuwkirk, born c.1839
      (3) Jacob Nieuwkirk, born c.1841
      (4) Anna Nieuwkirk, born c.1844
   f. Hannah Nieuwkirk, baptized 1811

4. Johannes Nieuwkirk, baptized October 17, 1767
5. Cornelius Nieuwkirk, born 1769
6. John Nieuwkirk, baptized July 2, 1772
7. Maria Nieuwkirk, baptized December 18, 1775

Cornelius Nieuwkirk
1710-1788

This son of Arien Gerritsen Nieuwkirk (1663) was baptized November 12, 1710 at Kingston, in Ulster County, New York; died February, 1788. Married October 29, 1731 to Dina Hoogteeling, baptized May 7, 1710 and died September 15, 1787; daughter of Philip and Jennette Roosa Hoogteeling. Cornelius was a trooper under Captain Johannes Ten Broeke, Ulster County Militia, in 1738. He lived at Hurley in Ulster County, where he made his will, dated September 15, 1787. The will is printed on page 16, of the March, 1984 issue of *Newkirk Notes*, by Gil and Mary Alford, and makes for interesting reading, even though heavily in the original Dutch. Children, all born at Kingston, included:

1. Elizabeth Nieuwkirk, baptized October 1, 1732; died single
2. Jannetjen Nieuwkirk, baptized October 20, 1734; married November 18, 1759 to Benjamin Roosa of Hurley and had children:
    a. Elizabeth Roosa, baptized November 9, 1760
    b. Leah Roosa, baptized December 25, 1765
3. Arie Nieuwkirk, baptized September 11, 1737; an infant death
4. Philip Nieuwkirk, or Philippus, baptized April 3, 1740 at Kingston, New York, and died some time after executing his will on July 29, 1793. Married Jannetje Roosa October 30, 1773, who was baptized August 17, 1746, a daughter of Heyman and Jannetje Frear Roosa. They had children, all born at Hurley, in Ulster County, New York:
    a. Jannetjen Nieuwkirk, baptized March 23, 1775; died young
    b. Dina Nieuwkirk, baptized June 30, 1776; died young
    c. Cornelius P. Nieuwkirk, baptized February 1, 1778 and married January 5, 1800 Ballie (or Maria) Roggen. At least two children, born at Kingston, in New York:
        (1) Peter Nieuwkirk, born September 29, 1800
        (2) Jane Ann Nieuwkirk, baptized June 20, 1801
    d. Mareitje Nieuwkirk (Maria), baptized October 5, 1781; died young
    e. Elizabeth Nieuwkirk, baptized June 10, 1787

5. Arie Nieuwkirk, a second use of the name after the earlier infant death, baptized October 3, 1742 in Kingston. Died before September 15, 1787. Married November 18, 1768/69 Maria Crispell, daughter of Peter and Lea Roosa Crispell, baptized February 24, 1751. Two children, born at Hurley, Ulster County:
    a. Cornelius Nieuwkirk, baptized June 1, 1771; died young
    b. Petrus Nieuwkirk, baptized August 13, 1775
6. Leah Nieuwkirk, baptized April 29, 1744, and married December 8, 1764 to Garret C. Newkirk (1739), son of Cornelius Newkirk (1715) and Neeltjen DuBois Newkirk (1716). They had five children, described in the section devoted to his family.
7. Hendricka Nieuwkirk, baptized March 9, 1746, and married October 30, 1785 to Cornelius Dumont
8. Ariantje Nieuwkirk, baptized January 8, 1748 and died August 25, 1805. Married December 23, 1779 to Petrus DuBois, born March 28, 1749 and died April 2, 1830, son of Johannes DuBois and Judike Wynkoop DuBois. Four children; all died single:
    a. Judike DuBois, born March 18, 1784; died August 1, 1845
    b. Petrus DuBois, baptized October 1, 1786
    c. Dina DuBois, born February 2, 1789
    d. John P. DuBois, born December 4, 1791; died July 21, 1854
9. Cornelius C. Nieuwkirk, baptized October 15, 1752, of whom more.

Cornelius C. Nieuwkirk
1752-1832

This son of Cornelius Nieuwkirk (1710) was baptized October 15, 1752 at Kingston, in Ulster County, New York, and died June 22, 1832, leaving a will dated just four days earlier. Revolutionary War Pension Records, S.14006, New York, report that he served in the company commanded by Captain Moses Contine in the Newark Line as Lieutenant of infantry for five months, and as a Lieutenant of cavalry for nineteen months. He was granted a pension of four hundred dollars and nineteen cents per year, commencing March 4, 1834; two years after his death. The papers contain the date of his death, and the names of his wife and several of his children and grandchildren. Some records indicate that he was commissioned Cornet of Kingston Company of Horse; Lieutenant on June 16, 1778; and Captain on October 23, 1779. He was married January 12, 1779/80 to Sarah Kierstede, baptized September 2, 1759 and died April 29, 1818, the daughter of Christoffel and Catharine deMeier Kierstede. He had five children:

1. Cornelius C. Nieuwkirk, Jr., clearly styled in that manner in the pension papers of his father; baptized November 26, 1780 in Ulster County, New York, and died there October 20, 1867. Married December 6, 1802 Magdalena Hardenberg, born August, 1782 at Ulster and died November 3, 1815. Married second September 5, 1828 in Dutchess County, New York, to Eleanor Wynkoop, who died between 1843 and 1850, and was the widow of his son, Christopher (1805). The Marriage Register contains the entry: "*Since the solemnization of the immediately above marriage, I have discovered it to be contrary to the word of God. He having married the widow of his son. I was deceived by the representations of the parties and I have entered my solemn protest.*" Children, six from the first marriage, and five from the second, all born in New York:
   a. Jacobus H. Nieuwkirk, born 1804, and died January 10, 1828. Married to Catryntje Elting
   b. Christopher Nieuwkirk, born c.1805; died January 10, 1828. Married Eleanor Wynkoop who, after his death, was married second to his father (above). Mormon IGI records report his christening on December 4, 1782, which may be more nearly correct.
   c. Catherine H. Nieuwkirk, born April 16, 1808. Married June 25, 1829 to Peter C. LeFevre, born November 16, 1805 in Ulster County and died 1891 in Queens
   d. Sarah Nieuwkirk, born 1810; died March 13, 1841
   e. Cornelius C. Nieuwkirk, III, born January 1, 1813 in Marbletown, Ulster County, New York, and moved to Michigan in the late 1830s, and died March 28, 1902 in

Sturgis (or at White Pigeon), Michigan, and of whom
more following

f. Bogardus Nieuwkirk, born March 27, 1815; married
    January 12, 1842 Catherine Newkirk, born January 30,
    1823, daughter of Benjamin Garrett Newkirk (1800)
g. Elizabeth Nieuwkirk, born 1829
h. Jane Nieuwkirk, born 1834; married James Perrine, and
    second to Charles L. Strong
i. Mary Nieuwkirk, born 1837, and married January 30,
    1856 to John Gillespie
j. John L. Nieuwkirk, born 1839; married April 23, 1861 to
    Sarah H. LeFevre
k. Henry Nieuwkirk, born 1839; single

2. Christopher Nieuwkirk, or perhaps Christoffel Nieuwkirk,
   born November 24, 1782. Married to Cornelia W. Ten Eyck,
   born c.1792; died June 15, 1859 at Saugerties, New York.
3. William Nieuwkirk, baptized August 3, 1788, and died June
   18, 1832
4. Philip Nieuwkirk, born January 4, 1791; married Phebe B.,
   born 1800. The 1850 Ulster County census includes two
   children:
   a. Edgar B. Nieuwkirk, born c.1829
   b. Catherine E. Nieuwkirk, born c.1832
5. Catharine Nieuwkirk, born November 24, 1793; died before
   June 18, 1832, when her father wrote his will, and named her
   husband and children. Married Ten Eyck DeWitt. Children:
   a. John DeWitt
   b. Newkirk DeWitt
   c. Matthew Paulding DeWitt
   d. Sarah Catharine DeWitt.

Cornelius C. Newkirk, III
1813-1902

This son of Cornelius C. Newkirk, Jr. (1780), was born
January 1, 1811 (or 1813, according to his obituary) in Marbletown, Ulster County, New York, and moved to Michigan in the late
1830's. Between 1841 and about 1845/46, he lived for a time on a

farm he had purchased near LaPorte, Indiana, returning to Michigan, where he died March 28, 1902 at White Pigeon. Married first at Marbletown to Mary Davis, born 1814 in New York, and died 1856; having had three sons and four daughters. Two sons and the eldest daughter predeceased their father. Married second in 1864 to Jane C. Shears, of Kingston, Ulster County, New York, born 1824 and died 1905. They apparently had no children. The known children included:

1. Mary Newkirk, born c.1842 in Indiana, according to the 1850 census of St. Joseph County, Michigan. Perhaps died young, and was the eldest daughter mentioned in her father's obituary as being deceased.

2. Emma Catherine Newkirk, born in October, 1843 at LaPorte, Indiana; died May 15, 1923 at Richmond, Virginia, and buried at White Pigeon, Michigan. The 1850 census of St. Joseph County, Michigan, carries only two children in the household; Mary, mentioned above, and a girl reported as "Unice," but questioned as to its accuracy, born c.1844 in Michigan. We can not explain the absence in the census of at least two more of the children, born prior to 1850. Could it be that "Unice" was in reality Emma? That being the case, we would then have the proper number of children for the family. However, the census states the place of birth as Michigan for this child, when the time frame would dictate Indiana. Married in White Pigeon to James Newell Sheap, born October 19, 1837 at Columbia, Montour County, Pennsylvania; died July 6, 1921 at Sturgis, Michigan, where he is buried. He was a son of Joseph Sheap and Jane McKinney Laird Sheap, and he and Emma Catherine were divorced, having had one child:
   a. Cornelius Newkirk Sheap, born November 20, 1874, of whom more.

3. Mary Louisa Newkirk, born c.1846 at White Pigeon, Michigan, and died c.1930 at Richmond, Virginia. Known as Mamie, or Aunt Mame, she never married.

4. Cornelius C. Newkirk, Jr., born c.1849 at White Pigeon. Known as Teely or Teelie, his father's obituary states he was "in unknown parts of the west." He appeared in the 1870

census of Michigan, but not thereafter. Family tradition relates that he was not contacted again after going west.

5. Sarah C. Newkirk, born April 24, 1853 at White Pigeon, Michigan, and died there March 22, 1937. Married 1875 to Fred C. Beisel, born April 13, 1852 and died April 11, 1943, at White Pigeon. The 1860 census lists his middle initial as C, but his tombstone lists it as G. Her obituary states that they moved to Chicago immediately after marriage, and stayed there for several years, before returning to White Pigeon about 1922. Her father's obituary indicates that they were then living at LaCrosse, Wisconsin, and had four sons and two daughters:

    a. Anne Beisel, born 1878; died 1921; single.

    b. Jane B. Beisel, born 1880; died 1965. Married J. H. Badger; buried in family plot at White Pigeon, Michigan.

    c. Fred Cornelius Beisel, died September 24, 1940. His tombstone at White Pigeon, Michigan, states he was a Lieutenant Commander in the Navy; his mother's obituary places him at Green Bay, Wisconsin.

    d. Harold Beisel, reportedly lived in Berkley, California.

    e. Sarah Margaret Beisel, born 1882; died 1971. Single.

    f. Florence Beisel, born 1884; a registered nurse, and died November 17, 1972 at White Pigeon, Michigan, single.

6. A son, predeceased his father.

7. A son, predeceased his father.

Cornelius Newkirk Sheap
1874-1947

This son of Emma Catherine Newkirk (1843) and James Newell Sheap (1837), was born November 20, 1874 at White Pigeon, Michigan, and died June 27, 1947 at Richmond, Virginia, where he is buried. Married January 16, 1906 at Minot, North Dakota, to Helen Beatty Scott, born March 21, 1883 at Nepean, Ontario, Canada, and died May 14, 1984 at Richmond, Virginia, where she is buried with her husband. Her birth certificate lists her first name as Ellen, and she was also known as Nellie or Nell. She was the daughter of John Scott and Evangeline Mary Ann Wilson Scott. They had one son:

1. Donald Scott Sheap, born December 27, 1908 at Minot, North Dakota, died November 12, 1986 at Harrisonburg, Virginia; buried at Richmond. Married June 5, 1929 Washington, D. C., to Rose Marie (Emma?) Snow, born August 14, 1910 at Dobson, Surry County, North Carolina, daughter of James Byrd Snow and Emma Irene Jones. The family Bible of the Snow family records the birth of Rose Emma (which uses the given name of her mother), and two of her sisters confirm that was her original name. At some point in her life, she adopted Rose Marie as her two given names. Two children:
    a. Donald Cornelius Sheap, born October 31, 1930 at Sandston, Virginia. Married March 2, 1957 at Richmond, Virginia, to Kathryn Lee Crosby, born October 1, 1929, and had children, born at Richmond:
        (1) Townley Scott Sheap, born June 10, 1960
        (2) Susan Elizabeth Sheap, a twin, born July 29, 1963
        (3) Courtney Lytell Sheap, a twin, born July 29, 1963
    b. Christopher Newkirk Sheap, born April 14, 1945 at Richmond, Virginia, a physician, and my correspondent for this family group. Married August 2, 1969 at Ft. Belvoir, Virginia, Norma Jean McNair, born September 13, 1947 Corpus Christi, Texas, daughter of William Donald McNair and Jean Eleanor Davis. They had five children, the first born at Charlottesville, Virginia; the second at Heidelberg, Germany; and the last three at Harrisonburg, Virginia:
        (1) Stephanie Marie Sheap, born May 17, 1973; married April 29, 1995 at Harrisonburg, Virginia, George Andrew Fox, Jr., born January 29, 1970 at Richmond, Virginia.
        (2) Anne Christine Sheap, born January 24, 1977.
        (3) Jennifer Lynn Sheap, born May 2, 1979
        (4) Christopher Scott Sheap, born January 28, 1981
        (5) Kathleen McNair Sheap, born April 16, 1984

Adrian Newkirk
1720-

This son of Jan Newkirk (1690) and Dorothea Douw Newkirk (1701), was baptized June 12, 1720 at Kingston, Ulster County, New York. Married twice; first on November 7, 1741 to his first cousin, Marretjen Rutsen, baptized September 9, 1722, a daughter of Jacob Rutsen, Jr., and Lea Nieuwkirk Rutsen (1702). Adrian was married second October 27, 1765 to Tryntje Louw, baptized April 2, 1727. She was the widow of Philip Bevier, and the daughter of Petrus Matthew Louw and Catherine DuBois Louw. Nine children were born to the first marriage, and four to the second, all apparently at Kingston, Ulster County, New York:

1. Lea Newkirk, baptized January 23, 1743; married November 16, 1768 to Zachariah Hoffman
2. Henricus Newkirk, baptized July 29, 1744
3. Dorothea Newkirk, baptized October 27, 1745; married July 24, 1769 to Nathaniel Contine (his third wife), born October 1, 1724 and died c.1818
4. Elizabeth Newkirk baptized December 13, 1747, married John Dewy
5. Jacob Rutsen Newkirk, baptized April 1, 1750; married June 18, 1778 to Annatje Person, who was born December 15, 1748 and died February 23, 1837. There was a Jacob Newkirk commissioned March 23, 1778 as a Lieutenant Colonel, Second of South End Regiment, Ulster County, under Colonel James Clinton, which may have been this Jacob. Children, born in New York:
   a. John Person Newkirk, born April 30, 1780 and died February 17, 1855. Married November 28, 1802 Catherine Salisbury
   b. Deborah Newkirk, born December 5, 1784; died March 26, 1788
   c. Catharina Newkirk, born June 21, 1790; died April 8, 1881. She was married August 14, 1814 to Abraham A. Salisbury
6. Meyndert Newkirk, baptized September 2, 1753

7. Jan Newkirk, baptized January 1, 1755 (IGI records list a daughter, Maria, with this same date of christening; they do not list Jan)
8. Catharine Newkirk, baptized January 25, 1761
9. Johannes Newkirk, baptized July 1, 1764
10. Elias Newkirk, baptized September 14, 1766, a twin. Married July 23, 1791 at Rochester, New York, to Jennetye Cortrecht (or Jane Kortright), born November, 1770 and died June 6, 1835. Children, all born in Ulster County, New York:
    a. Marie Newkirk, who was baptized November 14, 1796 at Shawangunk
    b. Stephen Newkirk, born c.1796, according to census, and baptized January 27, 1799 at Rochester. Married in 1839 to Mary, born c.1810 in Virginia. They appear in the 1850 census of Mercer County, Virginia, (later West Virginia) with three children, all born in Virginia:
        (1) Samuel Newkirk, born c.1840
        (2) John Newkirk, born c.1842
        (3) William Newkirk, born c.1845
    c. Jacob Verner Newkirk, who was baptized May 30, 1803 at Rochester
    d. Adrientje Newkirk, baptized October 30, 1805 (or December 22, 1805; Mormon IGI records), at Rochester, Ulster County
11. Philip Newkirk, baptized September 14, 1766, a twin
12. Gerrit Newkirk, baptized November 13, 1768. Descendants were said to be living in Missouri and Illinois in 1870. Married July 7, 1796 to Annatje Burhans. He is possibly the same Gerrit A. Newkirk, whose 1812 will mentions a wife, Anna, and several children. The middle initial could be for Adrian, his father, and one of the children could have been named Tryntje for her grandmother. The children, all born in Ulster County, New York, born between about 1797 and 1805 or so, were:
    a. Gerrit Newkirk
    b. Pierpoint Newkirk
    c. Edward Newkirk
    d. Burhans Newkirk

e. Anne Newkirk
f. Maria Newkirk
g. Catherine Newkirk
h. Tryntje Bridget Newkirk

13. Daniel Newkirk, baptized May 10, 1772; almost surely the same Daniel Newkirk "from Shawangunk" who was married December 7, 1795 at Rochester, New York, to Elizabeth Mulks and had children. Mormon IGI records report their marriage as December 26, 1793. The 1850 census of La Porte County, Indiana, lists one Elizabeth Newkirk as head of household at age 74, born c.1776 in New York, which could be his widow. There are three girls in the household, the last three listed below. The family may have included all of the following, as reported in *Newkirk Notes* and in other sources:

a. Caterina Newkirk, baptized May 29, 1796 at Marbletown
b. Susanna Newkirk, baptized March 4, 1798 at Marbletown
c. Benoni Newkirk, baptized May 10, 1800 at Marbletown
d. Benoni Newkirk, a second use of the name, baptized August 30, 1802 at Rochester, New York. Probably the same Benoni in the 1850 census of La Porte County, Indiana, with a wife, Jane B., born c.1816; two children, born in Indiana:
   (1) Elizabeth Newkirk, born c.1842
   (2) James C. Newkirk, born c.1850
e. Catherine Newkirk, born c.1804 in New York
f. Sarah Newkirk, born c.1811 in New York
g. Caroline Newkirk, born c.1822 in New York

CHAPTER 10

Matheus Cornelisse Van Nieuwkirk, Jr.
1647-1705

This son of Mattheuw Cornelisse Van Nieuwkirk (1600) was born about 1647 at Slichtenhorst, Gelderland, Holland. When he was about twelve years old, he traveled to America with his brother Gerret Cornelisse (1635) aboard the Dutch vessel, *Moesman*, arriving in New York on April 25, 1659. He lived in Bergen, New Jersey, where he died May 12, 1705. He was married twice; first on December 14, 1670 at the Bergen Reformed Church, to Anna Lubi, the daughter of Jacob Lubi and Geertruyt Leons Lubi. She died in Bergen December 20, 1685, after having five children. Mattheuw married second August 15, 1686 to Catryna Paulus at Bergen. An entry in the Holland Society's Marriage Record states: *1686: Matheus Cornelison Van Newkirk, widower of Anna Lubi, born in Schlechtenhorst in Gelderland, and Catreyna Poulus, Y. D., from Bergen, New Jersey, both living at Bergen, married August 15 at Bergen by the Voorleezer R. Van Giesen in presence of the Court at Bergen in the Church.* She survived her husband, and her will dated September 30, 1731 was not probated until May 7, 1764. There were eight children born to the second marriage, and only they were mentioned in their mother's will. It appears that Mattheuw adopted the surname Cornelison, and his descendants are thereafter often known by that name. It should be pointed out here that Van, or Von, found in many Germanic surnames, simply means "of", as in Mattheuse Cornelissen Van Nieuwkercke, meaning Matthew Cornelison of Newkirk. Later generations of families with such names often dropped the latter part, anglicizing their names in America. The children of Mattheus, from both his marriages, all born at Bergen, New Jersey, were:

1. Geertruyt Van Nieuwkirk, born September 18, 1671; married Peter Lambertse Brink. He was a son of Lambert Huybertse Brink and Hendricke Cornelisse Brink, and was baptized June 26, 1670 at Kingston, Ulster County, New York. Ten children.

2. Geeretje Van Nieuwkirk, baptized June 23, 1673; married July 6, 1695 at New York to Aelt Juriaensen. He was a son of Juriaen Thomassen Van Ripen and Reyckje Harmens Coerten. They had a child:
    a. Annetje Juriaensen, baptized at Bergen May 1, 1696
3. Jacomyntje Van Nieuwkirk, baptized April 2, 1678. Married April 20, 1701 to Jacob Symonsen Van Winkle. He was born August 9, 1678 at Bergen, a son of Symon Jacobs Van Winkle and Annetje Ariaense Van Winkle. Three children, born Bergen County:
    a. Waling Van Winkle.
    b. Jacob Van Winkle
    c. Simeon Van Winkle; married Geertruydt Van der Houex and had thirteen children, born in Bergen County:
        (1) Annatje Van Winkle, born March 16, 1729
        (2) Sarah Van Winkle, born August 29, 1731
        (3) Johannes Van Winkle, born December 6, 1733
        (4) Michael Van Winkle, born April 6, 1736
        (5) Simeon Van Winkle, Jr.
        (6) Eleanor Van Winkle
        (7) Catharine Van Winkle, baptized June 17, 1739
        (8) Marianus Van Winkle, baptized June 5, 1741
        (9) Charity Van Winkle
        (10) Geertruydt Van Winkle
        (11) Johannes Van Winkle, baptized November 7, 1749
        (12) Benjamin Van Winkle, born December 6, 1756
        (13) Hannah Van Winkle
4. Cornelis Van Nieuwkirk, born March 11, 1680; died June 7, 1691
5. Jacob Matthuesen Van Nieuwkirk, born November 21, 1682. Married April 27, 1707 to Sara Cornelis of North Haarlem. Two children:
    a. Antje Van Nieuwkirk, baptized February 29, 1708 in Hackensack, New Jersey, and married May 30, 1747 to Johannes Bikelo
    b. Jacomyntje Van Nieuwkirk, born c.1710, and married May 30, 1747 to Abraham Van Winkle, son of Johannes and Helena Spier Van Winkle. They had children:

      (1)   Geertruyt Van Winkle, born February 15, 1747
      (2)   Jacob Van Winkle, born January 9, 1750
      (3)   Simeon Van Winkle, born December 22, 1755
      (4)   Helena Van Winkle, born February 28, 1758

6. Jannetye Van Nieuwkirk, born July 8, 1687; died May 5, 1691
7. Tryntje Van Nieuwkirk, baptized December 17, 1688; died February 16, 1689
8. Jan Van Nieuwkirk, born April 20, 1690. One account states that he died January 17, 1691.
9. Jannetje Van Nieuwkirk, born May 17, 1691; married April 21, 1733 Garret Diedricks, or Gerrit Didericks. He was born September 17, 1695, son of Wander Didericks and Aaltje Gerrits Didericks. They had a daughter:

a. Aaltje Diedericks, born June 6, 1736 at Schraalenburgh, New Jersey and married December 7, 1752 to Jacob Brinkerhoff. Five children, born in Bergen County:

    (1)   Jannette Brinkerhoff, born November 15, 1753 and died young
    (2)   Jannette Brinkerhoff, born January 1, 1755
    (3)   Hendrick Brinkerhoff, born August 17, 1756
    (4)   Gerrit Brinkerhoff, born April 4, 1762
    (5)   Elizabeth Brinkerhoff, born June 23, 1765

10. Pieter Van Nieuwkirk, born August 26, 1694. Married June 12, 1726 to Tryntje Dirckje, and had one child:

a. Tryntje Van Nieuwkirk, also shown in IGI records as Fytie, baptized June 16, 1732 at Belleville, New Jersey, and married to Jacob Garrabrant. One child:

    (1)   Maritie Garrabrant, who was baptized at Second River Church, July 11, 1756.

11. Gerret Van Nieuwkirk, born November 18, 1696 and of whom more
12. Paulus Van Nieuwkirk, born August 20, 1699, of whom more
13. Cornelis Van Nieuwkirk, born September 13, 1703 and died September 10, 1781. Married October 18, 1749 to Lea Maris, widow of Abraham Cammega Schraalenburg. She died March 17, 1757. They had no children.

Gerret Newkirk
1696-1785

Son of Mattheus Cornelisse Van Nieuwkirk, Jr. (1647), and his second wife, Catryna Paulus Nieuwkirk, Gerret was born November 18, 1696 at Bergen, New Jersey, and died there April 23, 1785. Married September 5, 1730 to Catrintje Kuyper, born at Ahasemus, and died September 14, 1751, daughter of Hendrick Kuyper of Bergen County. Four children, all born at Bergen:

1. Catharina Newkirk, born August 9, 1731 and died September 17, 1759. Named in the will of her grandfather Hendrick Kuyper, dated September 16, 1754
2. Matthew Newkirk, born March 3, 1734 and died July 10, 1811. Married c.1765 in Hudson County, New Jersey to Catlyntje Toers, born September 30, 1739, daughter of Arent and Annatje Spier Toers. DAR Patriot Index reports him as Lieutenant from New Jersey during the Revolution. Three children:
   a. Gerret M. Newkirk, born April 9, 1766, of whom more.
   b. Aaron Newkirk, or Arent Newkirk, born October 22, 1768 and died April 1, 1849. Married Jennetje Vreeland and had children, all born in New Jersey, probably Bergen County:
      (1) Catlyntje Newkirk, born November 6, 1792. Married on November 7, 1813 to Cornelius Van Ripen
      (2) Cornelia Newkirk, born October 2, 1794; died March 30, 1870. Married January 23, 1813 Daniel Vreeland
      (3) Matteus Newkirk, born May 22, 1799 and died November 10, 1799
      (4) Catharine Newkirk, born May 15, 1807. Married November 28, 1822 in Bergen County, New Jersey Cornelius M. Vreeland and moved to Lisbon, Illinois, where she died January 10, 1892, and he died July 17, 1877. They had eight children.
   c. Hendrick Newkirk, born June 22, 1771; died single

2. Jannette Newkirk or Jannetje, born May 5, 1737; died October 4, 1779.

3. Hendrick Newkirk, born April 4, 1741 in Bergen County, New Jersey, and died July 8, 1795. Married September 10, 1779 to Janneke Vreeland, who was born December 1, 1758, and after the death of her husband, married second May 26, 1798 to Joseph Van Winkle. Hendrick had three children, all born in Bergen County, New Jersey:

   a. Gerret H. Newkirk, born January 8, 1781; died October 21, 1860

   b. George Newkirk, born November 23, 1783 and died August 19, 1861. Married February 9, 1805 to Sarah Van Derhoff, a daughter of Garret (or George) Van Derhoff. She was born August 8, 1782 and died September 1, 1861. They appear in the 1850 census of Hudson County, New Jersey (formerly Bergen County), with their youngest son, George. Six children, all born in Bergen County:

      (1) Jane Newkirk, born December 6, 1805; died April 19, 1806

      (2) Henry G. Newkirk, born December 19, 1808. Married to Sarah Van Buskirk November 7, 1838. Children, all born in New Jersey:

         (a) Sarah Catharine Newkirk, born November 7, 1835 and married on December 24, 1855 to Cornelius Van Pelt

         (b) Arabella Newkirk, born November 23, 1843

         (c) John V. B. Newkirk, born April 11, 1848

         (d) George Newkirk, born May 30, 1851

         (e) John Henry Newkirk, born February 3, 1860

         (f) Eliza Jane Newkirk, born February 3, 1860

      (3) Garret G. Newkirk, born September 28, 1812, and died February 26, 1872. Married November 15, 1840 to Jane Van Ripen and had at least one son:

         (a) George Newkirk, born September 16, 1844 in New Jersey and married Catharine Seebach

      (4) Jane Maria Newkirk, born February 17, 1816, and married January 24, 1841 to David Burbank

(5)   Abraham P. Newkirk, born December 21, 1819. Married on September 11, 1844 to Maria Tallman. Listed in the 1850 census for Hudson County, New Jersey, with one of their sons. Also in the household is one Nancy Tallman, born c.1835 in New York; and Sarah E. DuBois, born c.1830 in New York. There were at least two children:

      (a)   George W. Newkirk, born April 29, 1847 in New York

      (b)   Eugene T. Newkirk, born March 17, 1858 in New Jersey and died October 23, 1868

(6)   George Newkirk, born May 8, 1826; married December 23, 1854 to Gertrude Vreeland. At least one son, born in New Jersey:

      (a)   Nicholas V. Newkirk, born November 23, 1857

c.   Catryntje Newkirk, born September 7, 1791; died July 25, 1848. Married August 16, 1812 to Hartman Van Wagenen, and had four children.

Gerret M. Newkirk
1766-1832

This son of Matthew Newkirk (1734) was born April 9, 1766 and died August 28, 1832. He was married to Polly Achermann, or Ackerman, and had children, born in New Jersey:

1.   Catharine Newkirk, born October 10, 1788; married June 17, 1809 in Hudson County, New Jersey, to George Vreeland

2.   Margaret Newkirk, born May 22, 1790; married November 10, 1811 to Garret Sip

3.   Sally Newkirk, born June 25, 1793; died December 9, 1794

4.   Sally Newkirk, second use of the name, born December 18, 1796; died August 15, 1797

5.   Henry Newkirk, born December 16, 1799; died July 29, 1861. Married July 24, 1818 to Eliza Provost, born September 9, 1800, died October 8, 1858. The family appears in the 1850 census of Hudson County, New Jersey, with four of their nine children, all born in New Jersey:

a. James M. Newkirk, born June 27, 1819; married May 27, 1840 to Sarah Jane Vreeland, born c.1819. They appear together in the 1850 census of Hudson County, New Jersey, with no children. Living with them is a couple, born in New York: John Franks, born c.1822, and a bookkeeper, and Anna Franks, born c.1829, presumably his wife.

b. Henry H. Newkirk, born March 22, 1823; married first Margaret Smith, born October 11, 1823 and died July 13, 1861. Married second March 22, 1871 to Anne M. Vermilye. Henry and Margaret appear in the 1850 census for Hudson County, New Jersey, with two small children, and one Sarah M. Newkirk, born c.1838, not otherwise identified. The children were:

    (1)   Eliza Jane Newkirk, born c.1846

    (2)   Phebe E. Newkirk, born c.1848

c. Mary Newkirk, born April 17, 1826; died January 12, 1858. Married February 5, 1846 to George V. DeMott

d. Garret Newkirk, born July 23, 1828, and married on September 20, 1848 to Catherine Ryerson. They are apparently the couple appearing in the 1850 census of the county, where he is listed as a teamster, with one son:

    (1)   James Ari Newkirk, born c.1849

e. John Newkirk, born November 10, 1830; listed in the census as a book-keeper. Married October 4, 1854 to Antje Boice

f. Eliza Newkirk, born October 10, 1832; married December 20, 1860 to Francis P. Gautier

g. Cornelius Newkirk, born May 20, 1835 and died October 16, 1838

h. George V. Newkirk, born December 1, 1838, and died February 12, 1859

i. Emma Matilda Newkirk, born c.1849; married May 27, 1868 to William H. Bronson

6. Gerret G. Newkirk, born October 17, 1808, and married October 25, 1828 to Rachel Van Houten, who died December 1, 1835, daughter of Halmigh Van Houten. Married second to Jane Fowler, widow of Abram Tice, who died October 6,

1849; and third on September 6, 1851 to Eliza Ann Beatty, born 1820, daughter of George E. Beatty. He appears in the 1850 census of Hudson County, New Jersey, at which time he was a widower. Also in the household was Cornelius A. Vreeland, a merchant, born c.1828; and Mary A. Vreeland, born 1831, one of Gerret's daughters, living at home with her young husband. Gerret had two children by his first marriage, ten by the second, five by the third, all born in New Jersey:

a. Catherine Newkirk, born February 11, 1829, and died January 22, 1830

b. Mary A. Newkirk, born September 1, 1831; married September 19, 1849 Cornelius A. Vreeland born c.1831

c. Catherine Elizabeth Newkirk, born June 30, 1838, and married February 3, 1856 Reuben Giberson

d. Rachel V. H. Newkirk, born September 9, 1839; married to George L. Darress

e. Gilbert F. Newkirk, born February 27, 1841, and died October 21, 1841

f. Henry Cornelius Newkirk, born February 27, 1841; died October 4, 1842

g. George V. Newkirk, born April 1, 1842

h. Garret S. Newkirk, born April 18, 1843; died July 30, 1843

i. Sarah Jane Newkirk, born October 17, 1844, and died October 29, 1869

j. William Henry Newkirk, born November 27, 1845

k. Margaret S. Newkirk, born April 8, 1847

l. Abraham Newkirk, born May 15, 1848

m. James S. Newkirk, born September 9, 1852; married October 29, 1873 to Mary Elizabeth Terhune, who died c.1878. He married second in 1881 to Annabella Meeker Randall, and had four children.

n. Franklin P. Newkirk, born November 10, 1853

o. Laura E. Newkirk, born August 3, 1855

p. Emma Rebecca Newkirk, born May 2, 1857; died August 6, 1860

q. Charles Edward Newkirk, born November 29, 1863; died July 18, 1864

Paulus Newkirk
1699-1763

This son of Matthew Cornelisse Van Nieuwkirk, Jr. (1647), and his second wife, Catryna Paulus Nieuwkirk, was born August 20, 1699 and died February 5, 1763, probably at Schraalenburgh, New Jersey. Married June 18, 1728 to Helena Spier, who died April 6, 1801, daughter of Barent Hendrickse Spier. Eight children, all born in New Jersey:

1. Catrina Newkirk, born May 10, 1729; died September 18, 1759; single
2. Catlyntje Newkirk, born May 7, 1733; perhaps died young
3. Matthew P. Newkirk, born April 30, 1735 at Belleville, New Jersey, and died November 12, 1818. Married February 16, 1766 to Geertje Kogh (or Koch), who died February 27, 1828. A son:
   a. John M. Newkirk, or Johannis, born May 18, 1781; died March, 1870 in Bergen County, New Jersey. Married February 1, 1806 his cousin, Maritje Newkirk; daughter of Jacob (1743) and Fitje Hennion Nieukirk (1744). She was born July 13, 1782 and died September 24, 1852. Four children, all born in Bergen County, New Jersey:
      (1) Gertrude Newkirk, born October 20, 1810, a twin
      (2) John Newkirk, born October 20, 1810, a twin, and died December 28, 1847. Married December 25, 1834 to Sarah Hedden
      (3) Sophia Newkirk, born May 31, 1813, and died February 14, 1815
      (4) Matthew Newkirk or Mathis, born June 20, 1816 and died August, 1873. Married January 16, 1845 Leah Demarest: children, born in Bergen County:
         (a) James Demarest Newkirk, born June 8, 1846
         (b) Maria Catharine Newkirk, born August 9, 1850
         (c) Anna Matilda Newkirk, born December 28, 1851
         (d) John Alfred Newkirk, born November 26, 1857, and christened October 12, 1860

     (e) John Newkirk, born May 9, 1861

     (f) Samuel Tyler Newkirk, born August 29, 1865

4. Barent Newkirk, born March 12, 1738 (or April 24, 1737) in Bergen County, New Jersey, died c.1805. Married April 6, 1765 to Antje Toers, born 1743, died 1805, daughter of Arent and Annatje Spier Toers. Seven children, all born New York:

   a. Lena Newkirk, baptized January 13, 1767 in New York

   b. Arent Newkirk, born September 1, 1768, and baptized October 2, 1768 in Bergen, New Jersey

   c. Annatje Newkirk, baptized July 1, 1770

   d. Matthew Newkirk, baptized May 24, 1772

   e. Barent Newkirk, baptized May 8, 1774

   f. Catharine Newkirk, born c.1775; died May 27, 1814. Married first February 1, 1795 Elihu Baldwin; second August 15, 1801 Ebenezer Bassett, born 1781, died 1815

   g. Jannetje Newkirk, born November 15, 1777, and died September 17, 1779

5. Jannetje Newkirk, baptized May 26, 1740, and died October 4, 1779. Married Jan Van Geisen; three children, born at Passaic, New Jersey:

   a. Rachel Van Geisen, born October 1, 1770

   b. Paulus Van Geisen, born March 16, 1773

   c. Johannes Van Geisen, born July 23, 1775

6. Jacob Newkirk, born November 22, 1743, of whom more.

7. Johannes Newkirk, born October 9, 1746 in New Jersey, and died September 29, 1749

8. Rachel Newkirk, born March 11, 1751 in Schraalenburgh, New Jersey; married Dirck Van Hooten. Three children, born at Patterson:

   a. Antje Van Hooten, born February 10, 1776

   b. Helmigh Van Hooten, born March 19, 1778

   c. Catalyntje Van Hooten, born October 6, 1781

Jacob Newkirk
1743-1818

This son of Paulus Newkirk (1699) was born November 22, 1743 in New Jersey, and died June 9, 1818. Married February 13,

1769 to Fitje Hennion, born April 20, 1744 and died January 23, 1808. Eight children, all born in New York:

1. Maritje Newkirk, born July 18, 1770; died August 1, 1776
2. Paulus Newkirk, born November 25, 1772; died young
3. Lena Newkirk, born c.1775; died July 25, 1776
4. Paulus Newkirk, second use of the name, born April 13, 1776, and died August 27, 1776
5. Jacob Newkirk, born April 28, 1778; died December 5, 1796
6. Garret J. Newkirk, born July 21, 1780, probably in Bergen County (later Hudson), New Jersey, and died there August 22, 1818. Married February 22, 1806 Rachel Shepard, daughter of George Shepard. She was born September 6, 1784 and died April 16, 1861. Children, probably born in Hudson County, New Jersey:

   a. Jacob Newkirk, born November 26, 1807. Married May 22, 1830 to Siba Brinkerhoff and had children, born in New Jersey. He apparently appears in the 1850 census for Hudson County, where his wife is listed as being Elizabeth, which suggests a second name for his wife; although his son, Jacob B., is also listed, seeming to identify the family properly. Children included:

      (1) Rachel Newkirk, born July 16, 1831; died July 10, 1852. Married February 13, 1850 to Jacob M. Merselis

      (2) Jacob B. Newkirk, born December 31, 1833; married October 26, 1859 to Date M. Spear

      (3) Garret Newkirk, born February 10, 1836; died July 17, 1873. Single

      (4) Jane Elizabeth Newkirk, born October 31, 1838. Married November 10, 1859 George W. Birdsall

      (5) John Henry Newkirk, born February 2, 1841; and married March 19, 1866 to Emma C. Coe

      (6) Mary Catherine Newkirk, born March 7, 1845 and married December 13, 1866 Abraham Vanderbeck

      (7) Abraham Newkirk, born November 16, 1847

      (8) William Edward Newkirk, born March 6, 1851

   b. George Newkirk, born June 19, 1809; married Ann Tappen

c.   Matthew Newkirk, born July 4, 1811; died May 29, 1812

d.   Sophia Newkirk, born November 24, 1812; died July 11, 1935. Married September 1, 1832 James Provost

e.   Garret Newkirk, born March 18, 1815; married Jane Brinkerhoff. Children, born in New Jersey:

    (1)   Sophia Newkirk, born September 24, 1856

    (2)   Gertrude Newkirk, born January 17, 1859

    (3)   Winfield Newkirk, born c.1860

    (4)   Ella Newkirk, born c.1861

    (5)   Annie Newkirk, born c.1862

    (6)   Edward Newkirk, born c.1863

f.   Catharine Newkirk, born March 14, 1817. Married to George Vreeland on February 23, 1837

7.   Maritje Newkirk, born July 13, 1782; died September 24, 1852. Married February 1, 1806 to her first cousin, John M. Newkirk, born May 18, 1781 and died March, 1870. He was a son of Matthew P. Newkirk (1735) and Geertje Kogh (or Koch) Newkirk. Their descendants are treated under the section devoted to his family

8.   John J. Newkirk, or Johannis Newkirk, born October 23, 1786, probably in Bergen, later Hudson, County, New Jersey; died August 15, 1860. Married May 14, 1814 to Gertrude Collard, born June 15, 1788 and died January 23, 1858; daughter of John Collard. They appear in the 1850 census of Hudson County, with four of their children. Also in the household is one David Danielson, born c.1842; and Effie Van Ripen, aged 78, born c.1772. Five children, all born in Hudson County:

a.   Jacob Newkirk, born May 29, 1815. Married October 24, 1839 to Aletta Riker, born March 27, 1820, and died January 14, 1850. He appears in the 1850 census of Hudson County, a widower, with two children. Also in the household is Charles Allen Newkirk, born c.1836, not identified. His children, born in New Jersey, were:

    (1)   Anna Maria Newkirk, born September 26, 1840; married October 16, 1861 John V. R. Vreeland

    (2)   John William Newkirk, born November 6, 1842, and married October 28, 1863 to Lavina Rino

      (3)   Lewis M. Newkirk, born April 26, 1846 and died July 19, 1847

      (4)   Lewis Newkirk, born May 18, 1848, and died February 27, 1849

b.   Abraham Newkirk, born October 2, 1817. Married October 23, 1839 to Mary Elizabeth Howell. Children, all born in New Jersey:

      (1)   Gertrude E. Newkirk, born June 29, 1841, and married February 14, 1861 to Lewis M. Crosby

      (2)   Catharine H. Newkirk, born September 25, 1843

      (3)   Henry B. Newkirk, born August 14, 1845; died young

      (4)   Sophia W. Newkirk, born September 19, 1847; married November 13, 1867 George A. Adams

      (5)   Frederick H. Newkirk, born October 14, 1851; married July 16, 1871 to Sophia Meeks

c.   Garret J Newkirk., born August 29, 1821, died August 11, 1851.

d.   Sophia Newkirk, born September 25, 1823. Married September 26, 1842 to Blakely Wison

e.   Effie Newkirk, born March 23, 1826; married June 22, 1847 to Daniel Van Winkle.

CHAPTER 11

Henry Newkirk
1740-1823

This Henry Newkirk was born about 1740, probably in Berkeley County, Virginia, but perhaps Washington County, Pennsylvania, where other members of his family lived. He apparently died c.1823 in Clermont County, Ohio. A print of a handwritten note of unkown origin was sent to me by Henry F. Turner of Hemet, California, which has written upon it, among other notes, that Henry died September 25, 1821. It is believed that he was a son of Henry Newkirk (1721), who was a son of Barent Newkirk (1689); as will be discussed. Much of the information here presented was derived from data found in the September, 1986 issue of *Newkirk Notes*, by Gil and Mary Alford; most of which was furnished by Aileen M. Whitt of New Richmond, Ohio, a Certified Genealogical Records Searcher; and from letters from Henry F. Turner, a descendant of this Henry.

Aileen Whitt states that some of the information reported has not been verified, and the reader should use caution in accepting it as fact, until documentary proof is uncovered.

He was reportedly and possibly married twice; first to Lydia Raredon, according to the mysterious note mentioned above, and second to Catherine, whose last name is not now known. There is, however, a deed in 1795, in which Henry and his wife conveyed land to Joseph Blackburn, and there she is listed as Catherine, as she is in his will.

One major piece of information helps to identify this individual. In 1774, Henry Newkirk obtained a patent on about 400 acres of land known as *The Legacy*, located in what is now Washington County, Pennyslvania. At that time, there were two other Henry Newkirks, besides the one now under discussion. This Henry was then 34 years old; his father, also Henry (1721), was then 53 years old, but not believed to be in Washington County at that time; and his first cousin, Henry Newkirk (1768), son of Abraham Newkirk,

(1724), was just six years old. Thus, it is reasonably apparent that our Henry Newkirk of 1740 was the owner of *The Legacy*.

Henry Newkirk appears in the 1783 Tax List of Somerset Township, Pennsylvania. At that time, he owned 500 acres of land, 3 horses, 6 cows, 3 sheep, 1 slave, and a distillery. In the 1790 census of Washington County, Pennsylvania, there are two Henry Newkirks listed. One lived on Mingo Creek and he and one other male in his household were over the age of 16. There was another male under 16 years, and two females of any age (a wife and daughter, probably). This is more than likely the family of our Henry of 1740. The second Henry had no children in his household and was probably Henry Newkirk (1768), at the age of 22, the son of Abraham (1724). The two Henrys were first cousins. In the 1800 census, Henry Newkirk (1740) appears again, this time with two males of 16 and up (himself and one son); 2 males under 16 years; and 4 females of any age.

In 1786, Henry Newkirk (1740) conveyed part of *The Legacy* to his cousin, Abraham Newkirk, Jr. (1764). Abraham later gave part of the land to his son, Henry Newkirk (1789), and about 1816, disposed of the last of his property, and left Pennsylvania.

Henry Newkirk (1740) apparently was called to service in the Revolution as a private, but furnished a substitute in at least two instances; he may not have personally served at all. References in the Pennsylvania Archives indicate that he was ordered to rendezvous March 4, 1782; that he found a suitable substitute for the term of 30 days relative to that order; that he was found on a roll of the company under Captain John Wall and Lieutenant David Hamilton; that he was ordered to rendezvous in that company June 22, 1782 as private first class; and that Daniel Devore served a tour as his substitute from June 22, 1782 to July 21, 1782. This family is reported in some notes from the collection of Dr. Adamson Bentley Newkirk, but the dates given there conflict with dates found in other sources, including the census records. Henry apparently had children from his first marriage, perhaps born in Pennsylvania:

1. Abraham Newkirk, born c.1774; died 1884 (reported by Dr. Newkirk as born c.1786 and died c.1829, which would appear to be more nearly correct), in Clermont County, Ohio; having served in the War of 1812. Married Elizabeth Coburn Kinner,

born c.1789 and died c.1877. This is probably the second male shown in the household in the 1790 census and, if so, requires that Henry, the father, was married prior to about 1773.

2. Rebecca Newkirk, born 1776; married William Barkley and lived on Bullskin, Brown County, Ohio. She is said to have lived to the age of 110 years.
3. Mary Newkirk, born 1778; married Joseph Jackson
4. Henry Newkirk, Jr., born 1781, of whom more.
5. John Newkirk, born August 16, 1784 in Clermont County, Ohio. On October 20, 1834, he purchased a farm in Marion County, Indiana, where he died August 22, 1864 of congestion of the bowels. Married Isabella Moore, born c.1779 and died September 3, 1870, also from a bowel disease. They appear in the 1860 census of Indiana, with several persons in their home, bearing the name Newkirk. There is also one John McLaren, born c.1846 in Indiana, living with them. It is possible that Catherine was a daughter, and that Augustus was a son, living at home with a wife Matilda and their first child. Those bearing the Newkirk name were:
   a. Catherine Newkirk, born c.1820, described as idiotic in the census, born in Ohio
   b. Augustus Newkirk, born c.1830, a farmer, born in Ohio.
   c. Matilda Newkirk, born c.1837 in Pennsylvania
   d. Inis Newkirk, a girl, born c.1857 in Indiana.
6. Lydia Newkirk, born 1783
7. George W. Newkirk, born 1784, of whom more
8. Joseph Newkirk, born 1785. Married March 23, 1815 Rebecca Johnson in Clermont County, Ohio. Four children, born in Ohio, had been reported to me, primarily from *Newkirk Notes*. A letter from Herbert C. Moyer of Batavia, Ohio, in 1995, reports that a paper in Probate Court of the county has other children in the family of Joseph. The paper is dated August 8, 1826, and reports Joseph as deceased. From these two sources, it appears that the family of Joseph could have included as many as seven children:
   a. Polly Newkirk, born 1816; according to Probate records
   b. Catharine Newkirk, born c.1818, according to the Probate records, who could possibly be the Catharine

235

Newkirk who was married March 7, 1839 in Brown County, Ohio to Andrew Myers, although not proven.

c. Mary Ann Newkirk, born April 3, 1819; died June 7, 1884 at Novelty, Knox County, Missouri. Married to William Porter and moved to Iowa. Her husband enlisted in the "Greybeards" during the War Between The States, and died at Rock Island, Illinois. She then moved her children to Novelty, where her brother lived. One or two of the children were born in Bracken County, Kentucky, and the rest in Iowa. She and other members of this family were reported in the September, 1986 issue of *Newkirk Notes*, by Gil and Mary Alford. The information was submitted by Frances Alma Newkirk Reber (1915), then living in Tulsa, Oklahoma; and by Katherine Barnett, then living at Kansas City, Missouri.

d. James Newkirk, born c.1820, according to the Probate records.

e. Margaret Newkirk, born 1823, reported from both sources, and married April 27, 1843 in Brown County, Ohio to Samuel Myers

f. Milton J. Newkirk, born 1824; died November 3, 1864 in Knox County, Missouri. Married September 27, 1849 in Brown County, Ohio, to Lydia Leach. He served in the Union Army in March, 1863, and died November 2, 1864 at Novelty, Knox County, Missouri, of typhoid fever. Lydia later went to Kansas, and on May 8, 1893, was living in Argonia, Sumner County, Kansas, when she applied for a widow's pension.

g. Joseph Newkirk, Jr., born 1825/33, and perhaps in Kentucky rather than Ohio; probably the same individual who was married September 23, 1864 in Bracken County, Kentucky, to Sarah Linville. Witnesses were Peter Haley and Samuel Myers. It appears that Joseph was married twice, first to Harriet Conrad, by whom he had at least three children. The 1860 census of Bracken County shows the family of Joseph, with Harriet and the first three children listed following. Also in the household is Rebecca Newkirk, age 65, apparently his mother. The

1870 census of the county lists Joseph with wife Sarah, two of the first three children, and three more apparently born to that second marriage. Children included:

(1)   Rebecca J. Newkirk, born April 4, 1852; probably married to Marshall Gordley and had a son:

    (a)   Marshall T. Gordley born December 12, 1875

(2)   John Newkirk, born c.1856

(3)   Mary M. Newkirk, born c.1859

(4)   Billy Newkirk, or more probably William, born c.1865

(5)   James Newkirk, born c.1868

(6)   Albert Newkirk, born c.1869

Henry Newkirk, Jr.
1781-1862

This son of Henry Newkirk (1740) was born 1781 in either Pennsylvania or Virginia, and died 1862 at Peach Grove, Pendleton County, Kentucky. Married about 1800 to Elizabeth McConnell, born c.1785 in Pennsylvania, and died in April, 1860. They are listed in the 1850 census of Pendleton County, Kentucky, with one of their sons, Perry (1824). The reader is asked to refer to a discussion in Chapter 3 of this study, wherein one Henry Newkirk, born 1781, is reported as a son of Elias Newkirk (1722), with a wife Pheby and four children. Aileen M. Whitt believes that my report is incorrect, and that Elias did not have a son Henry; the two I am reporting in this study being, in fact, a single individual. Please evaluate the data presented with care, pending final proof. The children of this Henry, as reported to me, included, at least:

1.   Abraham Newkirk, born c.1808 in Ohio. Married August 16, 1827 to Patsy Raredon in Pendleton, Kentucky. She was born c.1807 in Pennsylvania. They appear in the 1850 census for Pendleton County, in the household adjacent to that of his parents, with six of their children, born in Kentucky. The first child listed here is from information furnished by Shirley W. Mayhew of Tisbury, Massachusetts. The children were:

a.   Charles Newkirk, born c.1828 and the father of, at least:

    (1)   Abigail Newkirk, born c.1872 in Kentucky

b.   Catharine Newkirk, born c.1832
c.   Francis M. Newkirk, born c.1834
d.   Lorenzo J. Newkirk, born c.1835
e.   William J. Newkirk, born c.1842
f.   Perry N. Newkirk, born c.1844
g.   Hiram B. Newkirk, born c.1850

2.   Charles Wesley Newkirk, born c.1810 in Ohio; drowned June, 1836 in the Ohio River, and is thought to be buried at Ivor, Kentucky. Married November 25, 1830 in Pendleton County, Kentucky, to Sarah Powers, born 1816, daughter of Jeremiah Powers. After her husband's death, she was remarried to George M. Phillips and had a large family, most of whom lived in Pendleton and Campbell Counties, Kentucky. Charles Wesley was the father of several children, born in Kentucky:

a.   George Washington Newkirk, born November 6, 1831: died 1901

b.   Joseph Barker Newkirk, born November 12, 1833, of whom more.

c.   Charles Wesley Newkirk, Jr., born August 27, 1836; and died July 24, 1912. Married May 8, 1862 to Nancy E. Cookendorfer

3.   Mary Jane Newkirk, born October 29, 1820; died March 24, 1899. Married twice: first March 12, 1835 to Edmund Carnes in Pendleton County, Kentucky; second to Major John Wheeler

4.   Perry Newkirk, born 1824, single

5.   Hiram Newkirk, perhaps, born c.1825

6.   Joseph Newkirk, perhaps, born c.1826

7.   Henry Newkirk, perhaps, born c.1828

8.   Margaret Newkirk, perhaps, born c.1830; married to Samuel Peyton Moyer.

Joseph Barker Newkirk
1833-1916

This son of Charles Wesley Newkirk (1810) and Sarah Powers Newkirk (1816), was born November 12, 1833 in Campbell County, Kentucky, and died May 2, 1916 at New Richmond, in

Clermont County, Ohio. He was married January 22, 1857 in Pendleton County, Kentucky, to Rachel Ellen Amos (or Amiss). She was born January 7, 1841 in Pendleton County, Kentucky, and died March 2, 1881 near Vanceburg, in Lewis County, Kentucky.

As so often happens in genealogical research, just as I was putting the finishing touches to this manuscript, I received the new book, *Miller-Newkirk Family History, Ancestors & Descendants of Ben Miller & Sally (Newkirk) Miller and Related Families*, by Aileen Miller Whitt, 1995, Library of Congress 95-75750. Her given name was actually Eleanor Aileen Miller (1924), but she has generally dropped the first name in ordinary usage. In any case, her book is beautiful, and highly recommended. It is not just genealogy, as this study is, but contains numerous pictures, family stories, and other very interesting features. It covers in detail several generations of one branch of the Newkirk family, some of which will be summarized here. I have used it to verify my earlier information, and to fill in some of the missing names and dates. The book is available from Aileen at her home address: 1094 Fagin Road, New Richmond, Ohio 45157.

Joseph Barker Newkirk (1833) and Rachel Ellen Amos/Amiss (1841), had nine children, born in Kentucky:

1. Cynthia Newkirk, born October 5, 1858; died October 12, 1938. Married c.1880 William Thomas Cooper, son of Wyatt S. and Louisa Blankenship Cooper. They had three children:
   a. Elwood C. Cooper, born c.1881; married 1910 Bertha Aldridge and had two children.
   b. Nellie Cooper, born August 24, 1882; married 1913 to Harvey S. Kimble. No children.
   c. George Bruce Cooper, born February 29, 1884; died August 11, 1974. Married first to Anna Mae Blankenship and second to Ollie Blankenship Stafford, and third to Catherine Clayton. He had one son.
2. Josephine Newkirk, born July 19, 1859; died August 12, 1933. Married to Harry Harcum, son of Elisha Harcum and Mary Hitch. They had four children:
   a. Charles L. Harcum, born c.1876; married Amelia W. Fetzer.

b. Nora Harcum, born May 27, 1880, and married Frank Brooks.

c. George Melvin Harcum, born November 28, 1888; married to Lucille Seaman.

d. Goldie Harcum; married Robert Purdy.

3. Charles Amos Newkirk, born December 6, 1861; died January 25, 1918 in Franklin County, Indiana. Married 1885 Ida Fossett; second to Lida Barker. He had two children from his first marriage (and several infant deaths):

a. Wesley Everett Newkirk, married Georgeanna Ihrig; two children.

b. Ollie Mae Newkirk; married Howard Britton, and had five children.

4. Sarah Ellen Newkirk, born October 11, 1868, and died September 23, 1951. Married February 25, 1886 to Vincent Grant Miller, and had at least one son:

a. Herman Miller, born December 4, 1893; died May 15, 1978. Married to Lurena Hawkins, born August 19, 1895, and died February 1, 1974 in Cincinnati, Ohio, the daughter of Rezin Hawkins and Mary Ellen Leeds Hawkins. They had eight children, including:

(1) Eleanor Aileen Miller, born August 25, 1924; married April 26, 1946 to J. B. Whitt, born April 19, 1925, son of Estill V. and Sara Ann Johnson Whitt. She is the author of much of the information on this family. They have two daughters. The reader is again referred to her book on the Miller/Newkirk families for further details of later generations.

5. Joseph Franklin Newkirk, born August 14, 1871; died June 12, 1954. Married February 13, 1901 Anna Margaret Pell, daughter of Thomas and Mary Conley Pell. At least seven children:

a. Letha Newkirk, a twin, born May 14, 1902; married to Emmett Buskirk, and second to Willard Bigelow.

b. Lela Newkirk, a twin, born May 14, 1902; single.

c. Ellen Newkirk, an infant death

d. Hazel Newkirk, born August 13, 1907; married J. Frank Potts.

e. Edna Eilene Newkirk, born January 18, 1911; married to Norman Sullivan.

f. Mary Elizabeth Newkirk, born December 24, 1914; married James E. Murphy.

g. Hayden Elmo Newkirk, born May 14, 1918; died May 28, 1948.

6. Amanda Cordelia Newkirk, born February 8, 1874, and died February 17, 1918. Married September 15, 1892 to Jacob Ruckle in Lewis County, Kentucky. Two children:

a. Orville Ruckle; married Vivian Grimes and had a son.

b. Katie Ruckle, married Edgar Applegate; a son and a daughter.

7. Alice Melissa Newkirk, a twin, born February 4, 1877; died September 22, 1964. Married Claude H. Jackson, son of William Jackson and had three children:

a. Raymond Jackson, born c.1897, and died November 25, 1977. Married Bertie F. Poole. They had an infant death.

b. Mildred Jackson, born c.1903; died September 4, 1960. Married to Allen Ferguson, and had one son.

c. Claudia Jackson; married Blair Branham; two sons.

8. Agnes Mae Newkirk, a twin, born February 4, 1877; married Charles W. King. Three children:

a. Hubert King, born August 25, 1899; married Velma Hoggatt.

b. Leona King; married Louis Krekeler.

c. Elbert Harry King, born April 5, 1904; married Geneva Johns.

9. William Henry Newkirk, born June 25, 1880; died January 3, 1952. Married Ada Belle Burroughs and had three children:

a. Emmett Newkirk, born November 15, 1907; died August, 1969. Never married.

b. Ebert Ross Newkirk, born April 14, 1909; died October 31, 1938. Married Gladys Elizabeth Harris and had three children.

c. Lorraine Newkirk, born October 27, 1910; died August 31, 1912

George W. Newkirk
1784-1835

This son of Henry Newkirk (1740), was born c.1784, or as early as 1780; probably in Clermont County, Ohio; and died in September, 1835 of consumption. Married in 1808 to Margaret Johnson, born c.1794 in Clermont County, and died in 1874 at Indianapolis, Indiana. Margaret appears as head of household in the 1850 census of Marion County, Indiana, with four of her children: Joseph, Otto, Frances M. and Eliza Jane. They had at least twelve children, all born in Clermont County, Ohio:

1. John Newkirk, born June 8, 1811; died August 26, 1889 in Marion County, Indiana. Married there September 8, 1839 Eleanor Ann Johnson, born c.1818 in Ohio (listed as Eleanor in the 1850 census), and had children, born in Marion County:
    a. Charles J. Newkirk, born March 13, 1841. Married October 30, 1860 in Clinton County, Illinois, to Rebecca Ann Brown. She was born April 4, 1840 in Huntington County, Pennsylvania, a daughter of John W. Brown and Rebecca Inscho Brown, and died September, 1873 in Clinton County, Illinois.
    b. Margaret Jane Newkirk, born September 29, 1851
2. Joseph H. Newkirk, born October 12, 1813; died single in Clinton County, Illinois
3. James Madison Newkirk, born July 7, 1815, of whom more
4. Rebecca Newkirk, born January 9, 1817; died at Waterville, Kansas. Married first July 10, 1835 to John Bartley in Brown County, Ohio; second William Matis.
5. Nelson Newkirk, born November 21, 1819; died November 30, 1898 in Rice County, Kansas. (Henry F. Turner of Hemet, California reports that Nelson died April 6, 1904 at Drakesville, Iowa, taken from the notes of Dr. A. B. Newkirk). Married twice in Clermont County, Ohio: first October 7, 1840 Nancy Hicks, born May 22, 1819 in Clermont County, Ohio; died January 1, 1847 in Ohio of consumption. He married second September 30, 1847 to Eliza Hicks, born September 30, 1825 in Clermont County; died September 13, 1885 at Drakesville, Iowa of flu. He appears in the 1850 cen-

sus of Clermont County, with his second wife, and four of his children; he is there said to have been born in Indiana, rather than Ohio. In the 1850 census for Goshen, Orange County, New York, there is the family of Obediah Newkirk (1793) listed as household #0222 and family #0237. The next listing is for a second Nelson Newkirk, also in household #0222, and family #0234. He is there reported as having been born c.1797, having in his household one Mary Pelton, born 1833, not otherwise identified. He appears to be living in the same house with Obediah, who was a son of John Adam Newkirk (1763). Is it possible that this Nelson Newkirk (1797) is a brother of Obediah (1793)? It has been suggested that these two Nelsons are the same individuals, but that does not seem to be the case, with the disparity in ages, and appearance in census records of two different states in the same period. Nelson had three children from his first marriage, and five from the second, all in Clermont County, Ohio:

a. Harriet Eliza Newkirk, born 1841
b. John C. Newkirk, born 1843
c. William D. Newkirk, born 1844
d. James N. Newkirk, born 1849
e. Frances M. Newkirk, born 1852
f. Albert L. Newkirk, born 1854
g. Charles Newkirk, born 1858
h. Daniel L. Newkirk, born 1859

6. Gideon M. Newkirk, born September 16, 1820, and died July, 1889. Dr. A. B. Newkirk reported that Gideon died June 11, 1899 at Lawrence, Marion County, Indiana. He was married December 12, 1844 to Jane Marshall, born April 16, 1825; died June 10, 1900. Six children:

a. William Newkirk, born September 22, 1845, and died October 29, 1852
b. John Newton Newkirk, born August 8, 1849, and died November 4, 1849
c. James Thomas Newkirk, born July 4, 1853
d. Mary Ellen Newkirk, born May 22, 1856, and died May 3, 1857
e. Margaret Alice Newkirk, born September 2, 1858

f.   Richard Edward Newkirk, born September 13, 1863; a twin

g.   Sarah Frances Newkirk, born September 13, 1863; a twin

7.   Minerva Ellen Newkirk, born June 11, 1822 in Clermont County, Ohio; died Little Rock, Arkansas. Married Gabriel Lee, no children.

8.   Angeline Newkirk, born April 7, 1824, of whom more.

9.   George Washington Newkirk, born November 23, 1826; died c.1844

10. Oather Newkirk, or perhaps Otho, as he appears in the 1860 census of Indiana (a blacksmith), born February 18, 1829 in Clermont County, Ohio. Married July 5, 1851 in Indiana to Joanna Crawford, born there March 5, 1835; died August 15, 1875 at Truckee, California of a tumor in her neck. Six children:

a.   Margaret Ann Newkirk, born August 16, 1852 in Illinois

b.   Sarah Ellen Newkirk, born October 18, 1854 in Illinois

c.   Rosetta Newkirk, born March 10, 1861

d.   John B. Newkirk, born August 8, 1863 in Indiana

e.   James A. Newkirk, born June 5, 1867 in Marion County, Indiana, and died in Canada. At least one child:

    (1)   Adrian Newkirk, born 1890 and died in Canada

f.   William Nelson Newkirk, born March 4, 1870 in Adair County, Missouri and died February 9, 1939. Married in St. Clair County, Missouri, in 1898 to Fanny Herring, and had at least six children, born in Johnson County, Missouri:

    (1)   Harry Newkirk, born 1900

    (2)   George Newkirk, born 1902; died 1937. A son:

        (a)   George Newkirk, Jr., born 1923

    (3)   Merlee Newkirk, born 1905

    (4)   Charles Newkirk, born 1907

    (5)   Mary Newkirk, born 1911

    (6)   Hattie Newkirk, born 1915

11. Francis M Newkirk., born April 30, 1831, and died August 31, 1896 in Illinois. Married in 1857 to Almira Davis.

12. Eliza Jane Newkirk, born 1835, and married July 5, 1851 to Benjamin Eaton Thomas. Six girls and a boy.

James Madison Newkirk
1815-1898

This son of George W. Newkirk (1784), was born July 7, 1815 (or August 7), in Clermont County, Ohio, and died November 30, 1898 in Rice County, Kansas. He was buried at Kansas Center Cemetery at Frederick, Kansas. The final papers discharging his administrator; his son, Richard F.; were issued by the Court December 9, 1901; the appointment papers, dated January 30, 1900, listed all the heirs by name. Married November 13, 1834 in Clermont County, to Elizabeth Meyers, (or Moyer, said to be a daughter of Abraham Moyer), born February 15, 1818 in Ohio and died 1883 or 1887 in Rice County, Kansas. Their family appears in the 1850 census of Clermont County, with nine of their children. There, James Madison is listed only as James. In 1993, I received extensive information on this family from Henry Franklin Turner, of Hemet, California. Thirteen children, the first eleven born in Clermont County, Ohio; the last two in Clinton County, Iowa:

1. James Newkirk, born 1835; died young
2. Mary M. Newkirk (or W.), born March 25, 1836. Married July 14, 1859 in Clinton County, Iowa, to Frederick H. Clark. Apparently three children, all single and deceased by 1943:
    a. Ida Clark
    b. George Clark
    c. Alice Clark
3. Abraham H. Newkirk, born May 20, 1837, of whom more.
4. Elsie Ann Newkirk, born November 12, 1839; married May 26, 1857 Clinton County, Iowa, W. G. Himrod. Four children:
    a. Mary Grace Himrod; married Watkins.
    b. Estella Himrod; married Watkins, lived at Scranton, Pa.
    c. Elizabeth Christian Himrod, single
    d. Sally Himrod, single
5. John H. Newkirk, born January 30, 1840; died March 6, 1840
6. Kezia Catharine Newkirk, born December 15, 1841, died October 2, 1888. Married November 14, 1861 in Clinton County, Iowa, to Eli C. Gregory. At least two children:
    a. Arthur H. Gregory
    b. Ethel Gregory; married to Blunt. Lived in Iowa

7. George Sylvester Newkirk, born March 24, 1843. This is apparently the same George Newkirk listed on muster rolls of Company G, 59th Regiment Ohio Infantry, USA. His reports indicate that he was a private, enlisted October 2, 1861; on duty during January, 1862 as a brigade teamster; during May, 1863 as a cook; during March and April, 1864 as a corporal on Color Guard. He was reported missing in action as of May 27, 1864 at Picketts Mills in the Altoona Mountains, a prisoner of war, and known to be severely wounded, from which he died.

8. Susan Rebecca Newkirk, born May 1, 1844 and died September 11, 1897 Rice County, Kansas. Married December 6, 1865 in Clinton County, Iowa, to Gabriel B. Sellers, born October 20, 1840 in Ohio, and died July 5, 1907 in Rice County. They had at least two children, according to the division of estate of her brother James William Newkirk (1875-1943):

    a. Alfred L. Sellers; married and had at least eight children:
        (1) Bertha E. Sellers, married Jordan; lived Kingman, Kansas
        (2) Edith B. Sellers; married Quigley, lived Great Bend, Kansas
        (3) Gabe A. Sellers; lived at Wichita, Kansas
        (4) Mary A. Sellers; lived at Wichita, Kansas
        (5) Lester R. Sellers; lived at Knoxville, Tennessee
        (6) Dorothy E. Sellers, married King; lived Garden City, Kansas
        (7) Joe L. Sellers; lived at Grand Saline, Texas
        (8) Velma Sellers, an infant death.

    b. Alice Sellers; married Snodgrass; at least four children:
        (1) Benjamin H. Snodgrass, and lived at Wenatchee, Washington
        (2) Christopher C. Snodgrass, and lived at Chelan Falls, Washington
        (3) Susie E. Snodgrass; married Ives, lived Kirkland, Washington
        (4) Millie Snodgrass; married Hubbard, and lived at Hutchinson, KS

c. Joseph M. Sellers, lived at Lyons, Kansas
d. Emma Sophia Sellers; married Downing; three children:
   (1) Ruth Rebecca Downing; married Peverley, lived at Rawlins, Wyoming
   (2) Emma Blanche Downing; also married a Peverley; lived at Genesea, Kansas.
   (3) Olive Mildred Lee Downing; married Strohm and lived at Little River, Kansas.
e. James A. Sellers; married and had two children:
   (1) Grace Sellers; lived at Winfield, Kansas
   (2) William B. Sellers; lived at Winfield, Kansas
f. Susan Sellers; married to Taylor and had two children:
   (1) Florence Taylor; married McKenzie; lived at Los Angeles
   (2) Lola Taylor; married Cosand, lived at Imperial, California
g. Katie Sellers; married to Crawford. Lived at Little River, Kansas

9. Ellen Josephine Newkirk, born January 28, 1846; died 1905
10. Sophia Cinderella Newkirk, born August 17, 1848 (or February 19, 1847); married Moses L. Marsh.
11. Delilah Isabella Newkirk, born September 6, 1849. Married December 14, 1869 in Clinton County, Iowa, to Benjamin Franklin Shultz. Five children, named in her brother's estate:
    a. Letitia Mazettie Shultz, married Gregg and had children:
       (1) Bernice Iphagenia Gregg; married Cochran. Lived in New York City in 1943.
       (2) Dorothy Phyllis Gregg; married Shultz, and lived in Des Moines
       (3) Denton Bennie Gregg; married Anderson, and lived at Rockwell City, Iowa.
    b. Gavalah Shultz, single.
    c. Sophia Grace Shultz; married Henderson. Children:
       (1) David William Henderson; lived at Tipton, Iowa
       (2) Isabella Mary Henderson; lived at Tipton, Iowa
       (3) Dorothy Sophia Henderson; lived at Tipton, Iowa
    d. Paul Precious Shultz, deceased as of 1943, with children:

(1)   Earl Newkirk Shultz; lived at Petersborough, New Hampshire.

(2)   Kenneth Mitts Shultz; lived at Detroit, Michigan

(3)   Richard Paul Shultz; lived at Columbus, Ohio

  e.   Benjamin Franklin Shultz; lived at Gillette, Wyoming

12. James William Newkirk, born September 3, 1857, and died December 24, 1943 at Geneseo, Rice County, Kansas. I have received a paper which states that it is the division of the estate of James William, who apparently died intestate. It lists eleven of his brothers and sisters with the exception of James, the first-born, who was perhaps an infant death. James William was presumably unmarried, since no wife or children are mentioned. The list of heirs was so extensive that some of them received as little as 1/294 of the estate! That report forms the basis for the construction of some of the families of his siblings.

13. Richard Robert Newkirk, born February 11, 1859, of whom more.

Abraham H. Newkirk
1837-1913

This son of James Madison Newkirk (1815) was born May 20, 1837, and died February 25, 1913 in Wadsworth Soldiers Home, Leavenworth, Kansas. Abraham volunteered July 16, 1862 to serve three years, or for the war, and was discharged June 6, 1865. His certificate of discharge states that he served as a private in Company B, 26th Regiment, Iowa Infantry, USA. It further states that he was born in Clermont County, Ohio and was then 24 years old (which is probably his stated age at the time of enlistment), and was five feet eleven and a half inches tall, fair complexion, blue eyes, black hair, and by occupation, a farmer. Married December 31, 1867 in Clinton County, Iowa, to Orpha S. Gregory. She was born November 29, 1844 in Ohio, and died November 22, 1881 near Roscoe, Graham County, Kansas, a daughter of Isaac Gregory and Amy Clark Gregory. Her obituary appeared in the December 10, 1881 issue of *The Graham County Republican*, in which it is stated that: *"For many weeks before her death she was a great sufferer from ulcers which caused her death. At her home she leaves a husband and four interesting children to mourn their loss. There are other relatives whose hearts are made sad by her death."* They lived in Clinton County, Iowa, until about 1877, when they moved to Graham County, Kansas. There, on June 25, 1888, he received a Homestead grant of 160 acres of land (see Receiver's Final Receipt No. 10908). By Warranty Deed dated April 11, 1890, Abraham, a widower, conveyed the land to David M. Davis, Trustee. His children and grandchildren were all named in the division of estate of his brother James William Newkirk (1857), with their place of residence at that time, providing additional family information. They had children, born in Clinton County, Iowa:

1. Brent Newkirk, born c.1868 (which could, of course, be Barent from the old family name), according to Mormon IGI records.
2. Helen Josephine Newkirk, born August 18, 1870; died November 11, 1929 in Oklahoma. Married to Lee Troutman and had children:
   a. Orpha E. Troutman; married McKenzie. Lived at Santa Clara, California as of 1943
   b. Goldie R. Troutman; married Wright. Lived at Vellejo, California
   c. Martha E. Troutman; married to McEacharn. Lived at Waunette, Oklahoma.
   d. Robert L. Troutman; lived at Foyil, Oklahoma.
   e. Abraham N. Troutman; lived at Tecumseh, Oklahoma.
   f. Ethel A. Troutman; married Baldwin. Lived at Norman, Oklahoma.
   g. Alfred R. Troutman; lived at Purcell, Oklahoma.
   h. Walter J. Troutman; lived at Albuquerque, New Mexico.
3. Rebecca Elizabeth Newkirk, born September 9, 1873, and died November 18, 1914 at Belleville, Republic County, Kansas. Married to Alfred Gee Sanford. They had children:
   a. Carrie M. Sanford; married Porter, and lived at Elreno, Oklahoma.
   b. Nellie M. Sanford; married Nelson, and lived at Oketo, Kansas.

c. Ethel M. Sanford; married Howe, and lived at Colorado Springs.
d. Veda M. Sanford; married McCarty; lived at Wichita, Kansas.
e. Freda A. Sanford; married Collette; lived at Alameda, California
4. Estella Eldora Newkirk, born August 26, 1876, of whom more
5. Robert Richard Newkirk, born December 8, 1877; died December 23, 1943 at Topeka, Kansas, single. Buried at Little River, Rice County, Kansas.

Estella Eldora Newkirk
1876-1950

This daughter of Abraham H. Newkirk (1837), was born August 26, 1876 at Elwood, Clinton County, Iowa, and died September 7, 1950 in Kamiah, Lewis County, Idaho. Married September 25, 1898 at Southwest City, McDonald County, Missouri to Walter William Turner. He was born January 18, 1871 at Republic, Kansas, and died June 23, 1941 at Kamiah, Lewis County; a son of Isaac Turner and Erma Amanda Willis Turner. Their marriage license, dated September 19, 1898, executed by T. F. Downing, the minister, on the date of their wedding, indicates: *"Revenue Stamps for 10 cents canceled."* Four children:
1. Fred Melvin Turner, born October 17, 1899 at Southwest City, Missouri, and died December 22, 1988 at Maple Valley, King County, Washington. Married June 20, 1923 at Nezperce, in Lewis County, Idaho, to Blanche Rosalie Bovey. She was born April 3, 1900 at Nezperce, Idaho, daughter of William August Bovey and Ota May Poulson Bovey. Two children:
   a. Ruth Leota Turner, born March 19, 1924 at Craigmont, Lewis County, Idaho. Married January 1, 1943 at Brynmawr, King County, Washington, Harold Knutson, born September 1, 1915 at Minot, North Dakota, son of Olaf Knutson and Helga Marie Norum. Children, the first three born at Renton, Washington; the last two at Everett, Washington:

(1) Phyllis Marie Knutson, a twin, born March 24, 1946, and married February 23, 1968 at Everett, Washington Robert Glen Rhonemus. Two children, born at Seattle, Washington:
  (a) Mark Glen Rhonemus; December 9, 1971
  (b) Todd Allen Rhonemus; September 5, 1974

(2) A twin, stillbirth March 24, 1946.

(3) Judy Rosalie Knutson, born January 22, 1948.

(4) Roberta Lynn Knutson, born February 23, 1956; married May 19, 1979 Robert Thomas Maxwell, born January 24, 1950 at Pasco, Washington, a son of Robert Arthur Maxwell and Wanda Jean Pickering Maxwell. They have two children, born at Everett, Washington:
  (a) Brian Allen Maxwell, born July 21, 1982
  (b) Spencer Curtis Maxwell; December 14, 1983

(5) Roland Lee Knutson, born February 23, 1956; married June 18, 1977 to Amy Allison Keith, born June 19, 1956 Everett, Washington. Two children:
  (a) Keith Lee Knutson, born July 9, 1980 Seattle
  (b) Alex Marshall Knutson, born May 18, 1982 at Everett

b. Henry Franklin Turner, born June 29, 1926 at Craigmont; married October 28, 1949 at McMinnville, Yamhill County, Oregon, Betty Jane Dunwoody Ratcliff. She was born May 22, 1924 at Keystone, Keith County, Nebraska, daughter of Samuel Leon Dunwoody and Gertrude Sims Dunwoody. He is my correspondent for much of this family. There were two children born to her first marriage, and two to the marriage with Henry Franklin:
  (1) Naomi Jean Ratcliff, born February 11, 1945 at North Platte, Lincoln County, Nebraska. Married twice: August 8, 1965 to Randell Lee Prouse, and second to Robert Emmich
  (2) Gerald Clifford Ratcliff, born October 2, 1947 at Portland, Oregon
  (3) Melvin Douglas Turner, born July 25, 1950 at McMinnville, Yamhill County, Oregon

        (4)   Dale Wayne Turner, born October 1, 1953 at Renton, in King County, Washington, and married June 26, 1976 at Claremont, Los Angeles County, California, to Janice Laverne McDonnell

2.   Emma Elizabeth Turner, born April 11, 1904 in Athol, Idaho; married October 17, 1924 to William Hamilton

3.   Arvilla May Turner, born May 25, 1907 at Athol, Idaho

4.   Clara Imojean Turner, born August 29, 1913 at Winona, Idaho County, Idaho. Married October 4, 1933 at Julietta, Latah County, Idaho, to Mark Frederick Jay. Children:

    a.   Frederick Walter Jay, born December 12, 1935 at Kamish, in Lewis County, Idaho. Married June 24, 1955 at Kennewick, Washington, Carmen Marie Glendenning, born November 23, 1938 at Wenatchee, Douglas County, Washington, daughter of G. B. and Frances Marjorie Hill Glendenning. He married second Pat E. Griswold. Three children, the first two born at Kennewick and the third at Kent, in King County, Washington:

        (1)   Tana Rae Jay, born December 24, 1956; married in 1980 to Michael Lombardo.

        (2)   Michael James Jay, born June 26, 1958; married April 4, 1987 to Carlene Nickell.

        (3)   Mark Barnett Jay, born July 10, 1962, and married to Lori Holt.

    b.   Nanette E. Jay, born May 21, 1942 at Kamiah in Lewis County, Idaho. Married August 19, 1961 at Pasco, in Franklin County, Washington to Alfred Frederick Neels, born September 5, 1941 at Phillips, Wisconsin.

    c.   James Leroy Jay, born April 9, 1953 at Kennewick, Washington; married Linda Lee Whipmire.

In 1993, I received correspondence from Henry Franklin Turner (1926), which included several sheets of note paper, written by his grandmother, Estella Eldora Newkirk (1876). It is a rare piece of family history, describing her parents, and the struggles they overcame about the turn of the century in the plains country of the American west. I called Henry, and he has kindly permitted me to include her story here, just as she wrote it, with original spelling:

My parents were Iowa people, though my father was born in Clearmount County, Ohio. Abraham Newkirk volunteered and enrolled on the 16th day of July 1862 to serve 3 years or during the war. - (He was 24 years of age). While he was in service, my mother Orpha Gregory spent a share of her time preparing useful things. Now a days girls would say for their "Hope chest." When I was a child I remember of the feather beds, Down spreads & she & her mother Amy Gregory spun & wove what they called counterpanes, I remember a blue & white one also a pink & white one. I have the hair wreath she made during that time.

My father was discharged from the service at the close of the war on the 6th day of June, 1865. He was a farmer previous to this.

He took some of the money he received at the close of the war & bought a team of dapel gray colts from his father "James Newkirk".

I remember hearing him tell of how he & my mother (before they were married) went to Fairs, picnics & dances etc driving Frank & Joe to a lumber wagon....My parents were married Dec. 31, 1867 - I think in Clinton Co. near......

They lived there untill 1877 when they drove through by covered wagon & the gray team, to Graham Co. Kansas.

The only thing I remember in Iowa is my grandmothers Snowball tree, it seemed so large & full of big balls.

I was not well, had convulsions & an old Dr. McKinzy (their family doctor) told them if they would travel with me he thought I would get well (and I did). That pleased my father because he wanted to go to Kansas. I remember on the trip of staying over night with some friends of theirs who gave them eggs for on their way, packed them in oats. I remember them putting in a small one for me...There were four of we children Josephine 8, Rebeckie 6, Estella between 3 & 4, Robert Bertchard one year old.

(Note: the census records and other information indicate this child's name was Robert Richard; perhaps I have misread the old writing in these notes)

I had a wax doll with golden curls, they would tie her to a bow of the covered wagon at night, as we slept in the wagon. One night it rained, the water run down the string and melted the dolls head, that was the end of my first dolly.

Before we got to our journeys end we met up with a family by the name of Hall, he was driving dark colored horses "Rock & John". Papa said that I wanted to ride with them, so they put me on a small box in the front of the wagon, I either went to sleep, or we struck a rut, anyway out I went under the horses feet, they stopped suddenly. I was frightened but unhurt, I believe I remember the occasion...The Websters (Mrs. Webster was my mother's cousin) lived near Roscoe, Kansas. We stopped there & Papa took a homestead 3 miles from their place (we were taught to call them Aunt Kitty & Uncle Mell). They lived in a sod house with thatch roof, the ground for the floor.

My Papa built a sod house with board roof, floor & petitions & 5 windows. He set out a grove of Cottonwood trees for a wind break west & north of the house. He bought cook stove, dining table, 6 chairs, & two bedsteads, all quite nice for those days.

Uncle Mell made them a cupboard with doors, flour chest & bread board...They had brought a bureau with miror from Iowa (Mama's parents gave it to them when they were married). I believe Niece Nellie Nelson has it now.

There were springs & shallow wells not too far from our place, but it being on a divide, my Papa dug a deep deep well & walled it for many feet down from the top, as he dug, but no water. In geting the rock out of the quarry he got a small piece in his eye, I remember him being kept in a dark room, he almost lost his eye...Mother had to care for the horses, they jerked and hurt her.

We lived there 7 years & hauled water all the time. When we got cows & we children got older we would take the cows about 1/4 mile to a neighbors to water, sometimes we would ride them, & tie strips of bright colored calico around their horns, we could braid Pinks tail, we would put a ribbon on that too.

The other cows names were Pet, Queen & Roan. The buffalo grass on a school section joining us was very good pasture, we would keep the cows two on a rope (with swivels).

We & most of our neighbors burned what we called buffalo chips...but Papa would go in the Fall over on Bow Creek 5 miles away & haul wood for Winter...Some years he would have a good corn crop, but others there would be drought, hot winds & no corn at all...Some years he would raise millet & rye, would have the latter thrashed with a horse power machine, the neighbors would exchange work, the horses went round & around, we children thought it great fun to learn all of the horses names.

We usually had two hogs to butcher in the Fall, Mr. Hall would come help Papa butcher, they would blow up the bladder & put pebbles in so it would rattle, their daughter Minnie & we four would play with them out in the moon light, & enjoyed them as the children of today do their balloon.

My mother was in poor health about 18 months. Papa had 3 doctors for her one come 5 mile, one 8 mile on horseback, one come 15 miles with horse & buggy (from Logan) Kansas.

On Christmas eve in 1880 they had a neighbor tree for the children, I do not remember what the others received, but for me twas a yellow haired, china dolly. My mother named her Sophia Belle for two of my Papa's sisters (I have her yet). In the programme I remember a conundrum, brother Bert held a cat & a pretty little girl with curls held a pillow (cat-a-pillow.)

On Thanksgiving Day in 1881 my mother died of tumor, then the doctors did not know what was the matter. The day of the funeral was a terrable blizzard, I remember they took the lines from Frank & Joes harness to lower the casket into the grave.

It was sad & very hard for Papa in a new country with 4 small children.

Before Mother died she put Papas and Aunt Kittys hands together & made them promise they would keep we 4 children together until the older girls were old enough to get married.

Papas enpenses had been so great, & crop failure (I dont remember if it was the grasshopper year or not.) Anyway our cows were sold one by one to pay doctor bills & funeral expenses, & something to eat....Papa couldn't have we children without milk so there was a sad day when he took Frank & Joe & traded them for a team of mules & two cows to boot...Hard for him as they seemed a part of the family. Papa did not care for the mules so traded them for a black team Prince & Pete. I remember two years in particular that we had such a failure of crops, that Papa took we children in covered wagon to Rice County, where his folks lived.

255

There he would work with a thrashing machine for wages (so we would have something to live on through the Winter.)

His brother uncle Dick was a vocal music teacher, sister Josie picked up potatoes etc for him to pay her way to the Singing school. We other children were not old enough to go. Though when uncle had a concert..he had brother Bert and I sing. Papa was very proud of we childrens singing qualities.

When back home in Winter when the snow was deep (drifts 8 and 10 feet deep) he would lock the wheels of the wagon with chains so they would slide, put straw in wagon box, spread a heavy comforter down, have we children get in, then spread another heavy quilt over our heads & would say "now dont get your heads out & breathe the cold air." (I am telling you it was <u>cold</u>) He would take us 3 mile to a neighbors....and sometimes when not so cold he would take us five miles, we would spend the evening singing.

We children would sing "Old Jones Singing School", "Farmer John", "Whistling John", "Trill Bird Up in the Apple Tree," "Come Down in the Meadow". Bert & I would sing together "Dont Slam the Gate" and the dutch song.

We had some neighbors by the name of Chapman. There were three boys & one girl in their family. Mr. C. was a violin player, they would come to our house to spend evenings (because we had a board floor) & we eight children would dance Square dances (Sister Beckie and Jennie C. could waltz real pretty). Sometimes we would make molases candy & pull it, sometimes we would parch sweet corn.

We children liked the wild sand plums dried too...I thing we had apples on one tree just two years out of the seven we lived on the homestead,....and one year we had peaches & cherries, but the fruit trees winter killed.

I remember one Summer my father cut out some of the Cottonwood trees in the grove for a "croquet ground." & put benches around it. In Summer young people would come miles on horseback & in buggies to play croquet, usually on Sundays.

Estella Eldora must have been a very inquisitive child, and very interested in details, as witnessed by entries in her diary. The entries following were written when she was thirteen years old, and traveled with her family from Kansas to Arkansas. On July 19, 1942, she wrote an explanation of those entries:

This is of our trip from Graham County, Kansas to Arkansas by teams and wagons. My father, we four children, Aunty and Uncle Webster and George Webster. Three teams. I was thirteen, my brother Bert and I rode horseback as far as Geneseo.

Saw first train at Stocton September the 17th.

September 13th hard storm of rain and hail this morning moved on the Bunker Hill and took dinner, worse than Graham County. No crops but wheat, camped at night at Lorrance.

September 14th went through Wilson and took dinner just this side. Camped at night about a mile from Ellsworth.

September 15th. Took dinner 3 miles northwest of Tomas and on to Genesea done some traiding. Went to Grandpa stayed Sunday the 16th went to Sunday school, seen some of our old schoolmates. Stayed at Grandpa's till Monday afternoon then went to Uncle Gabe's and stayed till Monday night; had a splendid time.

September 18th. Took dinner near Windom camped at night at Cow Creek.

September 19th. Camped for dinner 4 miles west of Hutchenson went up to town done some traiding went on across the Arkansas River. On the Hutchenson Bridge about a quarter of a mile long saw the first street cars in Hutchenson. Crops are looking better. Beautiful groves and orchards. Beautiful county.

September 20th. Camped for dinner between Mt. Hope and Haven ate dinner in the shade of a honey locust tree, camped at night 20 miles from Hutchenson.

September 21st. Went through Collwitch camped for dinner about one and 1/2 mile from the Valley Grove schoolhouse. Then went on to Witchita, done some traiding, went out east of town and camped over night. We met Uncle Gabe and Isaac at the O. K. schoolhouse. Uncle Gabe stayed all night with us then took the train for home in the morning.

September 22nd. Rained all morning. It was so muddy that we did not travel all day. We went down town in the streetcars in the evening.

September 23rd. Sunday, stayed all day in the same place.

September 24th. Drove on, stopped for dinner between Udall and Winfield and hitched up and went on.

September 25th. Went to Winfield done some traiding. Drove out and camped about 4 miles at a schoolhouse, met nine loads of apples and one of pawpaws going west.

September 26th. Camped for dinner in the shade of an elm tree, first cotton we saw was at Dexter. Camped over night between Dexter and Cedarvale near Elgin.

September 27th. Went on through Cedarvale camped for dinner near west Kena. Went on to Wenena and camped over night at middle Kena, went on; first persimmons we saw were at middle Kena.

September 28th. Went through Sedan camped at Peru, splendid crops and lots of cotton. Went through Union City, camped at night at China.

September 29th. Went through Union City, camped for dinner six miles west of Coffeeville at a schoolhouse, went about 2 and 1/2 miles and camped over night and Sunday on Onion Creek. Had a swing in a walnut tree, had squirrel for supper for Sunday night.

October 1st. 1888. Started on again went through Coffeeville camped for dinner at Snow Creek, camped over night nine miles west of Catalpa.

October 2nd. Went through Catalpa, done some traiding, went on camped for dinner in the edge of the Nation. Drove on till about 4 o'clock then we stopped in a grove and went hickory hunting. Got two pails could of got more, stayed there over night.

October 3rd. Camped for dinner about 10 miles west of Harland's Fairy, went on about 2 miles, saw two bears, went on, camped over night three quarters mile west of Harland's Fairy.

October 4th. Camped for dinner at Maysville, went to Cherokee City. Met Mr. and Mrs. Bins, Mrs. Wilkins and family.

And now we are in Missouria, we got here the 21st day of August, 1889.

When Nation was mentioned, that meant Indian Territory, sometimes referred to as the Indian Nation. All spelling, grammar and phrases were left as nearly like the original as possible.

Family of Richard Robert Newkirk
c.1905, Rice County, Kansas
Left to right, rear: Ethel Elverne, Clare Sparks and Arthur Reid.
Left to right, front: Ray Hobart, Mary Alma Sparks Newkirk, Lella Belle and Richard Robert.

Richard Robert Newkirk
1859-1953

This son of James Madison Newkirk (1815) was born February 11, 1859 in Clinton County, Iowa, near Dewitt, and died February 15, 1953 in Rice County, Kansas. His biography appears in Volume 1, page 534, *Biographical History of Central Kansas*, 1902. Married February 11, 1884 at Elwood, Clinton County, Iowa, to Mary Alma Sparks, born June 20, 1861 and died November 8, 1924 in Harvey County, Kansas. An extensive biography appears in the September, 1986 issue of *Newkirk Notes*. Children, born in Rice County:

Clare Sparks Newkirk & Alice Irene Kiser Newkirk
Wedding photos, 1914

1. Clare Sparks Newkirk, born April 25, 1886, and died October
    31, 1962. Married October 14, 1914 Alice Irene Kiser, born
    October 14, 1890 in Rice County; died November 18, 1960 in
    Reno County. Children, born in Rice County:
    a. Frances Alma Newkirk, born December 25, 1915;
        married July 7, 1940 Matthew Allen Reber, born
        September 23, 1916
    b. Marjorie Ellen Newkirk, born August 22, 1918, and
        married November 5, 1944 to Laverne C. Schmidt, who
        was born September 21, 1920
    c. Phyllis Irene Newkirk, born September 11, 1921, and
        married April 20, 1941 to Gerald Leslie Fry
    d. Ralph Lawrence Newkirk, born October 11, 1925.
        Married August 14, 1948 in Pratt, Kansas, to Ima Jean
        Geffert. It is of some interest to note here that the author

is the son of Josephine Davis Pratt Hurley and, on a western trip in 1975, spent a night in Pratt, Kansas, seeking haven from a tremendous storm. At the time, I inquired as to the origin of the name, hoping for a genealogical connection, of course. I learned that it was one of many towns or counties named after the Civil War for individuals who served, primarily Union. Pratt was named for an obscure Lieutenant from Massachusetts who was killed soon after he enlisted, and never set foot in Kansas! There was a son, born at Pratt:

  (1)   Alan Dean Newkirk, born May 20, 1952

2.   Ethel Elverne Newkirk, born October 14, 1889, and died April 2, 1976. Married December 30, 1915 to Archer F. Kiser, born January 3, 1886; died August 19, 1959 in Sedgwick County, Kansas

3.   Arthur Reid Newkirk, born September 21, 1893. Married June 1, 1918 to Eunice Holdren, born January 23, 1895 in Rice County, Kansas. Children, born there:

a.   Donald Ray Newkirk, born July 16, 1919. Married May 9, 1947 to Helen K. Lindsay, born October 9, 1922 and died June 20, 1978. Children, born in Sedgwick County, Kansas:

  (1)   Katherine Ann Newkirk, born July 22, 1950; married to William Lorton

  (2)   David Lindsay Newkirk, born May 26, 1952. Married 1977 to Janet Souder, born September 18, 1952

  (3)   Douglas Robert Newkirk, born May 13, 1957

b.   Howard Lyle Newkirk, born April 13, 1923. Married June 12, 1943 to Norma Lee Wilkinson in Orange County, California, born July 17, 1923. Children:

  (1)   Richard Lee Newkirk, born February 10, 1945 in Jefferson County, Illinois. Married in Jackson County, Missouri, November 23, 1974 to Mary Jo Gladow

  (2)   Susan Ann Newkirk, born February 1, 1958 in Rock Island County, Illinois. Married November 24, 1978 to Brian E. Taylor; divorced

c.   Marilyn Ruth Newkirk, born December 21, 1928, and married September 9, 1951 to Stuart M. Hutchison

4.   Ray Hobart Newkirk, born May 26, 1897, of whom more

5.   Lella Belle Newkirk, born March 18, 1900 in Rice County, Kansas. Married there November 10, 1921 to Richard Roscoe Ball.

Ray Hobart Newkirk
1897-1961

This son of Richard Robert Newkirk (1859), was born May 26, 1897 and died May 13, 1961. Married September 6, 1919 to Hazel Robinson, who was born March 28, 1899 and died May 20, 1974. Children:

1.   Elwin Earl Newkirk, born September 17, 1923 in Rice County, Kansas, and died July 18, 1983 in Alameda County, California; buried at sea. Married 1942 Sylvia Berry in Denton, Texas; annulled

2.   Billie Ray Newkirk, born October 31, 1926 in Los Angeles, California. Married August 22, 1948 in Victoria County, Texas, to Helen Slawson, born December 23, 1929. They had five children:

    a.   Linda Joan Newkirk, born June 28, 1949 in Oregon and married June 15, 1974 in Cook County, Illinois, to Lester B. Knutson, born April 5, 1953 in Malaya

    b.   Patricia Susan Newkirk, born January 7, 1952 in Larimer County, Colorado. Married March 10, 1974 in Cook County, Illinois, to David A. Coffman, born October 20, 1952 in Oklahoma

    c.   James Alan Newkirk, born October 9, 1953 in Larimer County, Colorado. He was married September 2, 1977 in Australia to Karen E. Clover, born July 25, 1956 in England. They had children:

        (1)   Anway Ameranto Newkirk, born December 1, 1981 in Peru

        (2)   Martin Rafael Newkirk, born May 14, 1984 in Australia

d.   David Richard Newkirk, born February 19, 1958 in Lawrence County, South Dakota. Married in San Diego County, California, August 5, 1983 to Susan L. Glenn, born January 19, 1956, and had children, including:

    (1) Amanda Sue Newkirk, born January 19, 1985 in San Diego County, California

e.   Lisa Susan Newkirk, born June 7, 1963 Denver County, Colorado

3.   Patricia Ann Newkirk, born July 25, 1928. Married May 22, 1949 to Robert W. Stolper.

Angeline Newkirk
1824-1898

This daughter of George W. Newkirk (1784) was born April 7, 1824; died August 16, 1898 in Marion County, Indiana. Married there May 20, or June 1, 1839 Andrew Bolander, and had children:

1.   Margaret Bolander, born June 20, 1840 in Marion County and died September 27, 1911. Married at Oaklandon, Indiana (not on my maps) November 15, 1866 to Sylvester Ellis Hamilton, and had eight children:

a.   Andrew A. Hamilton, born September 4, 1867, and married March 21, 1894 at Castleton, Indiana, to Mary Tate. They had three children.

b.   Martha E. Hamilton, born June 22, 1869; married June 11, 1891 to Joseph E. Meads. Six children.

c.   Guy D. Hamilton, born October 27, 1871; married April 18, 1900 to Lillie M. Bronson. Four children.

d.   Emma B. Hamilton, born September 24, 1873; married Otis Sowers February 21, 1890. Three children.

e.   John F. Hamilton, born May 15, 1876; died September 29, 1905. Married November 8, 1903 Mary Pressel; one child.

f.   Arla C. Hamilton, born September 24, 1878; single.

g.   Elma Gertrude Hamilton, born February 9, 1881, and married December 10, 1895 Andrew Raymond Harper and had eight children.

h. Edward Hamilton, born April 10, 1884; died July 19, 1884

2. Sarah Bolander, born May 8, 1842 in Marion County, Indiana died June 1, 1895. Married November 2, 1863 to Julius C. Bunnell. They had no children.

3. Eliza Bolander, born January 17, 1843 in Marion County, and died May 13, 1898. Married November 7, 1866 to Francis M. Christian. Eight children, born in Marion County:

   a. Nora Christian, born August 4, 1867; married February 6, 1885 to Louis F. Allen. Four children.

   b. Anna Christian, born September 22, 1869; died January 11, 1907. Married September 24, 1887 Allen Z. White and had ten children.

   c. Grace Christian, born June 26, 1870 at Indianapolis, Indiana and married May 25, 1892 James Huffman. Four children.

   d. Joseph Christian, born October 22, 1872; married July 28, 1896 to Clara Harman. Three children.

   e. Nellie Christian, born April 6, 1874 at Indianapolis, and married April 7, 1895 to Ernest Newhouse. Six children.

   f. Sallie Christian, born July 16, 1877 at Brightwood, Indiana; married September 8, 1897 to John McKenzie. Three children.

   g. Maude Christian, born November 12, 1881; single.

   h. Hugh Christian, an infant death.

4. Martha Bolander, born October 30, 1845 at Castleton, Indiana, and married March 25, 1877 Austin Hamilton. Three children:

   a. Cora May Hamilton, born in Marion County, Indiana, and married to Henry C. F. Koch.

   b. Acy Hamilton, born August 11, 1878 in Marion County, and married November 12, 1910 to Lilian M. Morris.

   c. Lula Hamilton, born March 30, 1880 in Hancock County, and married to Walter Offenbacker.

5. Elizabeth Bolander, born November 8, 1847 at Castleton, Indiana; married October 18, 1866 to William Kane. One son:

   a. Julius C. Kane, born February 4, 1867, and married December 28, 1892 Cora E. Baker. Five children.

6. Kesiah Bolander, born May 20, 1850 in Marion County, Indiana, and died December 10, 1858.
7. John A. J. Bolander, born in Clinton County, Illinois, August 10, 1853; died March 3, 1892. Married March 1, 1882 Alice McIlvaine, born January 6, 1860 in Marion County. They had children, born in Marion County, Indiana:
   a. Breton Bolander, born April 19, 1883; married December 23, 1903 to Clara May Young. One son.
   b. Anna Mary Bolander, born February 15, 1885, and married September 12, 1909 Charles Flanagan. One son.
   c. Ethel Kissire Bolander, born February 1, 1887, and married December 25, 1906 to Lester J. Roberts. They had two children.
   d. James Andrew Bolander, born June 18, 1889, single.
   e. Emma Rebecca Bolander, born June 5, 1892; married May 9, 1909 Birchie L. Young. One son.
   f. Lester Bolander, born November 5, 1894; single.
8. Electa Bolander, born February 9, 1855 in Clinton County, Illinois and married February 11, 1880 John Messersmith. Two children, born in Indiana:
   a. Walter D. Messersmith, born August 27, 1881 at Indianapolis, Indiana; married November 16, 1901 Dora Wadsworth. Two children.
   b. Murry A. Messersmith, born at Castleton, Indiana on May 13, 1888; married October 4, 1911 Mabel Murffy.
9. James Bolander, born August 3, 1857 in Marion County, Indiana; died December 20, 1857.
10. Frank Bolander, born Apirl 10, 1861 in Marion County, and died November 17, 1900. Married Fredericka Burch, and had three children:
    a. Charles Bolander
    b. Joseph Bolander
    c. Paul Bolander

CHAPTER 12

Johann Heinrick Neukirk
1674-

One of the earliest Newkirks mentioned in America was Johann Heinrick Neukirk, appearing on *Governor Hunter's Ration List* of 1710. There, Johann is shown as being age 36 (born c.1674); his wife Anna Maria is 33 (born c.1677); Johannes is 11 (born c.1699); and John had died at age 8 (born c.1702). Johann appears in *The Simmendinger List of MacWeathys Book of Names*, and in Reverend Josiah Kockerthal's *Baptism Records of the Moravian Church in the Mohawk Valley*, which includes baptism records of two more of his children. Early Ulster County, New York, records report that, in November, 1734, Robert Cane was indicted for assault *"at the mansion house of Hendrick New Kerk at New Witt in the Southern District of Ulster County, upon Mary New Kerk, the wife of Hendrick; William Cumberford was indicted for assault at the house of Hendrick New Kerk upon Johannis New Kerk; and Johannis New Kerk of New Witt, yeoman, was indicted for assault upon William Cumberford."* The results of these indictments do not appear in the record, but they suggest a severe disturbance in the Newkirk household. It should be noted that, throughout the colonies, early settlers were highly prone to litigation, dragging neighbors into court on the flimsiest of excuses.

Many Palatines who fled Germany were wealthy, educated people; what was Johann's status? The indictments state he had a "mansion house" so he was apparently of the landed gentry. Who was Anna Maria? Some correspondents believe that she was a Maul, and perhaps a sister of Christopher Maul or Friederich Maul. The Mauls and the Newkirks were frequently witnesses of the baptism of the children of each family. Mormon IGI records list her name as Anna Maria Almenroder. The children were:
1. Johannes Neukirk, born c.1699 in Germany, of whom more
2. Johann Hendrick Neukirk, born c.1702 in Germany; died by 1710

3. Maria Catharina Neukirk, baptized December 11, 1713 in New York.
4. Anna Benigma Neukirk, born December 23, 1715 at the West Camp on the Hudson River, and married Alexander Patterson. She became a member of the Montgomery German Reformed Church August 11, 1732, at its inception. One writer states that the parentage of Alexander Patterson is not known, but there is a story that some of the Pattersons of Orange County, New York, were descended from a colonial New Jersey governor's illegitimate son. The children of Anna included:
   a. Johannes Patterson, baptized October 7, 1735; died young
   b. Johannes Patterson, the second to bear the name after the infant death, baptized June 27, 1738 and died in 1785. His baptism was at the Lutheran Church of New York. His will, written August 3, 1785, and proved December 29, 1785, mentions his brother James, and a daughter:
      (1) Mary Patterson
   c. Hendrick Patterson, born September 16, 1740; married to Christian Morrison, born 1761, perhaps in Scotland, a daughter of James Morrison. They bought 700 acres of land in Wallkill and settled at Hamptonburgh
   d. James Patterson, baptized May 17, 1743; apparently died young
   e. Maria Patterson, baptized May 20, 1745; married her cousin, Jacob Newkirk (1737), son of Johannes Neukirch (1699) and Geertje Klaarwater. See family reported under his name.
   f. James Patterson, second of this name, baptized May 5, 1747
   g. Susanna Patterson, baptized May 9, 1750
   h. Ann Patterson, baptized May 26, 1752; married to James Bells?
   i. Anna Patterson, baptized January 13, 1754, and married Jacob Their.
   j. Alexander Patterson, born March 16, 1756; died April 18, 1796 or 1797. Served in the 4th Regiment, Orange County Militia

5. Anna Ursula Neukirk (probably), born about 1718 in New York. She was married twice: first to Robert Huey, who died by May, 1744; and second to William Huey, or Hughes. Five children from the first marriage, and two from the second:
    a. James Huey, baptized at Montgomery April 11, 1738
    b. John Huey, perhaps
    c. Anna Huey, perhaps, who married Philippus DuPuis, at the Dutch Reformed Church of Kingston, March 22, 1757
    d. Susanna Huey, perhaps.
    e. Margaret Huey, baptized at Montgomery, September 7, 1742, and married to William Patterson
    f. Henry Huey, baptized at Montgomery, April 29, 1746
    g. Mary Huey, baptized at Montgomery, June 7, 1748

Johannes Neukirch
1699-1777

This son of Johann Heinrick Neukirch (1674) and Anna Maria Neukirch (1677), was born c.1699, probably in Germany. He was brought to America, probably to New York, by his parents, and perhaps with a group of Palatines transported by, or through the efforts of, Reverend Joshua Von Kocherthal. These people arrived first in New York on June 14, 1710, and were quarantined for a time on Governor's Island, due to disease among them. Among the survivors of that group, reported by Kocherthal, were the parents of this Johannes, who was listed with them at the age of 11 years in 1710. He was married before 1726 to Geertje Klaarwater, who was a daughter of Jacob Klaarwater and Mayke Crom Klaarwater. The Klaarwater (or later Clearwater) families were among the oldest in Holland, founders of the Dutch Republic, and owners of estates near Rotterdam. The founder of the family in America was Theunis Jacobsen Klaarwater, who was born at Baarn in 1624 and died 1715 in Ulster County, New York. In 1709, Queen Anne of England granted to him, his son Jacob, and others, a patent of 4,000 acres of land east of the Wallkill River in southern Ulster County.

Johannes Neukirch was one of the founders of the German Reformed Church of Montgomery County, New York; was elected the second deacon on October 23, 1734, and served as an elder in 1755 and 1768. He was apparently quite well-to-do, and wrote his will October 5, 1771, proven February 7, 1777 (Deed Book VII, page 490, Ulster County, New York). His wife is not mentioned, so she must have died between 1761 and 1771.

In his work, *Ulster County, New York Probate Records*, Volume 1, page 141, Gustave Anjou states that this Johannes was the son of Cornelis Gerretse Van Nieuwkercke (1662), and that he was married to Dorothea Douw, but does not quote the source of that statement. That does not appear to be correct, in light of other information available. We believe that the husband of Dorothea Douw was Jan, or Johannes Nieuwkirk, born 1690, son of Arien Gerritsen Nieuwkirk (1663), as reported in Chapter 9 of this study. Anjou lists at least four more children not found in other sources, including: Adrian, baptized June 12, 1720; Gerrit, baptized December 20, 1724; Myndert, baptized April 17, 1726; and Neeltjen, baptized April 7, 1728. Recognizing the fact that the will was dated 1771 and probated 1777, long after the reported births of these four children, and none of them were mentioned in the will, one must conclude that they were either not children of Johannes, or were all deceased at the time of the making of the will. It appears more likely that they were children of Jan, or Johannes Nieuwkirk, born 1690, son of Arien Gerritsen Nieuwkirk (1663), as reported in Chapter 9 and above, and his wife Dorothea Douw. The children of this Johannes included, at least:

1. Hendrick Newkirch, born November 21, 1721, and of whom more in Chapter 13

2. Anna Maria Newkirch, born c.1725/30; died some time after 1787, when she was mentioned in her husband's will. Married Johan Yoest German, born 1726 and died December 17, 1790. Members of the Montgomery German Reformed church; he joined May 15, 1754, she joined November 4, 1769. They had eight children:

   a. Geertje German, baptized August 27, 1757; married Jacob Pitts

   b. Elizabeth German, baptized August 25, 1759; married to Moses Letts

    c.   Hendrick German, baptized August 29, 1761; married to Rachel Amy

    d.   Johannis German, baptized May 7, 1763

    e.   Anna Maria German, baptized April 23, 1765; married Levi Hill

    f.   Catherine German, baptized February 14, 1767, and died young

    g.   Catherine German, baptized November 4, 1769; married Abraham Rosencrans

    h.   Andries German, baptized June 20, 1773; married to Elizabeth Clark

3.   Adam Newkirch, born c.1730, of whom more

4.   Elizabeth Newkirch, baptized October 22, 1734 at the Montgomery German Reformed church, and died March 21, 1812. Married to Jacob Bodine; four children:

    a.   Rachel Bodine, baptized 1766; died 1821; married John Sears

    b.   Charles Bodine, born June 30, 1771; married Maria Eager

    c.   Frances Bodine, born April 1, 1776; married Alexander Kidd, Jr.

    d.   Lewis Bodine, born February 19, 1784; married twice: Mary Kidd, and Mary Burns

5.   Jacob Newkirch, baptized April 26, 1737, of whom more

6.   Johannes Newkirch, Jr., baptized February 5, 1740, of whom more

7.   Petrus Newkirch, perhaps, baptized September 6, 1743; died young?

8.   Rachel Newkirch, baptized May 5, 1747 and died February 16, 1830. She married Stevanus Crist, Jr., and they were admitted to the German Reformed church at Montgomery, March 22, 1774. He died February 16, 1830, and she apparently married second William Smith. Four children, born to her first marriage:

    a.   Lorens Crist, baptized January 23, 1768

    b.   Catherine Crist, baptized May 12, 1770

    c.   Johannes Crist, born June 27, 1773

d.   Elizabeth Crist, born June 25, 1786. On September 5, 1806, both of her parents sponsored the baptisms of "Harriet and Virgil, illegitimate children of Elizabeth Crist"

Adam Newkirk
1730-1800

This son of Johannes Neukirch (1699) and Geertje Klaarwater Neukirch, was born c.1730 in New York, and died October, 1800 in Orange County, New York. Married June 10, 1756 to Magdaline Kimburg, born March 8, 1736 at Newburg, New York, daughter of Johannes Matthiue Kimburg and Anna Maria Friend. She survived her husband, being named in a Letter of Administration on his estate, dated October 10, 1800, filed in Liber C, page 56, at Orange County, New York. They were admitted as members of the Montgomery German Reformed church on March 22, 1774. Adam served in the War of the Revolution with his brothers, as a private in the 2nd Regiment of the Ulster County Militia. Their children, all born in New York, included:

1.   Johannis Newkirk, baptized August 28, 1756
2.   Matthys Newkirk, baptized February 27, 1758
3.   Anna Maria Newkirk, baptized August 25, 1759
4.   John Adam Newkirk, born February 25, 1763, of whom more
5.   Catherine Newkirk, born February 14, 1767. Married June 16, 1791 to John Goldsmith, who died in 1812
6.   Petrus Newkirk, or Peter Newkirk, born November 5, 1771. Married December 4, 1795 in Orange County, New York, to Margaret Graham and had five children:
    a.   Hannah Graham Newkirk, born February 28, 1796; died young
    b.   Hannah Graham Newkirk, second to use the name, baptized July 18, 1798
    c.   Andrew Graham Newkirk, baptized May 26, 1799, and married December 27, 1823 to Roxanna Newkirk, born c.1804. She was surely a cousin, but not now identified. The census of 1850 for Orange County indicates one son:
        (1)   David Newkirk, born c.1836 in New York

d. Adam Newkirk, born April 28, 1801
e. Leentje Newkirk, baptized May 4, 1802
f. Maria Graham Newkirk, baptized April 21, 1807
g. Eliza Jane Newkirk, born June 5, 1816, perhaps married Alfred Perrine September 12, 1844 at Montgomery
7. Adam Newkirk, Jr., born December 31, 1774, of whom more
8. Elizabeth Newkirk, born August 16, 1777
9. Hannah Newkirk, born October 22, 1780. Married February 7, 1804 Moses Bodine in Ulster County, New York. Children:
   a. Sally Bodine, baptized June 4, 1804
   b. Ethalinda Bodine, baptized August 2, 1806
   c. Catherine Bodine, baptized February 12, 1808
   d. Eliza Bodine, baptized March 13, 1810
   e. Hiram Bodine, baptized March 22, 1812
   f. Elahaur Bodine, baptized June 17, 1814
   g. Harriette Bodine, baptized February 26, 1816
   h. William Stitt Bodine, baptized October 21, 1819
10. Rachel Newkirk, possibly. Married to William Smith and had children:
    a. Jemima Smith, born January 2, 1787
    b. Adam Smith, born c.1787
    c. Betsey Smith, baptized September 24, 1792
    d. Edward Smith, baptized August 18, 1794

John Adam Newkirk
1763-1837

This son of Adam Newkirk (1730) and Magdaline Kimburg Newkirk (1736), was baptized in New York, February 25, 1763 and died August 31, 1837. Married February 25, 1791 to Catherine Bodine at Montgomery, Ulster County, New York. She was born c.1778 and died September 20, 1823 in Orange County, New York. Their children were all born in Orange County, New York:

1. Julia Newkirk, born December 7, 1791; married February 20, 1813 at Shawangunk Reformed Dutch Church in Ulster County to Thomas Booth.
2. Obediah Newkirk, born November 2, 1793 and died October 26, 1870. Married June 22, 1816 in Orange County, New

York, to Sarah Daily, born c.1798 in New York. He appears in the 1850 census of Orange County, with his wife and three of their children. Also in the household is Ida Daily, age 70 (born c.1780), probably the mother of Sarah. Also, there is Thomas Powers at the age of 12, born c.1838 in Ireland; and E. Van Steenburgh at age 18, born c.1832 in New York; neither of them being further identified. Their children, born in Orange County, New York, included:

a.   Alexander Yates Newkirk, born January 21, 1817; died December 7, 1882
b.   Mary Ann Newkirk, born February 10, 1820
c.   Henry Newkirk, born April 13, 1823
d.   Ida Catherine Newkirk, born October 14, 1826
e.   Margaret Gridley Newkirk, born July 4, 1828
f.   George Newkirk, born July 4, 1831
g.   Sarah Leonora Halsey Newkirk, born August 31, 1836

3.   Peter Newkirk, born August 25, 1794 and died June 19, 1850 in Orange County, New York. Married September 23, 1815 to Dolly Smith, born September 5, 1789 and died September 9, 1879. The family appears in the 1850 census of New York City, with Peter listed as a clerk. Only one of their daughters, Martha, is included in the household at the time. There are other individuals: Nancy Osborn, age 57, born c.1793; John Aker, age 43, born c.1807; and Frances Henry, age 25, born c.1825; all born in New York. Peter's children, the first four born in Orange County, New York, and the last two in New York City, were:

a.   Mary Allin Newkirk, born December 15, 1816
b.   James Smith Newkirk, born July 19, 1818
c.   Jacob Bodine Newkirk, born December 22, 1820, and had a son:
       (1)   Jacob Newkirk, born c.1850, died after 1940. Married April 5, 1883 to Elizabeth Raymond; at least a daughter:
               (a)   Louise N. Newkirk, born on September 26, 1885 at Kingston, Ulster County, New York (or by some records, in Brooklyn, New York),

died September 27, 1948. Married December
27, 1904 to Claude Ferry Howell.
- d.   William Newkirk, born February 17, 1823
- e.   Mary Agnes Newkirk, born January 15, 1830
- f.   Martha Whelan Newkirk, born October 14, 1833
4. Maria Newkirk, born July 22, 1797
5. John Adam Newkirk, Jr., born July 11, 1799
6. Caty Lena Newkirk, born January 28, 1801
7. Elsie Newkirk, born April 18, 1803
8. William Newkirk, born May 11, 1805
9. Melissa Newkirk, born July 12, 1807
10. Ann Eliza Newkirk, born December 2, 1812
11. Rachel Crist Newkirk, born August 22, 1815

Adam Newkirk, Jr.
1774-1861

This son of Adam Newkirk (1730), was born December 31,
1774, probably at Montgomery, Orange County, New York, and
baptized there January 22, 1775; died February 19, 1861. Married
October 17, 1801 to Hannah Shafer (IGI records of the Mormon
church show her name as Annatje Shafer) at Montgomery, and she
died September 12, 1830. Children, born in Orange County, were:
1. Daniel Newkirk, born February 9, 1802; died March 2, 1868.
   Married February 13, 1823 to Rachel Crist, born c.1804; died
   August 31, 1856. The family appears in the 1850 census of
   Orange County; he is a farmer. Children, all born New York:
   - a.   Clarissa Newkirk, born June 19, 1824, and married
     September 27, 1843 to John L. Smith
   - b.   Eveline Newkirk, born August 5, 1826
   - c.   Hannah Newkirk, born November 7, 1828
   - d.   Albert Crist Newkirk, born October 27, 1829
   - e.   Catherine Maria Newkirk, born November 25, 1831
   - f.   Henry L. Weller Newkirk, born July 18, 1834; died
     March 9, 1865
   - g.   Daniel Irving Newkirk, born October 21, 1836
   - h.   Hamlet Newkirk, born September 3, 1839
   - i.   Mary Elizabeth Newkirk, born January 7, 1842

2. Catherine Newkirk, born October 26, 1803
3. Matthew Newkirk, born October 8, 1805; died May 14, 1881 in Orange County, New York. Married February 21, 1833 to Catherine Maria Bodine, born c.1811; died March 18, 1888 in Orange County. See also the 1850 census of the county. At that time, the household included: Elizabeth Bodine, age 62, born 1788, probably the mother of Matthew's wife; James Peck, age 48, born c.1802; and Ann Miller, age 16, black, born c.1834; all in New York. The children, born in New York, included:
   a. Elizabeth Newkirk, born July 3, 1834; died February 18, 1903. Married Charles Weller
   b. Howard Newkirk, born February 28, 1836
   c. Ellen Newkirk, born June 15, 1838
   d. Mary Newkirk, born February 12, 1845; died November 19, 1900. Married Moses R. McMonagle
   e. Edna Newkirk, born January 25, 1852
4. Adam Newkirk, III, born April 25, 1808; died April 20, 1872. Married December 4, 1834 to Catherine Millspaugh, born c.1809. See the 1850 census for Orange County. In the household was Harvey Milligan, age 18, black, born c.1832 in New York. The children, born in New York, included:
   a. Hannah Catherine Newkirk, born October 12, 1835
   b. Rachel Millspaugh Newkirk, born December 31, 1839; died 1896
   c. Sarah Frances Newkirk, born December 12, 1841
   d. Mary Elizabeth Newkirk, born April 22, 1846
5. Morris Newkirk, born December 7, 1810
6. Elsie Maria Newkirk, born May 19, 1813; married October 22, 1833 to Robert Bell.
7. Moses Newkirk, born August 23, 1815
8. Marcus Newkirk, born March 11, 1818.
9. Frederick Shafer Newkirk, born June 18, 1820; died July 26, 1896 in Orange County, New York. Married December 27, 1848 to Mehitable K. Bodine at Montgomery, Orange County. She was born December 2, 1822; died March 8, 1884. The census of 1850 includes in the household: Nancy Bronson, age 24, born c.1826 in New York, with her son, Charles Bronson,

born c.1850, both black; and Robert Thompson, age 14, born c.1836 in New York, not otherwise identified. Children, born in New York, included:

    a.   Mary Fonda Newkirk, born c.1838

    b.   Melissa Newkirk, born c.1849

10. Matilda Smith Newkirk, born September 7, 1822

11. Priscilla Newkirk, born January 21, 1825; died June 30, 1887. Married January 28, 1846 Harvey J. Rockefeller

12. Dustan Newkirk, born August 25, 1827

13. Moses Newkirk, born August 13, 1830, perhaps a second use of the name, if the earlier child was an infant death.

Jacob Newkirk
1737-1818

This son of Johannes Neukirch (1699) and Geertje Klaarwater was baptized April 26, 1737 at the German Reformed church in Montgomery, New York, and died January 16, 1817 in Orange County, New York. Married twice: first on December 22, 1768 to his cousin, Anna Maria Patterson, baptized May 20, 1745, who was a daughter of Alexander Patterson and Anna Benigma Newkirk Patterson (1715). Married second November 16, 1790 to Roxanna Babcock. Jacob was a Lieutenant Colonel in the War of the Revolution. He assumed command of the 2nd Regiment, Ulster County Militia, in 1777, after Colonel McClaughry was taken prisoner in the battle of Fort Montgomery. Jacob became a member of the Montgomery Reformed church March 22, 1774, and served as an elder and a deacon. His will, found in Orange County, New York, Liber F, page 107, was written December 4, 1816 and proven February 8, 1817. His children, born in Orange County, New York, included:

1.   David Newkirk, baptized October 12, 1771. Married December 10, 1800 to Nancy Moore at Montgomery, Orange County, New York, and had two children, born there:

    a.   Mary Patterson Newkirk, born September 7, 1800; died March 14, 1880. Married July 22, 1821 in Orange County Abraham Taylor, born August 7, 1799 and died January 22, 1846

b.   Hannah Newkirk, born 1812; died July 15, 1849
2.   Abraham Newkirk, born May 15, 1774; died April 18, 1816
3.   Peninah Newkirk or Benina Newkirk, born June 15, 1776; and baptized August 11, 1776. Married December 30, 1797 to Daniel Cahill, Jr. They had at least one child:
a.   Jacob Newkirk Cahill, baptized October 12, 1799
4.   Joseph Newkirk, baptized May 30, 1779
5.   Susannah Newkirk, baptized October 28, 1781. Married March 2, 1806 to Robert Thompson, and had one child:
a.   Nancy Thompson
6.   Catherine Newkirk, baptized June 5, 1784

Johannes Neukirch, Jr.
1740-1820

This son of Johannes Neukirch (1699) and Geertje Klaarwater Neukirch, was baptized at the Montgomery Reformed Church on February 5, 1740, and died October 11, 1820 in Orange County, New York. His will, written April 27, 1818 and proven October 23, 1820, is filed in Liber F, page 359, Orange County. He apparently served as private in the Second Regiment, Ulster County Militia; listed in DAR Patriot Index as Lieutenant during the Revolution. Married Susannah Bodine, who died November 21, 1815, and they were parents of eleven children, all born in New York:
1.   Susanna Neukirch, baptized October 18, 1766; married first March 3, 1791 to First Lieutenant Philip P. Millspaugh, and second on May 8, 1800 to Alexander Holliday, by whom she had a child:
a.   John Newkirk Holliday, born April 13, 1801
2.   Anna Maria Neukirch, baptized April 15, 1769
3.   Mary Neukirch, baptized February 5, 1772; died July 15, 1853. Married December 15, 1791 Frederick P. Millspaugh, and lived at Montgomery, Orange County, New York. Nine children:
a.   Susanna Millspaugh, born July 31, 1792
b.   Nancy Millspaugh, baptized May 8, 1794
c.   Lucas Elmendorf Millspaugh, baptized February 9, 1797
d.   Nancy Millspaugh, baptized March 25, 1799

e. Mathilda Millspaugh, born October 4, 1801
f. Elsje Millspaugh, born July 11, 1803
g. Cortland Millspaugh, baptized May 20, 1808
h. Clifford Millspaugh, baptized December 23, 1810
i. Mary Millspaugh, baptized July 23, 1813
4. Nellie Neukirch, born July 1, 1774 and died young
5. Absalom Neukirch, born June 22, 1777
6. Sally Neukirch, baptized September 19, 1779; died March 16, 1868. Married January 4, 1798 to Jacob C. Moore; lived at Montgomery, in Orange County, New York. Nine children:
   a. Susannah Moore, baptized April 19, 1799
   b. Maria Moore, born October 1, 1801
   c. Selah Moore, baptized November 12, 1803
   d. Coenradt Moore, baptized December 13, 1806
   e. Elsie Newkirk Moore, baptized January 30, 1809
   f. Amos Millspaugh Moore, baptized March 17, 1812
   g. Joel Moore, baptized March 18, 1816
   h. Ellen Moore, baptized August 13, 1818
   i. Charles Moore, baptized June 25, 1823
7. Nellie Neukirch, baptized March 3, 1782
8. Catherine Neukirch, baptized September 28, 1783; died May 25, 1859. Married November 10, 1801 to Jeremiah Brown, and lived at Montgomery, Orange County, New York. Seven children:
   a. Mary Brown, baptized November 17, 1802
   b. Charles Newkirk Brown, baptized December 13, 1804
   c. James Brown, baptized August 30, 1808
   d. Frederick Lucier Brown, baptized December 3, 1810
   e. Sally Moore Brown, baptized October 11, 1812
   f. Charlotte Smith Brown, baptized June 7, 1817
   g. Susan Ann Brown, baptized January 7, 1821
9. William Neukirch, born March 27, 1786
10. Charles Neukirch, baptized October 20, 1788, and died July 13, 1841. Married March 15, 1810 to Ann Crist; lived at Montgomery in Orange County, New York. Two children:
    a. John Neukirch, born September 26, 1810. This is possibly the John Newkirk listed in the 1850 census of

Livingston County, Michigan as a blacksmith, with wife
Betsey, born c.1811, and four children, born New York:

    (1)   Laura Neukirch, born c.1834

    (2)   Charles Neukirch, born c.1836

    (3)   Clarissa Neukirch, born c.1838

    (4)   Edmund Neukirch, born c.1844

  b.   Elizabeth Neukirch, baptized July 7, 1812. Married February 17, 1831 to Levi Vanderlyn

11. Elsie Neukirch, baptized November 18, 1791. Married September 26, 1809 at Pine Bush, Orange County, New York, to Jeremiah Decker, and lived at Montgomery. Three children:

  a.   Nelson Decker, born June 15, 1810

  b.   Charles Newkirk Decker, born December 4, 1811

  c.   Bartholomew Sears Decker, born August 15, 1814

CHAPTER 13

Hendrick Newkirk
1721-1797

This son of Johannes Neukirck (1699) and Geertje Klaarwater Neukirck, perhaps their eldest, was born November 21, 1721 in Ulster County, New York, and died about December, 1797. Under his father's will, he received a tract of land containing 200 acres "in the Precinct of Wallkill." Married March 24, 1751 to Angenietje White at Montgomery, where he died. His will was dated June 19, 1797, and proven December 14, 1797. It is repeated for interest in the September 1, 1983 issue of *Newkirk Notes*, by Mary and Gil Alford. In his will, he refers to his wife as Agnes, rather than the original German spelling, and leaves her some of the stock on the farm, his negro man called Caesar, the negro boy named Barna, part of the growing crops, and two rooms in the house.

The will also mentions a grandson, Henry McBride, son of Archibald McBride. We have accounted below for the marriage of each of his daughters, other than Jane or Isabella, one of whom must have been married to McBride. The will also mentions a grandson, Henry, but I do not now know whose son he was. It appears that he broke with the German Reform Church, and associated himself and his family with the Goodwill Presbyterian Church of Montgomery. He was the father of nine children, all born in New York:

1. John Newkirk, baptized January 18, 1753, of whom more
2. Angenietje Newkirk, baptized January 13, 1754, and married Alexander McGregor. Called Agnes in her father's will, she received a servant girl named Dinah and personal items.
3. Geertje Newkirk, also known as Charity Newkirk, born February 3, 1756, and baptized at the Montgomery Reformed Church. Married May 14, 1778 at Goshen Presbyterian Church in Orange County, New York, to James Moore. His will, dated April 12, 1799, and proven April 14, 1800, lists several of their children. The will of her father named a

granddaughter, Agnes, listed here with the other children, for a total of seven:

- a. David Moore.
- b. William Moore.
- c. Henry Moore.
- d. James Moore.
- e. Agnes Moore.
- f. Jane Moore.
- g. Ann Moore.

4. Jane Newkirk, birth unknown, married Archibald McBride, Jr., who was baptized September 23, 1759, son of Archibald, McBride and his wife Jane. The couple lived in Mamakating, Sullivan County, New York, and had children:

- a. Jane McBride, born June 17, 1776; married December 15, 1793 to Isaac Slaughter.
- b. Patrick McBride, baptized September 20, 1778, and married first September 11, 1806 to Elizabeth Toulon, and second June 24, 1815 to Nancy Pitts.
- c. James McBride, baptized December 26, 1779, and died January 15, 1817. Married Catherine Clark.
- d. Agnes McBride, baptized May 13, 1781
- e. Nancy B. McBride, born 1783, and died May 10, 1863. Married James McNeal.
- f. Henry McBride, born February 20, 1787; died January 10, 1860. Married Mary Seybolt.

5. James Newkirk, baptized July 6, 1760; apparently died young

6. Mary Newkirk, baptized April 22, 1762. Married first James Young, and second George Embler, Jr. She was mother of a total of seven children:

- a. Sally Young, born July 30, 1780; died May 22, 1854. Married November 20, 1799 to Moses Millspaugh.
- b. Luca Young, born December 16, 1781
- c. Cati Young, born July 3, 1783
- d. Catherine Embler, born April 3, 1785; married February 26, 1803 to John Traphagen.
- e. John Embler, born July 5, 1789; died August 30, 1861. Married Lucretia (perhaps Rockefeller).
- f. Henry Embler, born January 9, 1791; married Mary.

g.   Crey Embler, born November 18, 1793. Married James McDonald on January 17, 1814.

7.   Isabella Newkirk, baptized February 24, 1765.

8.   Henry C. Newkirk, baptized June 20, 1767, who is believed to be more properly Henry Conkright, of whom more

9.   James Newkirk, baptized October 27, 1771 at the Reformed Church in Montgomery, New York, and died January 15, 1815. Baptized at the Goodwill Presbyterian Church. He was the second child to bear the name; apparently the first died quite young. This James received two lots in the division of the five thousand acres tract of his father's estate, his parcel containing one hundred and forty acres. He also received certain farms tools and stock. He was married March 16, 1794 to Hannah Thompson, born c.1773 and died May 27, 1846. She is buried at the Phillipsburg Cemetery, Orange County, New York. They had four children, all born in New York:

a.   John Thompson Newkirk, born February 8, 1797; died young.

b.   Nancy J. Newkirk, born March 17, 1799; married July 20, 1831 to Samuel S. John.

c.   Hannah F. Newkirk, born February 26, 1802. Married October 28, 1832 to Stoddard Pelton, his second wife. He was the fifth son of Peleg Pelton, and was born July 1, 1787 at Mount Hope, Orange County, New York, and died November 15, 1846 on the homestead of his father, on which he lived. He had been first married to Fannie Tuthill. Three children born to his first marriage and four to his marriage to Hannah F. Newkirk. The family is reported in *The Pelton Family in America*, by J. M. Pelton, published by Joel Munsell's Sons, 1892. That report, which may well be more accurate, gives the date of birth of Hannah as February 2, 1800 and her death as September 27, 1847. Stoddard is there reported as being born July 1, 1797 and died November 15, 1846, as reported above, although another account lists his death as July 27, 1847. The reader is again cautioned in their acceptance of certain "facts" found in this or other studies.

d. Morris Newkirk, born April 22, 1803; married Hannah N., born 1814 in New York. They appear in the 1850 census of Orange County, with six children, all born in New York:

    (1)   Horace N. Newkirk, born 1839
    (2)   George N. Newkirk, born 1841
    (3)   Mary E. Newkirk, born 1843
    (4)   Abigail Newkirk, born 1845
    (5)   Adelia Jane Newkirk, born 1846
    (6)   Spencer Newkirk, born 1849

John Newkirk
1753-1840

This son of Hendrick Newkirk (1721) was baptized January 18, 1753 at Montgomery, New York, and died June 2, 1840. He was a Captain in the Second Regiment, Ulster County Militia during the Revolution. Reports in DAR *Grandparent Papers* state that he commanded the crew that laid the famous iron chain across the Hudson River to prevent British frigates from reaching West Point. At the close of the Revolution, he settled a few miles west of Montgomery in the village of Bloomingburgh, Sullivan County, New York. In 1992, I received a letter from Stanley C. Newkirk of Ulster Park, New York, in which he included an article about the town of Bloomingburgh, which is near the Pennsylvania border. The article dealt with problems of the local government, but there was a photo of an historical marker, which is of interest to us.

The marker reads: *"Bloomingburgh, named July 4, 1812 by James Newkirk. First settler Captain John Newkirk prior to 1776. First school 1784, taught by Mr. Campbell."* The James Newkirk who named the town is Captain John's son, born c.1786. We do not know how he chose the name, which may in some way be related to his first wife, whose maiden name we do not now know.

Under his father's will, John Newkirk (1753) received a lot of land which he then possessed, under an earlier deed from his father. He was married three times, and perhaps four. First, on May 1, 1776, he was married at Shawangunk Dutch Reformed Church to Sarah Van Keuren. She was born December 23, 1753, died April

26, 1786, a daughter of Benjamin Van Keuren and Maria Van Belnschoate Van Keuren. Some sources say that he married second Mrs. Vail Taylor. His third, or perhaps fourth, marriage was September 11, 1836 to Mrs. Ruth Tuthill, widow of Benjamin Tuthill, at Montgomery. At the time, John was reported as being 84 years of age. See *Marriages and Deaths from The New Yorker 1836-1841*, 1980, the National Genealogical Society. The March, 1984 issue of *Newkirk Notes*, by Mary and Gil Alford, contains, on page 10, reports of several deeds involving Captain John Newkirk and Katurah, his wife, in Sullivan County, New York, between 1810 and 1812, leading to the speculation of the fourth marriage. His children were all born in New York, perhaps Orange County:

1. Henry Newkirk, or Hendrick Newkirk, born August 2, 1777; died March 6, 1859. Married May 27, 1802 Frances Reeves. Children, born in New York:

    a. Katurah Newkirk, apparently named for her grandmother, born on March 31, 1803; died May 2, 1890. Married July 28, 1821 to Jacob D. Stringham.

    b. John S. Newkirk, born February 7, 1805; died March 10, 1809

    c. Elijah Newkirk, born March 22, 1807; died December 11, 1887. Married October 9, 1834 to Margaret Weller, born 1810 in New York. They appear together in the 1850 census for Sullivan County, New York, with no children.

    d. John Newkirk, born February 10, 1809; died April 3, 1809

    e. Sally M. Newkirk, born February 15, 1810; died 1885. Married Wilson Rath.

    f. Catherine O. Newkirk, born June 6, 1812, a twin, died November 9, 1854

    g. Leah Newkirk, Catherine's twin, born June 6, 1812; died August 22, 1815

    h. Abraham Westbrook Newkirk, born December 12, 1814, and died August 31, 1901. Married October 30, 1839 to Adline Stickney, born 1813 and died 1905. They appear in the 1850 census of Sullivan County, New York, with four of their five children:

(1)   Frederick S. Newkirk, born January 15, 1842; died October 29, 1911. Married on May 27, 1868 to Gabelle Hasbrouck.

(2)   Clement Botsford Newkirk, born December 26, 1844; died May, 1920 in New York. Married April 2, 1873 to Mary L. Seybolt, born 1842 and died 1913. They had three children, probably all born at Kingston, Ulster County, New York:

(a)   Frank Seybolt Newkirk, born 1876; married to Ellen Louise Morris.

(b)   James Warren Newkirk, born April 27, 1883; married December 1, 1910 to Edith Marion White, who was born February 11, 1888 at Kingston. Two children:

1.   Shirley Newkirk, born January 9, 1913

2.   Dorothy Newkirk; September 6, 1916

(c)   Clement Ray Newkirk, born 1884

(3)   Mary F. Newkirk, born August 21, 1846; married December 26, 1872 to David S. Strong.

(4)   Charles H. Newkirk, born January 3, 1850; and married twice: first Ellen J. Wakeman, and second Sarah K. Skinner.

(5)   Venti Newkirk, born April 15, 1853; married October 23, 1872 to Edgar A. Hawthorn.

i.   Henry B. Newkirk, born September 19, 1816; died May 12, 1895. Married January 13, 1842 to Christine Lockwood, born 1818 in New York. They appear in the 1850 census for Sullivan County, with two children, born in New York:

(1)   Charles B. Newkirk born June 29, 1841; died June 30, 1845

(2)   Sarah S. Newkirk, born September 18, 1846; died May 30, 1881

j.   Hannah Newkirk, born February 27, 1819, a twin; died April 2, 1854. Married James McCrosky.

k.   Fanny Newkirk, born February 27, 1819, a twin; married to Fulton Comfort

1. Samuel D. Newkirk, a carpenter, born November 18, 1820; died April 24, 1901. Married first December 21, 1845 Anna Benedict; married second December 21, 1868 to a widow, whose name is not reported to me. See the 1850 census of Sullivan County, New York. At that time, they had only the first child listed below; also in the household was Moses S. Benedict, a silversmith, age 18, born 1832, probably a brother of Anna. Children were born to the first marriage only, in New York:

    (1)   Catherine J. Newkirk, born 1846; perhaps died young.

    (2)   Ella Newkirk, born May 8, 1851; married Francis Cameron.

    (3)   Smith B. Newkirk, born 1854; perhaps died young.

    (4)   John W. Newkirk, born July 31, 1857; died June 30, 1917

    (5)   Hannah N. Newkirk, born September 17, 1861; married on October 5, 1893 to Charles G. Holmes.

m.   Aseneth D. Newkirk, born November 8, 1820; married three times. First, March 13, 1831 Harmon Brown; second Alfred Wood; third Elijah Tucker.

2. Jacob Newkirk, or Jacobus Newkirk, baptized June 18, 1780 at the German Reformed Church at Montgomery. Reportedly, he "went west" and nothing further was heard from him.

3. Cornelius Newkirk, baptized June 25, 1782 in New York, and died December 4, 1842. Married first in 1802 to Ruth Smith, and second on July 4, 1821 to Susan Hovey. Five children from first marriage; four from the second, all born New York:

a.   Sarah Newkirk, born March 15, 1811; died September 8, 1878. Married c.1840 to Horace Tenney.

b.   Francis Newkirk, born June 12, 1813, and died October 3, 1862. Married to Lockwood Purdy. It is possible the spouse here was Purdy Lockwood, with the names reversed; the surname Lockwood appears elsewhere in family records.

c.   Maria Newkirk, born June 16, 1815; died January 7, 1901. Married September 29, 183? to Braddick Decker.

d. Nancy B. Newkirk, born March 29, 1817; married McNeal

e. Ruth A. Newkirk, born June 20, 1819; died December 24, 1896. Married September 13, 1849 to William Young McVey.

f. Catherine Newkirk, born April, 1822; married Jewel

g. John K. Newkirk, born c.1823; died at age nine

h. Henry Van Keuren Newkirk, born October 8, 1825; died March 25, 1883 in Orange County, New York. Married March 13, 1858 to Sarah Ellen McVey, born July 25, 1832 and died July 1, 1895 in Orange County. Six children, born in New York:

    (1) Mary F. Newkirk, born October 16, 1859; married Robert P. Sears.

    (2) Cornelius Newkirk, born November 15, 1862, and married December 17, 1890 to Elizabeth Cochran, born September, 1866

    (3) Anna C. Newkirk, born February 10, 1865

    (4) Henry V. Newkirk, born January 3, 1868; died April 15, 1916

    (5) Sarah E. Newkirk, born February 7, 1872; died November 13, 1911. Married Henry F. Frost.

    (6) Jane E. Newkirk, born January 18, 1874, and died April 1, 1914. Married August 9, 1898 Albert S. Embler.

i. Elizabeth Newkirk, born c.1826; married McVey.

4. Leah Newkirk, born March 12, 1784; died December 22, 1864. Married October 17, 1807 George Smith, born March 1, 1780 and died October 21, 1853.

5. James Newkirk, born c.1786; died January 18, 1828 in Sullivan County, New York. Some papers received on these families list this individual as James (Jacobus) Newkirk, with the same birth date assigned above to Jacob (Jacobus), who is believed to be his brother. The only confusion remaining is whether or not there were two individuals as here reported. The lineage remains the same in either case. Married to Mahala, born c.1785, who, after his death, was married to Aaron Hendricks about 1829. Mahala died November 4, 1863

at the age of 78 years, and is buried in South Cemetery, Lyons, Wayne County, New York. It appears that members of this family lived in both Wayne County, New York, and Wayne County, Michigan; apparently moving back and forth between the two. James and Mahala had eight children:

a. Leonard Charles Newkirk, born c.1806, of whom more.
b. Peter B. Newkirk, born c.1812
c. Charles H. Newkirk, born c.1819; married Philora, born c.1824 in New York. They are listed in the 1850 census of Ontario County, New York, with children, born in New York:
    (1) John Newkirk, born c.1839
    (2) Jane Newkirk, born c.1841
d. Fanny Jane Newkirk, born c.1820
e. Catherine Newkirk, born c.1822
f. Lemuel J. Newkirk, born c.1823; married c.1846 Abigail, born about 1828 in New York. They were divorced c.1878 and she lived with her son Albert in her later years. In the 1850 census for Phelps, Ontario County, New York, they had two children, both born in New York. Also in their household was one Charles Newkirk, born c.1836 in New York. Their children appear to have included:
    (1) John A. Newkirk, born c.1849
    (2) Theodore Newkirk, born c.1848
    (3) George A. Newkirk, born c.1852
    (4) Charles W. Newkirk, born c.1853
    (5) Oscar E. Newkirk, born 1854/60
    (6) Ellen Newkirk, born c.1862
    (7) Lemuel J. Newkirk, Jr., born c.1865
    (8) Albert C. Newkirk, born c.1868
g. Sarah Newkirk, born c.1825
h. Elizabeth Newkirk, born c.1827

6. Sarah Newkirk, born July 16, 1788; died April 3, 1791.

Leonard Charles Newkirk
1806-1889

This son of James Newkirk (1786), was born c.1806 in Sullivan County, New York, and died July 25, 1889 in Detroit, Michigan; buried at South Cemetery, Lyons, New York, with other family members. By occupation, he was a peppermint broker. Married to Mercy Walters, one child; second to Melinda Brown, born about June 11, 1811 and died December 11, 1846. Married third to Harriet after 1846, who died July 29, 1864. The census of 1850 for Wayne County lists his family, with no wife, but five of his children. In the household, there are two other individuals: Amy Alfred, born c.1815 in New York; and William Gillette, a miller, born c.1828 in England. One child born to the first marriage; five to the second, probably all in Wayne County:

1. Oliver Lysander Newkirk, baptized March 1, 1831 in the Presbyterian church in Lyons, New York. Married Elizabeth Blinn; divorced in 1880. They had at least one daughter:
    a. Luella W. Newkirk, born May 8, 1873 at Redford, Michigan, and died December, 1956 in Wayne County, Michigan. She was first married to Riley. She married second October 2, 1939 to her first cousin, William Leonard Newkirk, born August 13, 1865, his second wife. No children.
2. James Newkirk, born November 25, 1831; died July 25, 1843.
3. Charles Newkirk, born May 22, 1835; died November 16, 1912 in Michigan. Married c.1860 to Elizabeth. Both buried in Selden Cemetery, Wayne County, Michigan.
4. Daniel B. Newkirk, born September 7, 1837; died October 15, 1934 in Los Angeles, California; buried in Glenwood Cemetery, Wayne County, Michigan. He was a miner; married December 11, 1862 Nancy L. Zimmerman, born March 26, 1841 in New York; died February 16, 1913 in Wayne County, Michigan. Married second to Frances in California; no children. Children from his first marriage, all born in Wayne County, Michigan:
    a. Daniel L. Newkirk, born September 28, 1863; died May 19, 1865.

b. William Leonard Newkirk, born August 13, 1865, of whom more.

c. George O. Newkirk, born July 14, 1867 and died 1938. Married March 27, 1888 to Mattie E. Collins, born 1863, and died c.1942. Both buried at Glenwood Cemetery.

d. Emma M. Newkirk, born January 19, 1869, and died October 8, 1883; buried Glenwood Cemetery

5. Emily Newkirk, born September 1, 1842; died October 15, 1927. Married Jonas Gurnee, born 1832 and died 1908. Buried in South Cemetery in Lyons, New York, and had children:

a. Charles Gurnee, born c.1861

b. Alice Gurnee, born c.1864; died March 4, 1937. Married to Charles E. Craft, born 1858 and died 1891.

6. Celestia Newkirk, born May 29, 1843; died October 29, 1850.

William Leonard Newkirk
1865-1963

This son of Daniel B. Newkirk (1837) was born August 13, 1865 in Wayne County, Michigan, and died December 30, 1963 at El Paso, Texas; buried in Houston, Texas, where he was a road construction contractor. Married November 16, 1886 in Wayne County, Michigan to Laura Atkins Harrison, born October 8, 1864 at Mt. Clemens, Michigan; died March 6, 1939 at Detroit, daughter of Charles Harrison, Jr. and Lucy M. Atkins. Married second October 2, 1939 to his first cousin, Louella W. Newkirk Riley, born May 8, 1873 at Redford, Michigan; died December, 1956, daughter of Oliver Lysander Newkirk (1831) and Elizabeth Blinn Newkirk. Two children born in Wayne County, Michigan to first marriage:

1. Daniel Leighton Newkirk, an engineer, born December 28, 1887; died July 3, 1961 at Houston, Texas. Married June 28, 1913 at Calumet, Michigan to Mary Sherman, born September 17, 1892 in Lake Orion, Michigan, and died August 18, 1988 at El Paso, Texas. Three children:

a. Mary Julia Newkirk, born April 17, 1914 in Detroit, died November 15, 1996 at El Paso, Texas.

b. William Sherman Newkirk, born August 13, 1916 at Calumet, Michigan. Married at Houston, February, 1939, to Jane Elledge, and second October 28, 1990 Vicki Irene Moore. A son, born at Houston to the first marriage:

    (1)   William Sherman Newkirk, Jr., born June 6, 1957; married September, 1984 to Cathy Campbell, born December, 1957 at Chicago, and had children:

        (a)   Lauren Ann Newkirk, born 1985 Fort Worth

        (b)   Daniel E. Newkirk, born 1987 Fort Worth

        (c)   Katie Newkirk, born 1992 in Houston

c.   Charles Abner Newkirk, a musician, born June 26, 1918 in Detroit, and died March, 1983 at El Paso, Texas.

2.   Charles Harrison Newkirk, born March 26, 1890; died November 13, 1960 at Wayne City, Michigan. Married November 28, 1922 to Minnie Lillian Helm, born February 4, 1901 at Dearborn, Michigan. One daughter. After his death, she married second November 30, 1961 to Lloyd Prosise, and died November 11, 1985 in Howell, Michigan. Lloyd died January 19, 1985 in Howell. The daughter of Charles Harrison was:

a.   Laura Wilhelmina Newkirk, born February 19, 1925 in Dearborn, Wayne County, Michigan. Married December 23, 1944 in Dallas, Texas, to Clemens William Ziegler, born April 16, 1919 in Dearborn, son of William Ziegler and Hattie Schraeder Ziegler. Divorced October 30, 1947 after one child. Married second November 23, 1949 to George Frederick Merwin, born June 8, 1922, died April 9, 1996 at Grosse Pointe, Michigan. An artist and writer, he was the son of Lewis James Merwin and Irene Edith Gish Merwin. He adopted her first child, and they had two, born in Detroit, Wayne County, Michigan:

    (1)   Vicki Lyn Merwin, born October 7, 1945; married first January 10, 1964 at Livonia, Michigan, Richard Leon Hurlburt; divorced February 4, 1974. Married second April 27, 1974 at Novi, Oakland County, Michigan, to George Clifford Petrosky, born August 7, 1939 in Westmoreland County, Pennsylvania, who adopted both children from the first marriage. They had a child:

        (a)   Dawn Laurette Petrosky, born January 18, 1965 at Pontiac, Michigan. Married August

21, 1982 to Rick Allen Crim, born February 5, 1964 at Saginaw, Michigan. Two children:

1. Joseph Douglas Crim, born December 21, 1985 at Maui, Hawaii
2. Jessica Rose Crim, born March 17, 1995 at Mesa, Arizona.

(b) Collette Lee Petrosky, born September 7, 1967 at Pontiac, Michigan; married September 13, 1986 Michael Gundry, born July 29, 1966 at Niagara Falls, New York. Three children; first born at Camp Pendleton, last two at Oceanside, California:

1. Jonathan Matthew Gundry, born June 24, 1988
2. Kirsten Faith Gundry; October 18, 1991
3. Bailey Renee Gundry; February 3, 1995

(c) George Merwin Petrosky, born May 12, 1975 at Howell, Michigan. Married December 21, 1995 at Mesa, Arizona, to Zane Buchan, born August 25, 1976, and divorced.

(2) Mimi Laurette Merwin, born November 16, 1955 at Detroit; married September 2, 1974 at Northville, Michigan, Thomas Francis McDonald, born January 19, 1955 at Norfolk, Virginia. Divorced August 3, 1993 after three children:

(a) David Lee McDonald, born February 13, 1975 in Houghton County, Michigan; died September 27, 1994 at Novi, Oakland County
(b) Christina Lynn McDonald, born February 9, 1978 at Ann Arbor; died December 26, 1978 at Milford, Livingston County, Michigan.
(c) Tonni Michelle McDonald, born March 1, 1980 at Ann Arbor, Michigan.

(3) Jacqueline Lee Merwin, born June 9, 1958 at Detroit, and married there September 5, 1981 to William Terry Gonterman, born November 11, 1952 at Detroit, an auto mechanic.

Henry Conkright Newkirk
1767-1839

This son of Hendrick Neukirck (1721) was baptized June 20, 1767 at Montgomery German Reformed Church in Orange County, New York, and died October 26, 1839 in Franklin County, Indiana. His middle initial has been accepted by most researchers to stand for Conkright, or possibly Courtright, which was a prominent name in the Montgomery area. Under the will of his father, he was given one hundred acres which had been deeded to him, and which he had already disposed of; plus two notes for outstanding debts. He was married to Julia Anna Taylor, who was born September 20, 1770 in New York, and died September 25, 1836; buried in the Little Cedar Cemetery, Brookville, Indiana. It appears that he first settled in western Orange County, New York, near his father and his brother, Captain John Newkirk. He is listed in the 1800 census for Deer Park Township, Orange County. In the 1820 census, he is found in Sycamore Township, Hamilton County, Ohio. In that township, there was a village named Montgomery, which was settled by former inhabitants of Montgomery, Orange County, New York. In his pension claim in 1835, Henry lists his residence as Brookville Township, Franklin County, Indiana. His pension claim was rejected; many veterans of the Revolution were unable to provide written evidence of service or discharge when the pension was authorized in the early 1800s, having lost their records over that length of time.

It should be pointed out here that the information reported as to this family was taken largely from data sent to me by Gil and Mary Alford, as presented in the September and December, 1983 issues of their publication, *Newkirk Notes*. That information has not been personally authenticated by the author. Further, in 1995, a letter has been received from Bernice Emma Woodworth Teeter, one of the descendants of this line, who was an original contributor to the data published by the Alfords. She has pointed out that the parentage of Henry C. Newkirk (here under discussion), has not been proven to her complete satisfaction. She also sent me a copy of a letter written August 29, 1911 from Dr. A. B. Newkirk to Thomas J. Newkirk, in the course of their collaboration on the manuscript with which we are all familiar. In that letter, although it is outside his own lineage, and not reported in the final study found in *Genealogies of Pennsylvania Families* from The Pennsylvania Genealogical Magazine, Volume II, Hinman-Sotcher, 1982, Dr. Newkirk makes this comment: "I have records of another Henry who was born in Orange County, New York about 1730, who had a brother John and a sister Isabella. She married a man by the name of Anderson and lived near Bloomingburg, New York, and had a grandson, named Clem Anderson who lived at Fort Jarvis, N. Y. This Henry's wife, I think, was named Stuyvesant. He had a son Henry Conkright, born 1761, died in Hamilton County, Ohio, 1839. His wife's name was Julia Ann Taylor, and had the following children..." Dr. Newkirk then names the various children whom we report following. We present all this detail here to caution the reader that some questions remain relative to the exact lineage within some branches of the family. It should also be noted that we have reported a brother John and a sister Isabella as siblings of Henry Conkright Newkirk, which is one generation later than the family reported by Dr. A. B. Newkirk. It is possible that he has confused the families himself. In any case, the children were:

1. Katurah Newkirk, born June 30, 1789 and died September 12, 1862 in Franklin County, Indiana. Married November 30, 1805 to Riley, or Ryleigh, Woodworth, born August 1, 1782 in Litchfield, Connecticut, and died February 25, 1855 in Franklin County. Thirteen children, of whom one was:
   a. Dyer Dilavan Woodworth, born May 17, 1810, of whom more.
2. Malinda Newkirk, born c.1790; married Zeala Yoast.
3. Elizabeth Newkirk, born c.1791; died 1872. Married John W. Weller, born c.1795 in New York, and had ten children.
4. Temperance Newkirk, born March 28, 1792; died December 1, 1832. Married Henderson Haggerty.
5. Abraham Taylor Newkirk, born May 16, 1793, of whom more.
6. Sarah Van Keuren Newkirk, born c.1794. Married first Andrew Smith and second to Garrett. Two children.
7. Absolom W. Newkirk, born c.1795, of whom more.

8. Charles G. Newkirk, born November 11, 1800, of whom more.
9. Cornelius S. Newkirk, born March 24, 1803, of whom more.
10. Artimadoris W. Newkirk, or Artimus D. Woodworth Newkirk, born May 31, 1805, of whom more.
11. Mary Ann Newkirk, born August 9, 1807; married John Bell.

Dyer Dilavan Woodworth
1810-1891

This son of Ryleigh Woodworth (1782) and Katurah Newkirk Woodworth (1789) was born May 17, 1810 in Ontario, New York, and died December 15, 1891 at Mattoon, Coles County, Illinois. Married June 10, 1834 at Brookville, Franklin County, Indiana, to Abigail St. John, born March 25, 1812 at Port Jervis, Orange County, New York, and died February, 1885 at Birch Tree, Shannon County, Missouri, daughter of Daniel St. John (1777) and Mary Oakley St. John (1782). They had at least one son:

1. Edwin Ruthvin Woodworth, born April 21, 1837 Brookville, Indiana; died April 15, 1920 at Olathe, Johnson County, Kansas. Married August 3, 1860 at Marion, Indiana, to Mary Jane St. John, born February 4, 1843 in Indiana; died March 5, 1912 at Los Angeles, California. They had at least one son:

    a. Charles Elmer Woodworth, born January 27, 1872 at Newman, Douglas County, Illinois; died March 25, 1962 at Van Nuys, Los Angeles County, California. Married September 18, 1894 at Olathe, Johnson County, Kansas, to Rosetta Estella Hensey (or Hentze), born February 15, 1876 at Hampton, Rock Island County, Illinois; died July 24, 1941 at Van Nuys, California. At least one son:

        (1) John Charles Woodworth, born September 23, 1903 at Enid, Garfield County, Oklahoma; died December 10, 1939 at Santa Monica, California. Married March 7, 1924 at Arlington, California, to Emma Grace Lange, born March 13, 1909 at Keokuk, Lee County, Iowa; died November 3, 1967 at Portland, County, Oregon, daughter of

Frederick John Lange, Jr. (1869) and Dora Anna Wicke (1880). They had at least one daughter:

(a) Bernice Emma Woodworth, born October 25, 1925 at Van Nuys, California; married August 27, 1971 at Carson City, Ormsby County, Nevada, to Daniel Teeter. She is my correspondent for this family, and provided much of the original material found in *Newkirk Notes*.

Abraham Taylor Newkirk
1793-1890

This son of Henry C. Newkirk (1767) was born May 16, 1793 in New York, and died October 6, 1890. Married December 16, 1815 to Pamela Osborn, born August 21, 1796 in New York, and died May 10, 1863. Thirteen children, born in New York:

1. Mary Ann Newkirk, born February 22, 1817; died August 9, 1849.
2. Lydia Catherine Newkirk, born September 16, 1818; died October 5,0 1867. Married January 24, 1838 Anson Higley. Six children.
3. William Henry Newkirk, born May 16, 1820; died November 25, 1862. Married November 23, 1845 to Juliette Chapman, born c.1824 in New York. He married second in February, 1858 to Fidelia Farnham. Six children, five from the first, and one from the second marriage, all born in New York:
   a. Charles M. Newkirk, born February 13, 1846, and married June 1, 1882 to Sophia Voght.
   b. Ruth A. Newkirk, born December 20, 1847; married December 16, 1868 to Jeremiah Case.
   c. Silas Eugene Newkirk, born February 6, 1852, and died in August, 1895. Married December 27, 1882 Mary C. Clindince.
   d. Mary Cati Newkirk, born June 28, 1855; died October, 1886.
   e. George William Newkirk, born April 11, 1857; died August, 1895

 f. Lewis H. Newkirk, born July 27, 1859; married 1880 Della Bigler.

4. Julietta Newkirk, born March 15, 1822; died October 5, 1911. Married February 14, 1861 Jacob Watson. One child.

5. Adaline Newkirk (Sally?), born March 15, 1824; died 1907.

6. James Harvey Newkirk, born June 19, 1826; died February 23, 1844

7. Sarah Elenor Newkirk, born March 18, 1828, and died June 14, 1910. Married January 29, 1851 to Alfron W. Howe. Four children.

8. John O. Newkirk, born April 15, 1833, and died November 6, 1914. Married October 19, 1861 to Lillie Clapp. Nine children, all born in New York:

 a. William Ellis Newkirk, born August 6, 1862; died October, 1898. Married October 6, 1883 to Jennie Woods.

 b. Alsop O. Newkirk, born December 2, 1863; married February 16, 1888 to Luella Knap, and married second June 3, 1902 to Etta Martin.

 c. Frank Ellis Newkirk, born April 25, 1867; died May 11, 1914. He married November 2, 1892 to Etta Orr.

 d. Lottie Carrie Newkirk, born November 20, 1868, married November 3, 1887 to Richard C. Marshall.

 e. Ada May Newkirk, born July 1, 1871; married December 2, 1891 to Wallace J. Orr.

 f. Sarah Ellenor Newkirk, born September 24, 1873; died February 2, 1909.

 g. Susie Lydia Newkirk, born June 12, 1877, and died May 10, 1896. Married James D. Mock.

 h. Jessie A. Newkirk, born December 2, 1880, and married to Arthur Robinson.

 i. Gladys Newkirk, Jr., born September 12, 1882, and married to Horatio Harris.

9. Julia Newkirk, born c.1834.

10. David Harris Newkirk, born August 14, 1835; died June 23, 1885. Married March 16, 1871 to Helen E. Klock; one child:

 a. Alice May Newkirk, born January 31, 1881 New York.

11. Lewis Alonzo Newkirk, born May 6, 1837; died August 23, 1850
12. Rosetta Newkirk, born c.1837
13. Charles M. Newkirk, born March 24, 1844; died January 29, 1845.

Absolom W. Newkirk
1795-

This son of Henry C. Newkirk (1767) was born about 1795. Married, perhaps for the second time, August 19, 1824 in Warren County, Ohio, to Elizabeth Taylor. The first child reported below is accepted as being a child of Absolom and his first wife, and was born in New York. The last three are conjecture, and perhaps do not belong here, born in Ohio. As can be seen from the information provided following with James and Nelson Newkirk, it is at best questionable if they belong to this family at all. In any case, until further study sorts them out, the four children were:

1. David Newkirk, born c.1815 in New York. Married Charlotte, born c.1821 in Ohio. The family is included in the 1850 census for Clinton County, Ohio. Children, born in Ohio:
   a. Absalom Newkirk, born 1841 (census lists Abraham C.)
   b. Nancy A. Newkirk, born c.1842
   c. Hannah Newkirk, born c.1844
   d. Israel A. Newkirk, born c.1847
2. James Newkirk, born c.1816. Some reports list James in this family, and as having been married to Elizabeth Moyer, born c.1820 in Ohio. However, that marriage has been assigned by most records to James Madison Newkirk, born July 17, 1815, a son of George W. Newkirk (1784), reported earlier in these papers. The 1850 census of Clermont County, Ohio, includes the family, with a number of children, all born in Ohio, and I have reported them with the family of James Madison Newkirk.
3. Besaleel Locy Newkirk, born August 26, 1819, of whom more.
4. Nelson Newkirk, born c.1820 in Ohio. Once again, this child is not definitely identified as belonging to this family. He is re-

ported earlier in this study as a son of George W. Newkirk (1784), as was his brother James. It does not appear that there was a second Nelson Newkirk (nor a second James Madison Newkirk), and some records have apparently just confused the relationships. We can not now say precisely where Nelson and James belong; the families of both have been reported earlier, with descendants of George W. Newkirk (1784), which see.

James Wills Newkirk
1850-1927

Besaleel Locy Newkirk
1819-1899

This son of Absalom W. Newkirk (1795) was born August 26, 1819 in Indiana; died October 17, 1899 in Medical Lake, Washington. Married January 29, 1846 in Clinton County, Ohio to Martha

Wills, born August 24, 1826 in Warren County, Ohio, and died September 10, 1910 in Story County, Iowa; daughter of James and Ann Hart Wills. See also the census of 1850 for Clermont County, Ohio. Between 1993 and 1995, I received letters from Doris E. Wastradowski, a descendant of this family, living in Vancouver, Washington. She corrected some of my earlier information, and provided more. Children, born in Ohio:

1. Mary Ann Newkirk, born July 22, 1847 in Clinton County, and died March 17, 1923 in Ames, Story County, Iowa. Married January 26, 1865 in Ames to Simon Cope Stratton.
2. James Wills Newkirk, born January 10, 1850 in Clermont County, Ohio; died April 14, 1927 at Spokane, Washington. Married to Sarah Ellen McKinzie.
3. Ellen Locy Newkirk, born July 20, 1852 in Clinton County, Ohio, and died June, 1932 in Des Moines, Iowa. Married October 30, 1879 in Story County, Iowa, Clarence E. Person.
4. Sarah Elizabeth, born May 26, 1856 in Clinton County, Ohio, and died September 27, 1952 in Clark County, Washington. Married July 22, 1873 in Nevada, Story County, Iowa, to Thomas Edward Tueth. He was born May 6, 1850 in Macon County, Illinois, and died April 15, 1928 at Clarkston, Washington; son of Edward Tueth and Mary Wheeler Fields Tueth. Seven children, the first four born at Nevada, Story County, Iowa; last three at Mayview, Garfield County, Washington:
    a. Frances E. Tueth, born April 11, 1874; died August 25, 1875.
    b. Jesse Edward Tueth, born October 29, 1875, and died January 9, 1938.
    c. Daniel Joshua Tueth, born October 15, 1878, and died January 30, 1960.
    d. Martha Lenora Tueth, born February 7, 1881, and died July 27, 1950 at Vancouver, Washington. Married December 11, 1898 at Mayview, Washington, to William Leachman, born October 5, 1869 Ursa, Adams County, Illinois, died October 14, 1957, Vancouver. Six children:
        (1) William Thomas Leachman, born December 28, 1899 at Mayview, Washington, and died May 17, 1981 at Vancouver, Washington.

(2) Versa Mae Leachman, born January 22, 1902 at Cul de Sac, Nez Perce County, Idaho; died June 21, 1917 at Boise, Ada County, Idaho.

(3) Neil Kenneth Leachman, born November 2, 1903 at Cul de Sac, Idaho, and died June 25, 1967 at Portland, Oregon.

(4) Pearl Norine Leachman, born June 17, 1906 at Lewiston, Idaho, and died November 2, 1991 at Tacoma, Washington. Married June 12, 1932 to Clyde Cornelius Cannon at Vancouver.

(5) Marion Ethel Leachman, born March 17, 1909 at Lewiston, Idaho, and died January 12, 1995 at Bellevue, Washington. Married November 11, 1933 to George P. Jullion at Weiser, Idaho.

(6) Doris Eleanor Leachman, my correspondent, born December 17, 1919 at Boise, Iowa. Married September 21, 1940, Carl Roger Wastradowski, born November 12, 1913 at Bayard, Saskatchewan, Canada; died May 17, 1990 at Vancouver, a son of Christian Wastradowski and Catherine Ruhr. Doris also stated that in each census, Besaleel reported his parents born in Kentucky. Six children, all but the second born at Vancouver, Washington; the second child born at Farragut, Idaho:

   (a) Carol Jean Wastradowski, born May 18, 1942, and married February 20, 1965 at Vancouver, Paul Terrence Godsil (divorced).

   (b) Jane Marie Wastradowski, born May 6, 1945, and married January 14, 1967 to Edward Herbert Sheridan at Vancouver, Washington.

   (c) William Carl Wastradowski, born September 30, 1947

   (d) Lynn Martha Wastradowski, a twin, born February 16, 1951; married July 4, 1987 to Walter Boyd Hollow at Seattle, Washington.

   (e) Louise Catherine Wastradowski, a twin, born February 16, 1951; married April 20, 1980 Michael Joseph Kirkland at Reno, Nevada.

(f)   Patricia Doris Wastradowski, born March 1, 1957; married January 5, 1980 at Vancouver to Gary Allen Leaf.

e.   Ray Tueth, a twin, born March 10, 1885; died July 19, 1969 at Vancouver, Washington.

f.   Roy Tueth, a twin, born March 10, 1885; died November 18, 1960 at Portland, Oregon.

g.   Oril Eugene Tueth, born August 28, 1894, and died November 2, 1967 at Clarkston, Washington.

Sarah Elizabeth Newkirk
1856-1952

Sarah Elizabeth Newkirk and Thomas Edward Tueth
Married 1873 in Story County, Iowa

Charles G. Newkirk
1800-1850

This son of Henry C. Newkirk (1767) was born November 11, 1800 and died December 8, 1850. Married April 11, 1826 to Margaret Millholland, born May 14, 1809 and died September 20, 1877. They appear in the 1850 census for Marion County, Indiana, with seven of their children, reported to total ten, born in Indiana:

1. Julia Ann Newkirk, born March 23, 1827 and died March 6, 1904. Married September 8, 1844 to William Dickey.
2. Mary Jane Newkirk, born July 1, 1829; died September 10, 1898. Married March 3, 1852 in Marion County, Indiana David P. Millholland.
3. Joseph Newkirk, born July 24, 1831 and died December 13, 1908. Married February 18, 1854 to Mary E. Bowerman. Children, all born in New York:
   a. David M. Newkirk, born December 25, 1854; married November 14, 1881 to Alice J. Clapp.
   b. William Ellis Newkirk, born March 25, 1857, and died December 11, 1912.
   c. Charles A. Newkirk, born September 25, 1859; married November 14, 1884 to Clara E. Rush.
   d. Laura L. Newkirk, born January 23, 1862, and married September 1, 1885 to Martin Z. McBee.
4. Caroline Newkirk, born February 4, 1834; died May 27, 1842
5. Catherine Newkirk, born July 4, 1836; died September 12, 1892. Married twice: first January 25, 1859 to Foster W. Willy, and second September 25, 1865 to John W. Jeeney.
6. Abner M. Newkirk, born January 1, 1839; died 1916. Married September 20, 1868 to May Jane Piggot, born August 2, 1836 in Clinton County, Indiana; died April 15, 1911 in Montgomery County. Children:
   a. Samuel P. Newkirk, born August 13, 1869, and married to Goldie Hoageland.
   b. Clara Newkirk, born June 18, 1871; died August 18, 1871
   c. Charles W. Newkirk, born August 9, 1872; died 1942. He married Elna Dettbrenner.

d.   Walter Newkirk, born August 22, 1874; died February
      23, 1875.

e.   Willard Newkirk, born April 5, 1877, and died February
      21, 1895

7.   Margaret Newkirk, born April 21, 1841; died May 31, 1907.
      Married September 7, 1859 to John B. Sprager.

8.   Sarah Elizabeth Newkirk, born December 14, 1843. Married
      May 17, 1866 to John F. Stevenson.

9.   Eliza Newkirk, born February 9, 1847; died October 23, 1864

10. Naomi Newkirk, born September 5, 1849. Married September
      24, 1871 to James H. Reed.

Cornelius S. Newkirk
1803-1885

This son of Henry C. Newkirk (1767) was born March 24,
1803 and died January 28, 1885; buried in Dade County, Ohio.
Married December 11, 1823 in Hamilton County, Ohio, to Mary E.
Lackey, born April 16, 1807 and died February 16, 1866. The
family appears in the 1850 census for Jennings County, Ohio, with
five of their children. Seven children, most of them born in
Hamilton County, Ohio:

1.   Andrew Lackey Newkirk, a cooper, born December 4, 1824,
      and died September 3, 1892. Married February 26, 1847 in
      Jackson County, Indiana, to Mary W. Compton, who died
      January 29, 1883. Married second April 30, 1890 to Mahala
      M. Cross. His children, all born in Indiana, were:

a.   Hamilton R. Newkirk, born February 28, 1848; died
      September 14, 1876.

b.   Indiana Laura Newkirk, born March 8, 1850; died
      November 28, 1853

c.   Thomas J. Newkirk, born April 23, 1852; died 1889.
      Married first Mary Eal, and second Alpha Patrick.

d.   Olinda Newkirk, born October 23, 1854; married George
      Talley.

e.   Martha Ann Newkirk, born October 18, 1857 and died
      November 26, 1874.

2. Julia W. Newkirk (or Ann), born September 1, 1826; died July 10, 1904. Married January 1, 1846 in Franklin County, Indiana to William D. Brown.
3. James H. Newkirk (or E.), born July 19, 1829, and died June 17, 1901. Married November 20, 1856 in Jennings County, Indiana to Louisa J. Brown. Children, born in Ohio or Illinois:
    a. Elva M. Newkirk, born March 4, 1860; died January 29, 1880. Married Charles Burkhart.
    b. Jennie N. Newkirk, born May 5, 1862, and married Isaiah Stover.
    c. Lizzie Alice Newkirk, born June 4, 1864; died in November, 1899.
    d. Helen Mae Newkirk, born September 23, 1866, and died September 4, 1891. Married Samuel Gardner.
    e. William Wallace Newkirk, born December 31, 1867; died October 14, 1892.
    f. Dott Grace Newkirk, born January 8, 1869, and married to S. Henderston.
    g. George J. Newkirk, born April 1, 1871
    h. Harry B. Newkirk, born January 5, 1873; married Ella Prather.
    i. E. Layton Newkirk, born March 21, 1875, and died September 9, 1901.
    j. Martha Newkirk, born September 23, 1877; married to Hill Wood.
4. Abraham Taylor Newkirk, born 1831, of whom more.
5. John Elliott Newkirk, born April 17, 1835 in Ohio, or Illinois, and died October 12, 1899. Married November 13, 1870 to Elizabeth T. Marr. Children, born in either Ohio or Illinois:
    a. Jackson Newkirk, born September 7, 1871
    b. Lillie Belle Newkirk, born June 16, 1875
6. Absolom Wallas Newkirk, born October 17, 1837 in Knox County, Illinois; died August 10, 1921 in Larimer County, Colorado. Married May 17, 1857 Nancy E. Springstel, born September 23, 1841 in Clermont County, Ohio, and died September 9, 1883 at Boulder, Colorado. Nine children, the first four born in Knox County, Illinois; fifth not known; the last four born in Chase County, Kansas:

a. Milo Cornelius Newkirk, born October 28, 1857; died April 28, 1922 at Boulder, Colorado.
b. Mary E. Newkirk, born July 24, 1859, and died May 15, 1901. Married twice: first to Alva Parker, second to Al Harris.
c. John W. Newkirk, born November 2, 1863; died 1919 in Carbon County, Wyoming. Married Cara Sankey.
d. James H. Newkirk, born September 10, 1865 and died January 24, 1893, Bent County, Colorado. Married to Mattie J. Wilkes.
e. Andrew L. Newkirk, born March 14, 1869; married Sada Sankey.
f. Charles F. Newkirk, born November 30, 1871, married to Gertrude Pursel.
g. Samuel T. Newkirk, born January 14, 1874; married Olive N. Zon
h. Carrie Frances Newkirk, born February 22, 1876; died April 18, 1961 at Boulder, Colorado. Married September 3, 1895 to Charles C. Johnson.
i. Jennie Rena Newkirk, born March 13, 1878; died October 10, 1938 at Denver, Colorado. Married there March 5, 1893 to William Massey, born April 9, 1866 in Jefferson County, Colorado, and died April 26, 1951.

7. William Hamilton Newkirk, born April 23, 1842 in Illinois; died April 12, 1895. Married October 27, 1863 to America A. Marr and had children, all born in Illinois:
a. James C. Newkirk, born January 9, 1867; married Alice A. Strong
b. Cora A. Newkirk, born January 31, 1869
c. Olla Bell Newkirk, born September 7, 1871
d. Leon Lewis Newkirk, born January 9, 1876, and married to Sophie Shearer
e. Charles N. Newkirk, born January 10, 1878
f. William F. Newkirk, born July 4, 1884
g. Myrta C. Newkirk, born December 1, 1886

Abraham Taylor Newkirk
1831-1902

This son of Cornelius S. Newkirk (1803) was born September 13, 1831 and died January 7, 1902 in Dade County, Missouri. Married Elizabeth Ruddick November 28, 1858 in Jackson County, Indiana. She was born there August 8, 1831 and died January 10, 1918 in Dade County, Missouri. Children; the first five born in Jackson County, Indiana; the next four in Chase County, Kansas; and the last in Dade County, Missouri:

1. John Franklin Newkirk, born November 10, 1858 and died November 7, 1960 in Cherokee County, Kansas. Married in Dade County, Missouri, December 6, 1883 to Mary Minnesota Nott, born September 25, 1865 and died January 18, 1959 in Lafayette County, Missouri. Children:
    a. Arbuth E. Newkirk, born June 22, 1888, reportedly in Missouri; died August 27, 1910 in Cherokee County, Kansas.
    b. A twin brother to Arbuth E., stillbirth June 22, 1888
    c. Sarah Edna Newkirk, born March 28, 1892 in Missouri, died December 14, 1979 in Shawnee County, Kansas. Buried in Cherokee County, as were her brothers and sisters. Married first in Cherokee County, Kansas, July 13, 1913 to Thomas B. Estabrooks, and married second in Newton County, Missouri to Arthur Estabrooks. It has been suggested that there was only one marriage here, but it seems that she did marry twice, perhaps to brothers.
    d. Alta Elizabeth Newkirk, born September 3, 1903 in Delaware County, Oklahoma; died July 27, 1976 in Jasper County, Missouri. Married October 30, 1922 in Cherokee County, Kansas, to Albert P. Cutright. He was born March 6, 1905 and died August 15, 1957. He was adopted by a family named Pulley, and he and his descendants used that name.
    e. Frank Newkirk, born April 11, 1908; died April 20, 1908.

2. William Lindley Newkirk, born January 16, 1860 in Jackson County, Indiana. Married September 27, 1883 to Mary Bell Marsh.
3. Mary Elnora Newkirk, born March 6, 1861 in Jackson County; married October 26, 1882 to William D. Sturdy.
4. Jacob Elwood Newkirk, born November 4, 1862 in Jackson County, and married first September 4, 1889 to Myrtle Renfro; second December 29, 1901 to Ollie Neal. She was born October 31, 1878 in Gallia County, Ohio. He had four children from his first marriage, listed below, and five from the second, whom we have not identified. The children were probably born in Dade County, Missouri:
   a. Mary Elna Newkirk, born April 6, 1891
   b. Lewis A. Newkirk, born August 6, 1893; married Hazel E. Speer.
   c. Jacob Elwood Newkirk, Jr., born November 28, 1895; married to Nettie Terrell and had children:
      (1) Richard D. Newkirk, born c.1920
      (2) Jack Terrell Newkirk, born 1923, and had at least one daughter:
         (a) Theda Jo Newkirk, born 1940
   d. Grace B. Myrtle Newkirk, born September 5, 1898; died February 29, 1899.
5. Elmer Andrew Newkirk, born September 26, 1864 in Chase County, Kansas. Married first October 4, 1884 to Louella Moore, and second December 26, 1900 to Stella Hunter.
6. James H. Newkirk, born August 11, 1866; died November 13, 1871
7. Jerusha Elva Newkirk, born April 1, 1868 in Chase County, Kansas, and died February 26, 1889. Married c.1887 Price Hudspeth.
8. Julia B. Newkirk, born November 14, 1873 in Dade County, Missouri, and died there August 11, 1958. Married May 10, 1898 to Leroy Moore, born March 7, 1875; died December 20, 1962.

Artimus D. Woodworth Newkirk
1805-1872

This son of Henry C. Newkirk (1767) was born May 31, 1805 and died April 19, 1872. His name has been reported as either Artimadoris and Artimus, the latter being the more likely spelling. Married twice; first to Julia Ann Montgomery, born c.1823 in Pennsylvania, and second on August 6, 1843 to Lucretia Ann Thurston in Franklin County, Indiana. She was born c.1823 and died July 31, 1890. From the dates of birth of some of his children, it would appear that the first wife of Artimus was born as much as ten to twenty years earlier than the 1823 date reported; or he may have been married yet a third time before the marriage to Julia Ann Montgomery. He appears in the 1850 census for Franklin County, Indiana, with his second wife, Lucretia, and several other family members. In the household is Nancy Compton, born c.1828, who is not identified, but may be a married daughter from the first marriage. The dates of some of the children are different in the census from other reports, which will be noted. Nine children, one born to the first marriage (or at least two, if Nancy Compton is a married daughter); and the last eight to the second marriage:

1. Nancy Newkirk, perhaps, born c.1828; married Compton
2. Christopher, born February 22, 1836 (c.1830 by the census) in Pennsylvania, and died c.1855.
3. Thomas Jefferson Newkirk, born June 10, 1844 in Indiana, and married September 3, 1868 Lizzie Morris. Two children:
   a. Mary E. Newkirk, born August 19, 1869; married to Christopher Lindner.
   b. Cornelius S. Newkirk, born June 30, 1872, and married to Sarah J. Stillwagon.
4. Hadley Douglas J. Newkirk, born November 9, 1845 in Indiana, married January 12, 1870 to Sarah Morris. Children, born in Indiana or Illinois:
   a. Mary Louise Newkirk, born February 13, 1872, and married to Frank Abbey.
   b. James Oran Newkirk, born January 19, 1880
   c. Emily Ann Newkirk, born April 25, 1881; died January 15, 1893

d. Delcina Pearl Newkirk, born April 17, 1883, and married to Josie Anderson.

5. Artimus D. Newkirk, born October 12, 1847 in Indiana.

6. Cornelius S. Newkirk, born January 12, 1850 in Indiana, and died November 21, 1912 in Knox County, Illinois. Married September 10, 1868 to Sarah M. Fisher, born October 15, 1852 in Indiana and died March 4, 1922 in Knox County. Children:

   a. Ann Elizabeth Newkirk, born March 17, 1877; married to Charles Vanarsdal.

   b. Julietta E. Newkirk, born July 11, 1878

   c. James A. Newkirk, born January 29, 1880, and married to Maude E. Williamson.

   d. Charles W. Newkirk, born November 6, 1882, and died October 18, 1886.

7. Julia Ann Newkirk, born September 12, 1852 in Indiana. Married three times: first January 28, 1869 to Conrad Miller; married second November 6, 1880 to Thomas Watson; and third January 19, 1888 to Charles Rosencrans.

8. Christopher C. Newkirk, born April 19, 1854 in Indiana, and died April 14, 1872.

9. May C. Newkirk, born June 4, 1855 in Indiana; died February 17, 1901. Married February 28, 1875 to Robert Goddard.

10. Robert J. Newkirk, born March 9, 1860; died April 4, 1873.

BIBLIOGRAPHY

Much of the information appearing in the study was derived from many years of research by the author in courthouses, libraries and archives where family members were known to have lived. Much more is based on correspondence over the years with other researchers, far too many to acknowledge individually here. Suffice to say that without their assistance, the record would be woefully inadequate. In the course of research and correspondence, many publications, public records and personal collections were investigated, most of which are listed following.

Alford, Mary and Gil. *Newkirk Notes,* A series of newsletters published during the late 1980s, with extensive family history and genealogy.

American Historical Society. *History of Virginia, 1924*

Andrews, A. T. *History of the State of Kansas.* 1883.

Anjou, Gustave. *Ulster County, New York, Probate Records,* Volumes I & II. 1992, Bowie, Maryland; Heritage Books, Inc.

Barnes. *Maryland Marriages, 1634-1777*

_____. *Maryland Marriages, 1778-1800*

_____. *Marriages and Deaths From the Maryland Gazette*

Beitzell. *Point Lookout Prison Camp for Confederates*

Berkeley County, Virginia/West Virginia. *Wills, estates, inventories, births, deaths, marriages, deeds and other reference works.*

_____. *The Christine Bergen Papers, Historic Records Books.* Volumes 1 thr 25.

_____. Public Library records.

Bible, Neikirk family of southwest Virginia. Now held by David Pennington Hurley, Gulfport, Mississippi.

Blackburn and Welfley. *Bedford and Somerset Counties, Pa.*

Bockstruck, Lloyd DeWitt. *Virginia's Colonial Soldiers*

Brumbaugh. *Maryland Records.* 1915 and 1928 issues; Washington County Marriages.

_____. *Maryland Records, Colonial, Revolutionary, County and Church.* Volume 1.

_____. *Census of Maryland, 1776*

Burke. *Burke's Peerage and Baronetage.*

_____. *The General Armory*

Coldham, Peter Wilson. *The Bristol Register of Servants Sent to Foreign Plantations 1654-1686,* 1988

_____. *Complete Book of Emigrants, 1607-1660*

Crozier. *The General Armory*

Davis. *Marriage Records of Frederick County, Virginia, 1771-1825*

Douglas, Ben. *History of Wayne County, Ohio, Pioneers and First Settlers to the Present Time.* 1878, Indianapolis, Indiana.

Farquhar. *Directory of Bedford County, Pennsylvania, 1886*

Filby. *Passenger and Immigration Lists Index.*

Frederick County, Virginia. Wills, estates, inventories, births, deaths, marriages, deeds and other reference works.

Fry, Joshua & Jefferson, Peter. *Map of Virginia, North Carolina, Pennsylvania, Maryland, New Jersey 1751.* Montgomery County, Md. Library, Atlas Archives.

Greenwalt. *Records of St. Paul's Methodist Episcopal Church, 1825-1910.* Public Library, Hagerstown, Maryland.

_____. *Church and Cemetery Records of Washington County.* Public Library at Hagerstown, Maryland.

_____. *Williamsport Evangelical Congregation, Ledger of Dr. Samuel Weisel, 1848-1872.* Public Library at Hagerstown, Maryland.

Gregory, Peggy H. *Judd, Primarily Descendants of Rowland Judd, Esquire, of Wilkes County, North Carolina.* 1984, Houston, Texas.

Groff Book, A Family Genealogy. Washington County, Maryland Historical Society Library.

Harvey, Cornelius Burnham. *Genealogical History of Hudson and Bergen Counties, New Jersey.* 1900. Reprint 1996, Heritage Books, Inc., Bowie, Maryland.

Heidgerd, William. *The American Descendants of Chretien DuBois of Wicres, France,* Parts 14 through 20, 1977-1983, Hugenot Historical Society, New Paltz, New York.

Hinke and Reinecke. *Evangelical Reformed Church, Frederick, Maryland*

313

Hinman-Sotcher. *Genealogies of Pennsylvania Families.* Pennsylvania Genealogical Magazine, Volume II

Hoffman, Jacob L. *Matthias and Mary Hoover Hoffman and their Descendants.* Washington County Public Library, Hagerstown, Md.

Holdcraft, Jacob Mehrling. *Names In Stone 75,000 Cemetery Inscriptions From Frederick County, Maryland,* Volume 2. 1966, Ann Arbor, Michigan.

Hutchison, Mrs. Omega Charles. *Newkirk Genealogy, personal papers.*

Kansas. *Biographical History of Central Kansas.* 1902, Volume 1.

Keesecker, Guy L. *Berkeley County, Virginia 1850 Census*

_____ *Marriage Records of Berkeley County, Virginia/West Virginia.* Three volumes.

_____ *Marriage Records of Morgan County, Virginia, and West Virginia, 1820-1865.*

Klinkenberg, Audrey M. *Obituaries, Death Notices and Genealogical Gleanings From The Saugerties Telegraph* (New York), Volume 2, 1853-1860. 1990, Heritage Books, Inc., Bowie, Maryland.

_____: *Obituaries, Death Notices and Genealogical Gleanings From The Saugerties Telegraph* (New York), Volume 3, 1861-1870. 1994, Heritage Books, Inc., Bowie, Maryland.

Liebegott. *The Liebegott Collection (247 volumes).* Martinsburg public library, Martinsburg, Blair County, Pennyslvania

Link. *Marriages, Jefferson County, Virginia and West Virginia, 1801-1890*

Maryland State. *Archives of Maryland,* all volumes.

Morgan, Claritta H. *Births and Deaths, 1853-1871, Pulaski County, Virginia.* Pulaski public library.

_____. *Marriage Licenses Issued 1850-1900, Pulaski County, Virginia.* Pulaski public library.

Mormon Church, Genealogical Library. Archival family group sheets and other records.

_____. *International Genealogical Index.* North Carolina, Tennessee, Maryland, Pennsylvania, Ohio, Kentucky, Alabama, Virginia and other states.

Morrow and Morrow. *Marriages of Washington County, Maryland, An Index, 1799-1866.* DAR library, Washington, D. C.

National Archives, Washington, D. C. *Original microfilm census records, muster rolls of the Civil War, pension and other records of the War of the Revolution.*

Neikirk, Floyd Edwin. *Neikirk, Neukirch, Newkirk.* Genealogical library of the Mormon Church in Salt Lake, and DAR library, Washington, D. C.

Neikirk, Joseph C. *Personal papers collection of genealogical research in western Maryland.* Donated to my collection.

Neikirk, Sarah Alberta Clementine. *Personal papers and scrapbook.* Radford, Virginia.

Newkirk, Dr. Adamson Bentley. *Personal papers collection.* Washington County, Maryland Historical Society Library.

Newkirk, Estella. *Personal Diary.* c.1879 to 1889

Newspaper, western Maryland. *American Herald and Elizabeth Town Advertiser*

_____. *Republican Banner.* Marriages and deaths, 1830-1837, printed in Williamsport, Maryland

North Carolina State Division of Archives and History. *North Carolina Troops, 1861-1865, A Roster,* Volumes I through XIII, Wilmington, North Carolina: Broadfoot Publishing Company, 1990

_____. Wills, estates, inventories, births, deaths, marriages, deeds and other reference works relative to counties of North Carolina.

Pennsylvania, author unknown. *History of Bedford, Somerset and Fulton Counties, Pennsylvania.* 1884

_____. *History of Huntington and Blair Counties, Pennsylvania.* 1883

_____. *History of Washington County, Pennsylvania*

Pennsylvania. Miscellaneous court records, local courthouses; wills, estates, inventories, deeds, estates, etc.

Perrin. *History of Kentucky.*

Pioneer Historical Society and Library, Bedford, Pennsylvania. Collections of genealogical importance; obituaries, newspapers, family folders, cemetery records, publications, etc.

Poole, Hubert A. *Personal papers of the Newkirk families.* Washington County, Maryland Public Library.

Preston. *History of Southwest Virginia*

Pritchard, Claudius Hornby, Jr. *Colonel D. Wyatt Aiken, 1828-1887.*

Ross, James. *Life and Times of Elder Reuben Ross.* Philadelphia. Grant, Faires and Rodgers. Reprinted Nashville, Tennessee, McQuiddy Printing Company 1977.

Ross, Sarah Esther; Gribb, Mrs Lewis. *Ross-McCulloch.* Asheboro, North Carolina. Manuscript.

Scharff. *History of Western Maryland.* Two volumes.

Schermerhorn, Richard, Jr. *New York Genealogical and Biographical Record.* Issue of January, 1934.

Schreiner-Yantis, Nettie. *Archives of the Pioneers of Tazewell County, Virginia.*

_____. *Wythe County, Virginia, 1800 Tax Lists and Abstracts of Deeds, 1796-1800*

Seibmacher. *Waffenbuch.* New York Genealogical Library. Volume 3. *The Newkirks in the Fatherland.* (Original Dutch)

Simmendinger, Ulrich. *The Simmendinger Register.* St. Johnsville, New York: Reprinted by the Enterprise and News, 1934.

Skordas, Gust. *Early Settlers of Maryland*

_____. (Perhaps). *Servants to Foreign Plantations*

St. Clair. *St. Clair's Bedford: The History and Genealogy of Bedford County, Pennsylvania.* Several volumes, Pioneer Library, Bedford, Pa.

Tepper, Michael. *Emigrants to the Middle Colonies*

_____. *Passengers to America*

Virginia State Library and Archives, Richmond. Wills, estates, inventories, births, deaths, marriages, deeds and other reference works relative to counties of Virginia.

van der Linde, A. P. G. Jos. 1983; Genealogical Publishing Company, Inc. *New York Historical Manuscripts, Old First Dutch Reformed Church of Brooklyn, New York. First Book of Records, 1660-1752.*

Vogt. *Marriage Records of Frederick County, Virginia, 1738-1850*

Washington County, Maryland. Folder files of the County Historical Society; correspondence and family records; courthouse
records of wills, estates, church records, deeds, births, deaths
and marriages.

Washington County, Maryland Library. *Church Records, Zion
Reformed Church at Hagerstown.*

_____. *American Descendants of Chretien DuBois
of Wicres, France.* Twenty volumes.

_____. *Maryland Historical Trust Inventory.*
Library File WA-11-107, Henry Neikirk home, Antietam Battlefield site.

_____. *Washington County Cemetery Records.*
Seven volumes.

_____. *Western Maryland Genealogy.* Quarterly
publications since 1985.

_____. *Western Maryland Newspaper Abstracts,
1799-1805.* Volume 2.

Wayland, John W. *Virginia Valley Records*

Williams, T. J. C. *History of Frederick County, Maryland.* Two
volumes.

_____. *History of Washington County, Maryland*

Wright, F. Edward. *Maryland Militia, War of 1812.*

INDEX

All names in the text have been indexed, with each page on which they appear. Generally, a date will follow the given name entry, indicating the actual or approximate birth year. Occasionally, the date of marriage or death will appear, such as m/1825 or d/1778, in order to differentiate between individuals having the same name. Common names; such as John, Mary and Elizabeth; will often appear with numerous page entries. If no date is specified, they are without much question references to more than one individual. As mentioned earlier, all of the principal names are indexed under the more common spelling of Newkirk, without regard to the variant of the base name that may have actually been used by that family member. Reference to the text will list the original spelling that the author has found, or been given.

Allegar, Mary, 30, 33
Alleman, Susan Emaline, 122
Allen, Emma 1833, 128
Allen, Linda 1943, 182
Allen, Louis F., 264
Almenroder, Anna Maria, 266
Amiss, Rachel Ellen 1841, 239
Amos, Rachel Ellen 1841, 239
Amy, Rachel, 270
Anderson, Clem, 294
Anderson, David, 166
Anderson, Elizabeth, 92
Anderson, Emma, 178
Anderson, Hannah, 90
Anderson, Josie, 311
Anderson, Louisa, 176
Anderson, Mary, 166
Anderson, Mary Elizabeth 1839,
    166
Anderson, No given name, 247,
    294
Anderson, Temperson 1818, 60
Andrews, Marie 1876, 99
Angell, Augustus, 203
Anjou, Gustave, 2, 17, 21, 197,
    269
Apple, Thelma, 80
Applegate, Edgar, 241
Applegate, Samuel, 192
Applegate, Sarah 1795, 192
Applewhite, Elizabeth Ann, 205
Ariens, Jennette, 9
Arle, Samuel 1837, 49
Armstrong, Sarah 1805, 44
Arnold, David A., 167
Arnold, Louise 1916, 167
Arnold, Sallie R., 167
Asher, Levy, 192
Atkins, Lucy M., 290
Atkinson, Ruth, 104
Atz, James E., 78
Austin, Beatrice 1893, 154

Austin, George J., 153
Austin, Gilbert 1890, 154
Austin, Jeannette 1888, 153
Ayars, Susannah 1797, 59
Ayers, Sarah 1762, 48
Aylesworth, Almon, 110
Aylesworth, Flora C. 1844, 110
Aylesworth, Leslie Norman, 122

—B—

Babbington, Elsie, 202
Babcock, Roxanna, 276
Backer, Annah Deamute, 28
Bacon, Martha Reeve 1826, 46
Badger, J. H., 215
Bailey, Lemira Susanna, 16
Bailey, William, 102
Baker, Cora E., 264
Baker, Lucy Mary Taliaferro
    1826, 137
Baldwin, Elihu, 229
Baldwin, No given name, 249
Baldwin, Robert A., 119
Ball, Richard Roscoe, 262
Ballard, Amy Christina 1974,
    185
Ballard, Curtis, 185
Ballard, Jeanette Elizabeth 1972,
    185
Ballenger, Susannah, 137
Bandel, John, 179
Banks, Arthur Waddell, 101
Banks, Elizabeth 1952, 101
Banks, Gayle 1948, 101
Banks, Mary Ann, 171, 172
Banks, Minnie, 84
Banks, Oscar Page 1900, 101
Banks, Walter Page 1953, 101
Banks, Zeagler Newkirk 1922,
    101
Barber, Emily, 121

Barber, Virginia, 102
Barclay, John P., 157
Barclay, Maria, 157
Barfeld, Mary Ann 1828, 131, 132
Barker, Alice, 97
Barker, Lida, 240
Barkley, William, 235
Barkmeier, Tully 1878, 39
Barndon, Malinda 1812, 82
Barnes, Cathrine Storm, 203
Barnes, David, 203
Barnes, No given name, 85
Barnes, Sarah Keese 1810, 203
Barnes, William D., 129
Barnett, Katherine, 236
Barth, Omar, 56
Barth, Warren S., 56
Bartle, Ransom, 110
Bartley, John, 242
Basden, Rachel Wells, 86
Bassett, Ebenezer 1781, 229
Bates, Elizabeth 1833, 59
Bates, Henry, 193
Bates, Mary Katherine, 193
Baumgarner, Otto 1843, 128
Bayless, Daniel, 142
Bayless, Mary 1808, 142
Beall, George P., 119
Beard, Samuel H., 139
Beatty, Eliza Ann 1820, 226
Beatty, George E., 226
Beaudet, Amy 1981, 185
Beaudet, Kelley Ann 1977, 185
Beck, Clarice Aileen, 127
Beekman, Hendrickus, 9
Beezly, Lucinda, 171
Behymer, Rebecca, 147
Behymer, William, 147
Beisel, Anne 1878, 215
Beisel, Florence 1884, 215
Beisel, Fred C. 1852, 215

Beisel, Fred Cornelius, 215
Beisel, Harold, 215
Beisel, Jane B. 1880, 215
Beisel, Sarah Margaret 1882, 215
Bell, Almeta A. 1870, 153
Bell, Cassett M. 1902, 154
Bell, Cora A. 1865, 153
Bell, Corena J. 1870, 151
Bell, Edward C. 1895, 153
Bell, Edward E. 1878, 154
Bell, George P., 119
Bell, Gladys A. 1904, 154
Bell, Harvina J. 1862, 153
Bell, Ida J. 1872, 151
Bell, John, 151, 295
Bell, Joseph M., 153
Bell, Josie M. 1884, 152
Bell, Julius E. 1867, 151
Bell, LeRoy 1886, 152
Bell, Lowell W. 1883, 154
Bell, Margaret 1879, 151
Bell, Mary M. 1915, 154
Bell, Maude E. 1902, 153
Bell, Otho Gano 1907, 154
Bell, Robert, 275
Bell, Safrona P. 1863, 151
Bell, Samuel J. 1839, 151
Bell, Vern W. 1897, 153
Bell, Viola Henrietta, 204
Bell, Walter 1882, 151
Bell, William M. 1868, 153
Bells, James, 267
Benedict, Anna, 286
Benedict, Moses S. 1832, 286
Benham, Bernice M., 205
Bennett, Eliza 1840, 36
Bennett, Maria 1797, 115, 128
Benson, Albert B. 1907, 146
Benson, Albert L. 1877, 146
Benson, Eugene W. 1911, 146
Benson, Florence L. 1910, 146
Benson, Gertrude L. 1908, 146

Benson, Harley Allen 1913, 146
Benson, Herbert E. 1874, 146
Benson, Lenna P. 1904, 146
Benson, Loter D. 1906, 146
Benson, Pearl M. 1904, 146
Benson, Richard, 146
Bentley, Amanda, 115
Bentley, Hannah 1792, 136
Bentley, Henry Cabbell, 105
Berger, Robert Keith, 204
Berkley, Sarah F. 1848, 71
Berry, Emma Ova, 150
Berry, James, 150
Berry, Sarah O., 150
Berry, Sylvia, 262
Beudet, Dean, 185
Bevier, Cornelia 1755, 13
Bevier, Philip, 217
Bevier, Samuel, 13
Bigelow, Willard, 240
Biggs, Millie, 104
Bigler, Della, 297
Bikelo, Johannes, 221
Bill, Elizabeth D., 55
Birdsall, George W., 230
Bishop, Hamilton 1839, 142
Bishop, John Wesley, 142
Bishop, Lewis R., 153
Bishop, Mulford, 51
Bishop, William, 51
Bitner, Priscilla, 147
Bixler, Lottie W., 110
Black, Victor, 74
Blackburn, Joseph, 233
Blankenship, Anna Mae, 239
Blankenship, Louisa, 239
Blankenship, Ollie, 239
Blanshan, Catherine, 7
Blanshan, Elizabeth, 201
Blanshan, Maria, 3
Blinn, Elizabeth, 289, 290
Bloodgood, Judith, 198

Blunt, No given name, 245
Boden, Henry Clark, 44
Bodine, Catherine 1778, 272
Bodine, Catherine 1808, 272
Bodine, Catherine Maria 1811, 275
Bodine, Charles 1771, 270
Bodine, Elahaur 1814, 272
Bodine, Eliza 1810, 272
Bodine, Elizabeth 1788, 275
Bodine, Ethalinda 1806, 272
Bodine, Frances 1776, 270
Bodine, Harriette 1816, 272
Bodine, Hiram 1812, 272
Bodine, Jacob, 270
Bodine, Lewis 1784, 270
Bodine, Mehitable K. 1822, 275
Bodine, Moses, 272
Bodine, Rachel 1766, 270
Bodine, Sally 1804, 272
Bodine, Susannah d/1815, 277
Bodine, William Stitt 1819, 272
Bogaard, Aaltjen 1688, 25
Bogaard, Hendrick, 25
Bogardus, Evert, 8
Bogardus, Petrus 1699, 8
Bogart, Antjen 1746, 202
Bogart, Cornelius, 202
Bogart, Cornelius 1736, 202
Bogart, Jacob 1741, 202
Bogart, Jan Cornelius 1702, 202
Bogart, Margriette, 202
Bogart, Rachel 1753, 202
Bogart, Sarah 1744, 202
Bogart, Willemtje 1739, 202
Boice, Antje, 226
Bolander, Andrew, 263
Bolander, Anna Mary 1885, 265
Bolander, Breton 1883, 265
Bolander, Charles, 265
Bolander, Electa 1855, 265
Bolander, Eliza 1843, 264

Bolander, Elizabeth 1847, 264
Bolander, Emma Rebecca 1892,
    265
Bolander, Ethel Kissire 1887,
    265
Bolander, Frank 1861, 265
Bolander, James 1857, 265
Bolander, James Andrew 1889,
    265
Bolander, John A. J. 1853, 265
Bolander, Joseph, 265
Bolander, Kesiah 1850, 265
Bolander, Lester 1894, 265
Bolander, Margaret 1840, 263
Bolander, Martha 1845, 264
Bolander, Paul, 265
Bolander, Sarah 1842, 264
Bolenbaugh, Peter 1816, 132
Boling, Karl Denver, 122
Bonham, Mary Ann Gufford
    1832, 91
Bonham, Nathaniel 1814, 91
Boon, Martha, 64
Booth, Thomas, 272
Borhans, Willem, 11
Borton, Mary Chapman, 46
Bosch, Annatje, 5
Bosch, Henrich, 5
Boschma, Linda Sue 1958, 182
Bouchie, Marjorie Lou 1933, 133
Bovey, Blanche Rosalie 1900,
    250
Bovey, William August, 250
Bowen, Dicie 1815, 194
Bowen, Thomas 1786, 194
Bowerman, Mary E., 304
Bowers, Mary Catherine, 178
Bowman, James, 162
Bowne, Maude, 150
Boyer, Pauline, 74
Bradford, Thomas, Rev., 96
Branch, Hiram 1830, 45

Brandon, Malinda 1812, 82
Brandon, Margaret Ann, 82
Branham, Blair, 241
Bratton, Jack 1965, 181
Bratton, Robert, 180
Brentlinger, Jonathan, 193
Brentlinger, Susannah, 193
Brewer, Jack, 76
Brickle, Thomas, 86
Brickley, Barbara Jane 1949, 159
Briley, James 1798, 68
Brill, Linda 1954, 181
Brink, Hendricke Cornelisse,
    197, 220
Brink, Lambert Huybertse, 197,
    220
Brink, Lysbeth Lambertse 1666,
    3, 8, 197
Brink, Peter Lambertse 1670,
    220
Brinkerhoff, Abraham, 10
Brinkerhoff, Aeltje 1740, 10
Brinkerhoff, Elizabeth 1765, 222
Brinkerhoff, Gerardina, 10
Brinkerhoff, Gerrit 1762, 222
Brinkerhoff, Hendrick 1756, 222
Brinkerhoff, Isaac, 10
Brinkerhoff, Jacob, 222
Brinkerhoff, Jane, 231
Brinkerhoff, Jannette 1753, 222
Brinkerhoff, Jannette 1755, 222
Brinkerhoff, Siba, 230
Brinkman, Beryl, 98
Briskell, Cyrus, 189
Bristow, Amanda Jane, 157
Britton, Howard, 240
Broadhead, Anna Jane 1737, 14
Broadhead, Henry, 15
Broadhead, Henry 1752, 16
Broadhead, Margaret 1749, 13
Broadhead, Mary, 21
Broadhead, Richard 1749, 13

Broadus, Adam 1813, 166
Broadus, Adam 1851, 166
Broadus, Emily 1861, 166
Broadus, Henrietta 1856, 166
Broadus, Jane 1820, 166
Broadus, Noah 1853, 166
Brock, Frances E., 36
Brock, Margaret 1811, 190
Brockne, Barent, 87
Bronson, Callie 1870, 105
Bronson, Charles 1850, 275
Bronson, Gustavus Adolphus
    1837, 105
Bronson, Laura 1879, 105
Bronson, Lillie 1876, 105
Bronson, Lillie M., 263
Bronson, Mamie Bryan 1871,
    105
Bronson, Nancy 1826, 275
Bronson, William H., 226
Brooks, Frank, 240
Brooks, Hannah 1820, 61
Broom, Austin Joshua 1992, 182
Brosard, Mary Ann, 87
Brosard, Penelope, 86
Brosard, Peter Androus, 87
Bross, Mary E., 157
Brown, Aaron 1737, 31
Brown, Charles Newkirk 1804,
    278
Brown, Charlotte Smith 1817,
    278
Brown, Elisha, 177
Brown, Frederick Lucier 1810,
    278
Brown, Harmon, 286
Brown, James 1808, 278
Brown, Jeremiah, 278
Brown, Jesse, 86
Brown, John, 118
Brown, John W., 242
Brown, Louisa J., 306

Brown, Lydia Ellen 1873, 177
Brown, Mary, 176
Brown, Mary 1802, 278
Brown, Mary 1813, 195
Brown, Melinda 1811, 289
Brown, Milly 1805, 77, 78
Brown, Nancy A. 1840, 177
Brown, Rebecca Ann 1840, 242
Brown, Ruey M. 1871, 177
Brown, Sally Moore 1812, 278
Brown, Sandy M. 1828, 177
Brown, Susan Ann 1821, 278
Brown, William D., 306
Bruce, Lydia A., 120
Bryant, Dorothy, 101
Bryson, Rachel, 192
Buchan, Zane 1976, 292
Bunnell, Julius C., 264
Bunts, Cora Edith, 204
Burbank, David, 224
Burch, Fredericka, 265
Burgoon, Franklin Wayne, 204
Burgoon, John Michael 1951,
    205
Burgoon, Kathleen Ann 1948,
    204
Burgoon, Patricia Jean 1946, 204
Burgoon, Ranaldo Orla 1918,
    204
Burgoon, Shannon 1963, 205
Burhans, Aaltje 1739, 25
Burhans, Amy 1807, 15
Burhans, Annatje, 218
Burhans, Barent, 5
Burhans, Cornelius 1746, 25
Burhans, Elizabeth, 5
Burhans, Helena 1732, 6
Burhans, Helena 1750, 25
Burhans, Hendricus 1735, 25
Burhans, Hendricus 1748, 25
Burhans, Jacomyntje 1755, 25
Burhans, Jannetje 1753, 25

Burhans, Johannes 1709, 25
Burhans, Johannes 1733, 25
Burhans, Johannes 1742, 25
Burhans, Margriet 1744, 25
Burhans, Saartje, 25
Burhans, William, 6, 11
Burkhart, Charles, 306
Burlingame, Charles H. 1853, 37
Burlingame, Clifford, 37
Burlingame, Elizabeth, 37
Burlingame, Franklin, 37
Burlingame, Henry, 37
Burlingame, Jane Evans, 37
Burlingame, Mildred, 37
Burlingame, Robert C., 37
Burlingame, Vera Gertrude
    1892, 37, 38
Burnett, Nicki, 205
Burns, Mary, 270
Burroughs, Ada Belle, 241
Burroughs, Catherine 1767, 43,
    47
Burroughs, Elizabeth, 30, 49
Burroughs, Joseph F., 30
Burt, Julia Ann, 40
Buskirk, Emmett, 240
Buyce, Leon, 85

—C—

Cade, John, 48
Cahill, Daniel, Jr., 277
Cahill, Jacob Newkirk 1799, 277
Cain, Barbara, 17
Cain, Bernard M., 17
Cain, Elizabeth, 17
Cain, Emily, 17
Cain, Richard, 17
Caldwell, Maxine, 180
Calsam, Diane J. 1965, 52
Calsam, Robert, 52
Cambern, Claude, 149

Cameron, Francis, 286
Cameron, No given name, 78
Campbell, Annie, 120
Campbell, Cathy 1957, 291
Campbell, Thomas, 21
Cane, Robert, 266
Cannady, William, 91
Cannon, Amelia 1788, 22
Cannon, Clyde Cornelius, 301
Cantine, Elizabeth 1762, 18, 201
Cantine, Jane, 18
Cantine, Leah 1758, 201
Cantine, Nathaniel 1724, 201
Cantine, Peter, 201
Cantine, Peter Jacob, 18
Caress, Ezekial Logan, 178
Carmichel, Eloise, 104
Carmody, Margaret Agnes 1898,
    39
Carnes, Edmund, 238
Carothers, Amanda, 171
Carpenter, John P., 152
Carpenter, Lillian A. 1897, 152
Carpenter, Ruby L. 1896, 152
Carrigan, Thomas, 85
Carrol, Adolph D., 133
Carrol, Grace D. 1915, 134
Carrol, Lurene V. 1902, 134
Carrol, Violet M. 1905, 134
Carrol, Walter E. 1901, 134
Carroll, Rhoda 1765, 113, 128
Carson, Sarah C., 43
Carson, Vista M., 147
Carson, Zaccheus 1813, 59
Carter, Benjamin, 178
Carter, Benjamin, Jr. 1844, 178
Carter, Patricia Noe, 129
Carty, Geraldine L., 101
Caruthers, James S. 1782, 45
Case, Jeremiah, 296
Cassady, Florence, 51
Cassady, Harry, 51

Cassady, Helen, 56
Cassady, Mary Lizzie, 51
Cassady, Sarah, 51
Cassidy, Hannah J., 59
Chapman, Juliette 1824, 296
Chappell, Adaline Orvanda, 178
Charles, Horace T., 96
Chilton, Mamie, 74
Christian, Anna 1869, 264
Christian, Francis M., 264
Christian, Grace 1870, 264
Christian, Hugh, 264
Christian, Joseph 1872, 264
Christian, Maude 1881, 264
Christian, Nellie 1874, 264
Christian, Nora 1867, 264
Christian, Sallie 1877, 264
Churchill, Genevieve, 180
Clapp, Alice J., 304
Clapp, Lillie, 297
Clare, Steve, 84
Clark, Alice, 245
Clark, Amanda 1839, 59
Clark, Amy, 248
Clark, Betty Lou 1931, 185
Clark, Catherine, 281
Clark, Cora Rosalee 1882, 102
Clark, Elizabeth, 270
Clark, Fanny, 174
Clark, Frederick H., 245
Clark, George, 245
Clark, Ida, 245
Clark, Sanford S., 110
Clark, William Arward, 102
Clary, Isaac N. 1819, 137
Clary, John B., 138
Clary, John C. 1826, 137
Clary, Margaret 1820, 137
Clary, Rachel A. 1826, 137
Clary, William D. 1828, 138
Clayton, Catherine, 239
Clifton, Ethel May, 146

Clifton, Nellie M., 153
Clindince, Mary C., 296
Clinton, James, Colonel, 217
Clouse, Christena 1781/91, 116
Clover, Karen E. 1956, 262
Clute, Rachel, 206
Cochran, Elizabeth 1866, 287
Cochran, John, 157
Cochran, No given name, 247
Cochran, Thomas, 139
Code, Charity Priscilla, 91
Coe, Emma C., 230
Coerten, Reyckje Harmens, 221
Coffman, David A. 1952, 262
Cole, Nancy 1821, 20
Coles, Anna Elizabeth, 56
Collard, Gertrude 1788, 231
Collard, John, 231
Collard, Marie Bernice, 129
Collette, No given name, 250
Collier, Nellie, 206
Collins, John Stedman, 105
Collins, Mattie E., 290
Colson, Lovina, 113
Colvey, William, 114
Colvin, John Howard, 174
Colvin, William, 114
Colwell, Asah Feison, 93
Comer, John, 112
Comfort, Claude E. 1898, 36
Comfort, Elroy 1892, 36
Comfort, Fulton, 285
Comfort, Robert L. 1896, 36
Comfort, Sadie M. 1894, 36
Comfort, Vincent, 36
Compton, Mary W., 305
Compton, Nancy 1828, 310
Compton, No given name, 310
Conklyn, William 1797, 60
Conkright, No given name, 293
Conley, Mary, 240
Connahey, No given name, 55

Conner, Charles, 74
Conrad, Harriet, 236
Contine, Moses, Captain, 211
Contine, Nathaniel 1724, 217
Contyne, Elizabeth 1762, 18
Cook, Edith 1916, 180
Cook, Margaret Elizabeth 1918, 180
Cookendorfer, Nancy E., 238
Coombs, Albert, 51
Cooper, Elwood C. 1881, 239
Cooper, George Bruce 1884, 239
Cooper, James Hubbard 1934, 99
Cooper, James T., 99
Cooper, Maria, 25
Cooper, Nellie 1882, 239
Cooper, William Henry, 131
Cooper, William Thomas, 239
Cooper, Wyatt S., 239
Cope, Mariah Jane, 79
Corathers, Clyde Benjamin 1920, 54
Corathers, Frances Ann 1947, 54
Corbett, Archibald Haywood 1869, 105
Corbett, Charles Sprunt, 97
Corbett, John 1798, 105
Corbett, John Archibald 1841, 105
Corbett, Mary Jeannette 1865, 105
Corbett, No given name, 112
Cornelis, Sarah, 221
Cornelison, Gerritt 1631, 3
Cortrecht, Jennetye 1770, 218
Cosand, No given name, 247
Coston, Mollie, 97
Cotnam, No given name, 84
Courtright, No given name, 293
Cox, Courtney Noelle 1978, 158
Cox, Ethel Keziah 1878, 158, 159

Cox, James B. 1842, 159
Cox, James B. 1842, Dr., 158
Cox, James Baker 1905, 158
Cox, James C. W., Rev., 158
Cox, James Earl 1875, 158
Cox, Lena Winifred 1867, 158
Cox, Leroy Eldridge 1873, 158
Cox, Ralph Earl 1909, 158
Cox, Ralph Newkirk 1868, 158
Cox, Stephanie Nicole 1976, 158
Cox, Thomas Earl 1947, 158
Craft, Charles E. 1858, 290
Craig, Norma Musgrove, 187
Craig, Rebecca, 30
Craven, John, Captain, 107
Crawford, Ernest, 144
Crawford, Joanna 1835, 244
Crawford, William, Capt., 114
Crim, A. M., 165
Crim, Jessica Rose 1995, 292
Crim, Joseph Douglas 1985, 292
Crim, Nina Virginia 1905, 165
Crim, Rick Allen 1964, 292
Crispell, Albert 1728, 4
Crispell, Albert 1743, 4
Crispell, Anthony, 3
Crispell, Anthony 1692, 3
Crispell, Ariantje 1694, 4
Crispell, Arriantje 1734, 4
Crispell, Cornelius, 4
Crispell, Elizabeth 1738, 4
Crispell, Johannes, 4
Crispell, Johannes 1695, 4
Crispell, Johannes 1745, 5
Crispell, Lea 1740, 4
Crispell, Maria 1751, 211
Crispell, Neeltje, 4
Crispell, Peter, 211
Crispell, Peter 1664, 3
Crispell, Petrus 1727, 4
Crispell, Petrus 1736, 4
Crispell, Rachel 1732, 4

Crist, Ann, 278
Crist, Catherine 1770, 270
Crist, Elizabeth 1786, 271
Crist, Harriet, 271
Crist, Johannes 1773, 270
Crist, Lorens 1768, 270
Crist, Rachel 1804, 274
Crist, Stevanus, Jr., 270
Crist, Virgil, 271
Critchlow, Elizabeth 1802, 190
Critchlow, Elvira 1816, 177
Critchlow, Mary Ann 1815, 172
Crom, Mayke, 268
Cromartie, Nancy 1873, 99
Crooks, Sarah 1811, 57
Crosby, Kathryn Lee 1929, 216
Crosby, Lewis M., 232
Cross, Mahala M., 305
Cross, Malinda J., 144
Cross, Polly Ann, 152
Cumberford, William, 266
Cunningham, John, 77
Cunningham, Nancy, 78
Cunningham, Olive, 77
Cunnings, Michael Swagler, 157
Curl, Frances Loretta 1914, 133
Currie, Ida Bell 1872, 91
Curry, Ann 1753, 33
Curtis, Gordon Patrick, 186
Curtis, Mike Allen 1966, 186
Curtis, Steven Patrick 1969, 186
Cutler, No given name, 24
Cutright, Albert P. 1905, 308
Czerniel, Barbara Marie 1956,
    133

—D—

Daily, Ida 1780, 273
Daily, Sarah 1798, 273
Danielson, David 1842, 231
Dare, Albert 1840, 59

Dare, Helene Vivian 1916, 54
Darling, George H. 1833, 140
Darress, George L., 227
Daugherty, Henry Clinton, 122
Davey, Marjorie, 106
Davey, Violet, 106
David, Wesley P., 139
Davis, Almira, 244
Davis, Brenda Christine 1965,
    184
Davis, Charles Richard 1946,
    184
Davis, Cynthia Jane 1969, 184
Davis, Edward, 108
Davis, George Thomas 1906, 184
Davis, George Thomas, Jr. 1943,
    184
Davis, George W., 175
Davis, James Steven 1953, 184
Davis, Jean Eleanor, 216
Davis, Joe 1805, 176
Davis, John B., 88
Davis, Lela 1878, 175
Davis, Lena Williams, 86
Davis, Mary 1814, 214
Davis, Mary Ann 1830, 176
Davis, Rebecca 1771, 155
Davis, Sarah 1813, 176
Davis, William Lance 1968, 184
Dawson, Lucinda 1795, 70
Dawson, Martha 1797, 69
Dawson, Sarah U. 1820, 43
Day, Leanah Houston 1814, 190
de Bethune, Andre Jacques 1919,
    39
de Lamater, Batah 1742, 18
De Mont, Egbert, 200
De Reimer, Elsie 1777, 202
De Reimer, Petrus, III, 202
Decker, Bartholomew Sears
    1814, 279
Decker, Braddick, 286

Decker, Charles Newkirk 1811, 279
Decker, Jeremiah, 279
Decker, Nelson 1810, 279
Deckers, Titjen, 3
Delaps, Allen, 30
Demarest, Leah, 228
Demarest, Sarah, 202
Demarest, Sietsye, 202
deMeier, Catharine, 212
DeMott, George V., 226
Denbo, Roy, 78
Dendall, Bessie, 80
Denelsbeck, Lydia, 51
Denton, Gilbert, 79
Denton, Minnie B., 80
DePeyster, Jacob, 10
Dettbrenner, Elna, 304
Devane, Jane Madeline 1843, 97
Devaux, Reginald, 102
Devens, Abram, 16
Devore, Daniel, 234
Dewey, Georgia Ann, 182
DeWhitt, Johannes E. 1733, 12
DeWitt, Aagje, 6
DeWitt, Anne 1725, 21
DeWitt, Blandina 1800, 19
DeWitt, Cornelia 1837, 20
DeWitt, Egbert 1699, 12
DeWitt, Eli, 13
DeWitt, Jacobus, 13
DeWitt, Johannes, 21
DeWitt, John, 213
DeWitt, John E. 1733, 12
DeWitt, Matthew Paulding, 213
DeWitt, Newkirk, 213
DeWitt, Sarah Catharine, 213
DeWitt, Stephen, 14
DeWitt, Ten Eyck, 213
Dewy, John, 217
Dickenson, No given name, 30
Dickey, William, 304

Dickson, Marcus Lonzo, 85
Didericks, Aaltje 1736, 222
Diedricks, Garret 1695, 222
Diedricks, Wander, 222
Dilgard, William, 117
Dilks, Norman J. 1910, 55
Dillon, Cyrus, 37
Dillon, Edna 1901, 36
Dillon, Ella 1854, 37
Dillon, Ellis 1857, 37
Dillon, Lewis 1855, 37
Dillon, Matthew 1795, 155
Dillon, Nathan 1790, 34
Dillon, Orlando, 36
Dillon, Ruth 1813, 34
Dillon, Walter 1859, 37
Dirckje, Tryntje, 222
Dixon, Mary, 178
Dixon, Thomas, 190
Dobbie, J. J., Dr., 98
Dobbie, Jane Stewart, 98
Dobbie, John Graham, 98
Dobbs, Anna 1736, 24
Dobbs, Isaac 1743, 24
Dobbs, Jenneke 1738, 24
Dobbs, John 1734, 24
Dobbs, John J. m/1733, 24
Dodd, Martha Virginia 1894, 167
Dodd, Samuel L., 167
Dodd, Sarah, 167
Dorland, Joseph, 10
Dorman, Alice, 196
Dougherty, Rebecca, 152
Douglass, Anna D., 120
Douglass, Ben, 117, 120
Douglass, J. Mabel, 120
Douthitt, Robert 1802, 156
Douw, Dorothea 1701, 197, 217, 269
Douw, Kendrick, 197
Downing, Emma Blanche, 247

Downing, Martha Ann, 140
Downing, No given name, 247
Downing, Olive Mildred Lee,
247
Downing, Ruth Rebecca, 247
Drake, Catharine 1775, 193, 196
Du Bois, Johannes 1710, 198
Du Mont, John, 200
DuBois, Abigail 1795, 33
DuBois, Abraham 1792, 33
DuBois, Aleda 1763, 27
DuBois, Andrew, 30
DuBois, Ann 1793, 33
DuBois, Anna 1757, 30
DuBois, Barent, 29
DuBois, Barent 1693, 7
DuBois, Benjamin 1767, 31
DuBois, Benjamin 1770, 31
DuBois, Catharine 1706, 7
DuBois, Catherine, 217
DuBois, Catherine 1751, 30
DuBois, Cornelius 1762, 30
DuBois, David, 47
DuBois, David 1724, 31, 32, 49
DuBois, David 1761, 30
DuBois, Dina 1789, 211
DuBois, Eleanor, 30
DuBois, Eleazer, 33
DuBois, Elizabeth, 30
DuBois, Elizabeth 1730, 41
DuBois, Elizabeth 1804, 33
DuBois, Elizabeth d/1943, 51
DuBois, Garret, 4
DuBois, Gerret 1700, 7
DuBois, Gerret 1704, 7
DuBois, Gerretje, 4
DuBois, Gieltjie 1697, 7
DuBois, Hendrica 1746, 8, 13
DuBois, Hendricus 1765, 27
DuBois, Hezekiah, 27
DuBois, Hezekiah 1727, 27
DuBois, Isaac, 49

DuBois, Isaac 1702, 7
DuBois, Jacob 1661, 7, 12
DuBois, Jacob 1719, 29
DuBois, Jacob, Reverend, 30, 33
DuBois, Jacomyntje 1693, 7
DuBois, Johannes, 13, 211
DuBois, Johannes 1710, 8
DuBois, John, 30
DuBois, John 1752, 30
DuBois, John 1780, 40
DuBois, John P. 1791, 211
DuBois, Jonathan 1757, 30
DuBois, Joseph 1737, 31
DuBois, Josiah, 33
DuBois, Josiah 1762, 32
DuBois, Judike 1784, 211
DuBois, Lewis 1755, 30
DuBois, Louis, 7, 41
DuBois, Louis 1695, 7
DuBois, Lydia 1761, 30
DuBois, Maria 1756, 27
DuBois, Mary 1790, 33
DuBois, Matthew 1722, 30
DuBois, Matthew 1765, 31
DuBois, Michele 1789, 49, 50,
54, 55
DuBois, Minche 1789, 49
DuBois, Neeltjen 1716, 8, 12,
211
DuBois, Peter 1789, 42
DuBois, Peter, Captain, 11
DuBois, Petrus 1749, 211
DuBois, Petrus 1786, 211
DuBois, Phebe 1807, 33
DuBois, Rachel 1749, 29
DuBois, Rachel 1759, 30
DuBois, Rachel 1765, 32
DuBois, Rebecca, 30
DuBois, Rebecca 1708, 8
DuBois, Rebecca 1786, 49
DuBois, Rebecca 1796, 33
DuBois, Samuel, 30

DuBois, Sarah, 30
DuBois, Sarah 1713, 8
DuBois, Sarah 1753, 30
DuBois, Sarah 1754, 30
DuBois, Sarah 1788, 33
DuBois, Sarah 1833, 49
DuBois, Sarah E. 1830, 225
DuBois, Solomon, 7, 8
DuBois, Thomas, 42
Dudley, Bessie O., 35
Dudley, Carr, 35
Dudley, Charles E., 35
Dudley, Frederick A., 35
Dudley, John T., 35
Dudley, Lewis H., 35
Dudley, Lulu F., 35
Dudley, Rosanna B., 35
Dudley, William N., 35
Dumond, Philippus 1707, 198
Dumond, Walran, 198
Dumont, Cornelius, 211
Dumont, Jacob, 202
Dunham, Elizabeth, 165
Dunham, Narcissa W., 137
Dunham, William C., 165
Dunham, Wilmer 1893, 165
Dunkin, Abraham 1824, 140
Dunkin, Amos, 140
Dunkin, Emma 1830, 140
Dunkin, Harkless 1816, 138
Dunkin, Henry 1818, 138
Dunkin, Hercules 1826, 140
Dunkin, Jane 1832, 140
Dunkin, John, 138
Dunkin, John 1825, 138
Dunkin, Joshua 1835, 138, 139
Dunkin, Margaret 1820, 138
Dunkin, Margaret 1834, 140
Dunkin, Reason 1836, 140
Dunkin, Sarah 1828, 140
Dunkin, Sarah J. 1832, 138
Dunlap, Bathsheba, 45

Dunwoody, Betty Jane 1924, 251
Dunwoody, Samuel Leon, 251
DuPuis, Philippus, 268

—E—

Eager, Maria, 270
Eakins, Alva, 152
Eal, Mary, 305
Edgerly, Thomas, 22
Edwards, Lena, 79
Ehrs, Bryan Edward 1976, 180
Ehrs, Heather Lee 1971, 180
Ehrs, Joe Ed, 180
Eiler, Susan C., 140
Eldridge, No given name, 51
Elias, No given name, 170
Elledge, Jane, 291
Ellis, George, 165
Ellis, Jacob, Col., 46
Ellis, Mary Susan 1871, 167
Ellis, Nannie, 165
Ellis, Nellie V. 1878, 165
Elmendorf, Aaltje, 7
Elmendorf, Abraham, 4
Elmendorf, Antje 1775, 200
Elmendorf, Ariaan Gerritse
    1728, 200
Elmendorf, Arriantje 1724, 199,
    202
Elmendorf, Arriantje 1777, 200
Elmendorf, Carlintje 1783, 200
Elmendorf, Coenrad, 11, 21, 199
Elmendorf, Coenrad Edmundus
    1763, 200
Elmendorf, Coenradt, 7, 8, 198
Elmendorf, Coenradt Jacobus
    1726, 200
Elmendorf, Conrad 1710, 8
Elmendorf, Cornelius 1778, 200
Elmendorf, Cornelius 1787, 200
Elmendorf, Cornelius J., 4

Elmendorf, Cornelius J. 1738, 201
Elmendorf, Elizabeth 1723, 199
Elmendorf, Elizabeth 1772, 200
Elmendorf, Gerrit 1696, 11
Elmendorf, Gerrit 1734, 200
Elmendorf, Jacobus 1694, 199, 200
Elmendorf, Jacobus 1736, 200
Elmendorf, Jacobus 1771, 200
Elmendorf, Jacobus 1774, 200
Elmendorf, Jacobus C. 1772, 200
Elmendorf, Janneke, 200
Elmendorf, Lucas 1718, 198
Elmendorf, Margaret, 4
Elmendorf, Margaret 1708, 7
Elmendorf, Margaret 1732, 200
Elmendorf, Maria 1780, 200
Elmendorf, Maria 1795, 201
Elmendorf, Petrus 1742, 201
Elmendorf, Sarah 1785, 200
Elmendorff, Conrad 1734, 11
Elmendorff, Garret 1736, 11
Elmendorff, Garret 1743, 11
Elmendorff, Margrietje 1737, 11
Elting, Catryntje, 212
Elwell, Annie, 54
Elwell, Benjamin, 56
Elwell, Catherine, 41, 47
Elwell, Dorothy, 47
Elwell, Elizabeth, 56
Elwell, Elizabeth 1783, 48
Elwell, Isaac, 47
Elwell, Joast, 47
Elwell, Laura Frances, 56
Elwell, Laura Frances 1909, 55
Elwell, Levi, 47
Elwell, Lydia 1816, 59
Elwell, Lydia V. 1921, 56
Elwell, Matthew, 47
Elwell, Minnie, 56
Elwell, Otis H., 55, 56

Elwell, Samuel, 47
Elwell, Sarah Ann 1805, 59
Elwell, Sarah E., 50
Elwell, William, 47
Embler, Albert S., 287
Embler, Catherine 1785, 281
Embler, Crey 1793, 282
Embler, George, Jr., 281
Embler, Henry 1791, 281
Embler, John 1789, 281
Emmich, Robert, 251
Epple, Jane Louise, 101
Ervin, No given name, 112
Essinger, No given name, 45
Estabrooks, Arthur, 308
Estabrooks, Thomas B., 308
Etheridge, Beatrice Marple 1941, 39
Evans, Anna Jane 1822, 96
Evans, Frank, 56
Evans, Horatio, 130
Evans, Leola, 56
Everett, John, 76
Everhart, Annie V., 168
Everhart, C. E., 168
Everhart, Mary Belle 1900, 168
Everman, Mary, 70
Evers, Sarah, 118
Evertse, Arent, 2

—F—

Fainey, Jane 1798, 114
Faison, Julien Poydras, Rev., 93
Faith, No given name, 112
Fanguery, Alfred, 58
Farnham, Fidelia, 296
Farris, Nancy 1811, 83
Fassett, Marjorie 1897, 132
Fayhe, Kate 1857, 148
Fayhe, Michael, 148
Fear, Anna 1833, 138, 139

Fear, Cyrus 1829, 139
Fear, Francis 1824, 139
Fear, John F. 1831, 139
Fear, Margaret 1822, 138
Fear, Maria 1820, 138
Fear, Matilda 1836, 139
Fear, Orpha 1827, 139
Fear, Peter, Dr. 1795, 138
Fear, William 1838, 139
Fellows, Virginia Frances, 141
Fennell, Annie Thomas, 98
Fennell, David Carey 1884, 98
Fennell, Jane Newkirk, 98
Fennell, Margaret Howey, 98
Fennell, Mary Madeline, 98
Fennell, Nell Stewart, 98
Ferguson, Allen, 241
Ferris, Phoebe, 204
Fetzer, Amelia W., 239
Fields, Mary Wheeler, 300
Fish, Tryphenia 1776, 58
Fisher, Frederick, Colonel, 208
Fisher, Sarah M. 1852, 311
Fisler, Joseph Atwood 1843, 62
Fithian, Anna Frances 1907, 53
Fithian, George, 53
Fithian, George O., 55
Fithian, Marguerite 1894, 55
Fizzetie, Wayne 1929, 180
Flanagan, Charles, 265
Fleek, Mary E., 45
Floyd, Eda A. 1850, 176
Floyd, James, 176
Floyd, Martha Ann, 141
Focken, Tryntje, 7
Foote, Ellen, 111
Ford, Mary 1811, 163, 164, 165, 166
Ford, Rachel Rice 1850, 62
Fossett, Ida, 240
Foster, Elizabeth, 45
Foster, Jonathan, 45

Foster, Leah, 118
Foster, Louisa Ellen 1863, 177
Foster, Sarah, 42
Foster, William, 177
Foules, Mamie, 39
Fountain, Eleanor 1814, 171
Fowler, Jane, 226
Fox, Armenis B. 1856, 174
Fox, George Andrew, Jr. 1970, 216
Fox, Hannah Etta 1844, 174
Fox, Henrietta 1844, 174
Fox, Isaac, 174
Fox, Jonathan, 174
Fox, Joseph, 174
Fox, Joseph 1853, 174
Fox, Louise, 80
Fox, Nancy J. 1842, 174
Fox, Richard M. 1859, 174
Fox, William A. 1856, 174
Fox, William W. 1849, 174
Foy, Susannah, 137
Franks, Anna 1829, 226
Franks, John 1822, 226
Frazer, Phebe K., 51
Frear, Jannetje, 210
Freeland, Miriam, 136
Freer, Alida 1796, 14
Friend, Anna Maria, 271
Froelich, Minnie, 128
Frost, Constance, 17
Frost, Douglas V., Dr., 17
Frost, Henry F., 287
Frost, Melodie, 17
Frost, Nancy, 17
Frost, Ray, 17
Fry, Gerald Leslie, 260
Fry, Mary M., 144
Funk, Mildred 1912, 134
Funk, Paul, 134

—G—

Gardenier, Lysbeth, 9
Gardinier, Rachel 1763, 208
Gardner, Berney 1892, 36
Gardner, Charles H. 1901, 36
Gardner, H., 36
Gardner, Henry B. 1899, 36
Gardner, Kingsley E. 1890, 36
Gardner, Martha 1895, 36
Gardner, Samuel, 306
Gardner, Sarah 1897, 36
Gardner, Stanley 1893, 36
Garrabrant, Jacob, 222
Garrabrant, Maritie 1756, 222
Garrett, No given name, 294
Garrison, Darlene, 182
Garrison, Eunice, 35
Garrison, Joel, 30
Garrison, Tamson, 32
Garrison, William, 31
Garritson, Maria 1769, 209
Garsling, Mary, 10
Gartin, Lowell C. 1891, 152
Gartin, Omar, 152
Gartin, William R. 1889, 152
Garton, Anna Lorena 1883, 52
Garton, Oliver, 52
Gary, Anthony Patrick 1992, 181
Gary, Brian, 181
Gatin, Roy, 99
Gaunt, Dorothy R., 56
Gaunt, Oscar 1884, 56
Gaunt, Stanley, 56
Gautier, Francis P., 226
Geffert, Ima Jean, 260
Gehagen, Harry 1890, 39
Gentry, Samuel C., 188
Gerin, No given name, 84
German, Andries 1773, 270
German, Anna Maria 1765, 270
German, Catherine 1767, 270

German, Catherine 1769, 270
German, Elizabeth 1759, 269
German, Geertje 1757, 269
German, Hendrick 1761, 270
German, Johan Yoest 1726, 269
German, Johannis 1763, 270
Gerrits, Aaltie, 2
Gerrits, Aaltje, 222
Gerrits, Bijtie, 1, 2
Gibbon, Sarah O., 119
Gibbon, Tobias M., 118
Gibbs, Jack, 78
Giberson, Reuben, 227
Gibson, Beverly Ann, 159
Gibson, Dayton R., 52
Gidley, Ricketson, 203
Gieger, Albert Jack, 102
Gilbert, Frank, 99
Gilbert, Margaret Elizabeth
    1908, 99
Gilbert, Sarah Evans 1918, 100
Gilbert, William Francis 1911,
    100
Giles, Jacob, 104
Giles, Sarah, 73
Gillespie, John, 213
Gillette, William 1828, 289
Gilliland, Sarah, 156
Gillis, James, 105
Gilpin, Eliza, 136
Gilson, Jesse B., 149
Gilson, William J. 1910, 149
Gish, Irene Edith, 291
Gladow, Mary Jo, 261
Glasbey, Mary F. 1839, 61
Glendenning, Carmen Marie
    1938, 252
Glendenning, G. B., 252
Glenn, C. T., 84
Glenn, Sallie 1869, 84
Glenn, Susan L. 1956, 263
Goddard, Robert, 311

Godsil, Terrence, 301
Goelzer, Friedrich Ludwig, 123
Goff, Dora, 78
Goldman, Chauncey, 78
Goldsmith, John, 271
Gonterman, William Terry 1952, 292
Gonya, Cleone, 103
Gonzales, Joseph Earl 1989, 186
Gonzales, Lisa Louise 1981, 186
Gonzales, Matthew Jason 1986, 186
Gonzales, Richard 1941, 186
Goodson, No given name, 78
Gordley, Marshall, 237
Gordley, Marshall T. 1875, 237
Gore, Ada, 92
Goss, Harry, 79
Graff, Bertha Reed 1879, 53
Graham, Kathie, 70
Graham, Margaret, 271
Graham, No given name, 70
Graves, Mary Jane 1922, 180
Graves, No given name, 74
Gray, Amy 1962, 157
Gray, Harry Pauldin, 56
Gray, Henrietta, 56
Gray, John H., 153
Gray, Josephine, 56
Gray, Kenneth Everett, 159
Gray, Lena B. 1886, 153
Gray, Mark Everett 1960, 157, 159
Gray, Mary J. 1893, 153
Gray, Rebecca J. 1849, 141
Greathouse, Eliza Ann, 58
Green, Lester Maxwell, 104
Green, Lester Maxwell, II, 104
Green, Lester Maxwell, III 1954, 104
Green, Mary Jane, 84
Gregg, Bernice Iphagenia, 247

Gregg, Denton Bennie, 247
Gregg, Dorothy Phyllis, 247
Gregg, No given name, 247
Gregoire, Opheilia 1902, 159
Gregoire, William, 159
Gregory, Amy Clark, 248
Gregory, Arthur H., 245
Gregory, Eli C., 245
Gregory, Esther L., 79
Gregory, Ethel, 245
Gregory, Isaac, 248
Gregory, Orpha S. 1844, 248
Gregory, Wilbur, 78
Greig, Norman, 102
Griffis, David 1945, 180
Grimes, Eliza Ann, 141
Grimes, Vivian, 241
Griswold, Pat E., 252
Groff, Garret, 40
Grubbs, Asa, 164
Grubbs, Leslie C. 1900, 164
Grubbs, Nannie, 164
Grubhoffer, Kathryn, 158
Guess, Emma L., 81
Gufford, Mary Ann 1832, 91
Gundry, Bailey Renee 1995, 292
Gundry, Jonathan Matthew 1988, 292
Gundry, Kirsten Faith 1991, 292
Gundry, Michael 1966, 292
Gurnee, Alice 1864, 290
Gurnee, Charles 1861, 290
Gurnee, Jonas 1832, 290
Guyll, Bob, 76

—H—

Hagaman, Ulysses Grant 1868, 56
Hager, Jonathan, 167
Haggerty, Henderson, 294
Haley, Peter, 236

334

Hall, Albert G., 93
Hall, Alfred, 93
Hall, Elizabeth 1780, 189
Hall, Garrett 1792, 68
Hall, Margaret, 76
Hall, Martin 1821, 68
Hall, No given name, 107
Hall, Rebecca 1779, 187, 188
Ham, Alice Titus 1899, 205
Ham, Eugene, 203
Ham, John Fredrick 1896, 205
Ham, John Milton 1861, 204
Ham, Milton Conrad, 204
Ham, Milton Conrad 1891, 205
Hamilton, Acy 1878, 264
Hamilton, Andrew A. 1867, 263
Hamilton, Arla C. 1878, 263
Hamilton, Austin, 264
Hamilton, Cora May, 264
Hamilton, David, Lt., 234
Hamilton, Edward 1884, 264
Hamilton, Elma Gertrude 1881,
    263
Hamilton, Emma B. 1873, 263
Hamilton, Guy D. 1871, 263
Hamilton, Jeff Patrick 1987, 184
Hamilton, Jennifer Michelle
    1982, 184
Hamilton, John F. 1876, 263
Hamilton, Josiah, Col., 46
Hamilton, Kevin Edward 1981,
    184
Hamilton, Linda Marie 1985,
    184
Hamilton, Lula 1880, 264
Hamilton, Martha E. 1869, 263
Hamilton, Mary 1829, 145
Hamilton, Phillip Andrew 1987,
    184
Hamilton, Polly 1829, 145
Hamilton, Said 1953, 184
Hamilton, Sylvester Ellis, 263

Hamilton, William, 252
Hamilton, William John 1984,
    184
Hammond, Billy, 80
Hanna, Abigail 1757, 41
Hansen, Annie Joyce, 104
Hansen, Julius, 104
Hansen, Thomas Julius, 104
Hanson, Alexander, 175
Harcum, Charles L. 1876, 239
Harcum, Elisha, 239
Harcum, George Melvin 1888,
    240
Harcum, Goldie, 240
Harcum, Harry, 239
Harcum, Nora 1880, 240
Hardenberg, Magdalena 1782,
    212
Hardenbergh, Catrina 1729, 200
Hardenbergh, Gerardus, 200
Hardenbergh, Janneke, 199
Hardy, Susan Jane, 76
Harman, Clara, 264
Harper, Andrew Raymond, 263
Harris, Al, 307
Harris, Frances 1809, 188
Harris, George Daniel 1956, 181
Harris, Gladys Elizabeth, 241
Harris, Horatio, 297
Harris, John 1929, 181
Harris, Lorelie 1939, 182
Harris, Michelle Marie 1954, 181
Harris, Rosalie Ann 1957, 181
Harris, Taryn Danielle 1988, 181
Harris, Tori Wilson 1983, 181
Harris, Trace Oliver 1992, 181
Harrison, Asbury J., 152
Harrison, Charles, Jr., 290
Harrison, Laura Atkins 1864,
    290
Harrison, Randolph, 133
Harsin, Balli 1759, 21

Harsin, Margaret 1759, 21
Harsin, Maria 1759, 21
Hart, Ann, 300
Hart, David, 118
Hart, Jane 1801, 118
Hart, Joseph M., 52
Hart, Sarah, 118
Harter, Henry 1883, 34
Harter, William 1910, 34
Harwood, Lee Curtis 1881, 168
Harwood, Mary, 168
Harwood, Thomas, 168
Hasbrouck, Gabelle, 285
Haskett, Melissa A., 139
Hassett, Ann Elizabeth 1855, 111
Hawes, Edmond Alexander, II, 95
Hawes, Elizabeth A. 1801, 90
Hawes, Enoch, 90
Hawes, John, 90
Hawes, Mary Catherine 1803, 95
Hawk, Abraham, 142
Hawk, Marcus, 140
Hawkins, Lurena 1895, 240
Hawkins, Mary, 170
Hawkins, Rezin, 240
Hawthorn, Edgar A., 285
Hay, John, Honorable, 108
Hay, Susannah 1781, 108, 112, 161
Hay, William, 108
Hayes, Eliza, 58
Hayes, Robert, 58
Hayes, Rutherford B., Pres., 123
Hayford, Cora, 134
Hayman, Elizabeth, 29
Hays, Benjamin F., 196
Hays, No given name, 72
Hearder, Peter 1826, 27
Heberton, George,, 43
Heberton, Margaret 1799, 43

Heberton, Margaret Catherine 1799, 44
Heberton, Mary 1766, 44
Hedden, Sarah, 228
Heermaantsen, Neeltje 1767, 22
Heggens, Covilla, 58
Heights, Alexander, 156
Helm, Minnie Lillian 1901, 291
Helmy, Louise, 103
Hemple, Erwin Newkirk 1939, 54
Hemple, George Richard 1908, 54
Hempy, Elizabeth 1812, 131
Henderson, Benjamin Franklin 1865, 177
Henderson, David William, 247
Henderson, Dorothy Sophia, 247
Henderson, Elizabeth 1804, 175
Henderson, Elmer Le Roy 1887, 176
Henderson, Emaline 1850, 176
Henderson, Freeman 1870, 177
Henderson, Isabella Mary, 247
Henderson, James 1852, 176
Henderson, Jasper Henry 1867, 177
Henderson, John C. Breckenridge 1857, 176
Henderson, Joseph 1770, 170, 175, 176
Henderson, Joseph Benjamin 1854, 176
Henderson, Joseph Benjamin 1856, 176
Henderson, Joseph, Jr. 1808, 176
Henderson, Marian Isabelle, 177
Henderson, No given name, 247
Henderson, Permelia Ann 1855, 176
Henderson, Polly 1797, 173, 175
Henderson, Robert 1795, 175

Henderson, Robert Michael 1863, 177
Henderson, Robert, Jr. 1827, 176
Henderson, Sarah Jane, 177
Henderson, William 1794, 170, 175
Henderson, William 1859, 177
Henderston, S., 306
Hendricks, Aaron, 287
Hendrix, Charles L. 1879, 144
Hendrix, Dora A. 1878, 144
Hendrix, George W. 1837, 144
Hendrix, Kendall E. 1908, 144
Hendrix, Laura A. 1882, 144
Hendrix, Mary Etta 1866, 144
Hendrix, Robert E. 1904, 144
Hendrix, William A. 1871, 144
Hennion, Fitje 1744, 228, 229
Henry, C. Thomas 1826, 105
Henry, C. Thomas, II, 105
Henry, Frances 1825, 273
Henry, Mary E., 103
Hensey, Rosetta Estella 1876, 295
Hermance, Abraham 1740, 24
Hermance, Goozen 1745, 24
Hermance, Jacob, 24
Hermance, Jacomyntje 1743, 24
Hermance, Jan, 24
Hermance, Jan 1738, 24
Hermens, Kil, 1, 2
Herr, Theresa 1813, 57
Herring, Alfred Taylor, 91
Herring, Ella King, 92
Herring, Fanny, 244
Herring, Stephen, 93
Herring, William B., 88
Hess, Claude, 164
Hess, Esther, 164
Hess, Helen F. 1910, 164
Hewyard, Elizabeth, 33
Hibler, Samuel, 41

Hicks, Eliza 1825, 242
Hicks, Nancy 1819, 242
Hight, Armintha M. 1842, 38
Hight, Stewart 1809, 38
Higley, Anson, 296
Hilflicker, Ruby May 1903, 179
Hill, Frances Marjorie, 252
Hill, Levi, 270
Hilt, Elizabeth, 138
Himrod, Elizabeth Christian, 245
Himrod, Estella, 245
Himrod, Mary Grace, 245
Himrod, Sally, 245
Himrod, W. G., 245
Hires, Sarah, 103
Hitch, Mary, 239
Hitchner, Christianna 1802, 58
Hitchner, Laura, 55, 56
Hitchner, Phebe, 56
Hoag, Mary Annette, 203
Hoageland, Goldie, 304
Hoagland, Henry, 63, 66, 67
Hoagland, Jacobus, 63
Hoagland, James, 66
Hoagland, John, 63, 65
Hoagland, William, 66
Hobson, Edythe S., 70
Hoff, Andries 1743, 24
Hoff, Catharine 1739, 24
Hoff, John 1741, 24
Hoff, Philipus, 24
Hoffman, Tjaetjen, 8
Hoffman, Zachariah, 217
Hoggatt, Velma, 241
Holdren, Eunice 1895, 261
Hollen, Nathan, 79
Holliday, Alexander, 277
Holliday, John Newkirk 1801, 277
Hollow, Walter Boyd, 301
Holme, Benjamin, Colonel, 46
Holmes, Charles G., 286

Holt, Joseph M., 52
Holt, Lori, 252
Hood, John, 63, 64, 109
Hood, John, Jr., 65
Hood, Tunis, 63
Hoogteeling, Dina 1710, 210
Hoogteeling, Kezia, 24
Hoogteeling, Philip, 210
Hook, Thomas Jefferson, 172
Hoopingarner, Jacob 1795, 189
Hopkins, Adam P., 120
Hopkins, Henry, 120
Hopkins, Mary, 120
Hopkins, Nancy W. 1829, 115
Hopper, Harry K., 81
Hopper, Mary Elizabeth, 81
Hoskins, Mary 1796, 34
Hostetler, Jonathan 1819, 122
Hostetler, Laura Alice 1858, 122
Hotten, Martha, 78
Houchens, Frances, 140
Hough, Austin, 188
Houlahan, Adrienne Elizabeth, 183
Hovey, Susan, 286
Howard, Amanda, 84
Howard, Docia, 196
Howard, William G. 1816, 196
Howden, Andrew, 129
Howden, No given name, 116
Howe, Alfron W., 297
Howe, No given name, 250
Howell, Benjamin F., 140
Howell, Claude Ferry, 274
Howell, Edward, 103
Howell, Mary Elizabeth, 232
Howsen, Peter, 117
Hubbard, George, 176
Hubbard, Martin, 128
Hubbard, Nancy Ann 1855, 176
Hubbard, No given name, 246
Hubert, AnnMarie Pulcherie, 159

Huckendublen, Lydia E. 1856, 117
Huckfeldt, Betty Lou 1930, 179
Huckfeldt, Ray 1908, 179
Hudson, Cordelia, 175
Hudspeth, Price, 309
Huey, Anna, 268
Huey, Henry, 268
Huey, James 1738, 268
Huey, John, 268
Huey, Margaret 1742, 268
Huey, Mary, 268
Huey, Robert, 268
Huey, Susanna, 268
Huey, William, 268
Huffman, Ann 1822, 90
Huffman, Harriet, 93
Huffman, James, 93, 264
Huffman, Lavinia, 93
Huffman, Mary 1813, 94
Hughes, Cordelia A., 195
Hughes, Jane 1810, 44
Hughes, Minne Vera, 53
Hughes, Nancy E., 193
Hughes, Samuel M., 193
Hughes, William, 268
Hull, Abraham 1809, 136
Hull, Cyrus 1811, 136
Hull, Elizabeth, 79
Hull, George Washington 1823, 136
Hull, John 1782, 135
Hull, Josiah 1813, 136
Hull, Lorinda 1815, 136
Hull, Margaret 1817, 136
Hull, Newkirk 1806, 136
Hull, No given name, 107
Hull, Orpha 1819, 136
Humphreys, Charles Levi 1912, 53
Humphreys, Charles William 1949, 53

338

Humphreys, John Albertus 1952, 53
Hunt, William 1801, 156
Hunter, Charlotte 1810, 44
Hunter, Stella, 309
Hurlburt, Richard Leon, 291
Hurley, W. M., 163
Hurst, Mary E., 51
Hurst, Susanna, 42
Hutchinson, Lydia 1798, 58
Hutchison, Stuart M., 262
Huybertse, Elizabeth 1666, 3
Huybertsen, Lambert, 21

—I—

Ihrig, Georgeanna, 240
Ingeburg, Martha 1936, 184
Ingram, Sallie, 104
Inscho, Rebecca, 242
Inscoll, Ruth 1796, 169, 186
Ireland, Mary Ann 1845, 61
Isaminger, Rebecca 1828, 137
Israel, Rebecca, 34
Ives, No given name, 246
Izatt, Anna 1901, 37
Izatt, Ida J. 1903, 37
Izatt, Mary F. 1907, 37
Izatt, Ralph E. 1912, 37
Izatt, Russell A. 1910, 37
Izatt, William, 37
Izatt, William A. 1905, 37

—J—

Jackson, Claude H., 241
Jackson, Claudia, 241
Jackson, Eliza 1834, 45
Jackson, Joseph, 235
Jackson, Mildred 1903, 241
Jackson, Raymond 1897, 241
Jackson, William, 241
Jacobus, Eliza Hayes, 44

James, Elizabeth, 6
James, Josiah, 6
Jamison, Judy Ann, 80
Jansen, Gerrit, 2
Jansen, Margaret, 41
Jansen, Margaret 1699, 7
Jansen, Matthys, 7
Jay, Frederick Walter 1935, 252
Jay, James Leroy 1943, 252
Jay, Mark Barnett 1962, 252
Jay, Mark Frederick, 252
Jay, Michael James 1958, 252
Jay, Nanette E. 1942, 252
Jay, Tana Rae 1956, 252
Jeeney, John W., 304
Jennings, Lucretia, 22
Jewel, No given name, 287
John, Samuel S., 282
Johns, Geneva, 241
Johnson, Charles C., 307
Johnson, Edward, 69
Johnson, Eleanor Ann 1818, 242
Johnson, Ethel B., 69
Johnson, Harriet 1796, 40
Johnson, Henry, Reverend, 54
Johnson, Hester Mae 1906, 53
Johnson, Lela Ruth, 76
Johnson, Louis, 51
Johnson, Margaret 1794, 242
Johnson, Rebecca 1795, 235, 236
Johnson, Sara Ann, 240
Johnson, Sherri Lynn 1960, 159
Jones, Anna, 136
Jones, Charles Lerrquine, 106
Jones, Charlotte 1816, 136
Jones, Emma Irene, 216
Jones, Esther, 138
Jones, George Henry, 182
Jones, Howard Lester 1909, 182
Jones, Howard Lester, Jr. 1953, 177, 182
Jones, No given name, 72

339

Kiser, Roxy V. 1897, 150
Kiser, Sarah Emeline 1865, 150
Kiser, Sophia H. 1896, 150
Kiser, William F. 1854, 150
Kiser, William F. 1902, 150
Kitchen, Hezzie L. M. 1881, 165
Kittle, Helena, 5
Klaarwater, Geertje, 267, 268,
   271, 276, 277, 280
Klaarwater, Jacob, 268
Klaarwater, Theunis Jacobsen
   1624, 268
Klock, Helen E., 297
Knap, Luella, 297
Knox, John, 107
Knox, Margaret d/1823, 135
Knutson, Alex Marshall 1982,
   251
Knutson, Harold 1915, 250
Knutson, Judy Rosalie 1948, 251
Knutson, Keith Lee 1980, 251
Knutson, Lester B. 1953, 262
Knutson, Olaf, 250
Knutson, Phyllis Marie 1946,
   251
Knutson, Roberta Lynn 1956,
   251
Knutson, Roland Lee 1956, 251
Koch, Geertje, 228, 231
Koch, Henry C. F., 264
Kogh, Geertje, 228, 231
Koofman, Jacob, 169
Kool, Annetje 1713, 17
Kool, Catharine, 27
Kool, Jacob, 17
Kortright, Jane 1770, 218
Krekeler, Louis, 241
Krig, Ada L., 190
Krom, Aagje, 4, 7
Krom, Abraham, 5
Krom, Hendrick, 5
Krom, John, 29

Krom, John Hayman 1741, 29
Kuhn, Katherine 1886, 129
Kunst, Barent 1667, 6
Kunst, Hillitje Jans, 9
Kunst, Jacomyntje m/1713, 6
Kunst, Jan Barentsen, 6, 9
Kunst, Jannetje, 6
Kunst, Jennetje Jansz 1664, 3, 9,
   23, 25, 29, 63
Kuyper, Catrintje, 223
Kuyper, Hendrick, 223

—L—

Lackey, Mary E. 1807, 305
Ladd, Fannie Bird 1879, 126
Laird, Jane McKinney, 214
Lambertsen, Lysbeth 1666, 21
Lamont, Lara 1967, 183
Lamont, William 1924, 183
Landiss, Elizabeth, 72
Lange, Emma Grace 1909, 295
Lange, Frederick John, Jr. 1869,
   296
Lanier, Ben, 87
Lantz, John W., 158
Larkins, Sophia W., 96
Lauffer, Matthew Scott, 127
Lawill, Frances, 140
Lawill, John, 140
Lawrence, Robert, 85
Le Fevre, Sarah 1717, 13
Leach, Lydia, 236
Leachman, Doris Eleanor 1919,
   301
Leachman, Marion Ethel 1909,
   301
Leachman, Neil Kenneth 1903,
   301
Leachman, Pearl Norine 1906,
   301
Leachman, Versa Mae 1902, 301

341

Leachman, William 1869, 300
Leachman, William Thomas 1899, 300
Leaf, Gary Allen, 302
Leake, Rachel, 30
Leavenworth, Mary Louise, 16
Lee, Gabriel, 244
Leeds, Mary Ellen, 240
Leekins, William W., 157
LeFever, Peter, 14
LeFevre, Peter C. 1805, 212
LeFevre, Sarah H., 213
Lefferts, Edward V. 1815, 31
Lefferts, Elizabeth V. 1811, 31
Lefferts, Henry Wynkoop 1813, 31
Lefferts, James L. 1818, 31
Lefferts, John 1779, 31
Lefferts, Mary Helen Wynkoop 1825, 31
Lefferts, Reading Beatty 1822, 31
Lefferts, Sarah W. 1809, 31
Lefferts, Worth 1828, 31
Legg, Sarah, 17
Leggett, George, Dr., 110
Lehman, Mattheus, 28
Leimeister, Anton, 126
Leimeister, Greg Edward 1965, 121, 127
Leimeister, Kelsey Lynn 1989, 127
Leimeister, Kurt Alan 1961, 127
Leimeister, Mark Andrew 1958, 127
Leimeister, Paul Anthony 1932, 126
Leimeister, Ryan Thomas 1991, 127
Leons, Geertruyt, 220
Lesch, Laura, 50
Letts, Moses, 269

Lewars, Kenneth Brumbaugh, 177
Lewis, Delaine Kay, 158
Leyda, Benjamin, 117
Leyda, George 1794, 116
Leyda, James 1801, 116
Leyda, Margaret 1793, 121
Lindamood, Joalta, 151
Lindner, Christopher, 310
Lindsay, Helen K. 1922, 261
Linn, Anna B. 1854, 119
Linton, Eva Estelle, 78
Linton, Mary, 78
Linville, Sarah, 236
Lippincott, William, 48
Lockwood, Christine 1818, 285
Lockwood, Purdy, 286
Logan, Frank L., 153
Logan, Frank W. 1915, 153
Logan, Ross, 153
Logan, Russell W. 1911, 153
Logan, William John 1913, 153
Lohse, Allen, 133
Lombardo, Michael, 252
Long, Edith Elmetta, 144
Long, Mamie, 103
Longfellow, Virgil T. 1876, 147
Loper, Grace 1788, 57
Lorenz, James Edward, 127
Lorenz, Karen Louise 1965, 127
Lorton, William, 261
Loudon, David Bostwick, 178
Loughrey, Clare 1946, 184
Lounsberri, Sarah, 66
Louw, Catharine, 198
Louw, Janneke, 23
Louw, Magdalena, 8
Louw, Petrus Matthew, 217
Louw, Tryntje 1727, 217
Love, Eliza M., 100
Lovett, Martha Ann, 141
Lovfald, Steven Keith, 133

Lowe, Jane, 78
Lowe, Joe, 80
Loyd, Earl, 180
Lubi, Anna, 1, 220
Lubi, Jacob, 220
Lucas, Giles, 104
Ludlow, James, 155
Lykens, Alfred 1825, 40
Lykens, Edwin 1843, 40
Lytle, Elizabeth Mary, 126

—M—

MacLeod, Captain, 87
Maddle, Delila, 194
Mahaffey, Samuel, 139
Mahaffy, Andrew, 136
Maria, Sister 1922, 129
Maris, Lea, 222
Maris, Mary Louisa 1866, 46
Marple, Frances Eva 1894, 176
Marple, Mason, 176
Marr, America A., 307
Marr, Elizabeth T., 306
Marsh, Mary Bell, 309
Marsh, Moses L., 247
Marshall, Jane 1825, 243
Marshall, Richard C., 297
Martens, Jennette, 25
Martin, Elizabeth, 169, 186
Martin, Etta, 297
Mason, Festus Arthur, 92
Mason, Floyd W., 81
Mason, George William 1824, 138
Mason, Lillian Lametha 1889, 183
Mason, Martha 1781, 162, 163
Mason, Mary 1781, 162
Mason, Mary Martha 1781, 162
Mason, Maude, 146
Massey, No given name, 71

Massey, William 1866, 307
Mathews, Bartlett Marion 1903, 53
Mathews, Carey Beryl 1942, 98
Mathews, David Daniel 1948, 99
Mathews, Donald Reuben 1932, 53
Mathews, Glen Alfred 1926, 53
Mathews, Ivey, 98
Mathews, John Dudley 1944, 98
Mathews, Marion Wayne 1928, 53
Mathews, Timothy Ivey 1946, 99
Matis, William, 242
Matthews, Lydia, 138
Matthis, Edmond, 90
Matthis, James 1764, Major, 90
Matti, Henry Louis 1881, 126
Matti, Maude Evelyn 1906, 126
Mattingley, Minnie K., 144
Maul, Christopher, 266
Maul, Friederich, 266
Maurer, Anna 1900, 38
Maurer, Clark James 1935, 39
Maurer, Clark Lewis 1897, 39
Maurer, Hazel Anna 1893, 38
Maurer, Jakob 1833, 38
Maurer, Leone, 39
Maurer, Margaret Ann 1927, 39
Maurer, Nelson Edward 1894, 39
Maurer, Pansy Mae 1890, 38
Maurer, Peggy 1927, 39
Maurer, Rolla 1891, 38
Maurer, Rudolph Frederick 1888, 37, 38
Maurer, Samuel Henry 1868, 38
Maxwell, Brian Allen 1982, 251
Maxwell, Robert Arthur, 251
Maxwell, Robert Thomas 1950, 251
Maxwell, Spencer Curtis 1983, 251

May, Mary Berkeley Murphy, 105
Mayer, Walker, 157
Mayhew, Rebecca 1784, 45
Mayhew, Uriah 1746, 32
McBee, Martin Z., 304
McBride, Agnes 1781, 281
McBride, Archibald, 281
McBride, Archibald, Jr. 1759, 280, 281
McBride, Elizabeth 1794, 155
McBride, Ethel J. 1890, 151
McBride, Henry, 280
McBride, Henry 1787, 281
McBride, James 1779, 281
McBride, Jane, 281
McBride, Jane 1776, 281
McBride, Nancy B. 1783, 281
McBride, Orno H., 151
McBride, Patrick 1778, 281
McBride, Verna B. 1892, 151
McBride, William C. 1894, 151
McBroom, Sean 1964, 182
McCallum, Donald Malcolm, 52
McCallum, Donald Malcolm, Jr. 1963, 52
McCarty, Matilda J., 174
McCarty, No given name, 250
McCarty, Pearl A., 154
McConnell, Elizabeth 1785, 237
McCool, Margaret Joy 1902, 52
McCormick, James, 190
McCrosky, James, 285
McDade, Franklin, 173
McDonald, Abner, Jr. 1805, 68
McDonald, Christina Lynn 1978, 292
McDonald, David, 72
McDonald, David Lee 1975, 292
McDonald, Eli, 72
McDonald, Hugh, 74
McDonald, James, 68, 282

McDonald, Jane, 72
McDonald, Lori 1952, 180
McDonald, Mary, 72
McDonald, No given name, 72
McDonald, Susie, 72
McDonald, Thomas Francis 1955, 292
McDonald, Tonni Michelle 1980, 292
McDonnell, Janice Laverne, 252
McEacharn, No given name, 249
McGee, Jane 1780, 170, 176
McGinnis, William, Capt., 198
McGlasson, Maurice A., 80
McGregor, Alexander, 280
McIlvaine, Alice 1860, 265
McIntosh, Alberta, 79
McIntyre, Agnes, 134
McIntyre, Clifford, 134
McIntyre, Leona, 134
McKay, Alice Newkirk 1915, 149
McKay, Napoleon B., 149
McKeaigg, James H., 191
McKee, Bruce D., 81
McKenzie, John, 264
McKenzie, No given name, 247, 249
McKenzie, Roxanne, 127
McKinley, William, Pres., 123
McKinzie, Sarah Ellen, 300
McKitchen, Hezzie L. 1881, 165
McKnight, Joann, 127
McKnight, Susan Diane 1958, 127
McKnight, Thomas Fred, 127
McKoy, Annie, 105
McKoy, Carrie 1855, 104
McKoy, Edward B., 104
McKoy, Erskine Alexander, 103
McKoy, Josephine 1863, 104
McKoy, Margaret 1865, 104

McKoy, Usher, 104
McKoy, Willie, 105
McLaren, John 1846, 235
McMannis, Nellie, 154
McMillen, Thomas, Gen., 118
McMillin, Edith Belle 1886, 153
McMillin, Nellie Josephine 1887, 153
McMillin, Rubie Mae 1889, 153
McMillin, William H., 153
McMonagle, Moses R., 275
McNair, Norma Jean 1947, 216
McNair, William Donald, 216
McNeal, James, 281
McPherson, John 1824, 195
McPherson, Mary 1824, 195
McVey, No given name, 287
McVey, Sarah Ellen 1832, 287
McVey, William Young, 287
Meacham, Frank B., 104
Meacham, Frank Parker 1927, 104
Meacham, Frank Richard 1952, 104
Meacham, G. A., 106
Meacham, Jo Ann 1934, 104
Meads, Joseph E., 263
Meek, Becky Lynn, 185
Meeks, Sophia, 232
Megaw, George, 99
Meier, David 1950, 181
Meier, Lisa Kristine 1976, 181
Meier, Sara Renee 1978, 181
Mercer, Florence 1863, 96
Mercer, John W. 1812, 96
Merriott, Arkansas, 84
Merriott, J. Vander, 85
Merriott, Missouri, 84
Merriott, Walker J., 85
Merriweather, Randolph, 97
Merselis, Jacob M., 230
Mertine, Lena 1912, 20

Merwin, George Frederick 1922, 291
Merwin, Jacqueline Lee 1958, 292
Merwin, Lewis James, 291
Merwin, Mimi Laurette 1955, 292
Merwin, Vicki Lyn 1945, 291
Messersmith, John, 265
Messersmith, Murry A. 1888, 265
Messersmith, Walter D. 1881, 265
Meyer, Aaltjen 1741, 26
Meyer, Benjamin 1755, 26
Meyer, Christian, 26
Meyer, Christian 1738, 26
Meyer, Christian 1739, 26
Meyer, Edwin C., 153
Meyer, Hendricus 1742, 26
Meyer, Johannes 1746, 26
Meyer, John William 1714, 26
Meyer, Leah 1754, 26
Meyer, Maria 1743, 26
Meyer, Petrus 1750, 26
Meyer, Robert E. 1909, 153
Meyer, Samuel 1757, 26
Meyer, Tobias 1751, 26
Meyer, William C. 1913, 153
Meyers, Elizabeth 1818, 245
Miars, Ollie, 37
Michael, Thornley, 137
Michael, William, 137
Michaels, Nancy Ann 1806, 112
Miles, George, 108
Miles, George, Jr., 108
Miles, Margaret 1759, 108, 161
Millat, Mary, 209
Miller, Ann 1834, 275
Miller, Conrad, 311
Miller, Edna L., 68

Miller, Eleanor Aileen 1924, 239, 240
Miller, Herman 1893, 240
Miller, John 1728, 24
Miller, Mary, 108
Miller, Mary 1739, 43, 46
Miller, Michael, 108
Miller, Nancy 1815, 45
Miller, Rebecca, 58
Miller, Sinai Pearl 1880, 132
Miller, Vincent Grant, 240
Miller, William m/1727, 23
Millholland, David P., 304
Millholland, Margaret 1809, 304
Milligan, Elizabeth Jane 1821, 191
Milligan, Harvey 1832, 275
Mills, Catharine, 90
Mills, Erma Irene 1907, 185
Mills, Mary 1815, 171
Millspaugh, Catherine 1809, 275
Millspaugh, Clifford 1810, 278
Millspaugh, Cortland 1808, 278
Millspaugh, Elsje 1803, 278
Millspaugh, Frederick P., 277
Millspaugh, Lucas Elmendorf 1797, 277
Millspaugh, Mary 1813, 278
Millspaugh, Mathilda 1801, 278
Millspaugh, Moses, 281
Millspaugh, Nancy 1794, 277
Millspaugh, Nancy 1799, 277
Millspaugh, Philip P., 277
Millspaugh, Susanna 1792, 277
Milot, Mary, 209
Miner, Lester, 38
Mire, Donn Thomas 1934, 186
Mix, Dolly, 80
Mock, James D., 297
Monger, Bessie Mae 1894, 179
Montfort, Katherine, 74

Montgomery, Julia Ann 1823, 310
Moody, Merley Miller, 129
Moody, Nancy A., 140
Moore, Agnes, 281
Moore, Amos Millspaugh 1812, 278
Moore, Ann, 281
Moore, Charles 1823, 278
Moore, Charlotte, 32
Moore, Coenradt 1806, 278
Moore, David, 281
Moore, Ellen 1818, 278
Moore, Elsie Newkirk 1809, 278
Moore, Eugenia Estelle 1884, 97
Moore, George Leithton 1887, 97
Moore, Hannah 1808, 59
Moore, Henry, 281
Moore, Isabella 1779, 235
Moore, Ivey, 106
Moore, J. A. 1845, 97
Moore, Jacob C., 278
Moore, James, 280, 281
Moore, James Upham 1874, 97
Moore, James, Col., 87
Moore, Jane, 281
Moore, Joel 1816, 278
Moore, Joel J. 1884, 97
Moore, Jonathan 1987, 184
Moore, Julian Harrison 1882, 97
Moore, Leroy 1875, 309
Moore, Louella, 309
Moore, Maria 1801, 278
Moore, Marina Michelle 1986, 184
Moore, Martha Hawes 1891, 97
Moore, Mary S. 1872, 97
Moore, Nancy, 276
Moore, No given name, 52
Moore, Reno C., 122
Moore, Sarah 1828, 49
Moore, Selah 1803, 278

Moore, Steven, 184
Moore, Susannah 1799, 278
Moore, William, 281
Morehouse, Mildred, 20
Morgan, James, 6
Morris, Ellen Louise, 285
Morris, James, 139
Morris, Lilian M., 264
Morris, Lizzie, 310
Morris, Sarah, 310
Morrison, Christian 1761, 267
Morrison, James, 267
Morse, No given name, 75
Motz, Catharine, 117
Moyer, Abraham, 245
Moyer, Elizabeth 1818, 245
Moyer, Elizabeth 1820, 298
Moyer, Herbert C., 235
Moyer, Samuel Peyton, 238
Muggles, Oliver B., 36
Muggles, Oliver B. 1908, 36
Mulford, Joseph L. 1844, 62
Mulks, Elizabeth 1776, 219
Munat, Charles E., 57
Murffy, Mabel, 265
Murphy, James E., 241
Murphy, Mary Berkeley, 105
Myers, Andrew, 236
Myers, John B., 115
Myers, Kenneth Paul, 182
Myers, No given name, 140
Myers, Patricia Lee, 182
Myers, Samuel, 236
Myers, Zelma Elizabeth, 182
Myndertse, Neeltye, 197
Myrick, Mary, 126

—N—

Neal, Eva 1902, 35
Neal, John, 35
Neal, Ollie 1878, 309

Neels, Alfred Frederick 1941,
    252
Nelson, No given name, 249
Nesbit, Anna, 141
Nesbit, Sarah S., 141
Neuman, Fred 1876, 147
Neuman, John J. 1911, 147
Neuman, Robert M. 1902, 147
Newell, Carolyn Ann 1932, 185
Newell, Charles Nelson 1890,
    184
Newell, Charles Richard 1931,
    185
Newell, Cheryl Lee 1958, 185
Newell, Edward Brook 1885, 178
Newell, Geraldine Mae 1915,
    184
Newell, Jeff Allen 1955, 185
Newell, Judy Ann 1952, 185
Newell, Ruby Mae 1908, 179
Newhouse, Anna B. 1884, 152
Newhouse, Daisy M. 1878, 152
Newhouse, Elbert O. 1855, 152
Newhouse, Ernest, 264
Newhouse, Eva, 151
Newhouse, Iva A. 1879, 152
Newkirk, A. B., Dr., 137, 242,
    293
Newkirk, A. Forest, 84
Newkirk, Aaltjen 1758, 28
Newkirk, Aaron 1768, 223
Newkirk, Aaron 1794, 27
Newkirk, Aaron 1801, 18
Newkirk, Aaron 1850, 60
Newkirk, Abe Gasbeck, 20
Newkirk, Abigail 1800, 189
Newkirk, Abigail 1828, 288
Newkirk, Abigail 1845, 283
Newkirk, Abigail 1872, 237
Newkirk, Abner M. 1839, 304
Newkirk, Abraham (son/Henry)
    1774, 234

Newkirk, Albert 1914, 79
Newkirk, Albert Almaytron 1854, 157
Newkirk, Albert C. 1868, 288
Newkirk, Albert Crist 1829, 274
Newkirk, Albert H. 1871, 144
Newkirk, Albert L. 1854, 243
Newkirk, Albert S. 1854, 157
Newkirk, Alberta 1897, 51
Newkirk, Albertus 1876, 52
Newkirk, Alda 1911, 53
Newkirk, Aleene, 78
Newkirk, Alexander 1787, 86
Newkirk, Alexander 1802, 60
Newkirk, Alexander Yates 1817, 273
Newkirk, Alexandra Elle 1990, 127
Newkirk, Alice, 51
Newkirk, Alice 1886, 73
Newkirk, Alice 1918, 177, 183
Newkirk, Alice A. 1850, 132
Newkirk, Alice Marie 1959, 81
Newkirk, Alice May 1881, 297
Newkirk, Alice Melissa 1877, 241
Newkirk, Allen H. 1888, 57
Newkirk, Alley E. 1849, 83
Newkirk, Alma, 71
Newkirk, Almaytron 1828, 157
Newkirk, Alonzo P. 1848, 195
Newkirk, Alsop O. 1863, 297
Newkirk, Alta Elizabeth 1903, 308
Newkirk, Amanda 1835, 190
Newkirk, Amanda 1848, 172
Newkirk, Amanda Carolina, 57
Newkirk, Amanda Cordelia 1874, 241
Newkirk, Amanda Melvina 1837, 178
Newkirk, Amanda Sue 1985, 263

Newkirk, America 1834, 131
Newkirk, Amilda 1833, 190
Newkirk, Andrea 1786, 26
Newkirk, Andreas 1768, 23
Newkirk, Andreas 1786, 26
Newkirk, Andreas 1790, 27
Newkirk, Andrew 1748, 21
Newkirk, Andrew 1773, 48, 58
Newkirk, Andrew 1827, 59
Newkirk, Andrew 1838, 48
Newkirk, Andrew A. 1786, 26
Newkirk, Andrew Graham 1799, 271
Newkirk, Andrew L. 1869, 307
Newkirk, Andrew Lackey 1824, 305
Newkirk, Andries 1712, 24
Newkirk, Angeline 1824, 244, 263
Newkirk, Angeline 1827, 189
Newkirk, Angenietje 1754, 280
Newkirk, Anissa James 1993, 127
Newkirk, Anita 1950, 76
Newkirk, Ann 1764, 32, 40
Newkirk, Ann 1777, 41
Newkirk, Ann 1781/82, 21
Newkirk, Ann 1793, 36
Newkirk, Ann 1795, 45
Newkirk, Ann 1834, 14
Newkirk, Ann 1835, 59
Newkirk, Ann 1837, 15
Newkirk, Ann DeWitt 1861, 20
Newkirk, Ann Eliza 1812, 274
Newkirk, Ann Elizabeth 1877, 311
Newkirk, Ann Jane 1796, 89, 92
Newkirk, Ann Julia 1826, 96
Newkirk, Ann Rachel 1831, 94
Newkirk, Anna 1726, 206
Newkirk, Anna 1759, 22
Newkirk, Anna 1781, 21

Newkirk, Anna 1785, 14
Newkirk, Anna 1786, 109
Newkirk, Anna 1792, 137
Newkirk, Anna 1802, 112
Newkirk, Anna 1814, 132
Newkirk, Anna 1844, 209
Newkirk, Anna 1874, 74
Newkirk, Anna Bacon 1862, 46
Newkirk, Anna Benigma 1715,
    267, 276
Newkirk, Anna C. 1865, 287
Newkirk, Anna De Witt 1796, 23
Newkirk, Anna Eliza 1873, 51,
    52
Newkirk, Anna Maria 1677, 266,
    268
Newkirk, Anna Maria 1725/30,
    269
Newkirk, Anna Maria 1759, 271
Newkirk, Anna Maria 1769, 277
Newkirk, Anna Maria 1840, 231
Newkirk, Anna Mary 1867, 166
Newkirk, Anna Mary 1905, 168
Newkirk, Anna Matilda 1851,
    228
Newkirk, Anna Ursula 1718, 268
Newkirk, Annatje 1710, 23
Newkirk, Annatje 1763, 206
Newkirk, Annatje 1770, 229
Newkirk, Annatje 1776, 28, 206
Newkirk, Annatje 1790, 22
Newkirk, Annatje 1795, 26
Newkirk, Anne, 219
Newkirk, Anne 1780, 13
Newkirk, Anne 1842, 113
Newkirk, Anne E., 56
Newkirk, Anne Julia 1857, 96
Newkirk, Anne Marie 1936, 99
Newkirk, Annetje 1799, 209
Newkirk, Annie 1862, 231
Newkirk, Annie Agnes 1913, 102
Newkirk, Annie M. 1872, 165

Newkirk, Antje 1708, 221
Newkirk, Antoinette 1849, 137
Newkirk, Anway Ameranto
    1981, 262
Newkirk, Appollis McHenry
    1835, 34
Newkirk, Arabella 1843, 224
Newkirk, Arbuth E. 1888, 308
Newkirk, Archie 1908, 79
Newkirk, Arent 1768, 223, 229
Newkirk, Ariaan 1687, 25
Newkirk, Ariaantje 1699, 199
Newkirk, Ariantje 1748, 211
Newkirk, Arie 1663, 8
Newkirk, Arie 1737, 210
Newkirk, Arie 1742, 211
Newkirk, Arie 1753, 26
Newkirk, Arie Gerritsen 1773,
    206
Newkirk, Arien Gerritsen 1661,
    21
Newkirk, Arien Gerritsen 1663,
    3, 197, 205, 210, 269
Newkirk, Armanda 1871, 83
Newkirk, Armenis Benjamin
    1834, 175
Newkirk, Arrilla 1840, 35
Newkirk, Arthur Clinton 1856,
    120
Newkirk, Arthur Reid 1893, 261
Newkirk, Artimadoris
    Woodworth 1805, 295, 310
Newkirk, Artimus D. 1847, 311
Newkirk, Artimus D. Woodworth
    1805, 295, 310
Newkirk, Arward Theodore
    1906, 102
Newkirk, Ary 1721, 205
Newkirk, Asa H. 1811, 188
Newkirk, Aseneth D. 1820, 286
Newkirk, Attelia Whitted 1867,
    92

Newkirk, Audrey Anna 1920, 53
Newkirk, Augustus 1830, 235
Newkirk, B. Hayes 1879, 49
Newkirk, Barent 1689, 9, 63, 64, 65, 85, 107, 109, 160, 161, 169, 233
Newkirk, Barent 1736/55, 64, 65
Newkirk, Barent 1738, 229
Newkirk, Barent 1774, 229
Newkirk, Barent 1799, 68, 69
Newkirk, Barent 1868, 249
Newkirk, Barnet 1799, 68
Newkirk, Bathsheba 1792, 45
Newkirk, Bathsheba 1799, 155
Newkirk, Beatrice Graf 1902, 53
Newkirk, Becki Lynn 1967, 182
Newkirk, Bella, 52
Newkirk, Benina 1776, 277
Newkirk, Benjamin, 54
Newkirk, Benjamin 1720, 11, 19
Newkirk, Benjamin 1748, 18
Newkirk, Benjamin 1750, 21
Newkirk, Benjamin 1752, 13
Newkirk, Benjamin 1776, 27
Newkirk, Benjamin 1780, 48
Newkirk, Benjamin 1791, 35, 42
Newkirk, Benjamin 1794, 23, 43, 48
Newkirk, Benjamin 1808, 34
Newkirk, Benjamin 1810, 68, 77, 78, 79, 80
Newkirk, Benjamin 1829, 172
Newkirk, Benjamin 1835, 74
Newkirk, Benjamin 1849, 173
Newkirk, Benjamin 1870, 92
Newkirk, Benjamin A. 1794, 48
Newkirk, Benjamin Franklin 1754, 169, 170, 173, 175, 177
Newkirk, Benjamin Franklin 1841, 178
Newkirk, Benjamin Franklin 1870, 77

Newkirk, Benjamin Franklin, Jr. 1812, 172
Newkirk, Benjamin Garret 1800, 19, 20
Newkirk, Benjamin Garret 1858, 20
Newkirk, Benjamin Garrett 1800, 213
Newkirk, Benjamin Henry 1837, 94
Newkirk, Benjamin Leroy 1925, 80
Newkirk, Benjamin Oral 1900, 80
Newkirk, Benjamin Phillip 1869, 80
Newkirk, Benjamin Rhodes 1801, 89, 93
Newkirk, Benjamin Richard 1810, 171, 172
Newkirk, Benjamin W. 1830, 70
Newkirk, Benjamin William L. 1833, 77, 78
Newkirk, Benjamin, Jr. 1778, 13
Newkirk, Benoni 1800, 219
Newkirk, Benoni 1802, 219
Newkirk, Benton 1840, 77
Newkirk, Bernard Fulton 1909, 102
Newkirk, Besaleel Locy 1819, 298, 299, 301
Newkirk, Besse Mabel, 127
Newkirk, Bessie 1883, 122
Newkirk, Betsey 1811, 279
Newkirk, Betsy Ann 1957, 133
Newkirk, Betty Jane N., 71
Newkirk, Billie Ray 1926, 262
Newkirk, Billy 1865, 237
Newkirk, Birchard Hayes 1879, 53
Newkirk, Birdie 1886, 34
Newkirk, Blandina 1764, 22

Newkirk, Blandina 1789, 22
Newkirk, Bogardus 1815, 19, 213
Newkirk, Boone 1845, 193
Newkirk, Bowman 1841, 48
Newkirk, Brent 1868, 249
Newkirk, Brockdon 1980, 182
Newkirk, Bryan 1794, 89, 92, 95
Newkirk, Bryan Benjamin Rhodes 1829, 97
Newkirk, Bryan Winslow 1853, 96
Newkirk, Bryant Benjamin 1834, 91
Newkirk, Burhans, 218
Newkirk, Burilla 1835, 171
Newkirk, Burt Leroy, 16
Newkirk, Byrant 1794, 92
Newkirk, C. B. 1826, 92
Newkirk, C. C . 1824, 69
Newkirk, Calvin C., 84
Newkirk, Carey F. 1868, 144
Newkirk, Carlisle R. 1892, 149
Newkirk, Carol Dawn 1936, 133
Newkirk, Caroline 1822, 219
Newkirk, Caroline 1833, 110, 114
Newkirk, Caroline 1834, 304
Newkirk, Caroline 1843, 158
Newkirk, Caroline A. 1838, 58
Newkirk, Caroline E. 1851, 61
Newkirk, Caroline E. m/1837, 41
Newkirk, Caroline M. 1837, 15
Newkirk, Carolyn 1911, 53
Newkirk, Carolyn m/1937, 56
Newkirk, Carrie Frances 1876, 307
Newkirk, Cassandra 1793, 192
Newkirk, Cassilda 1842, 190
Newkirk, Caterina 1796, 219
Newkirk, Catharina 1731, 223
Newkirk, Catharina 1750, 18

Newkirk, Catharina 1757, 26
Newkirk, Catharina 1790, 217
Newkirk, Catharina Dorothea 1799, 23
Newkirk, Catharine 1738, 12
Newkirk, Catharine 1761, 218
Newkirk, Catharine 1775, 229
Newkirk, Catharine 1788, 225
Newkirk, Catharine 1793, 213
Newkirk, Catharine 1807, 223
Newkirk, Catharine 1817, 231
Newkirk, Catharine 1818, 235
Newkirk, Catharine 1823, 19
Newkirk, Catharine 1831, 70
Newkirk, Catharine 1832, 238
Newkirk, Catharine H. 1843, 232
Newkirk, Catherine, 18, 86, 219, 233
Newkirk, Catherine 1737, 31
Newkirk, Catherine 1767, 271
Newkirk, Catherine 1782, 207
Newkirk, Catherine 1783, 40, 278
Newkirk, Catherine 1784, 277
Newkirk, Catherine 1789/1800, 86
Newkirk, Catherine 1792, 155
Newkirk, Catherine 1803, 275
Newkirk, Catherine 1804, 219
Newkirk, Catherine 1820, 235
Newkirk, Catherine 1822, 287, 288
Newkirk, Catherine 1823, 213
Newkirk, Catherine 1829, 227
Newkirk, Catherine 1831, 27
Newkirk, Catherine 1836, 304
Newkirk, Catherine 1837, 130
Newkirk, Catherine 1839, 209
Newkirk, Catherine Alice 1912, 149
Newkirk, Catherine Ann 1979, 186

Newkirk, Catherine E. 1832, 213
Newkirk, Catherine Elizabeth
  1838, 227
Newkirk, Catherine G. 1846, 131
Newkirk, Catherine H. 1808, 212
Newkirk, Catherine J. 1846, 286
Newkirk, Catherine Maria 1831,
  274
Newkirk, Catherine O. 1812, 284
Newkirk, Catherine R. 1851, 191
Newkirk, Catlyntje 1733, 228
Newkirk, Catlyntje 1792, 223
Newkirk, Catrina 1729, 228
Newkirk, Catryntje 1791, 225
Newkirk, Caty Lena 1801, 274
Newkirk, Caty Rusten 1795, 19
Newkirk, Cecil Edward 1915,
  180
Newkirk, Celestia 1843, 290
Newkirk, Charity 1756, 280
Newkirk, Charles, 96
Newkirk, Charles 1753, 22
Newkirk, Charles 1771, 170
Newkirk, Charles 1788, 278
Newkirk, Charles 1792, 22
Newkirk, Charles 1793, 22
Newkirk, Charles 1795, 194
Newkirk, Charles 1828, 237
Newkirk, Charles 1835, 289
Newkirk, Charles 1836, 72, 279,
  288
Newkirk, Charles 1837, 195
Newkirk, Charles 1846, 45
Newkirk, Charles 1858, 243
Newkirk, Charles 1879, 190
Newkirk, Charles 1882, 73
Newkirk, Charles 1907, 244
Newkirk, Charles 1920, 129
Newkirk, Charles A. 1859, 304
Newkirk, Charles Abner 1918,
  291
Newkirk, Charles Allen 1836,
  231
Newkirk, Charles Amos 1861,
  240
Newkirk, Charles B. 1841, 285
Newkirk, Charles C. 1820, 188
Newkirk, Charles D. 1855, 115
Newkirk, Charles David 1918,
  168
Newkirk, Charles DeWitt 1836,
  20
Newkirk, Charles Drake 1845,
  196
Newkirk, Charles Edward 1863,
  227
Newkirk, Charles F. 1839, 51
Newkirk, Charles F. 1865, 164
Newkirk, Charles F. 1871, 307
Newkirk, Charles G. 1800, 295,
  304
Newkirk, Charles Gilbert 1882,
  144
Newkirk, Charles H. 1819, 288
Newkirk, Charles H. 1850, 285
Newkirk, Charles H. 1881, 117
Newkirk, Charles Hamilton
  1907, 164
Newkirk, Charles Harrison 1890,
  291
Newkirk, Charles Henry 1830,
  90
Newkirk, Charles Henry 1858,
  61
Newkirk, Charles J. 1841, 242
Newkirk, Charles L. 1840, 188
Newkirk, Charles M. 1844, 298
Newkirk, Charles M. 1846, 296
Newkirk, Charles N. 1878, 307
Newkirk, Charles R. 1858, 61
Newkirk, Charles Virgil 1946, 76
Newkirk, Charles W., 103
Newkirk, Charles W. 1853, 288

Newkirk, Charles W. 1872, 304
Newkirk, Charles W. 1882, 311
Newkirk, Charles Wesley 1810, 238
Newkirk, Charles Wesley, Jr. 1836, 238
Newkirk, Charles, Jr. 1846, 194
Newkirk, Charley L., 70
Newkirk, Charlotte 1821, 298
Newkirk, Charlotte 1831, 34
Newkirk, Charlotte Grace 1983, 186
Newkirk, Chester L. 1917, 80
Newkirk, Chester L., Jr. 1953, 80
Newkirk, Christiana 1765, 48
Newkirk, Christiana 1791, 43, 47
Newkirk, Christiana 1824, 155
Newkirk, Christie 1973, 76
Newkirk, Christina Brooks 1968, 17
Newkirk, Christoffel 1782, 213
Newkirk, Christopher 1782, 212, 213
Newkirk, Christopher 1805, 212
Newkirk, Christopher 1830/36, 310
Newkirk, Christopher C. 1838, 140
Newkirk, Christopher C. 1854, 311
Newkirk, Christopher Cornelius 1760, 64, 66
Newkirk, Christopher Cornelius 1770, 67
Newkirk, Clara 1870, 152
Newkirk, Clara 1871, 304
Newkirk, Clara Estelle 1864, 128
Newkirk, Clare Sparks 1886, 260
Newkirk, Clarence A. 1875, 71
Newkirk, Clarence L. 1871, 171
Newkirk, Clarence T., 112
Newkirk, Clarinda 1833, 57

Newkirk, Clarissa 1824, 274
Newkirk, Clarissa 1838, 279
Newkirk, Clarissa 1839, 58
Newkirk, Clarissa 1841, 57
Newkirk, Clarke 1876, 39
Newkirk, Claude, 71
Newkirk, Claude 1880, 149
Newkirk, Claude Mason 1899, 165
Newkirk, Clay McTyre 1903, 71
Newkirk, Clement 1815, 49, 50
Newkirk, Clement Botsford 1844, 285
Newkirk, Clement H. 1867, 51
Newkirk, Clement Ray 1884, 285
Newkirk, Clementine H. 1843, 40
Newkirk, Cleora McFarland 1908, 52
Newkirk, Clifton 1834, 191
Newkirk, Clifton H. 1823, 188
Newkirk, Clinton 1971, 76
Newkirk, Cloyd A. 1905, 79
Newkirk, Clyde, 112
Newkirk, Clyde Almaytron 1883, 157
Newkirk, Clyde F. 1889, 70
Newkirk, Clyde Newton 1870, 115
Newkirk, Coenradt 1722, 12, 21
Newkirk, Coenradt 1766, 22
Newkirk, Coenradt C. 1766, 22
Newkirk, Conrad 1783, 22
Newkirk, Cora A. 1869, 307
Newkirk, Cora Louise 1869, 128
Newkirk, Cornelia 1719, 24
Newkirk, Cornelia 1794, 22, 223
Newkirk, Cornelia 1800, 189
Newkirk, Cornelia 1825, 19
Newkirk, Cornelis 1680, 221
Newkirk, Cornelis 1703, 222

Newkirk, Cornelis Gerretse 1662, 3, 9, 11, 23, 25, 29, 269
Newkirk, Cornelis Gerretse 1689, 63
Newkirk, Cornelius 1696, 11, 29, 31, 41, 46
Newkirk, Cornelius 1710, 12, 21, 202, 210, 211
Newkirk, Cornelius 1710 s/o Jan, 23
Newkirk, Cornelius 1711, 11
Newkirk, Cornelius 1712, 24
Newkirk, Cornelius 1715, 8, 11, 12, 211
Newkirk, Cornelius 1716, 64, 65
Newkirk, Cornelius 1717, 26
Newkirk, Cornelius 1723, 25
Newkirk, Cornelius 1725, 26
Newkirk, Cornelius 1733, 31, 42, 43, 46, 57, 58, 60
Newkirk, Cornelius 1756, 41, 43, 47
Newkirk, Cornelius 1761, 48
Newkirk, Cornelius 1769, 209
Newkirk, Cornelius 1770, 64, 66, 67, 69, 70, 71, 72, 77
Newkirk, Cornelius 1771, 211
Newkirk, Cornelius 1772, 13
Newkirk, Cornelius 1775, 48, 60, 86
Newkirk, Cornelius 1780, 19
Newkirk, Cornelius 1782, 286
Newkirk, Cornelius 1794, 15
Newkirk, Cornelius 1817, 50, 55
Newkirk, Cornelius 1832, 18
Newkirk, Cornelius 1835, 226
Newkirk, Cornelius 1840, 72
Newkirk, Cornelius 1862, 287
Newkirk, Cornelius B. 1783, 14
Newkirk, Cornelius C. 1752, 211
Newkirk, Cornelius C., III 1813, 212, 213

Newkirk, Cornelius C., Jr. 1780, 212, 213
Newkirk, Cornelius C., Jr. 1849, 214
Newkirk, Cornelius H. 1834, 15
Newkirk, Cornelius M., 54
Newkirk, Cornelius M. 1792, 49, 50, 54, 55
Newkirk, Cornelius P. 1778, 210
Newkirk, Cornelius P. 1831, 73
Newkirk, Cornelius S. 1803, 295, 305, 308
Newkirk, Cornelius S. 1850, 311
Newkirk, Cornelius S. 1872, 310
Newkirk, Cornelius S., Jr. 1780, 19
Newkirk, Cortlyn Garton 1906, 52
Newkirk, Cynthia 1858, 239
Newkirk, Cynthia Dial 1826, 70
Newkirk, Cynthia H. 1829, 129
Newkirk, Cyrus 1799, 115
Newkirk, Cyrus 1800, 130
Newkirk, Cyrus 1810, 141
Newkirk, Cyrus 1821, 118, 137
Newkirk, Cyrus 1838, 132
Newkirk, Cyrus M. 1819, 187
Newkirk, Cyrus Napoleon 1840, 71
Newkirk, Daisy B. 1878, 133
Newkirk, Dan, 131
Newkirk, Dan Allen 1945, 133
Newkirk, Dan Christopher 1955, 186
Newkirk, Dana 1912, 79
Newkirk, Dana Shelton 1906, 16
Newkirk, Danette Lynn 1960, 182
Newkirk, Daniel 1772, 219
Newkirk, Daniel 1802, 274
Newkirk, Daniel Aaron 1981, 186

Newkirk, Daniel B. 1837, 289, 290
Newkirk, Daniel B. 1876, 147
Newkirk, Daniel B., Jr. 1906, 147
Newkirk, Daniel Bayless 1825, 143, 145
Newkirk, Daniel E. 1987, 291
Newkirk, Daniel Irving 1836, 274
Newkirk, Daniel L. 1859, 243
Newkirk, Daniel L. 1863, 289
Newkirk, Daniel Leighton 1887, 290
Newkirk, Daniel Thomas 1959, 21
Newkirk, Darius Histaspus 1826, 110
Newkirk, David 1771, 276
Newkirk, David 1815, 298
Newkirk, David 1829, 130
Newkirk, David 1836, 271
Newkirk, David 1840, 195
Newkirk, David 1843, 172
Newkirk, David 1851, 75
Newkirk, David 1872, 52
Newkirk, David Bonnett 1843, 110
Newkirk, David E. 1862, 50
Newkirk, David H. 1825, 120
Newkirk, David H. 1868, 167
Newkirk, David Harris 1835, 297
Newkirk, David Harvey 1868, 92
Newkirk, David Ivan 1938, 182
Newkirk, David Lindsay 1952, 261
Newkirk, David M. 1854, 304
Newkirk, David Rhodes 1870, 99
Newkirk, David Rhodes, II 1913, 99
Newkirk, David Richard 1958, 263

Newkirk, David Seaton 1811, 195
Newkirk, Dawn Diane 1964, 182
Newkirk, Deborah 1784, 217
Newkirk, Delcina Pearl 1883, 311
Newkirk, Delila C. 1825, 173, 174
Newkirk, Delilah 1798, 130
Newkirk, Delilah 1837, 18
Newkirk, Delilah Isabella 1849, 247
Newkirk, Delphina 1843, 117
Newkirk, Demaris Ellen 1868, 80
Newkirk, DeWitt 1799, 22
Newkirk, Diana 1765, 13
Newkirk, Diatha 1844, 83
Newkirk, Dicey Jane 1851, 196
Newkirk, Dina 1765, 13
Newkirk, Dina 1776, 210
Newkirk, Disje 1658, 2, 3
Newkirk, Donald, 34
Newkirk, Donald E. 1910, 168
Newkirk, Donald Ray 1919, 261
Newkirk, Donald William 1913, 180
Newkirk, Dora, 78
Newkirk, Dora 1903, 79
Newkirk, Dorcas 1836, 86
Newkirk, Dorothea 1745, 217
Newkirk, Dorothy 1745, 201
Newkirk, Dorothy 1916, 285
Newkirk, Dott Grace 1869, 306
Newkirk, Douglas, 79
Newkirk, Douglas Robert 1957, 261
Newkirk, Drake 1802, 194
Newkirk, Drusilla 1752, 107
Newkirk, Dudley Richman 1907, 53
Newkirk, Dustan 1827, 276

Newkirk, E. Hogan 1863, 84
Newkirk, E. Layton 1875, 306
Newkirk, Earl, 54, 78
Newkirk, Ebert Ross 1909, 241
Newkirk, Edgar 1824, 15
Newkirk, Edgar 1888, 72
Newkirk, Edgar A. 1866, 128
Newkirk, Edgar B. 1829, 213
Newkirk, Edith 1874, 171
Newkirk, Edith Blanche 1888, 119
Newkirk, Edmund 1807, 59
Newkirk, Edmund 1844, 279
Newkirk, Edna 1852, 275
Newkirk, Edna Eilene 1911, 241
Newkirk, Edward, 55, 218
Newkirk, Edward 1840, 40
Newkirk, Edward 1841, 45
Newkirk, Edward 1863, 231
Newkirk, Edwin Lewis 1852, 131, 132
Newkirk, Effie 1826, 232
Newkirk, Effie Dale 1879, 119
Newkirk, Eileen, 16
Newkirk, Elbert 1818, 61
Newkirk, Elbert L., 70
Newkirk, Eldridge 1836, 157
Newkirk, Eleanor 1777, 13
Newkirk, Eleanor 1828, 14
Newkirk, Elias 1722, 64, 66, 67, 81, 86, 169, 237
Newkirk, Elias 1766, 218
Newkirk, Elias 1809, 68, 72, 76
Newkirk, Elias, Jr. 1785, 67
Newkirk, Elijah 1807, 284
Newkirk, Elijah 1823, 187
Newkirk, Elijah 1849, 187
Newkirk, Elisabet 1793, 26
Newkirk, Elisie, 74
Newkirk, Eliza 1805, 40
Newkirk, Eliza 1812, 60
Newkirk, Eliza 1832, 226

Newkirk, Eliza 1833, 155
Newkirk, Eliza 1847, 305
Newkirk, Eliza J. 1834, 144
Newkirk, Eliza J. 1846, 146
Newkirk, Eliza Jane 1816, 272
Newkirk, Eliza Jane 1830, 174, 175
Newkirk, Eliza Jane 1835, 242, 244
Newkirk, Eliza Jane 1846, 226
Newkirk, Eliza Jane 1860, 224
Newkirk, Eliza Maria 1828, 110
Newkirk, Elizabeth, 170, 289
Newkirk, Elizabeth 1719, 205
Newkirk, Elizabeth 1723, 197
Newkirk, Elizabeth 1732, 210
Newkirk, Elizabeth 1734, 270
Newkirk, Elizabeth 1735, 31, 32, 49
Newkirk, Elizabeth 1746, 32
Newkirk, Elizabeth 1747, 217
Newkirk, Elizabeth 1754, 41
Newkirk, Elizabeth 1757, 107
Newkirk, Elizabeth 1776, 13, 33
Newkirk, Elizabeth 1777, 48, 272
Newkirk, Elizabeth 1779, 41
Newkirk, Elizabeth 1783, 13
Newkirk, Elizabeth 1787, 26, 210
Newkirk, Elizabeth 1789, 45
Newkirk, Elizabeth 1791, 294
Newkirk, Elizabeth 1798, 188
Newkirk, Elizabeth 1799, 194
Newkirk, Elizabeth 1803, 14
Newkirk, Elizabeth 1805, 68, 192
Newkirk, Elizabeth 1812, 117, 191, 279
Newkirk, Elizabeth 1816, 191
Newkirk, Elizabeth 1817, 187
Newkirk, Elizabeth 1822, 19

Newkirk, Elizabeth 1824, 187
Newkirk, Elizabeth 1825, 139
Newkirk, Elizabeth 1826, 287
Newkirk, Elizabeth 1827, 28,
    288
Newkirk, Elizabeth 1829, 213
Newkirk, Elizabeth 1830, 15
Newkirk, Elizabeth 1831, 77
Newkirk, Elizabeth 1834, 275
Newkirk, Elizabeth 1836, 188
Newkirk, Elizabeth 1842, 219
Newkirk, Elizabeth 1843, 54
Newkirk, Elizabeth 1846, 187
Newkirk, Elizabeth 1862, 77
Newkirk, Elizabeth 1888, 56
Newkirk, Elizabeth Ann 1846,
    83
Newkirk, Elizabeth Ann 1942,
    52
Newkirk, Elizabeth Hannah
    1837, 74
Newkirk, Elizabeth J. 1841, 130
Newkirk, Elizabeth N. 1859, 75
Newkirk, Elizabeth Thompson
    1857, 46
Newkirk, Ella, 99
Newkirk, Ella 1851, 286
Newkirk, Ella 1861, 231
Newkirk, Ella 1868, 122
Newkirk, Ella 1878, 171
Newkirk, Ellen, 240
Newkirk, Ellen 1838, 275
Newkirk, Ellen 1857, 73
Newkirk, Ellen 1862, 288
Newkirk, Ellen Josephine 1846,
    247
Newkirk, Ellen Locy 1852, 300
Newkirk, Ellery Lynn 1992, 127
Newkirk, Ellis 1841, 35
Newkirk, Ellis M. 1903, 165
Newkirk, Elmer Andrew 1864,
    309

Newkirk, Elmira 1840, 157
Newkirk, Elonson 1843, 173
Newkirk, Elsa Ora 1873, 122
Newkirk, Elsie 1791, 279
Newkirk, Elsie 1803, 274
Newkirk, Elsie 1837, 172
Newkirk, Elsie Ann 1839, 245
Newkirk, Elsie I. 1846, 178
Newkirk, Elsie Maria 1813, 275
Newkirk, Elva M. 1860, 306
Newkirk, Elverta, 51
Newkirk, Elvira V. 1840, 112
Newkirk, Elvira Virginia, 164
Newkirk, Elwin Earl 1923, 262
Newkirk, Elwood, 79
Newkirk, Emaline 1839, 117
Newkirk, Emeline 1844, 195
Newkirk, Emeline S. 1844, 195
Newkirk, Emily 1800, 60
Newkirk, Emily 1813, 142
Newkirk, Emily 1842, 290
Newkirk, Emily A. 1827, 139
Newkirk, Emily Ann 1881, 310
Newkirk, Emily J. 1833, 120
Newkirk, Emily Josephine 1843,
    116
Newkirk, Emma 1872, 74
Newkirk, Emma Catherine 1843,
    214, 215
Newkirk, Emma Elizabeth Ellen
    1852, 142
Newkirk, Emma Jane 1853, 120
Newkirk, Emma M. 1869, 290
Newkirk, Emma Matilda 1849,
    226
Newkirk, Emma Pearl 1881, 147
Newkirk, Emma R. 1863, 36
Newkirk, Emma Rebecca 1857,
    227
Newkirk, Emmett 1907, 241
Newkirk, Engeltje 1716, 24
Newkirk, Enoch 1799, 58

Newkirk, Enoch 1847, 187
Newkirk, Enoch Boone 1806, 193
Newkirk, Enoch Boone 1809, 190
Newkirk, Enoch Boone 1813, 186
Newkirk, Enoch Boone 1854, 187
Newkirk, Enoch Dexter 1838, 187
Newkirk, Enoch, Jr. 1853, 59
Newkirk, Enos Edward 1890, 85
Newkirk, Ermin 1843, 69
Newkirk, Ernest, 79
Newkirk, Esila 1868, 122
Newkirk, Essie May 1903, 81
Newkirk, Esta 1868, 122
Newkirk, Estella Eldora 1876, 250, 252, 256
Newkirk, Esther, 170
Newkirk, Esther Virginia 1910, 102
Newkirk, Ethel 1884, 73
Newkirk, Ethel Dee 1888, 179
Newkirk, Ethel Elverne 1889, 261
Newkirk, Eugene T. 1858, 225
Newkirk, Eugene Wade 1859, 120
Newkirk, Eva 1875, 168
Newkirk, Eva 1888, 35
Newkirk, Eva Allen, 207
Newkirk, Eveline 1826, 274
Newkirk, Eveline 1855, 191
Newkirk, Evelyn, 112, 134
Newkirk, Evelyn Caledonia 1841, 105
Newkirk, Everett John 1892, 179, 183
Newkirk, Fanny 1819, 285
Newkirk, Fanny Jane 1820, 288

Newkirk, Fanny L. 1879, 147
Newkirk, Finey 1836, 82
Newkirk, Firman H. 1857, 59
Newkirk, Florence Mildred 1867, 38
Newkirk, Flossie 1887, 152
Newkirk, Flossie M. 1904, 144
Newkirk, Floyd 1894, 38
Newkirk, Francenia Caroline 1827, 93
Newkirk, Frances, 72, 289
Newkirk, Frances 1842, 193
Newkirk, Frances 1885, 54
Newkirk, Frances Alma 1915, 236, 260
Newkirk, Frances M. 1831, 242
Newkirk, Frances M. 1852, 243
Newkirk, Frances Virginia 1917, 168
Newkirk, Francis 1813, 286
Newkirk, Francis 1834, 195
Newkirk, Francis M. 1831, 244
Newkirk, Francis M. 1834, 238
Newkirk, Francis M. 1835, 77
Newkirk, Francis Marion 1850, 178
Newkirk, Francis Marion 1858, 132
Newkirk, Francis Van DeBogart 1799, 207
Newkirk, Francis W., 103
Newkirk, Frank, 21
Newkirk, Frank 1859, 73
Newkirk, Frank 1871, 20
Newkirk, Frank 1908, 308
Newkirk, Frank A. 1914, 144
Newkirk, Frank E. 1861, 128
Newkirk, Frank Ellis 1867, 297
Newkirk, Frank Seybolt 1876, 285
Newkirk, Franklin, 79
Newkirk, Franklin 1830, 91

Newkirk, Franklin P. 1853, 227
Newkirk, Fred T., 112
Newkirk, Frederick H. 1851, 232
Newkirk, Frederick Herbert
1874, 132
Newkirk, Frederick S. 1842, 285
Newkirk, Frederick Shafer 1820,
275
Newkirk, Fredia, 78
Newkirk, Furman 1805, 60
Newkirk, Furman 1813, 60
Newkirk, Fytie 1732, 222
Newkirk, Gap A. 1828, 18
Newkirk, Garret 1726, 29, 41,
43, 45
Newkirk, Garret 1758, 47
Newkirk, Garret 1783, 41
Newkirk, Garret 1815, 231
Newkirk, Garret 1828, 226
Newkirk, Garret 1834, 20
Newkirk, Garret 1836, 230
Newkirk, Garret 1898, 20
Newkirk, Garret C. 1739, 12,
211
Newkirk, Garret C. 1760, 206
Newkirk, Garret Cornelius 1826,
207
Newkirk, Garret G. 1812, 224
Newkirk, Garret Harsin 1787, 22
Newkirk, Garret J. 1780, 230
Newkirk, Garret J. 1821, 232
Newkirk, Garret L. 1760, 206
Newkirk, Garret S. 1843, 227
Newkirk, Garrett M. 1741, 18
Newkirk, Garth 1981, 182
Newkirk, Geeretje 1673, 221
Newkirk, Geertje 1756, 280
Newkirk, Geertjen 1758, 22
Newkirk, Geertrude Lansing
1809, 23
Newkirk, Geertruyt 1671, 220

Newkirk, George 1780, 108, 109,
161, 162, 163
Newkirk, George 1783, 224
Newkirk, George 1809, 230
Newkirk, George 1826, 224, 225
Newkirk, George 1831, 273
Newkirk, George 1839, 69, 163,
164, 165, 166
Newkirk, George 1842, 141
Newkirk, George 1844, 224
Newkirk, George 1847, 23
Newkirk, George 1848, 114
Newkirk, George 1851, 224
Newkirk, George 1873, 168
Newkirk, George 1875, 165
Newkirk, George 1902, 244
Newkirk, George A. 1852, 288
Newkirk, George Albert 1864, 76
Newkirk, George Bryan 1839, 94
Newkirk, George Clyde 1877,
119
Newkirk, George D. 1876, 51
Newkirk, George Enos 1866, 84
Newkirk, George Francis 1918,
129
Newkirk, George Grant 1862,
120
Newkirk, George H. 1896, 167
Newkirk, George Harold 1905,
53
Newkirk, George Heberton 1825,
44
Newkirk, George J. 1871, 306
Newkirk, George Jay 1960, 76
Newkirk, George M. 1837, 61
Newkirk, George M. 1900, 144
Newkirk, George Marshall 1849,
144
Newkirk, George N. 1841, 283
Newkirk, George O. 1867, 290
Newkirk, George R. 1880, 110

Newkirk, Hadley Douglas J. 1845, 310
Newkirk, Hamilton R. 1848, 305
Newkirk, Hamlet 1839, 274
Newkirk, Handish 1838, 193
Newkirk, Hannah, 52
Newkirk, Hannah 1780, 272
Newkirk, Hannah 1787, 135
Newkirk, Hannah 1789, 43, 47
Newkirk, Hannah 1798, 42
Newkirk, Hannah 1811, 209
Newkirk, Hannah 1812, 277
Newkirk, Hannah 1819, 285
Newkirk, Hannah 1828, 274
Newkirk, Hannah 1836, 131
Newkirk, Hannah 1844, 298
Newkirk, Hannah 1848, 54
Newkirk, Hannah A. 1846, 56
Newkirk, Hannah Catherine 1835, 275
Newkirk, Hannah F. 1802, 282
Newkirk, Hannah Graham 1796, 271
Newkirk, Hannah Graham 1798, 271
Newkirk, Hannah N., 283
Newkirk, Hannah N. 1861, 286
Newkirk, Harriet, 289
Newkirk, Harriet 1843, 114
Newkirk, Harriet Adelaida 1835, 94
Newkirk, Harriet Eliza 1841, 243
Newkirk, Harriet Emeline 1834, 116
Newkirk, Harriet Jane 1841, 116
Newkirk, Harriet L. 1820, 173, 174
Newkirk, Harriet O'Ella 1850, 115
Newkirk, Harriet Rachel Gufford 1872, 92
Newkirk, Harriet W. 1841, 55

Newkirk, Harriett 1847, 84
Newkirk, Harriett 1853, 54
Newkirk, Harris D. 1878, Dr., 16
Newkirk, Harrison 1831, 72
Newkirk, Harrison R. 1814, 196
Newkirk, Harry 1888, 77
Newkirk, Harry 1900, 244
Newkirk, Harry B. 1873, 306
Newkirk, Harry E., 112
Newkirk, Harvey 1845, 69
Newkirk, Harvey N. 1827, 129
Newkirk, Hattie 1915, 244
Newkirk, Hattie Carey 1863, 91
Newkirk, Hayden Elmo 1918, 241
Newkirk, Haywood Francis 1865, 96
Newkirk, Hazel 1907, 241
Newkirk, Helen, 51, 102
Newkirk, Helen C. 1832, 93
Newkirk, Helen Josephine 1870, 249
Newkirk, Helen Leyda 1818, 121
Newkirk, Helen M. 1908, 147
Newkirk, Helen Mae 1866, 306
Newkirk, Helen Ruth 1925, 80
Newkirk, Hendrick 1721, 269, 280, 283, 293
Newkirk, Hendrick 1741, 224
Newkirk, Hendrick 1771, 223
Newkirk, Hendrick 1777, 284
Newkirk, Hendrick Hermance 1802, 23
Newkirk, Hendricka 1746, 211
Newkirk, Hendricus, 197
Newkirk, Hendricus 1722, 26
Newkirk, Hendricus 1767, 28
Newkirk, Hendrikje 1692, 8, 198
Newkirk, Henricus 1744, 217
Newkirk, Henriette Louise 1922, 129
Newkirk, Henry, 63, 280

Newkirk, Henry 1721, 64, 66, 113, 233
Newkirk, Henry 1740, 82, 135, 233, 234, 237, 242
Newkirk, Henry 1750, 86
Newkirk, Henry 1768, 107, 155, 156, 157, 233, 234
Newkirk, Henry 1777, 284
Newkirk, Henry 1781, 67, 81, 109, 237
Newkirk, Henry 1784, 170
Newkirk, Henry 1789, 114, 118, 136, 234
Newkirk, Henry 1795, 170, 173, 175
Newkirk, Henry 1799, 225
Newkirk, Henry 1811, 83
Newkirk, Henry 1812, 131, 132
Newkirk, Henry 1823, 273
Newkirk, Henry 1828, 238
Newkirk, Henry 1832, 116
Newkirk, Henry 1833, 82, 157
Newkirk, Henry 1836, 155
Newkirk, Henry 1839, 213
Newkirk, Henry 1854, 103
Newkirk, Henry 1889, 38
Newkirk, Henry Allen 1869, 34
Newkirk, Henry B. 1816, 285
Newkirk, Henry B. 1845, 232
Newkirk, Henry C. 1767, 282, 293
Newkirk, Henry Clay 1840, 110
Newkirk, Henry Clay 1845, 131
Newkirk, Henry Conkright 1767, 282, 293, 296, 298, 304, 305, 310
Newkirk, Henry Cornelius 1841, 227
Newkirk, Henry Franklin 1859, 91
Newkirk, Henry G. 1808, 224
Newkirk, Henry H. 1823, 226

Newkirk, Henry Haywood 1834, 103
Newkirk, Henry Herbert 1893, 79
Newkirk, Henry John Thomas 1804, 89, 94
Newkirk, Henry L. Weller 1834, 274
Newkirk, Henry M. 1848, 119
Newkirk, Henry M. 1895, 119
Newkirk, Henry R. 1865, 55
Newkirk, Henry V. 1868, 287
Newkirk, Henry Van Keuren 1825, 287
Newkirk, Henry Warren 1870, 74
Newkirk, Henry, Jr. 1740, 66
Newkirk, Henry, Jr. 1781, 82, 235, 237
Newkirk, Hershell, 78
Newkirk, Hester Ann 1840, 72
Newkirk, Hetty 1840, 34
Newkirk, Hiram 1810, 82
Newkirk, Hiram 1825, 238
Newkirk, Hiram B. 1850, 238
Newkirk, Hiram Crabtree 1837, 83, 84
Newkirk, Hogan 1838, 83
Newkirk, Holliday S. 1847, 140
Newkirk, Horace Leavenworth 1911, 16
Newkirk, Horace N. 1839, 283
Newkirk, Horatio Wood 1863, 46
Newkirk, Howard 1836, 275
Newkirk, Howard Lyle 1923, 261
Newkirk, Howard Raymond 1899, 179, 185
Newkirk, Hugh 1813, 57
Newkirk, Hugh 1839, 195
Newkirk, Hugh R. 1840, 83
Newkirk, Ida 1891, 38
Newkirk, Ida A. 1876, 77
Newkirk, Ida Catherine 1826, 273

Newkirk, Ida May 1864, 157
Newkirk, Ida W. 1853, 119
Newkirk, Ileene, 78
Newkirk, Indiana Laura 1850, 305
Newkirk, Inis 1857, 235
Newkirk, Irene May 1900, 133
Newkirk, Irving John Richard 1918, 103
Newkirk, Isaac 1753, 32, 33
Newkirk, Isaac 1754, 114
Newkirk, Isaac 1754 son/Abraham, 107, 113, 114, 116, 118, 121, 128
Newkirk, Isaac 1754 son/Cornelius, 14
Newkirk, Isaac 1762, 170, 189
Newkirk, Isaac 1785, 35
Newkirk, Isaac 1795, 108, 109, 111, 161, 164
Newkirk, Isaac 1801, 40
Newkirk, Isaac 1821, 119
Newkirk, Isaac 1822, 191
Newkirk, Isaac 1825, 35
Newkirk, Isaac 1828, 15, 115
Newkirk, Isaac 1832, 34
Newkirk, Isaac 1835, 130
Newkirk, Isaac B. 1814, 172
Newkirk, Isaac B. 1863, 179
Newkirk, Isaac James 1826, 110
Newkirk, Isaac N. 1833, 70
Newkirk, Isaac N. 1867, 157
Newkirk, Isaac N., Jr. 1874, 70
Newkirk, Isaac Newton 1824, 128
Newkirk, Isaac R. 1833, 34
Newkirk, Isaac Roberts 1866, 46
Newkirk, Isabella, 294
Newkirk, Isabella 1765, 282
Newkirk, Isaiah 1832, 34
Newkirk, Isaiah McCallen 1829, 173, 174

Newkirk, Isaiah W. 1833, 50, 52
Newkirk, Israel A. 1847, 298
Newkirk, Israel F. 1815, 60
Newkirk, Iva, 52
Newkirk, Ivan, 57
Newkirk, Ivan Earl 1890, 179, 182
Newkirk, J. Herbert, 79
Newkirk, Jack Terrell 1923, 309
Newkirk, Jackson 1871, 306
Newkirk, Jacob, 30
Newkirk, Jacob 1723, 206
Newkirk, Jacob 1732, 206
Newkirk, Jacob 1737, 267, 270, 276
Newkirk, Jacob 1743, 228, 229
Newkirk, Jacob 1744, 8, 13
Newkirk, Jacob 1763, 32, 39
Newkirk, Jacob 1778, 230
Newkirk, Jacob 1780, 286
Newkirk, Jacob 1781, 48
Newkirk, Jacob 1788, 35
Newkirk, Jacob 1807, 230
Newkirk, Jacob 1815, 231
Newkirk, Jacob 1829, 35
Newkirk, Jacob 1836, 172
Newkirk, Jacob 1841, 209
Newkirk, Jacob 1850, 273
Newkirk, Jacob B. 1833, 230
Newkirk, Jacob Bodine 1820, 273
Newkirk, Jacob Elwood 1862, 309
Newkirk, Jacob Elwood, Jr. 1895, 309
Newkirk, Jacob Felix 1807, 89, 94
Newkirk, Jacob Matthuesen 1682, 221
Newkirk, Jacob Rutsen 1750, 217
Newkirk, Jacob Verner 1803, 218
Newkirk, Jacobus 1755, 26

Newkirk, Jacobus 1758, 18
Newkirk, Jacobus H. 1804, 212
Newkirk, Jacomyntje 1678, 221
Newkirk, Jacomyntje 1694, 10, 11
Newkirk, Jacomyntje 1710, 221
Newkirk, Jacomyntje 1722, 25
Newkirk, Jacomyntje 1727, 25
Newkirk, Jacomyntje 1729, 27
Newkirk, Jacomyntje 1731, 30
Newkirk, Jacomyntje 1755, 16
Newkirk, Jacomyntje 1758, 16
Newkirk, James 1760, 281
Newkirk, James 1771, 282
Newkirk, James 1786, 283, 287, 288, 289
Newkirk, James 1788, 108, 109, 161, 162
Newkirk, James 1803, 82
Newkirk, James 1816, 298
Newkirk, James 1831, 289
Newkirk, James 1835, 245
Newkirk, James 1841, 194
Newkirk, James 1842, 23
Newkirk, James 1849, 172
Newkirk, James 1865, 73
Newkirk, James 1868, 237
Newkirk, James A. 1867, 244
Newkirk, James A. 1874, 110
Newkirk, James A. 1880, 311
Newkirk, James Alan 1953, 262
Newkirk, James Ari 1849, 226
Newkirk, James B. 1829, 77
Newkirk, James Benjamin 1829, 77
Newkirk, James Buchanan 1856, 91
Newkirk, James C. 1850, 219
Newkirk, James C. 1867, 307
Newkirk, James Clifford 1869, 163, 165
Newkirk, James D., 129

Newkirk, James Demarest 1846, 228
Newkirk, James E., 72
Newkirk, James E. 1800, 60
Newkirk, James E. 1921, 66
Newkirk, James Edward 1841, 74
Newkirk, James Edward 1852, 178
Newkirk, James Ellis 1891, 167
Newkirk, James F. 1842, 171
Newkirk, James Garland 1892, 147
Newkirk, James H. 1829, 306
Newkirk, James H. 1865, 307
Newkirk, James H. 1866, 309
Newkirk, James H. 1869, 83
Newkirk, James Harvey 1826, 297
Newkirk, James Henry 1812, 69
Newkirk, James Henry 1871, 81
Newkirk, James L. 1840, 82
Newkirk, James L. 1842, 83
Newkirk, James L. J. 1852, 147
Newkirk, James Leonard 1809, 171, 177
Newkirk, James Leonard 1822, 90
Newkirk, James M. 1819, 225
Newkirk, James M. 1825, 189
Newkirk, James Madison 1815, 242, 245, 248, 259, 298
Newkirk, James Mason 1806, 162, 163, 165, 166
Newkirk, James Mason, Jr. 1837, 163, 164, 166
Newkirk, James Morrison 1836, 76
Newkirk, James N. 1849, 243
Newkirk, James Oran 1880, 310
Newkirk, James Polk 1845, 61

Newkirk, James Rhodes 1834, 100

Newkirk, James Richard 1832, 100

Newkirk, James Richard d/1991, 103

Newkirk, James Richard, Jr. 1870, 102

Newkirk, James Riley 1873, 190

Newkirk, James Ross 1832, 139

Newkirk, James S. 1852, 227

Newkirk, James Samson 1830, 115

Newkirk, James Samuel 1845, 175

Newkirk, James Smith 1818, 273

Newkirk, James Sylvester 1901, 81

Newkirk, James Thomas 1853, 243

Newkirk, James Vaughn 1963, 76

Newkirk, James Warren 1883, 285

Newkirk, James Wesley 1886, 84

Newkirk, James William 1857, 246, 248

Newkirk, James Wills 1850, 300

Newkirk, Jan 1666, 3

Newkirk, Jan 1685, 9, 23

Newkirk, Jan 1690, 197, 201, 217, 222, 269

Newkirk, Jan 1755, 218

Newkirk, Jan Gerretse 1666, 3

Newkirk, Jane, 281

Newkirk, Jane 1795, 115

Newkirk, Jane 1805, 224

Newkirk, Jane 1814, 69

Newkirk, Jane 1828, 207

Newkirk, Jane 1834, 213

Newkirk, Jane 1841, 191, 288

Newkirk, Jane 1842, 58

Newkirk, Jane 1963, 184

Newkirk, Jane Ann 1802, 210

Newkirk, Jane B. 1816, 219

Newkirk, Jane E. 1833, 48

Newkirk, Jane E. 1874, 287

Newkirk, Jane Elizabeth 1838, 230

Newkirk, Jane Juliane 1801, 23

Newkirk, Jane Maria 1816, 224

Newkirk, Jane R. 1843, 191

Newkirk, Janice Eileen 1938, 54

Newkirk, Janis 1948, 76

Newkirk, Jannetje 1691, 222

Newkirk, Jannetje 1714, 24

Newkirk, Jannetje 1737, 223

Newkirk, Jannetje 1740, 229

Newkirk, Jannetje 1777, 229

Newkirk, Jannetjen 1712, 11

Newkirk, Jannetjen 1713, 25

Newkirk, Jannetjen 1728, 29

Newkirk, Jannetjen 1734, 210

Newkirk, Jannetjen 1746, 13

Newkirk, Jannetjen 1750, 13

Newkirk, Jannetjen 1775, 210

Newkirk, Jannette 1737, 223

Newkirk, Jannette 1762, 22

Newkirk, Jannetye 1687, 222

Newkirk, Jared H. 1846, 113

Newkirk, Jean 1714, 64, 65

Newkirk, Jefferson 1829, 194

Newkirk, Jeffrey Burt 1959, 17

Newkirk, Jefsu H. 1828, 192

Newkirk, Jemima 1726/30, 67

Newkirk, Jemima 1730, 64, 86, 169

Newkirk, Jemima 1759, 87

Newkirk, Jemima 1797, 194

Newkirk, Jemima 1801, 170, 175

Newkirk, Jemima 1814, 193

Newkirk, Jemima 1833, 82

Newkirk, Jenneke 1746, 18

Newkirk, Jennie, 99

Newkirk, Jennie N. 1862, 306
Newkirk, Jennie Rena 1878, 307
Newkirk, Jennifer Elizabeth
1976, 186
Newkirk, Jeptha 1807, 112
Newkirk, Jeptha 1836, 171
Newkirk, Jeptha 1842, 113
Newkirk, Jeptha 1871, 168
Newkirk, Jeptha M. 1868, 164
Newkirk, Jeremiah Seavey 1871,
102
Newkirk, Jerusha Elva 1868, 309
Newkirk, Jesse 1878, 149
Newkirk, Jesse Barnett 1862, 78
Newkirk, Jesse D. 1885, 195
Newkirk, Jessie A. 1861, 36
Newkirk, Jessie A. 1880, 297
Newkirk, Jessie Ruth 1902, 81
Newkirk, Joast 1761, 47, 48
Newkirk, Joel 1869, 77
Newkirk, Joel Glen 1924, 80
Newkirk, Joel H., 16
Newkirk, Joel Rice 1847, 77, 80
Newkirk, Joel Rice, Jr. 1873, 81
Newkirk, Joey 1910, 99
Newkirk, Johann Heinrick 1674,
266, 268
Newkirk, Johann Hendrick 1702,
266
Newkirk, Johannes 1699, 266,
267, 268, 269, 271, 276, 277,
280
Newkirk, Johannes 1724, 205,
206
Newkirk, Johannes 1746, 229
Newkirk, Johannes 1751, 21
Newkirk, Johannes 1760, 27
Newkirk, Johannes 1764, 218
Newkirk, Johannes 1767, 209
Newkirk, Johannes 1774, 28
Newkirk, Johannes 1777, 8, 13
Newkirk, Johannes 1797, 207

Newkirk, Johannes, Jr. 1740,
270, 277
Newkirk, Johannia 1781, 228
Newkirk, Johannis 1690, 197
Newkirk, Johannis 1756, 271
Newkirk, Johannis 1786, 231
Newkirk, John, 48, 74, 112, 162,
294
Newkirk, John 1702, 266
Newkirk, John 1753, 280, 283,
293
Newkirk, John 1759, 42
Newkirk, John 1767, 206
Newkirk, John 1772, 209
Newkirk, John 1782, 42, 67
Newkirk, John 1783, 109
Newkirk, John 1784, 235
Newkirk, John 1786, 114, 116,
121
Newkirk, John 1789, 40
Newkirk, John 1799, 139
Newkirk, John 1800, 28
Newkirk, John 1802, 59
Newkirk, John 1803, 189
Newkirk, John 1804, 27
Newkirk, John 1808, 68, 71
Newkirk, John 1809, 284
Newkirk, John 1810, 228, 278
Newkirk, John 1811, 242
Newkirk, John 1828, 155
Newkirk, John 1830, 226
Newkirk, John 1832, 59, 112
Newkirk, John 1833, 131
Newkirk, John 1839, 288
Newkirk, John 1842, 218
Newkirk, John 1843, 60
Newkirk, John 1845, 54
Newkirk, John 1846, 18
Newkirk, John 1850, 207
Newkirk, John 1856, 237
Newkirk, John 1859, 72
Newkirk, John 1860, 78

Newkirk, John 1861, 228
Newkirk, John 1869, 96
Newkirk, John 1882, 77
Newkirk, John A. 1849, 288
Newkirk, John Abram 1830, 94
Newkirk, John Adam 1763, 243, 271, 272
Newkirk, John Adam, Jr. 1799, 274
Newkirk, John Alfred 1857, 228
Newkirk, John B. 1782, 14
Newkirk, John B. 1863, 244
Newkirk, John Bacon 1859, 46
Newkirk, John Barnett 1852, 69
Newkirk, John Benjamin 1927, 76
Newkirk, John Brooks 1843, 61
Newkirk, John Burt 1920, 17
Newkirk, John C. 1817, 132
Newkirk, John C. 1843, 243
Newkirk, John C. 1844, 187
Newkirk, John Carty 1922, 102
Newkirk, John David 1898, 168
Newkirk, John E. 1857, 36
Newkirk, John Elliott 1835, 306
Newkirk, John Forest 1794, 155
Newkirk, John Francis 1850, 142
Newkirk, John Franklin 1858, 308
Newkirk, John Gibbon 1855, 119
Newkirk, John Gray 1847, 15, 16
Newkirk, John H. 1807, 188
Newkirk, John H. 1810, 34, 36, 37, 38
Newkirk, John H. 1840, 245
Newkirk, John Henry 1841, 230
Newkirk, John Henry 1860, 224
Newkirk, John I. 1797, 15
Newkirk, John Irvin 1897, 70
Newkirk, John J. 1786, 231
Newkirk, John Jordan 1961, 17
Newkirk, John K. 1823, 287

Newkirk, John L. 1812, 83, 84
Newkirk, John L. 1839, 213
Newkirk, John Linn 1883, 119
Newkirk, John Lyman 1857, 122
Newkirk, John M. 1781, 228, 231
Newkirk, John M. 1880, 122, 126
Newkirk, John Morrison 1836, 74
Newkirk, John Newton 1849, 243
Newkirk, John O. 1833, 297
Newkirk, John P. 1843, 61
Newkirk, John Person 1780, 217
Newkirk, John Q. 1838, 188
Newkirk, John R. 1828, 114
Newkirk, John Rainey 1856, 117
Newkirk, John S. 1805, 284
Newkirk, John S. 1838, 82
Newkirk, John Smith m/1861, 82
Newkirk, John Ten Eyck 1866, 20
Newkirk, John Thompson 1797, 282
Newkirk, John V. B. 1848, 224
Newkirk, John W., 129
Newkirk, John W. 1813, 113
Newkirk, John W. 1840, 140, 190
Newkirk, John W. 1848, 70
Newkirk, John W. 1857, 286
Newkirk, John W. 1863, 307
Newkirk, John W. 1891, 71
Newkirk, John W., Jr. 1919, 71
Newkirk, John Washington 1826, 121, 123
Newkirk, John Wesley 1812, 83
Newkirk, John Wesley 1859, 84
Newkirk, John William, 142
Newkirk, John William 1842, 231
Newkirk, John, Jr. 1762, 206

Newkirk, Jonas 1836, 71
Newkirk, Jonathan Benton 1889, 80
Newkirk, Jonathan D. 1843, 77, 79
Newkirk, Jonathan H. 1843, 140
Newkirk, Joseph, 50, 54
Newkirk, Joseph 1779, 277
Newkirk, Joseph 1783, 49
Newkirk, Joseph 1785, 235
Newkirk, Joseph 1791, 89, 90, 92, 108, 109, 161, 162
Newkirk, Joseph 1799, 34
Newkirk, Joseph 1822, 110
Newkirk, Joseph 1823, 69
Newkirk, Joseph 1826, 238
Newkirk, Joseph 1831, 304
Newkirk, Joseph 1837, 34
Newkirk, Joseph 1838, 110
Newkirk, Joseph 1874, 85
Newkirk, Joseph 1913, 242
Newkirk, Joseph Alexander 1826, 115
Newkirk, Joseph Barker 1833, 238, 239
Newkirk, Joseph Franklin 1871, 240
Newkirk, Joseph H. 1813, 242
Newkirk, Joseph H. 1839, 61
Newkirk, Joseph H. 1876, 110
Newkirk, Joseph Harrison 1853, 196
Newkirk, Joseph Hezekiah 1853, 91
Newkirk, Joseph Lester 1955, 21
Newkirk, Joseph Seavey 1918, 103
Newkirk, Joseph Tyler 1993, 133
Newkirk, Joseph, Jr. 1825/33, 236
Newkirk, Josephine 1844, 105
Newkirk, Josephine 1859, 239

Newkirk, Josephine 1890, 149
Newkirk, Josephine Cecelia 1880, 103
Newkirk, Josephine E. 1840, 191
Newkirk, Josephine V. 1838, 40
Newkirk, Josiah 1847, 173
Newkirk, Joyce A. 1947, 52
Newkirk, Judeke 1771, 8, 13
Newkirk, Judice 1787, 8, 13
Newkirk, Julia 1791, 272
Newkirk, Julia 1834, 297
Newkirk, Julia A. 1845, 188
Newkirk, Julia Ann 1827, 304
Newkirk, Julia Ann 1852, 311
Newkirk, Julia B. 1873, 309
Newkirk, Julia Fulton 1915, 102
Newkirk, Julia Isabel 1876, 74
Newkirk, Julia W. 1826, 306
Newkirk, Julietta 1822, 297
Newkirk, Julietta E. 1878, 311
Newkirk, Karl Alfred 1963, 127
Newkirk, Karl Edward 1941, 127
Newkirk, Karl Ford 1906, 126
Newkirk, Katherine Ann 1950, 261
Newkirk, Katherine Brosard 1858, 91
Newkirk, Katherine Fulton 1860, 100
Newkirk, Kathie, 70
Newkirk, Kathleen Irene 1922, 180
Newkirk, Katie, 291
Newkirk, Katie Ethel 1889, 75
Newkirk, Katurah, 284
Newkirk, Katurah 1789, 294, 295
Newkirk, Katurah 1803, 284
Newkirk, Kenneth Charles 1913, 144
Newkirk, Kenneth Franklin 1915, 54

Newkirk, Kenneth Franklin 1940, 54
Newkirk, Kenneth Loyd 1916, 180
Newkirk, Kenneth Loyd, Jr. 1943, 180
Newkirk, Kezia Catharine 1841, 245
Newkirk, Keziah 1801, 140
Newkirk, Keziah 1802, 155, 156
Newkirk, Keziah 1813, 193
Newkirk, Keziah 1845, 158, 159
Newkirk, Kristine 1958, 184
Newkirk, L. 1839, 70
Newkirk, Lambert 1815, 60
Newkirk, Lambert, Jr. 1860, 61
Newkirk, Larry W., 142
Newkirk, Laura, 103
Newkirk, Laura 1834, 279
Newkirk, Laura 1860, 54
Newkirk, Laura 1871, 128
Newkirk, Laura 1880, 72
Newkirk, Laura 1885, 54
Newkirk, Laura Christine 1961, 186
Newkirk, Laura E. 1839, 105
Newkirk, Laura E. 1855, 227
Newkirk, Laura E. 1857, 157
Newkirk, Laura Elizabeth 1848, 113
Newkirk, Laura F. 1916, 165
Newkirk, Laura L. 1862, 304
Newkirk, Laura Marie 1966, 127
Newkirk, Laura Wilhelmina 1925, 291
Newkirk, Lauren Ann 1985, 291
Newkirk, Laverne 1901, 147
Newkirk, Lawrence 1870, 39
Newkirk, Lea 1702, 201, 217
Newkirk, Lea 1743, 217
Newkirk, Lea 1791, 26
Newkirk, Leah 1744, 12, 211

Newkirk, Leah 1784, 287
Newkirk, Leah 1800, 27
Newkirk, Leah 1812, 284
Newkirk, Leah 1831, 139
Newkirk, Lee 1879, 39
Newkirk, Leentje 1802, 272
Newkirk, Lela 1902, 240
Newkirk, Lella Belle 1900, 262
Newkirk, Lemuel 1831, 172
Newkirk, Lemuel 1838, 171
Newkirk, Lemuel C. 1848, 190
Newkirk, Lemuel J. 1823, 288
Newkirk, Lemuel J., Jr. 1865, 288
Newkirk, Lena 1767, 229
Newkirk, Lena 1775, 230
Newkirk, Leo G. 1892, 134
Newkirk, Leon Lewis 1876, 307
Newkirk, Leona Theresa 1905, 102
Newkirk, Leonard Charles 1806, 288, 289
Newkirk, Leonard Earl 1940, 182
Newkirk, Leslie Victor 1857, 119
Newkirk, Lester Forest 1907, 179
Newkirk, Lester Hayes 1909, 53
Newkirk, Lester Smoot 1884, 74
Newkirk, Letha 1902, 240
Newkirk, Leulla W. 1873, 289
Newkirk, Levi 1800, 27
Newkirk, Lewis 1808, 189, 190
Newkirk, Lewis 1843, 35, 38
Newkirk, Lewis 1848, 232
Newkirk, Lewis 1887, 38
Newkirk, Lewis A. 1893, 309
Newkirk, Lewis Alonzo 1837, 298
Newkirk, Lewis H. 1859, 297
Newkirk, Lewis M. 1846, 232
Newkirk, Lille 1883, 54
Newkirk, Lillian 1925, 183

Newkirk, Lillian L. 1869, 157
Newkirk, Lillie Belle 1875, 306
Newkirk, Lillie L. 1878, 36
Newkirk, Lillie M. 1883, 147
Newkirk, Lilly H. 1895, 71
Newkirk, Linda 1955, 76
Newkirk, Linda Joan 1949, 262
Newkirk, Linea 1804, 192
Newkirk, Lisa Christine 1969, 127
Newkirk, Lisa Susan 1963, 263
Newkirk, Lisly 1837, 18
Newkirk, Lizzie Alice 1864, 306
Newkirk, Lois Caroyl 1936, 52
Newkirk, Loraine, 180
Newkirk, Loren 1956, 133
Newkirk, Loren Fassett 1930, 133
Newkirk, Loren Grant 1872, 132
Newkirk, Loren Miller 1898, 132
Newkirk, Lorenzo 1841, 49, 51, 52
Newkirk, Lorenzo 1904, 52
Newkirk, Lorenzo J. 1835, 238
Newkirk, Lorinda, 136
Newkirk, Lorraine 1910, 241
Newkirk, Lottie Carrie 1868, 297
Newkirk, Louella W. 1873, 290
Newkirk, Louisa 1773, 170
Newkirk, Louisa 1834, 69
Newkirk, Louisa 1835, 34
Newkirk, Louisa 1844, 195
Newkirk, Louisa Adaline 1854, 142
Newkirk, Louisa C. 1853, 192
Newkirk, Louisa Hall 1809, 188
Newkirk, Louisa I. 1844, 113
Newkirk, Louisa J. 1841, 83
Newkirk, Louisarba 1810, 156
Newkirk, Louise 1826, 35
Newkirk, Louise N. 1885, 273
Newkirk, Louisiana 1803, 116

Newkirk, Louisiana 1812, 156
Newkirk, Lucille, 134
Newkirk, Lucinda 1835, 178
Newkirk, Lucinda 1844, 172
Newkirk, Lucinda Frances 1848, 69
Newkirk, Lucy 1807, 83
Newkirk, Lucy 1872, 80
Newkirk, Lucy H. 1839, 190
Newkirk, Lulu 1889, 122
Newkirk, Lulu May 1883, 133
Newkirk, Luzerba 1806, 116
Newkirk, Lydia 1783, 235
Newkirk, Lydia 1801, 59
Newkirk, Lydia 1828, 59
Newkirk, Lydia Catherine 1818, 296
Newkirk, Lydia Ellen 1888, 83, 85
Newkirk, Lynn Malinda 1839, 178
Newkirk, Mabel, 112
Newkirk, Mabel 1891, 51
Newkirk, Mable, 71
Newkirk, Mable 1885, 122
Newkirk, Macy S. 1833, 141
Newkirk, Madeline Shaw 1864, 99
Newkirk, Madge, 112
Newkirk, Madley 1828, 97
Newkirk, Magdalena 1782, 19
Newkirk, Magdelin 1804, 28
Newkirk, Mahala 1785, 287, 288
Newkirk, Malinda 1790, 294
Newkirk, Malinda 1801, 68
Newkirk, Malinda J. 1840, 144, 153
Newkirk, Malinda J. 1842, 83
Newkirk, Malinda Katherine 1843, 196
Newkirk, Malissa 1842, 194
Newkirk, Malissa 1846, 195

Newkirk, Marcia Jean 1958, 81
Newkirk, Marcus 1818, 275
Newkirk, Marcus Eugene 1930, 81
Newkirk, Marcus Joel 1905, 81
Newkirk, Marcus T. 1879, 74
Newkirk, Mareitje 1781, 210
Newkirk, Margaarita 1793, 15
Newkirk, Margaret, 52, 162
Newkirk, Margaret 1754, 22
Newkirk, Margaret 1762, 42
Newkirk, Margaret 1781, 41
Newkirk, Margaret 1790, 225
Newkirk, Margaret 1793, 156
Newkirk, Margaret 1801, 16
Newkirk, Margaret 1803, 68
Newkirk, Margaret 1823, 236
Newkirk, Margaret 1824, 40
Newkirk, Margaret 1830, 14, 238
Newkirk, Margaret 1835, 191
Newkirk, Margaret 1838, 191
Newkirk, Margaret 1839, 131
Newkirk, Margaret 1841, 305
Newkirk, Margaret 1852, 71
Newkirk, Margaret A. 1837, 139
Newkirk, Margaret A. 1845, 144
Newkirk, Margaret Alice 1858, 243
Newkirk, Margaret Ann 1830, 19
Newkirk, Margaret Ann 1852, 244
Newkirk, Margaret C. 1832, 195
Newkirk, Margaret E. 1845, 173
Newkirk, Margaret Gridley 1828, 273
Newkirk, Margaret Heberton 1867, 44
Newkirk, Margaret Howey 1867, 99
Newkirk, Margaret Jane 1840, 141

Newkirk, Margaret Jane 1851, 242
Newkirk, Margaret Laura 1854, 178
Newkirk, Margaret P. 1835, 82
Newkirk, Margaret S., 41
Newkirk, Margaret S. 1847, 227
Newkirk, Margaret Zuie 1852, 122
Newkirk, Margarete Huffman 1829, 93
Newkirk, Margaretta 1755, 18
Newkirk, Margretje 1742, 13
Newkirk, Margrietje 1769, 28
Newkirk, Margrietjen 1742, 13
Newkirk, Maria, 219
Newkirk, Maria 1755, 218
Newkirk, Maria 1756, 22
Newkirk, Maria 1763, 27
Newkirk, Maria 1775, 209
Newkirk, Maria 1797, 274
Newkirk, Maria 1798, 23
Newkirk, Maria 1802, 207
Newkirk, Maria 1815, 286
Newkirk, Maria 1864, 20
Newkirk, Maria 1874, 51
Newkirk, Maria Ann 1833, 207
Newkirk, Maria Catharina 1713, 267
Newkirk, Maria Catharine 1850, 228
Newkirk, Maria DeWitt 1828, 19
Newkirk, Maria Graham 1807, 272
Newkirk, Maria Harsin 1784, 22
Newkirk, Maria Love 1866, 102
Newkirk, Mariah 1813, 50
Newkirk, Mariah Louisa 1832, 129
Newkirk, Marian Alberta m/1949, 56
Newkirk, Marian E. 1849, 121

Newkirk, Marian Ethel 1849, 123
Newkirk, Marie 1796, 218
Newkirk, Marie Louise 1903, 99
Newkirk, Marie Thersa 1910, 101
Newkirk, Marigreta 1803, 209
Newkirk, Marilla 1843, 191
Newkirk, Marilyn 1953, 76
Newkirk, Marilyn Kay 1946, 79
Newkirk, Marilyn Ruth 1928, 262
Newkirk, Marion, 78, 134
Newkirk, Marion Ivan 1900, 34
Newkirk, Maritje 1770, 230
Newkirk, Maritje 1782, 228, 231
Newkirk, Marjorie Alicia 1952, 186
Newkirk, Marjorie Ellen 1918, 260
Newkirk, Marshall 1841, 69
Newkirk, Martha, 77, 78, 84, 129
Newkirk, Martha 1778, 35
Newkirk, Martha 1829, 110
Newkirk, Martha 1836, 28
Newkirk, Martha 1845, 82
Newkirk, Martha 1848, 191
Newkirk, Martha 1856, 171
Newkirk, Martha 1877, 306
Newkirk, Martha A. 1831, 189
Newkirk, Martha A. 1845, 187
Newkirk, Martha A. 1868, 36
Newkirk, Martha Ann, 193
Newkirk, Martha Ann 1857, 305
Newkirk, Martha C. 1847, 83
Newkirk, Martha D. 1866, 51
Newkirk, Martha E. 1888, 76
Newkirk, Martha Florence 1869, 74
Newkirk, Martha H. 1841, 58
Newkirk, Martha H. 1843, 58
Newkirk, Martha Jane 1848, 131
Newkirk, Martha Jane 1916, 168
Newkirk, Martha V. A. 1848, 131
Newkirk, Martha Whelan 1833, 274
Newkirk, Martin Rafael 1984, 262
Newkirk, Mary, 46, 55, 65, 72, 162
Newkirk, Mary 1740, 31
Newkirk, Mary 1748, 32
Newkirk, Mary 1756, 22
Newkirk, Mary 1762, 281
Newkirk, Mary 1772, 277
Newkirk, Mary 1775, 28, 66
Newkirk, Mary 1778, 235
Newkirk, Mary 1780, 42
Newkirk, Mary 1783, 48
Newkirk, Mary 1793, 40, 50, 137
Newkirk, Mary 1797, 36, 68
Newkirk, Mary 1798, 18
Newkirk, Mary 1800, 35, 192
Newkirk, Mary 1810, 218
Newkirk, Mary 1818, 15
Newkirk, Mary 1826, 226
Newkirk, Mary 1833, 23, 131
Newkirk, Mary 1834, 72
Newkirk, Mary 1835, 195
Newkirk, Mary 1837, 213
Newkirk, Mary 1842, 214
Newkirk, Mary 1845, 275
Newkirk, Mary 1846, 196
Newkirk, Mary 1849, 207
Newkirk, Mary 1862, 96
Newkirk, Mary 1867, 77
Newkirk, Mary 1870, 74
Newkirk, Mary 1884, 61
Newkirk, Mary 1897, 88
Newkirk, Mary 1911, 244
Newkirk, Mary A. 1814, 209
Newkirk, Mary A. 1831, 227
Newkirk, Mary A. 1834, 40

Newkirk, Mary A. 1840, 191
Newkirk, Mary A. 1844, 142
Newkirk, Mary A. 1853, 84
Newkirk, Mary A. 1891, 167
Newkirk, Mary Agnes 1830, 274
Newkirk, Mary Allin 1816, 273
Newkirk, Mary Ann 1787, 90
Newkirk, Mary Ann 1807, 295
Newkirk, Mary Ann 1817, 188, 296
Newkirk, Mary Ann 1819, 236
Newkirk, Mary Ann 1820, 273
Newkirk, Mary Ann 1836, 92
Newkirk, Mary Ann 1842, 131
Newkirk, Mary Ann 1844, 83
Newkirk, Mary Ann 1847, 300
Newkirk, Mary B. 1864, 103
Newkirk, Mary Bryan 1849, 105
Newkirk, Mary Bryant 1864, 91
Newkirk, Mary C. 1855, 173
Newkirk, Mary Catherine 1845, 230
Newkirk, Mary Cati 1855, 296
Newkirk, Mary d/1859, 48
Newkirk, Mary E. 1837, 128, 129
Newkirk, Mary E. 1843, 283
Newkirk, Mary E. 1845, 83
Newkirk, Mary E. 1846, 58, 114
Newkirk, Mary E. 1848, 191
Newkirk, Mary E. 1859, 307
Newkirk, Mary E. 1869, 310
Newkirk, Mary Eliza 1830, 93
Newkirk, Mary Eliza 1842, 175
Newkirk, Mary Elizabeth 1819, 46
Newkirk, Mary Elizabeth 1842, 274
Newkirk, Mary Elizabeth 1843, 178
Newkirk, Mary Elizabeth 1846, 275
Newkirk, Mary Elizabeth 1862, 77, 98
Newkirk, Mary Elizabeth 1914, 241
Newkirk, Mary Elizabeth 1928, 180
Newkirk, Mary Ellen 1834, 192
Newkirk, Mary Ellen 1856, 243
Newkirk, Mary Ellen 1868, 79
Newkirk, Mary Elna 1891, 309
Newkirk, Mary Elnora 1861, 309
Newkirk, Mary Emma 1910, 129
Newkirk, Mary F. 1830, 72
Newkirk, Mary F. 1846, 285
Newkirk, Mary F. 1859, 287
Newkirk, Mary Fonda 1838, 276
Newkirk, Mary H. 1786, 41
Newkirk, Mary Helen 1885, 119
Newkirk, Mary Imelda 1918, 102
Newkirk, Mary J. 1829, 143, 150
Newkirk, Mary J. 1840, 58
Newkirk, Mary Jane, 44
Newkirk, Mary Jane 1820, 238
Newkirk, Mary Jane 1829, 304
Newkirk, Mary Jane 1831, 57, 110
Newkirk, Mary Jane 1895, 85
Newkirk, Mary Jane 1947, 133
Newkirk, Mary Julia 1914, 290
Newkirk, Mary K. 1851, 119
Newkirk, Mary L. 1831, 91
Newkirk, Mary Lou 1946, 180
Newkirk, Mary Louisa 1846, 214
Newkirk, Mary Louise 1872, 310
Newkirk, Mary Louise 1874, 74
Newkirk, Mary M. 1836, 245
Newkirk, Mary M. 1846, 111
Newkirk, Mary M. 1848, 191
Newkirk, Mary M. 1859, 237
Newkirk, Mary Patterson 1800, 276
Newkirk, Mary Reed 1852, 62

Newkirk, Mary Richard 1855, 172

Newkirk, Maryte 1803, 209

Newkirk, Marytje 1765, 28

Newkirk, Mason Everett 1928, 184

Newkirk, Matheus 1749, 13

Newkirk, Matheus 1769, 42, 45

Newkirk, Matheus 1782, 207

Newkirk, Matheus Cornelisse, Jr. 1647, 220

Newkirk, Mathis 1816, 228

Newkirk, Matilda 1803, 16

Newkirk, Matilda 1826, 155

Newkirk, Matilda 1831, 50

Newkirk, Matilda 1837, 235

Newkirk, Matilda 1842, 157

Newkirk, Matilda Smith 1822, 276

Newkirk, Matteus 1799, 223

Newkirk, Mattheus Cornelisse 1600, 220

Newkirk, Mattheus Cornelisse 1647, 2

Newkirk, Mattheus Cornelisse, Jr. 1647, 1, 223

Newkirk, Mattheuse Cornelissen 1600, 1, 2

Newkirk, Matthew 1717, 11, 17

Newkirk, Matthew 1724, 29, 47

Newkirk, Matthew 1734, 223, 225

Newkirk, Matthew 1749, 13

Newkirk, Matthew 1764, 42, 43, 47

Newkirk, Matthew 1769, 42, 45

Newkirk, Matthew 1772, 229

Newkirk, Matthew 1784, 14

Newkirk, Matthew 1794, 42, 43

Newkirk, Matthew 1805, 275

Newkirk, Matthew 1811, 230

Newkirk, Matthew 1814, 45

Newkirk, Matthew 1816, 228

Newkirk, Matthew 1860, 46

Newkirk, Matthew Cornelisse, Jr. 1647, 228

Newkirk, Matthew P. 1735, 228, 231

Newkirk, Matthew, Jr. 1838, 44

Newkirk, Matthys 1758, 271

Newkirk, Maurice Dodd 1917, 167

Newkirk, May C. 1855, 311

Newkirk, May E. 1872, 39

Newkirk, McCardle 1861, 191

Newkirk, Melissa 1807, 274

Newkirk, Melissa 1849, 276

Newkirk, Melissa J. 1858, 175

Newkirk, Melissa Kay 1968, 79

Newkirk, Melvina J. 1860, 152

Newkirk, Merlee 1905, 244

Newkirk, Meyndert 1726, 198

Newkirk, Meyndert 1753, 217

Newkirk, Michael 1846, 178

Newkirk, Mildred Elizabeth 1899, 51, 52

Newkirk, Mildred L. 1888, 134

Newkirk, Millard 1848, 196

Newkirk, Millie 1866, 79

Newkirk, Millie 1868, 150

Newkirk, Millie M. 1865, 79

Newkirk, Milo Cornelius 1857, 307

Newkirk, Milton 1814, 117

Newkirk, Milton 1826, 15

Newkirk, Milton J. 1824, 236

Newkirk, Mina Carroll 1834, 123

Newkirk, Minche 1843, 56

Newkirk, Minerva 1840, 155

Newkirk, Minerva Ellen 1822, 244

Newkirk, Minnie, 180

Newkirk, Minnie 1864, 122

Newkirk, Minnie 1892, 84

Newkirk, Mira J. 1890, 147
Newkirk, Missouri 1809, 131
Newkirk, Missouri 1837, 132
Newkirk, Mitchell Joseph 1913, 129
Newkirk, Morris 1803, 283
Newkirk, Morris 1810, 275
Newkirk, Moses 1815, 275
Newkirk, Moses 1822, 15, 16
Newkirk, Moses 1830, 276
Newkirk, Moses 1840, 18
Newkirk, Moses Kirkendoll 1806, 171
Newkirk, Muriel Louise 1917, 17
Newkirk, Murle M. 1896, 145
Newkirk, Myndert 1726, 269
Newkirk, Myra Irine 1891, 119
Newkirk, Myrta C. 1886, 307
Newkirk, Myrtle, 71
Newkirk, Myrtle L. 1876, 133
Newkirk, Nadenia, 16
Newkirk, Nancy, 34
Newkirk, Nancy 1793, 207
Newkirk, Nancy 1796, 68, 138
Newkirk, Nancy 1828, 310
Newkirk, Nancy 1833, 141
Newkirk, Nancy 1838, 172
Newkirk, Nancy A. 1841, 173
Newkirk, Nancy A. 1842, 172, 298
Newkirk, Nancy A. 1848, 178
Newkirk, Nancy J. 1799, 282
Newkirk, Nancy Jane 1833, 74
Newkirk, Nannie V. 1904, 165
Newkirk, Nannie Victoria 1882, 74
Newkirk, Naomi 1849, 305
Newkirk, Napoleon B. 1847, 191
Newkirk, Nathan 1833, 35
Newkirk, Nathan 1835, 57
Newkirk, Nathaniel Reeve, Dr. 1817, 46

Newkirk, Neeltje 1667, 3, 5
Newkirk, Neeltje 1728, 198
Newkirk, Neeltje 1769, 13
Newkirk, Neeltje 1783, 14
Newkirk, Neeltje 1794, 207
Newkirk, Neeltje 1796, 209
Newkirk, Neeltje Meyer 1804, 23
Newkirk, Neeltjen 1728, 269
Newkirk, Nell Patricia 1927, 132
Newkirk, Nellie 1774, 278
Newkirk, Nellie 1782, 278
Newkirk, Nellie Graff 1881, 54
Newkirk, Nellie K., 112
Newkirk, Nellie Maria 1810, 14
Newkirk, Nellie Mason m/1906, 168
Newkirk, Nelly 1777, 8, 13
Newkirk, Nelly 1826, 15
Newkirk, Nelson 1797, 243
Newkirk, Nelson 1819, 242, 243
Newkirk, Nelson 1820, 298
Newkirk, Neltje 1802, 27
Newkirk, Nercissa L. 1834, 120
Newkirk, Neta 1894, 122
Newkirk, Newton 1816, 118
Newkirk, Newton M. 1843, 117
Newkirk, Nicholas C. 1842, 187
Newkirk, Nicholas V. 1857, 225
Newkirk, Nickson R. 1853, 189
Newkirk, Noah E., 112
Newkirk, Nola Jeanne 1932, 126
Newkirk, Noley G. 1888, 145
Newkirk, Nora 1868, 115
Newkirk, Nora 1876, 171
Newkirk, Nora Ann 1936, 181
Newkirk, Nora Pearl 1887, 178
Newkirk, Oather 1829, 244
Newkirk, Obediah 1793, 243, 272
Newkirk, Ohio State 1824, 121
Newkirk, Olinda 1854, 305

Newkirk, Olive Bilderbeck 1891, 56
Newkirk, Oliver 1834, 35, 36
Newkirk, Oliver Lysander 1831, 289, 290
Newkirk, Olivia 1820, 132
Newkirk, Olla Bell 1871, 307
Newkirk, Ollie Mae, 240
Newkirk, Omar H., 56
Newkirk, Omer 1891, 78
Newkirk, Onida 1879, 122
Newkirk, Ophelia 1892, 85
Newkirk, Orpha 1794, 138
Newkirk, Orpha 1901, 85
Newkirk, Osborne 1860, 70
Newkirk, Oscar E. 1854/60, 288
Newkirk, Otho 1829, 244
Newkirk, Otis Edward 1872, 74
Newkirk, Otto 1829, 242
Newkirk, P. H. 1807, 118
Newkirk, Patricia Ann 1928, 263
Newkirk, Patricia Lynn 1950, 54
Newkirk, Patricia Susan 1952, 262
Newkirk, Paulus 1699, 222, 227, 229
Newkirk, Paulus 1772, 230
Newkirk, Paulus 1776, 230
Newkirk, Paxton H. 1827, 120
Newkirk, Paxton H., Jr., 120
Newkirk, Pearl 1898, 85
Newkirk, Pearl C. 1890, 134
Newkirk, Pearson 1802, 192
Newkirk, Peggy 1794, 22
Newkirk, Penelope 1785, 89, 90
Newkirk, Penelope 1823, 92
Newkirk, Peninah 1776, 277
Newkirk, Permelia 1805, 130
Newkirk, Permelia 1806, 171, 175, 176
Newkirk, Permelia Jane 1838, 116

Newkirk, Perry 1824, 237, 238
Newkirk, Perry N. 1844, 238
Newkirk, Peter, 63
Newkirk, Peter 1727, 64, 65, 67, 85, 169, 170, 187, 189, 192, 193
Newkirk, Peter 1758, 18
Newkirk, Peter 1760, 87
Newkirk, Peter 1783, 170
Newkirk, Peter 1794, 273
Newkirk, Peter 1800, 210
Newkirk, Peter 1805, 195
Newkirk, Peter B. 1812, 288
Newkirk, Peter L. 1836, 48
Newkirk, Peter, II 1765, 170, 192
Newkirk, Peter, Jr. 1799, 18
Newkirk, Petrus 1743, 270
Newkirk, Petrus 1765, 27
Newkirk, Petrus 1771, 271
Newkirk, Petrus 1772, 28
Newkirk, Petrus 1775, 211
Newkirk, Phallysta 1838, 157
Newkirk, Phebe 1805, 40
Newkirk, Phebe 1808, 156
Newkirk, Phebe B. 1800, 213
Newkirk, Phebe E. 1848, 226
Newkirk, Pheby, 237
Newkirk, Phereby F. 1836, 83
Newkirk, Philip 1740, 210
Newkirk, Philip 1766, 218
Newkirk, Philip 1791, 213
Newkirk, Philo H. 1852, 117
Newkirk, Philora 1824, 288
Newkirk, Phoebe, 84
Newkirk, Phoebe F. 1836, 83
Newkirk, Phoebe m/1801, 82
Newkirk, Phyllis Irene 1921, 260
Newkirk, Pierpoint, 218
Newkirk, Pieter 1694, 222
Newkirk, Polly 1816, 173, 235
Newkirk, Priscilla 1825, 276
Newkirk, Quessie 1851, 103

Newkirk, Quinton K. 1856, 61
Newkirk, R. F. 1843, 188
Newkirk, Rachel, 65, 272
Newkirk, Rachel 1704, 202
Newkirk, Rachel 1728, 27
Newkirk, Rachel 1747, 270
Newkirk, Rachel 1751, 229
Newkirk, Rachel 1758, 87
Newkirk, Rachel 1759, 47
Newkirk, Rachel 1787, 42, 43, 47
Newkirk, Rachel 1790, 15
Newkirk, Rachel 1792, 207
Newkirk, Rachel 1799, 16
Newkirk, Rachel 1805, 209
Newkirk, Rachel 1831, 131, 230
Newkirk, Rachel 1842, 15
Newkirk, Rachel Ann 1826, 93
Newkirk, Rachel Ann 1911, 21
Newkirk, Rachel Catherine 1830, 90
Newkirk, Rachel Crist 1815, 274
Newkirk, Rachel Emma 1836, 103
Newkirk, Rachel Millspaugh 1839, 275
Newkirk, Rachel V. H. 1839, 227
Newkirk, Ralph, 79
Newkirk, Ralph Lawrence 1925, 260
Newkirk, Ralph Leon 1924, 102
Newkirk, Ralph T., 112
Newkirk, Ray Hobart 1897, 262
Newkirk, Raymond 1902, 165
Newkirk, Raymond Earl 1912, 180
Newkirk, Rebecca 1750, 32
Newkirk, Rebecca 1771, 48
Newkirk, Rebecca 1776, 235
Newkirk, Rebecca 1788, 49
Newkirk, Rebecca 1789, 35
Newkirk, Rebecca 1795, 40

Newkirk, Rebecca 1805, 59
Newkirk, Rebecca 1817, 242
Newkirk, Rebecca Elizabeth 1873, 249
Newkirk, Rebecca J. 1852, 237
Newkirk, Rebecca Jane 1829, 157
Newkirk, Rebecca L. 1860, 149
Newkirk, Rebecca V., 55
Newkirk, Reed 1810, 60
Newkirk, Reuben 1769, 107, 109, 130
Newkirk, Reuben 1791, 137
Newkirk, Reuben 1792, 114, 121
Newkirk, Reuben 1793, 108, 111
Newkirk, Reuben 1845, 131
Newkirk, Reuben 1852, 158
Newkirk, Reuben Franklin 1854, 122, 126
Newkirk, Rhoda 1796, 155
Newkirk, Rhoda 1825, 118
Newkirk, Rhoda 1834, 157
Newkirk, Rhoda 1900, 51
Newkirk, Rhoda C. 1838, 116
Newkirk, Rhoda Carroll 1821, 121
Newkirk, Rhoda J. 1835, 129
Newkirk, Rhoda Maria 1829, 120
Newkirk, Richard, 103
Newkirk, Richard 1760, 169, 186
Newkirk, Richard 1829, 69
Newkirk, Richard Albert 1925, 129
Newkirk, Richard Brent 1954, 186
Newkirk, Richard D. 1920, 309
Newkirk, Richard Dudley 1942, 53
Newkirk, Richard Edward 1863, 244
Newkirk, Richard James 1926, 185

Newkirk, Richard Lee 1945, 261
Newkirk, Richard Robert 1859, 248, 259, 262
Newkirk, Richard, Jr. 1784, 170, 186
Newkirk, Rilla 1840, 35
Newkirk, Robert, 56
Newkirk, Robert 1859, 96
Newkirk, Robert Allen 1925, 129
Newkirk, Robert Aloysius 1921, 103
Newkirk, Robert J. 1860, 311
Newkirk, Robert L. 1874, 147
Newkirk, Robert O. 1862, 120
Newkirk, Robert Richard 1877, 250
Newkirk, Robert S., 129
Newkirk, Robert Stewart 1835, 110
Newkirk, Robinson 1782, 35
Newkirk, Robyn Earl 1965, 182
Newkirk, Roger Sullivan 1939, 179
Newkirk, Rolla 1863, 38
Newkirk, Rolla Elbert 1910, 147
Newkirk, Romeo 1859, 189
Newkirk, Ronnie 1948, 79
Newkirk, Rosa, 103, 164
Newkirk, Rosanna 1865, 36
Newkirk, Roscoe, 71
Newkirk, Rose Ann 1820, 196
Newkirk, Rose Ann 1849, 196
Newkirk, Rosean 1820, 196
Newkirk, Rosean 1838, 195
Newkirk, Rosetta 1837, 298
Newkirk, Rosetta 1861, 244
Newkirk, Roxanna 1804, 271
Newkirk, Roy 1892, 38
Newkirk, Roy C. 1905, 85
Newkirk, Roy James 1914, 102
Newkirk, Roy Mason 1909, 164
Newkirk, Rozena, 71

Newkirk, Ruby A. 1897, 144
Newkirk, Rufus Marion 1849, 57
Newkirk, Ruphina 1841, 117
Newkirk, Ruth 1813, 34
Newkirk, Ruth A. 1819, 287
Newkirk, Ruth A. 1847, 296
Newkirk, Ruth B. 1903, 21
Newkirk, Ruth Ellis 1917, 165
Newkirk, Rutha Catherine 1850, 187
Newkirk, S. A. 1835, 70
Newkirk, Sally 1779, 278
Newkirk, Sally 1793, 225
Newkirk, Sally 1796, 225
Newkirk, Sally M. 1810, 284
Newkirk, Samuel 1760, 28
Newkirk, Samuel 1788, 41, 43, 47
Newkirk, Samuel 1840, 218
Newkirk, Samuel C. 1846, 61
Newkirk, Samuel D. 1820, 286
Newkirk, Samuel Floyd 1900, 81
Newkirk, Samuel H. 1838, 82
Newkirk, Samuel P. 1851, 75
Newkirk, Samuel P. 1869, 304
Newkirk, Samuel T. 1838, 112
Newkirk, Samuel T. 1874, 307
Newkirk, Samuel Tyler 1865, 228
Newkirk, Samuel, Jr. 1820, 42, 43
Newkirk, Sandra Kay 1969, 133
Newkirk, Sarah, 112
Newkirk, Sarah 1715, 26
Newkirk, Sarah 1742, 31
Newkirk, Sarah 1765, 35, 42, 206
Newkirk, Sarah 1780, 21, 35
Newkirk, Sarah 1786, 30, 40
Newkirk, Sarah 1788, 288
Newkirk, Sarah 1790, 49
Newkirk, Sarah 1791, 42

Newkirk, Sarah 1800, 45
Newkirk, Sarah 1805, 190
Newkirk, Sarah 1808, 195
Newkirk, Sarah 1810, 212
Newkirk, Sarah 1811, 219, 286
Newkirk, Sarah 1825, 288
Newkirk, Sarah 1832, 19
Newkirk, Sarah 1833, 28
Newkirk, Sarah 1865, 189
Newkirk, Sarah A. 1870, 37
Newkirk, Sarah Ann 1820, 110
Newkirk, Sarah Ann 1837, 35, 37
Newkirk, Sarah C., 43
Newkirk, Sarah C. 1853, 215
Newkirk, Sarah Catharine 1835, 224
Newkirk, Sarah E. 1872, 287
Newkirk, Sarah Edna 1892, 308
Newkirk, Sarah Elenor 1828, 297
Newkirk, Sarah Elizabeth 1843, 305
Newkirk, Sarah Elizabeth 1847, 196
Newkirk, Sarah Elizabeth 1855, 91
Newkirk, Sarah Elizabeth 1856, 300
Newkirk, Sarah Ellen 1854, 244
Newkirk, Sarah Ellen 1868, 240
Newkirk, Sarah Ellenor 1873, 297
Newkirk, Sarah Frances 1841, 275
Newkirk, Sarah Frances 1863, 244
Newkirk, Sarah J. 1831, 157
Newkirk, Sarah J. 1851, 78
Newkirk, Sarah Jane 1830, 144, 151
Newkirk, Sarah Jane 1844, 227
Newkirk, Sarah Jane 1848, 146

Newkirk, Sarah K. 1846, 142
Newkirk, Sarah Leonora Halsey 1836, 273
Newkirk, Sarah M. 1838, 226
Newkirk, Sarah P. 1819, 119
Newkirk, Sarah P. 1848, 111
Newkirk, Sarah S. 1846, 285
Newkirk, Sarah Van Keuren 1794, 294
Newkirk, Seymore 1869, 51
Newkirk, Sharon 1955, 133
Newkirk, Sharon S. 1856, 131
Newkirk, Shipman 1804, 156, 157, 158
Newkirk, Shipman 1807, 131
Newkirk, Shirley, 134
Newkirk, Shirley 1913, 285
Newkirk, Silas Eugene 1852, 296
Newkirk, Silas J. 1837, 70
Newkirk, Simeon 1841, 188
Newkirk, Simeon 1875, 79
Newkirk, Smith B. 1854, 286
Newkirk, Solomon 1840, 83
Newkirk, Sophia 1761, 107
Newkirk, Sophia 1812, 231
Newkirk, Sophia 1813, 228
Newkirk, Sophia 1823, 232
Newkirk, Sophia 1856, 231
Newkirk, Sophia Cinderella 1847/48, 247
Newkirk, Sophia W. 1847, 232
Newkirk, Sophie Wilkings 1855, 96
Newkirk, Spencer 1849, 283
Newkirk, Stanley C., 283
Newkirk, Stanley Clifton 1932, 19, 20
Newkirk, Stanley Tappen 1900, 20
Newkirk, Stansberry 1850, 113
Newkirk, Stella, 78
Newkirk, Stella 1873, 190

Newkirk, Stephen 1796, 218
Newkirk, Susan 1812, 34
Newkirk, Susan 1961, 184
Newkirk, Susan Ann 1958, 261
Newkirk, Susan Hill 1861, 91
Newkirk, Susan M., 110
Newkirk, Susan Patricia 1957, 21
Newkirk, Susan Rebecca 1844, 246
Newkirk, Susanna 1766, 277
Newkirk, Susanna 1798, 219
Newkirk, Susanna L. 1838, 112
Newkirk, Susannah 1781, 277
Newkirk, Susannah 1785, 49
Newkirk, Susannah 1807, 116
Newkirk, Susannah 1813, 49
Newkirk, Susannah C. 1830, 77
Newkirk, Susie Fay 1885, 122
Newkirk, Susie Lydia 1877, 297
Newkirk, Sylvanus 1829, 28
Newkirk, Tabitha 1861, 190
Newkirk, Tamson B. 1862, 51
Newkirk, Tanneke 1762, 206
Newkirk, Tanya 1975, 76
Newkirk, Telitha 1837, 69
Newkirk, Temperance 1792, 294
Newkirk, Ten Eyck 1839, 20
Newkirk, Teunis, 109
Newkirk, Teunis 1718, 64, 65, 67
Newkirk, Teunis 1750, 107, 108, 109, 161, 162, 164
Newkirk, Teunis 1768, 170, 193
Newkirk, Teunis 1794, 114
Newkirk, Teunis Shipman 1805, 140, 142, 143, 145, 150, 151, 152, 153
Newkirk, Thankful Jane 1832, 91
Newkirk, Theda Jo 1940, 309
Newkirk, Thelma A. 1906, 39
Newkirk, Theodore 1848, 288
Newkirk, Theodore 1877, 168
Newkirk, Thirsa 1906, 39

Newkirk, Thomas 1802, 68, 70
Newkirk, Thomas 1829, 196
Newkirk, Thomas 1832, 69
Newkirk, Thomas 1871, 85
Newkirk, Thomas 1880, 73
Newkirk, Thomas 1942, 182
Newkirk, Thomas A. 1941, 99
Newkirk, Thomas B. 1846, 113
Newkirk, Thomas B. 1859, 78
Newkirk, Thomas B. 1873, 99
Newkirk, Thomas Benton 1842, 196
Newkirk, Thomas Hopkins 1849, 115
Newkirk, Thomas Isaac 1866, 120
Newkirk, Thomas J., 293
Newkirk, Thomas J. 1852, 305
Newkirk, Thomas J. 1854, 149
Newkirk, Thomas Jefferson 1844, 310
Newkirk, Thomas Jefferson 1854, 148
Newkirk, Thomas Joel 1865, 77
Newkirk, Thomas N. 1856, 187
Newkirk, Thomas Stafford 1798, 192
Newkirk, Thomas W. 1840, 55
Newkirk, Thomas Wilmer 1905, 99
Newkirk, Thompson 1806, 40
Newkirk, Timothy 1791, 89
Newkirk, Timothy H. 1791, 92
Newkirk, Timothy H., Jr. 1828, 92
Newkirk, Timothy Henry Rhodes 1829, 90, 92
Newkirk, Timothy Rhodes 1874, 92
Newkirk, Tobias 1723, 64, 65, 67, 85, 87, 169
Newkirk, Tobias 1767, 170

Newkirk, Tobias 1841, 195
Newkirk, Tracy, 182
Newkirk, Tresse E. 1878, 77
Newkirk, Trintje 1665, 6
Newkirk, Trintje 1763, 28
Newkirk, Triphenia 1855, 59
Newkirk, Trisha Lynn 1963, 21
Newkirk, Tryntje 1688, 222
Newkirk, Tryntje 1732, 222
Newkirk, Tryntje Bridget, 219
Newkirk, Tunis 1750, 130
Newkirk, Tunis 1817, 109
Newkirk, Tunis 1843, 130
Newkirk, Tunis Ellis 1853, 111
Newkirk, Ursula 1818, 118
Newkirk, Velma June 1921, 80
Newkirk, Venila 1847, 207
Newkirk, Venti 1853, 285
Newkirk, Veral Anne 1934, 186
Newkirk, Verna Mae 1914, 49, 54
Newkirk, Vernon L. 1895, 134
Newkirk, Victor Lee 1870, 71
Newkirk, Victor M. 1811, 40
Newkirk, Victor M., Jr. 1847, 40
Newkirk, Victoria Louise 1964, 17
Newkirk, Vincent J., 78
Newkirk, Virgie, 180
Newkirk, Virgil, 78
Newkirk, Virginia 1817, 113
Newkirk, Virginia 1840, 163, 164
Newkirk, Virginia Bailey 1914, 17
Newkirk, Virginia Belle 1906, 164
Newkirk, Virginia Mae 1919, 180, 182
Newkirk, Wade Lee 1959, 182
Newkirk, Walker 1878, 103
Newkirk, Walter, 78

Newkirk, Walter 1874, 305
Newkirk, Walter 1899, 79
Newkirk, Walter Edwin 1885, 134
Newkirk, Walter Eugene 1924, 129
Newkirk, Walter L. 1891, 36
Newkirk, Walter Laurie 1879, 128
Newkirk, Warren B. m/1949, 56
Newkirk, Warren T. 1883, 149
Newkirk, Warren Webber 1913, 133
Newkirk, Wesley Everett, 240
Newkirk, Wilbert E. 1870, 51, 52
Newkirk, Willard 1877, 305
Newkirk, William, 55, 57
Newkirk, William 1735, 206
Newkirk, William 1758, 169, 187
Newkirk, William 1765, 206
Newkirk, William 1784, 35
Newkirk, William 1786, 278
Newkirk, William 1788, 213
Newkirk, William 1791, 40
Newkirk, William 1796, 192
Newkirk, William 1797, 58
Newkirk, William 1805, 274
Newkirk, William 1806, 140
Newkirk, William 1809, 57
Newkirk, William 1814, 14
Newkirk, William 1815, 191
Newkirk, William 1823, 274
Newkirk, William 1827, 15
Newkirk, William 1830, 14
Newkirk, William 1831, 130
Newkirk, William 1834, 207
Newkirk, William 1836, 141
Newkirk, William 1837, 131
Newkirk, William 1839, 113, 188
Newkirk, William 1840, 28

Newkirk, William 1844, 58, 194
Newkirk, William 1845, 15, 218, 243
Newkirk, William 1848, 45
Newkirk, William 1852, 187
Newkirk, William 1865, 237
Newkirk, William 1866, 77
Newkirk, William 1875, 128
Newkirk, William 1903, 85
Newkirk, William A. 1835, 114
Newkirk, William A. 1839, 59
Newkirk, William B. 1844, 83
Newkirk, William B. 1852, 157
Newkirk, William Beckett 1871, 51
Newkirk, William Brian Van Ryan 1912, 101
Newkirk, William Broadhead 1788, 14
Newkirk, William Brooks 1841, 61
Newkirk, William Bryan 1861, 101
Newkirk, William C. 1765, 209
Newkirk, William C. 1839, 172
Newkirk, William C. 1869, 79
Newkirk, William D. 1844, 243
Newkirk, William Daniel 1916, 129
Newkirk, William E. 1880, 77
Newkirk, William Edward 1851, 230
Newkirk, William Ellis 1857, 304
Newkirk, William Ellis 1862, 297
Newkirk, William F. 1884, 307
Newkirk, William H. 1842, 190
Newkirk, William H. 1849, 58
Newkirk, William Hamilton 1842, 307

Newkirk, William Henry 1795, 14
Newkirk, William Henry 1820, 296
Newkirk, William Henry 1834, 44
Newkirk, William Henry 1845, 227
Newkirk, William Henry 1867, 189
Newkirk, William Henry 1880, 241
Newkirk, William Hurrick 1866, 83
Newkirk, William J. 1842, 238
Newkirk, William J. 1847, 188
Newkirk, William J. 1904, 147
Newkirk, William John 1960, 184
Newkirk, William King 1909, 99
Newkirk, William L. 1835, 190
Newkirk, William L. 1849, 171
Newkirk, William Leonard 1858, 178, 179, 183, 184, 185
Newkirk, William Leonard 1865, 289, 290
Newkirk, William Lindley 1860, 309
Newkirk, William M. 1852, 75
Newkirk, William Nelson 1870, 244
Newkirk, William Riley 1837, 144, 152
Newkirk, William S. 1877, 190
Newkirk, William Seavey 1854, 96
Newkirk, William Sherman 1916, 290
Newkirk, William Sherman, Jr. 1957, 291
Newkirk, William T. 1839, 173

Newkirk, William Usher 1831, 97
Newkirk, William Wallace 1867, 306
Newkirk, Willshire 1835, 69
Newkirk, Winfield 1860, 231
Newkirk, Wyntje 1795, 15
Newkirk, Yonika 1728, 29
Newkirk, Zachariah 1816, 58
Newkirk, Zachariah Elias 1837, 77
Newkirk, Zed Jeffrey 1965, 182
Newkirk, Zelu 1804, 130
Newkirk, Zeriah 1852, 122
Niblick, Amanda F. 1822, 114
Nicholas, No given name, 30
Nickell, Carlene, 252
Niece, Christina, 176
Noblitt, Ella, 177
Norum, Helga Marie, 250
Nott, Mary Minnesota 1865, 308
Nottingham, Elizabeth, 205
Nottingham, Mary, 12

—O—

O'Keefe, Daniel, 146
Oakley, Mary 1782, 295
Oates, John Wesley, 84
Oates, Martha Isobel 1869, 84
Odle, Chester, 78
Offenbacker, Walter, 264
Oldham, Court F., 147
Oliver, Bessie Wyatt, 82
Oliver, Charles E., 74
Oliver, James, Dr., 18
Oliver, Matthew, 18
Oliver, William Henry, 44
Olmstead, Nicholas, 45
Olsen, Darlene, 103
Onstott, No given name, 78
Oosterhout, Marytjen, 28

Oram, Joshua, 117
Orndorf, Elizabeth, 166
Ornstein, Donna, 179
Orr, Etta, 297
Orr, Wallace J., 297
Osborn, Nancy 1793, 273
Osborn, Pamela 1796, 296
Osman, Charles, 142
Ostrander, Maes, 10
Ott, Clarabell, 101
Ovelette, Lynn 1946, 183
Overs, Ray Ella, 51
Overs, William, 51
Owens, Nancy, 171

—P—

Paddock, Catherine Louise 1960, 185
Paddock, Emily Marie 1991, 185
Paddock, Julie Ann 1958, 185
Paddock, Lindsay Ann 1981, 185
Paddock, Richard Rowell 1929, 185
Paddock, Richard Rowell, Jr. 1954, 185
Paddock, Sandra Lea 1956, 185
Paddock, William Jacob 1986, 185
Palmer, Delbert, 106
Parker, Alva, 307
Parker, Annie Laurie, 104
Parker, Edward B., 104
Parker, Elijah B., 104
Parker, Emma Pearle, 104
Parker, Irene McKoy, 104
Parker, John W., 104
Parker, Josephine, 104
Parker, Lydia, 67
Parker, Oda Lee, 104
Parker, Rebecca, 67
Parker, Sarah Ethel, 104

Parsons, J. G., 123
Pass, Clinton James 1975, 181
Pass, Darla Suzanne 1973, 181
Pass, Elizabeth Ashley 1983, 181
Pass, George 1956, 181
Pass, Katherine Lee 1980, 181
Pass, Paul 1931, 180
Pass, Paul Patrick 1970, 181
Pass, Phillip Patrick 1951, 180
Pass, Susan Marie 1954, 181
Pateway, Hester Ann, 105
Patrick, Alpha, 305
Patterson, Alexander, 267, 276
Patterson, Alexander 1756, 267
Patterson, Ann 1752, 267
Patterson, Anna 1754, 267
Patterson, Anna Maria 1745, 276
Patterson, Eloise, 149
Patterson, Hendrick 1740, 267
Patterson, James 1743, 267
Patterson, James 1747, 267
Patterson, Johannes 1735, 267
Patterson, Johannes 1738, 267
Patterson, Maria 1745, 267
Patterson, Mary, 267
Patterson, Robert, 41
Patterson, Susanna 1750, 267
Patterson, William, 268
Paulus, Catryna, 1, 220, 223, 228
Paulus, Hendrikje, 2
Pawling, Barent, 6
Pawling, Eleanor 1715, 6
Pawling, Elinor, 6
Pawling, Elizabeth 1719, 6
Pawling, Henry 1689, 6
Pawling, Henry 1714, 6
Pawling, John, 6
Pawling, John 1732, 6
Pawling, Levi, 6
Pawling, Mary, 6
Pawling, Sara 1716, 6
Paxton, Wilson N., 120

Peck, James 1802, 275
Pedrick, Anna F. 1905, 50
Pedrick, Chester 1881, 50
Pedrick, Evan C. 1910, 50
Pedrick, Joseph N. 1907, 50
Pedrick, Verna E. 1908, 50
Peek, Jacob, 202
Peek, Jacobus, 202
Pegram, Margie, 76
Pelaz, Gus, 102
Pell, Anna Margaret, 240
Pell, Thomas, 240
Pells, Clarissa Evertse, 5
Pelton, Mary 1833, 243
Pelton, Peleg, 282
Pelton, Stoddard 1787, 282
Pendigrass, Beulah, 99
Penny, Ann, 87
Pericone, Frances A., 49
Perricone, No given name, 54
Perrine, Alfred, 272
Perrine, James, 213
Perry, Patricia Jean, 127
Person, Ann, 27
Person, Annatje 1748, 217
Person, Clarence E., 300
Peters, Joseph D., 119
Peterson, George, 16
Petrosky, Collette Lee 1967, 292
Petrosky, Dawn Laurette 1965, 291
Petrosky, George Clifford 1939, 291
Petrosky, George Merwin 1975, 292
Peverley, No given name, 247
Phelps, Asa, 130
Philbrick, Ida Mae, 204
Philips, Asa, 130
Philipse, Pieterje, 206
Phillips, Cassa Ann 1814, 141
Phillips, George 1818, 138

Phillips, George M., 238
Phillips, Marjorie, 38
Phillips, Peterje, 206
Phillips, Robert, 38
Picker, Charlotte 1958, 186
Pickering, Wanda Jean, 251
Pickett, Noel, 79
Piggot, May Jane 1836, 304
Ping, Job, 176
Ping, Logan 1830, 176
Pitts, Jacob, 269
Pitts, Nancy, 281
Pocock, Sarah Ellen 1830, 120
Polhemus, Sarah, 10
Poole, Bertie F., 241
Porter, Armenus Benjamin 1851, 174
Porter, Elmer 1886, 150
Porter, Henry H., 174
Porter, John Hutson 1848, 174
Porter, Kellis 1894, 150
Porter, Lawrence G., 150
Porter, Martha J. 1841, 174
Porter, Mary G. 1841, 174
Porter, No given name, 249
Porter, Orval 1889, 150
Porter, William, 236
Porter, William H. 1849, 174
Porterfield, Mary, 109
Postell, Walter, 56
Potts, J. Frank, 241
Potts, Mary M., 119
Poulson, Ota May, 250
Poulus, Catreyna, 220
Powell, Ann, 68
Powell, Elizabeth 1770, 66, 67
Powell, Julia A., 190
Powell, Laurel Shanafelt, 156
Powell, Thomas, 68
Powers, Bill, 94
Powers, Jeremiah, 238
Powers, John D., Colonel, 93

Powers, Rosa J., 36
Powers, Sarah 1816, 238
Powers, Thomas 1838, 273
Prather, Ella, 306
Pratt, Daniel Lincoln 1820, 113
Pratt, Josephine Davis 1895, 261
Pratt, William 1793, 113
Pressel, Mary, 263
Price, Alfred, 127
Price, Charlotte Teresa 1941, 127
Price, Enoch 1834, 49
Prickett, Bessie, 50
Prickett, Clara Ray 1883, 50
Prickett, Evan S. 1886, 50
Prickett, Gladys R., 50
Prickett, Henry Howard 1858, 50
Prickett, Isaiah, 50
Prickett, Newkirk 1884, 50
Prickett, Ray, 50
Prickett, Verna, 51
Probasco, R. V., 35
Proctor, Mary 1810, 38
Proctor, Mary S. 1806, 189
Proctor, Sarah Jane 1839, 189
Prosise, Lloyd, 291
Prouse, Randell Lee, 251
Provost, Eliza 1800, 225
Provost, James, 231
Pruitt, Francis 1942, 100
Pruitt, Jane Elizabeth 1946, 100
Pruitt, Melvin, 100
Pudney, John, 10
Pudney, Phebe, 10
Pugh, Beulah Bell, 80
Pugh, Evan Preston, 81
Pulley, No given name, 308
Purdy, Lockwood, 286
Purdy, Robert, 240
Pursel, Gertrude, 307
Purvis, Nonene 1917, 102

Rino, Lavina, 231
Risner, Johnson Emerson, 127
Risner, Sharon Kay, 127
Rivenbark, Charley H., 90
Rivenbark, William W., 90
Roach, Bessie, 81
Roarback, Mary B. 1820, 186
Roberts, Carolina 1810, 191
Roberts, Carolyn, 126
Roberts, Florence, 71
Roberts, Harold Harrison, 126
Roberts, Lester J., 265
Roberts, Margaret 1836, 191
Roberts, Marian Esther, 126
Roberts, Mary Kate, 96
Roberts, Reno Eli, 126
Roberts, Richard Harold, 126
Roberts, Thomas, 126
Roberts, Thomas Dabney, 126
Roberts, Warren Thomas, 126
Roberts, Warren Wilcox, 126
Roberts, William Warren, 126
Robinson, Arthur, 297
Robinson, Catherine, 32
Robinson, Elizabeth Ann, 95
Robinson, Hazel 1899, 262
Robinson, John Winfield Scott, 105
Robinson, Kathy 1940, 182
Rockefeller, Harvey J., 276
Rockefeller, Lucretia, 281
Rockwall, Chester 1829, 92
Roe, Mary m/1782, 199
Rogalsy, Carol A. 1937, 53
Rogalsy, Peter Paul d/1959, 52
Rogers, Anne 1833, 44
Roggen, Ballie, 210
Roggen, Maria, 210
Rohrer, Elizabeth P., 83
Rolling, Christopher Michael 1981, 183

Rolling, Elizabeth Mae 1986, 183
Rolling, Harry Leo, 183
Rolling, Matthew Martin 1982, 183
Rolling, Richard 1940, 183
Roos, Isaac, 202
Roosa, Abraham d/1788, 201
Roosa, Albert, 4, 7
Roosa, Aldert 1745, 201
Roosa, Anna Margaret, 4
Roosa, Benjamin, 210
Roosa, Dirck, 4
Roosa, Elizabeth 1760, 210
Roosa, Heyman, 210
Roosa, Heyman Aldertse, 3
Roosa, Isaac 1751, 201
Roosa, Jacob 1749, 201
Roosa, Jannetje, 29
Roosa, Jannetje 1746, 210
Roosa, Jannette, 7
Roosa, Jenneke, 4
Roosa, Jenneken, 11
Roosa, Jennette, 210
Roosa, Lea, 3, 211
Roosa, Leah 1747, 201
Roosa, Leah 1765, 210
Roosa, Maria 1773, 19
Roosa, Neeltje, 6
Roosa, Neeltje 1713, 7
Roosa, Petrus, 4
Roosa, Rebecca, 5
Roosa, Rebecca 1755, 201
Roosa, Sarah 1757, 201
Roosevelt, Anna Margaret, 3
Roosevelt, Nicholas, 9
Roosevelt, Theodore, 9
Rose, Abraham, 32
Rose, Elizabeth, 47
Rose, Elizabeth 1798, 32
Rose, Ezekial 1745, 32
Rose, Isaac 1771, 32

Rose, John, 32
Rose, John 1774, 32
Rose, Mary, 32
Rose, Matthew, 170
Rose, Uriah 1770, 32
Rose, William S. 1791, 33
Rosecrans, Hendricus, Jr., 10
Rosenbaum, Julia S. 1857, 132
Rosencrans, Abraham, 270
Rosencrans, Charles, 311
Roush, George, 140
Rouwlen, Nancy, 207
Row, Wilhelmus, 27
Royynto, Vitto, 104
Rubeck, Jane L. 1879, 111
Ruckle, Jacob, 241
Ruckle, Katie, 241
Ruckle, Orville, 241
Ruddick, Elizabeth 1831, 308
Ruhl, Catherina, 199
Ruhl, Emily Louella 1916, 53
Ruhl, Gustav M., 199
Ruhr, Catherine, 301
Rush, Clara E., 304
Russell, Ann 1945, 183
Russell, Casey Ann 1972, 183
Russell, Frances Dale 1817, 136
Russell, Gary Dee 1948, 183
Russell, Kelly Michelle 1976, 183
Russell, Michael Aaron 1978, 183
Russell, William 1924, 183
Rutsen, Catherine, 19
Rutsen, Catherine 1729, 201
Rutsen, Elizabeth 1724, 201
Rutsen, Jacob, Colonel, 29
Rutsen, Jacob, Jr., 201, 217
Rutsen, Marretjen 1722, 201, 217
Rutsen, Sarah 1729, 201
Ryckman, Isaac, 24
Ryckman, Isaac 1743, 24

Ryckman, Johannes 1741, 24
Ryckman, Johannes 1746, 24
Ryerson, Catherine, 226

—S—

Salisbury, Abraham A., 217
Salisbury, Catherine, 217
Salisbury, Howard 1913, 183
Sammons, Elizabeth, 200
Sample, Damaris, 140
Samples, Charles, 74
Sanford, Alfred Gee, 249
Sanford, Carrie M., 249
Sanford, Ethel M., 250
Sanford, Freda A., 250
Sanford, Nellie M., 249
Sanford, Veda M., 250
Sankey, Cara, 307
Sankey, Sada, 307
Sapp, Lowell B., 101
Sayre, Ruth, 40
Schepmoe, Johannes, 29
Schepmoes, Dirck Jansen, 5
Schepmoes, Jo, 5
Schepmoes, Johannes 1672, 5
Schepmoes, Maria 1698, 5
Schmidt, Henrich, 5
Schmidt, Jonas, 5
Schmidt, Laverne C. 1920, 260
Schooler, Sherry, 80
Schoonmaker, Jan 1740, 25
Schoonmaker, Rachel, 200
Schoonmaker, Tyrrick 1699, 25
Schraalenburg, Abraham Cammega, 222
Schraeder, Hattie, 291
Schwichtenberg, John Michael 1948, 133
Schwichtenberg, Robert H. 1928, 132

389

Schwichtenberg, Susan 1949, 133

Scott, Helen Beatty 1883, 215

Scott, John, 215

Scott, Martha Ann, 192

Scott, Robert, 192

Scott, Velma E., 78

Scott, Winfield, 208

Seacrist, Charles, 39

Seacrist, Delphia, 39

Seacrist, Edna, 39

Seacrist, Harry, 39

Seacrist, Kenneth, 39

Seacrist, Ruby, 39

Seaman, Lucille, 240

Searing, Dorothy Louise 1930, 185

Sears, John, 270

Sears, Nathan, Dr., 57

Sears, Robert P., 287

Seavey, Eugenia F. 1847, 97

Seavey, Hannah 1848, 97

Seavey, Jeremiah Berry 1815, Dr., 96

Seavey, Jeremiah Berry, II 1867, 97

Seavey, Mary B. 1845, 97

Seebach, Catharine, 224

Segar, No given name, 22

Seibert, Ellen Ellis, 111

Sellers, Alfred L., 246

Sellers, Alice, 246

Sellers, Bertha E., 246

Sellers, Dorothy E., 246

Sellers, Edith B., 246

Sellers, Emma Sophia, 247

Sellers, Gabe A., 246

Sellers, Gabriel B. 1840, 246

Sellers, Grace, 247

Sellers, James A., 247

Sellers, Jeannette 1794, 105

Sellers, Joe L., 246

Sellers, Joseph M., 247

Sellers, Katie, 247

Sellers, Lester R., 246

Sellers, Mary A., 246

Sellers, Susan, 247

Sellers, Velma, 246

Sellers, William B., 247

Selsor, Margaret E. 1915, 129

Settle, Catherine, 188

Seybolt, Mary, 281

Seybolt, Mary L. 1842, 285

Seymour, Joyce 1934, 20

Shafer, Annatje m/1801, 274

Shafer, Hannah m/1801, 274

Shanafelt, Laurel, 156

Shaver, John, 108

Shaw, Colin Stewart 1944, 98

Shaw, David Carey 1911, 98

Shaw, Dudley Graham, 98

Shaw, Dudley Graham, II 1907, 98

Shaw, John Colin 1915, 99

Shaw, Lois Guenn 1945, 98

Shaw, Madeline Beryl 1940, 98

Shaw, Madeline J. 1913, 98

Shaw, Mary Nell 1941, 98

Shaw, No given name, 103

Shaw, Roberta 1946, 98

Shaw, Robin Elizabeth 1951, 98

Shaw, Robinson McGregor 1952, 98

Shaw, Roslin, 98

Shaw, Susan Christine 1948, 98

Shaw, William Graham 1936, 98

Shawn, William, 128

Sheap, Anne Christine 1977, 216

Sheap, Christopher Newkirk 1945, 216

Sheap, Christopher Scott 1981, 216

Sheap, Cornelius Newkirk 1874, 214

Sheap, Cornelius Newkirk, 1874, 215
Sheap, Courtney Lytell 1963, 216
Sheap, Donald Cornelius 1930, 216
Sheap, Donald Scott 1907, 216
Sheap, James Newell 1837, 214, 215
Sheap, Jennifer Lynn 1979, 216
Sheap, Joseph, 214
Sheap, Kathleen McNair 1984, 216
Sheap, Stephanie Marie 1973, 216
Sheap, Susan Elizabeth 1963, 216
Sheap, Townley Scott 1960, 216
Shearer, Sophie, 307
Shears, Jane C. 1824, 214
Shehan, Barbara, 207
Sheldon, Daniel 1950, 181
Sheldon, Leslie Ann 1981, 181
Sheldon, Natalie Rose 1984, 181
Sheldon, Scott Daniel 1987, 181
Shepard, George, 230
Shepard, Rachel 1784, 230
Shepherd, George, 105
Sheridan, Audry, 103
Sheridan, Edward Herbert, 301
Sheridan, Phyllis J., 103
Sherman, Laura 1802, 23
Sherman, Mary 1892, 290
Shields, Daniel T. 1867, 146
Shields, Thomas, 146
Shields, William 1845, 146
Shipman, Kezia, 107, 108, 130, 135, 155, 161
Shipman, Teunis, 107
Shockency, Sarah 1801, 194
Short, George L., 196
Shreve, James Wilford, 101
Shreve, James Wilford, II, 101

Shreve, Robert Fulton, 101
Shubrick, Starkey S., 98
Shull, Hoshell, 41
Shultz, Benjamin Franklin, 247, 248
Shultz, Earl Newkirk, 248
Shultz, Gavalah, 247
Shultz, Kenneth Mitts, 248
Shultz, Letitia Mazettie, 247
Shultz, Paul Precious, 247
Shultz, Richard Paul, 248
Shultz, Sophia Grace, 247
Shumway, Richard, 53
Shumway, Scott W. 1964, 53
Sidwell, James, Dr. 1814, 136
Silcox, Albert, 133
Silcox, Elmer Lee 1921, 133
Silcox, Loren Miller 1918, 133
Silcox, Pearl Olive 1922, 133
Silver, E. Gertrude, 172
Simmonds, John P., 139
Simpkins, Annette 1833, 61
Simpson, John 1822, 44
Sims, Gertrude, 251
Sinclair, Elizabeth, 72
Sinclair, George W., 72
Sinclair, Jane, 72
Sinclair, John, 78
Sip, Garret, 225
Sithins, Amy, 52
Skinner, Sarah K., 285
Slaughter, Isaac, 281
Slauson, James 1826, 15
Slave, April, 88
Slave, Barna, 280
Slave, Ben, 89
Slave, Bill, 89
Slave, Bob, 89
Slave, Caesar, 280
Slave, Caeser, 89
Slave, Charlie, 88
Slave, Charlotte, 88

Slave, Chloe, 89
Slave, Crease, 89
Slave, Daniel, 88
Slave, Dinah, 89, 280
Slave, Dolly, 89
Slave, Dover, 88
Slave, Else, 89
Slave, George, 88
Slave, Gilford, 89
Slave, Hannah, 88
Slave, Isaac, 89
Slave, John, 89
Slave, Juda, 89
Slave, Kate, 88
Slave, Keezy, 88
Slave, Mingo, 88
Slave, Minrod, 88
Slave, Peyton, 89
Slave, Rosetta, 89
Slave, Saffo, 89
Slave, Sam, 88, 89
Slave, Snooy, 89
Slave, Stella, 89
Slave, Stillar, 88
Slave, Tyge, 88
Slave, Virgil, 89
Slave, Zilph, 89
Slawson, Helen 1929, 262
Slecht, Abraham 1724, 199, 202
Slecht, Abraham 1755, 199
Slecht, Arreantje 1740, 199
Slecht, Arriantje 1757, 199
Slecht, Chieltje Cornelissen, 2, 197
Slecht, Elizabeth, 199
Slecht, Elizabeth 1762, 200
Slecht, Elsie De Reimer 1800, 203
Slecht, Frances 1864, 203
Slecht, Harriet Elmendorf 1807, 203

Slecht, Henry Augustus 1817, 203
Slecht, Jacob 1753, 202
Slecht, Jacobus 1753, 199, 202
Slecht, Jacomyntje, 6
Slecht, Jacomyntje Cornelis, 9
Slecht, James Edwin 1803, 203
Slecht, James Edwin 1829, 203, 204
Slecht, Jan, 199
Slecht, Jan 1760, 200
Slecht, Johannes 1719, 199
Slecht, Johannes 1752, 199
Slecht, Margaret, 199
Slecht, Margaret 1768, 200
Slecht, Mary Kate 1852, 203
Slecht, Peter Roosevelt 1804, 203
Slecht, Petrus 1764, 200
Slecht, Rhoda 1857, 203, 204
Slecht, Sarah 1858, 203
Smedes, Benjamin, 7
Smedes, Elizabeth, 199
Smedes, Petrus 1701, 7
Smith, Adam 1787, 272
Smith, Alberta, 99
Smith, Andrew, 294
Smith, Arthur 1817, 136
Smith, Betsey 1792, 272
Smith, Catherine, 188
Smith, Cecily, 159
Smith, Christine Marie, 133
Smith, David, Rev., 84
Smith, Dolly 1789, 273
Smith, Edward 1794, 272
Smith, George 1780, 287
Smith, Hattie M., 43
Smith, Henry, 174
Smith, Isaac R. m/1837, 41
Smith, Jemima 1787, 272
Smith, Jessie, 80
Smith, John L., 274
Smith, Lucy Ellen, 84

Smith, Margaret 1823, 226
Smith, Matilda S., 194
Smith, No given name, 126
Smith, Ruth, 286
Smith, Thomas, 69
Smith, Walter E., 153
Smith, Wilbur Robert, 123
Smith, William, 270, 272
Snodgrass, Benjamin H., 246
Snodgrass, Christopher C., 246
Snodgrass, Millie, 246
Snodgrass, No given name, 246
Snodgrass, Susie E., 246
Snook, William, Capt., 208
Snow, James Byrd, 216
Snow, Rose Emma 1910, 216
Snow, Rose Marie 1910, 216
Snowden, Joseph 1791, 68
Snowden, Nancy, 71
Snowden, Rachel 1814, 70
Snyder, Martinus 1698, 28
Snyder, Martinus 1748, 28
Snyder, Robert E. 1876, 167
Souder, Janet 1952, 261
Sousley, Cornelia 1730, 67, 169
Sousley, Isabella J. 1824, 195
Sousley, Sarah 1801, 194
Southerland, Daniel 1749, 87
Southerland, Jeremiah 1782, 87
Southerland, Nancy, 86, 94
Southerland, Rhoda, 87
Southerland, Samuel, 87
Southerland, Solomon, 87
Southworth, Elisha, 22
Sowers, Lydia Margaret, 80
Sowers, Otis, 263
Sparks, Alice 1777, 170
Sparks, Ellen, 139
Sparks, Mary Alma 1861, 259
Sparks, Pauline, 55
Spear, Date M., 230
Speck, Benjamin S., 165

Speck, John, 51
Speck, Lillian, 165
Speck, Winter N. 1916, 165
Speer, Hazel E., 309
Spence, Anna, 38
Spier, Annatje, 223, 229
Spier, Barent Hendrickse, 228
Spier, Helena, 221
Spier, Helena 1801, 228
Sprager, John B., 305
Spreng, Magdalena, 123
Springer, John G., 115
Sproule, Virginia, 138
Sptingstel, Nancy E. 1841, 306
St. John, Abigail 1812, 295
St. John, Daniel 1777, 295
St. John, Mary Jane 1843, 295
Stafford, Mary, 192
Stafford, Thomas, 192
Stallings Shadrack, Major, 92
Stallings, Elizabeth 1785, 92
Stanford, F. Burton, 101
Stansberry, Julia Ann 1820, 113
Staub, Christine, 53, 55
Stephens, Anna M., 149
Stephens, Mattie Lee, 96
Stevens, Alta, 147, 148
Stevenson, John F., 305
Steward, Scott E., 185
Stewart, Hugh 1784, 194
Stewart, Marcia 1766, 135, 141
Stickney, Adline 1813, 284
Stillwagon, Sarah J., 310
Stockholm, Abraham B., 203
Stolper, Robert W., 263
Storer, Rebecca 1807, 140
Stout, Milton, 142
Stover, Isaiah, 306
Strang, William, 51
Stratton, Simon Cope, 300
Stringham, Jacob D., 284
Strohm, No given name, 247

Strong, Alice A., 307
Strong, Charles L., 213
Strong, David S., 285
Stroud, Jane Reese, 43
Stuart, Frances 1803, 109
Stull, Jeremiah 1791, 45
Sturdy, William D., 309
Stuyvesant, No given name, 294
Sudam, Oke, 199
Sugar, Edward, 85
Sullivan, David, II, 178
Sullivan, Mary Elizabeth 1867,
    178
Sullivan, Norman, 241
Sutherland, David, 178
Swanson, Eleanor, 134
Swartwout, Catharine 1732, 10
Swartwout, Cornelius 1722, 10
Swartwout, Elizabeth 1717, 10
Swartwout, Jacobus 1692, 9
Swartwout, Jacobus 1734, 10
Swartwout, Jacomyntje 1728, 10
Swartwout, Jannetjen 1719, 10
Swartwout, Rudolphus 1724, 10
Swartwout, Samuel 1726, 10
Swartwout, Thomas, 9
Swartwout, Thomas 1715, 10
Swasic, James, 155
Sweat, Caleb, 22
Swing, Michael, 49
Swits, Ariatnje, 205

—T—

Taber, John M. 1791, 41
Taggart, James W., 174
Taggart, James Weddle, 173
Taggert, Elizabeth, 176
Talley, George, 305
Tallman, Maria, 224
Tallman, Nancy 1835, 225
Tappen, Ann, 230

Tappen, Rachel Ann 1868, 20
Tate, Mary, 263
Taylor, Abraham 1799, 276
Taylor, Anne Elizabeth, 91
Taylor, Brian E., 261
Taylor, Elizabeth, 298
Taylor, Florence, 247
Taylor, James B., 126
Taylor, Julia Anna 1770, 293
Taylor, Lola, 247
Taylor, Nellie Grace 1889, 126
Taylor, No given name, 247
Taylor, Vail, 284
Teeter, Daniel, 296
Ten Broeke, Johannes, Capt.,
    210
Ten Eyck, Abraham 1735, 4
Ten Eyck, Adrientje 1739, 4
Ten Eyck, Andries, 4
Ten Eyck, Andries 1727, 4
Ten Eyck, Cornelia W. 1792, 213
Ten Eyck, Gerritje, 6
Ten Eyck, Grietje 1689, 8, 11
Ten Eyck, Grietjen 1689, 8, 11
Ten Eyck, Jannetje 1722, 4
Ten Eyck, Johannes 1732, 4
Ten Eyck, Marytje, 4, 12
Ten Eyck, Mathys, 11, 29
Ten Eyck, Matthew, 4
Ten Eyck, Matthew 1720, 4
Ten Eyck, Neeltje 1717, 4
Ten Eyck, Petrus 1725, 4
Ten Eyck, Rachel 1699, 29
Tender, Alice, 190
Tenney, Horace, 286
Ter Bosch, Catharine, 10
Ter Bosch, Catrina, 198
Ter Bosch, Elizabeth, 10
Ter Bosch, Henry, 10
Terhune, Mary Elizabeth, 227
Terkoski, Eugene Gary, 205
Terrell, Nettie, 309

Terry, Alice, 85
Their, Jacob, 267
Theunyes, Ann Geertruyd, 26
Thomas Ruth, 51
Thomas, B. Triggs, 168
Thomas, Benjamin Eaton, 244
Thomas, Doris, 55
Thomas, Eva 1906, 168
Thomas, Hazel 1912, 55
Thomas, Howard, 168
Thomas, Howard H., 55
Thomas, Howard M. d/1953, 55
Thomas, John, 122
Thomas, Joseph Hill 1901, 55
Thomas, Loretta 1905, 55
Thomas, Rachel 1730, 87
Thomas, Ralph H. 1908, 55
Thomas, Ralph H. 1932, 55
Thomas, Ruth R., 52
Thomas, Samuel, 55
Thomas, Sarah, 60
Thomas, Velma 1902, 55
Thomas, William 1899, 55
Thomas, William H., 55
Thompson, Hannah 1773, 282
Thompson, James, 156
Thompson, Jane 1804, 156
Thompson, John, 40
Thompson, Mary, 40
Thompson, Nancy, 277
Thompson, Phebe, 40
Thompson, Robert, 277
Thompson, Robert 1836, 276
Thompson, Steven, 133
Thompson, William, 32
Thorn, Nancy Ann, 203
Thurman, Charlew 1812, 138
Thurston, Lucretia Ann, 310
Tice, Abram, 226
Tice, Virginia 1858, 111, 112
Tichenor, John Wesley, 139
Tillery, Nancy J., 73

Tillman, Frances E., 69
Tillman, Nancy, 72
Tipka, Josephine, 179
Titus, Elias, 203
Titus, Frances Hoag 1833, 203, 204
Toers, Annatje Spier, 223
Toers, Antje 1743, 229
Toers, Arent, 223, 229
Toers, Catlyntje 1739, 223
Totten, Edith, 78
Toulon, Elizabeth, 281
Traphagen, John, 281
Trollop, Clinton, 37
Trollop, Gertrude A., 37
Troutman, Abraham N., 249
Troutman, Alfred R., 249
Troutman, Ethel A., 249
Troutman, Goldie R., 249
Troutman, Lee, 249
Troutman, Martha E., 249
Troutman, Orpha E., 249
Troutman, Robert L., 249
Troutman, Walter J., 249
Tucker, Elijah, 286
Tucker, Mack, 72
Tueth, Daniel Joshua 1878, 300
Tueth, Edward, 300
Tueth, Frances E. 1874, 300
Tueth, Jesse Edward 1875, 300
Tueth, Martha Lenora 1881, 300
Tueth, Oril Eugene 1894, 302
Tueth, Ray 1885, 301
Tueth, Roy 1885, 302
Tueth, Thomas Edward 1850, 300
Tulkington, Monta, 177
Turner, Arvilla May 1907, 252
Turner, Clara Imojean 1913, 252
Turner, Dale Wayne 1953, 252
Turner, Emma Elizabeth 1904, 252

Turner, Fred Melvin 1899, 250
Turner, Henry F., 233, 242
Turner, Henry Franklin 1926, 233, 245, 251, 252
Turner, Isaac, 250
Turner, Matilda Ellen, 158
Turner, Melvin Douglas 1950, 251
Turner, Ruth Leota 1924, 250
Turner, Walter William 1871, 250
Tuthill, Benjamin, 284
Tuthill, Fannie, 282
Tuthill, Ruth, 284
Twigg, Louise, 176
Tyson, Patricia Lee Myers, 182
Tyson, Patrick William 1969, 183
Tyson, Shawn Michael 1970, 183
Tyson, William, 182

—U—

Usher, Mary Theresa 1841, 100

—V—

Van Belnschoate, Maria, 284
Van Bergen, Elizabeth, 198
Van Bergen, Peter 1721, 197
Van Borsum, Annetje, 23
Van Brestede, Andries, 23
Van Brestede, Jenneke 1683, 23
Van Buntschooten, Elias, 63
Van Buntschooten, Gerretje, 63
Van Buntschooten, Rebecca, 63, 64, 85, 107, 161, 169
Van Buskirk, Sarah, 224
Van den Berg, Ariantje Gerritse, 199
Van der Houex, Geertruydt, 221
Van Derhoff, Garret, 224
Van Derhoff, Sarah 1782, 224

Van Dusen, Jan, Jr., 198
Van Ette, Benjamin, 26
Van Ette, Catharina 1785, 26
Van Etten, Catharine 1758, 27
Van Etten, Elias, 27
Van Etten, Jacobus, 24, 27
Van Etten, Jacobus 1750, 27
Van Etten, Jenneke 1754, 24
Van Etten, Johannes 1721, 27
Van Etten, Lea, 26
Van Etten, Maria 1774, 27
Van Geisen, Jan, 229
Van Geisen, Johannes 1775, 229
Van Geisen, Paulus 1773, 229
Van Geisen, Rachel 1770, 229
Van Hooten, Antje 1776, 229
Van Hooten, Catalyntje 1781, 229
Van Hooten, Dirck, 229
Van Hooten, Helmigh 1778, 229
Van Houten, Halmigh, 226
Van Houten, Rachel, 226
Van Keuren, Abraham 1752, 12
Van Keuren, Benjamin, 284
Van Keuren, Catherine, 27
Van Keuren, Cornelius, 24
Van Keuren, Cornelius 1750, 24
Van Keuren, Garret 1746, 12
Van Keuren, Levi 1767, 12
Van Keuren, Margaret 1750, 12
Van Keuren, Margaret 1755, 12
Van Keuren, Marietje 1756, 12
Van Keuren, Martin 1762, 12
Van Keuren, Neeltje, 6
Van Keuren, Sarah 1753, 283
Van Keuren, Thomas, 6
Van Keuren, Thomas 1752, 24
Van Keuren, Tjerck 1760, 12
Van Keuren, Tjerck Matthysen, 12
Van Meter, Amy 1785, 42
Van Meter, Benjamin, 45

Van Meter, David 1761, 35, 42
Van Meter, Elizabeth 1788, 42
Van Meter, Ephraim 1791, 42
Van Meter, Henry, 45
Van Meter, James 1789, 42
Van Meter, Margaret 1801, 42
Van Meter, Mary 1770, 45
Van Meter, Nealy, 36
Van Meter, Rebecca, 45
Van Meter, Rebecca 1796, 35, 42, 48
Van Pelt, Cornelius, 224
Van Ripen, Cornelius, 223
Van Ripen, Effie 1772, 231
Van Ripen, Jane, 224
Van Ripen, Juriaen Thomassen, 221
Van Steenburgh, E. 1832, 273
Van Swearington, No given name, 65
van Voorhees, Willemtje, 202
Van Wagenen, Annatje 1732, 5
Van Wagenen, Clara 1721, 5
Van Wagenen, Gerret Aartsen, 5
Van Wagenen, Gerret Aartsen 1724, 5
Van Wagenen, Hartman, 225
Van Wagenen, Jacob 1728, 5
Van Wagenen, Johannes 1722, 5
Van Wagenen, Maria 1729, 5
Van Wagenen, Neeltje 1726, 5
Van Wagenen, Sarah 1734, 5
Van Wagenen, Simon, 5
Van Winkle, Abraham, 222
Van Winkle, Annatje 1729, 221
Van Winkle, Annetje Ariaense, 221
Van Winkle, Benjamin 1756, 221
Van Winkle, Catharine 1739, 221
Van Winkle, Charity, 221
Van Winkle, Daniel, 232
Van Winkle, Eleanor, 221
Van Winkle, Geertruydt, 221
Van Winkle, Geertruyt 1747, 222
Van Winkle, Hannah, 221
Van Winkle, Helena 1758, 222
Van Winkle, Jacob, 221
Van Winkle, Jacob 1750, 222
Van Winkle, Jacob Symonsen 1678, 221
Van Winkle, Johannes, 221
Van Winkle, Johannes 1733, 221
Van Winkle, Johannes 1749, 221
Van Winkle, Joseph, 224
Van Winkle, Marianus 1741, 221
Van Winkle, Michael 1736, 221
Van Winkle, Sarah 1731, 221
Van Winkle, Simeon, 221
Van Winkle, Simeon 1755, 222
Van Winkle, Simeon, Jr., 221
Van Winkle, Symon Jacobs, 221
Van Winkle, Waling, 221
Vanarsdal, Charles, 311
Vandament, Joseph, 149
Vandament, Laura Geneva 1911, 149
Vandament, Mary Della 1885, 149
Vandament, Millie E. 1892, 150
Vandament, Mina Pearl 1894, 150
Vandament, Walter T. 1887, 149
Vanderbeck, Abraham, 230
Vanderbeck, Jaques, 4
Vanderbeek, Femmetje Remsen, 10
Vanderlyn, Levi, 279
VanKeuren, Abraham 1711, 12
Vansant, Maria, 60
Veach, Emma, 81
Vedder, Elizabeth Seaman 1801, 207

Vedder, Maria, 207
Venard, Margaret A. 1820, 187
Vermilye, Anne M., 226
Vernooy, Elizabeth, 7
Vischer, Anna 1696, 205, 208
Vischer, Johannes, 205
Voght, Sophia, 296
Von Kocherthal, Joshua, Rev., 268
Vose, Catherine, 96
Vreeland, Cornelius A. 1828, 227
Vreeland, Cornelius M., 223
Vreeland, Daniel, 223
Vreeland, George, 225, 231
Vreeland, Gertrude, 225
Vreeland, Janneke 1758, 224
Vreeland, Jennetje, 223
Vreeland, John V. R., 231
Vreeland, Sarah Jane 1819, 225

—W—

Wadsworth, Dora, 265
Wagers, Mitch, 129
Waggoner, Hannah 1822, 173, 174
Wakeman, Ellen J., 285
Walker, Aaron, 151
Walker, Gladys, 154
Walker, Lucy Ann 1847, 152
Walker, Mary C. 1846, 151
Walker, Mary J., 142
Wall, Gertrude, 99
Wall, John, Captain, 234
Wallace, Lucy A., 109
Wallace, William, 41
Walls, J. Hence, 74
Walmsley, Sarah, 140
Walmsley, Sarah 1804, 139
Walter, Benjamin B., 195
Walters, Henry, 117

Walters, Mercy, 289
Walters, Sarah 1817, 132
Ward, Joseph, 94
Ward, Mary A., 203
Ward, Robert G., 151
Warren, Emma A. 1859, 148
Warren, Zina, 148
Warwick, Margaret Jane, 142
Wastradowski, Carl Roger 1913, 301
Wastradowski, Carol Jean 1942, 301
Wastradowski, Christian, 301
Wastradowski, Doris E., 300
Wastradowski, Jane Marie 1945, 301
Wastradowski, Louise Catherine 1951, 301
Wastradowski, Lynn Martha 1951, 301
Wastradowski, Patricia Doris 1957, 302
Wastradowski, William Carl 1947, 301
Watkins, No given name, 245
Watson, Barbara, 179
Watson, Jacob, 297
Watson, Joseph, 180
Watson, Thomas, 311
Watts, Virgie 1885, 39
Wayne, William W., 94
Weimer, Donald, 119
Weller, Charles, 275
Weller, John W. 1795, 294
Weller, Margaret 1810, 284
Wellman, Anna, 73
Wells, Camilla, 170, 194
Wells, Catherine, 87
Wells, Cornelia 1737, 28
Wells, Elizabeth, 116
Wells, James E., 93
Wells, Jane, 92

Wells, Lucinda, 93
Wells, Lucy Ellen, 92
Wells, Nancy, 93
Wells, Rachel, 86
Wells, Rebecca 1830, 121
Wells, Samuel, 28
Wells, Stokes, 93
Wells, William, 121
Welsh, Andrew J., 156
Welsh, Andrew John, 156
Welsh, Ira E., 156
Welsh, James P., 156
Welsh, John Wesley, 156
Welsh, Matthew 1794, 155, 156
Welsh, Seth McClure 1819, 156
Wendley, Eva St. Clair 1853, 91
Wentzell, Helen, 56
Wentzell, Ora, 56
West, Jehu, 128
West, Laura, 128
West, Lula Evelyn, 81
Wheeler, John, 238
Whipmire, Linda Lee, 252
Whitaker, Ambrose, 30
Whitaker, Freelove 1778, 30
Whitaker, No given name, 39
White, Allen Z., 264
White, Angenietje, 280
White, Cecil, 99
White, Edith Marion 1888, 285
White, Euphenia 1818, 172
White, Jane 1941, 99
White, Nancy 1934, 99
White, No given name, 78
White, Phoebe, 176
Whitney, Caroline Virginia, 96
Whitt, Aileen, 233
Whitt, Aileen M., 82, 233, 237
Whitt, Estill V., 240
Whitt, J. B. 1925, 240
Whitteker, J. Kenneth, 159

Whitteker, Mary Cecily 1939, 159
Wick, James L., 43
Wick, Sarah C. Carson, 43
Wicke, Dora Anna 1880, 296
Wiggins, Daniel Richard, 204
Wiggins, Patricia Burgoon, 199
Wildermuth, Catherine, 130
Wildermuth, David C., 132
Wilkes, Mattie J., 307
Wilkinson, Norma Lee 1923, 261
Willard, James, 74
Willard, Lafayette, 74
Willard, Lafe, 73
Willems, Maria, 5
Williams, Alberta, 105
Williams, Bryan Newkirk 1818, 93
Williams, Catherine 1816, 93
Williams, David, 92
Williams, David Henry 1828, 93
Williams, Elizabeth, 93
Williams, Harold, 180
Williams, Harriett A. 1836, 93
Williams, James M., 187
Williams, Joseph T. 1825, 93
Williams, Lena, 86
Williams, Mary Ann 1820, 93
Williams, Rachel Caroline 1836, 93
Williams, Samuel A. 1830, 93
Williams, Stephen 1791, 92
Williamson, Daniel, 108
Williamson, James Jones, 187
Williamson, John, 141
Williamson, Maude E., 311
Willis, Christopher Hampton, 167
Willis, Elizabeth Newkirk, 167
Willis, Erma Amanda, 250
Willis, Frances, 166
Willis, Frances Finley, 167

Willis, George Newkirk, 167
Willis, Hugh Finley, 167
Willis, Levin Charles, 167
Willis, Louis Orndorf, 166
Willis, Louis Orndorf, Jr., 167
Willis, Mary Anderson, 167
Willis, William, 166
Willis, William Brand, 167
Willkings, Mary Isabella, 96
Willkings, Winslow S., 96
Wills, James, 300
Wills, Martha 1826, 300
Willy, Foster W., 304
Wilson, Evangeline Mary Ann, 215
Wilson, Minnie E., 146
Wilson, Susan 1955, 181
Wilson, Uriah 1767, 67
Wilson, William E., 146
Wimple, Annatje 1747, 205
Wimple, Arriantje 1740, 205
Wimple, Catalina 1742, 205
Wimple, Isaac, 205
Wimple, Johannes, 205
Wimple, Johannes 1749, 205
Winchester, Henry Follett, 203
Winchester, Mary Ruth 1954, 186
Windsor, Edith Hazel 1922, 103
Wine, John Eugene, Dr., 98
Winkelman, Emma, 129
Winkler, Carl E. 1901, 151
Winkler, Herald L. 1899, 151
Winkler, Herman L. 1908, 151
Winkler, Lennie, 151
Winkler, Mamie B. 1903, 151
Winship, Margaret R. 1910, 152
Winship, William, 152
Wisemen, Logan, 78
Wismek, Rozalia, 127
Wison, Blakely, 232
Wittaker, Theodotia 1710, 25

Wittenmeyer, William, 138
Wolfe, William Howard, 80
Wood, Alfred, 286
Wood, Hill, 306
Wood, I. J., 168
Wood, Savilla T. 1883, 168
Woodman, Constant, 41
Woodridge, Brian Edward 1976, 181
Woodridge, Kenneth, 181
Woodridge, Melissa Sue 1975, 181
Woods, Harry, 78
Woods, Jennie, 297
Woodworth, Bernice Emma 1925, 293, 296
Woodworth, Charles Elmer 1872, 295
Woodworth, Dyer Dilavan 1810, 294, 295
Woodworth, Edwin Ruthvin 1837, 295
Woodworth, John Charles 1903, 295
Woodworth, Ryleigh 1782, 294, 295
Woolman, Frank, 52
Woolman, John M., 56
Woolman, Ralph, 56
Worl, Elizabeth J., 138
Wortham, Thomas A., 105
Wray, David W., 104
Wray, John David 1933, 104
Wright, No given name, 249
Wright, Sarah, 81
Wyatt, Bessie, 82
Wynkoop, Adriaan 1726, 198
Wynkoop, Catrina 1722, 198
Wynkoop, Cornelia 1717, 198
Wynkoop, Cornelis 1732, 198
Wynkoop, Cornelius, 17, 19

Wynkoop, Cornelius 1688, 8, 198
Wynkoop, Cornelius C. 1732, 199
Wynkoop, Eleanor, 212
Wynkoop, Elizabeth 1715, 198
Wynkoop, Henry 1737, Judge, 31
Wynkoop, Johannes, 198
Wynkoop, Johannes 1719, 198
Wynkoop, Judike, 13, 211
Wynkoop, Judike 1712, 8, 198
Wynkoop, Lea 1724, 198
Wynkoop, Lea 1728, 198
Wynkoop, Maria 1734, 199
Wynkoop, Petrus 1734, 199
Wynkoop, Susannah 1784, 31

—Y—

Yoast, Zeala, 294
Young, Birchie L., 265
Young, Cati 1783, 281
Young, Clara May, 265
Young, James, 281
Young, Jane S. 1815, 60
Young, Luca 1781, 281
Young, No given name, 193
Young, Sally 1780, 281

—Z—

Zalesky, Amelia, 159
Zalesky, Ann K. 1917, 159
Zalesky, Anne Marie 1962, 157, 159

Zalesky, Christine Courtney 1969, 159
Zalesky, Dean Richard 1938, 159
Zalesky, Emil R. 1880, 159
Zalesky, James E. 1908, 159
Zalesky, Jamie Lynn 1985, 159
Zalesky, Joseph, 159
Zalesky, Kellie Leigh 1988, 159
Zalesky, Mariann Jean 1935, 159
Zalesky, Marion M. 1911, 159
Zalesky, Michael Dean 1961, 159
Zalesky, Richard Cox 1906, Col., 159
Zeagler, Benjamin Hamilton 1860, 100
Zeagler, Edward, 101
Zeagler, Eleanor Catherine, 101
Zeagler, George Mindolf, 100
Zeagler, Katie Connor 1901, 101
Zeagler, Lois 1900, 101
Zeagler, Mary Esther 1898, 101
Zeagler, Paul, 101
Zeagler, Paul Crestwell 1903, 101
Ziegler, Clemens William 1919, 291
Ziegler, William, 291
Zimmerman, Dorothy 1913, 52
Zimmerman, Nancy L. 1841, 289
Zimmers, Howard L., 56
Zon, Olive N., 307
Zook, Bob 1926, 180
Zook, Patsy Kay 1949, 180
Zorne, Rollie E., 150

www.ingramcontent.com/pod-product-compliance
Lightning Source LLC
Chambersburg PA
CBHW070715280326
41926CB00087B/2118